Tradition and Dynamics in
Small-Farm Agriculture
Economic Studies in Asia, Africa, and Latin America

TRADITION AND Small-Farm

Economic Studies in Asia,

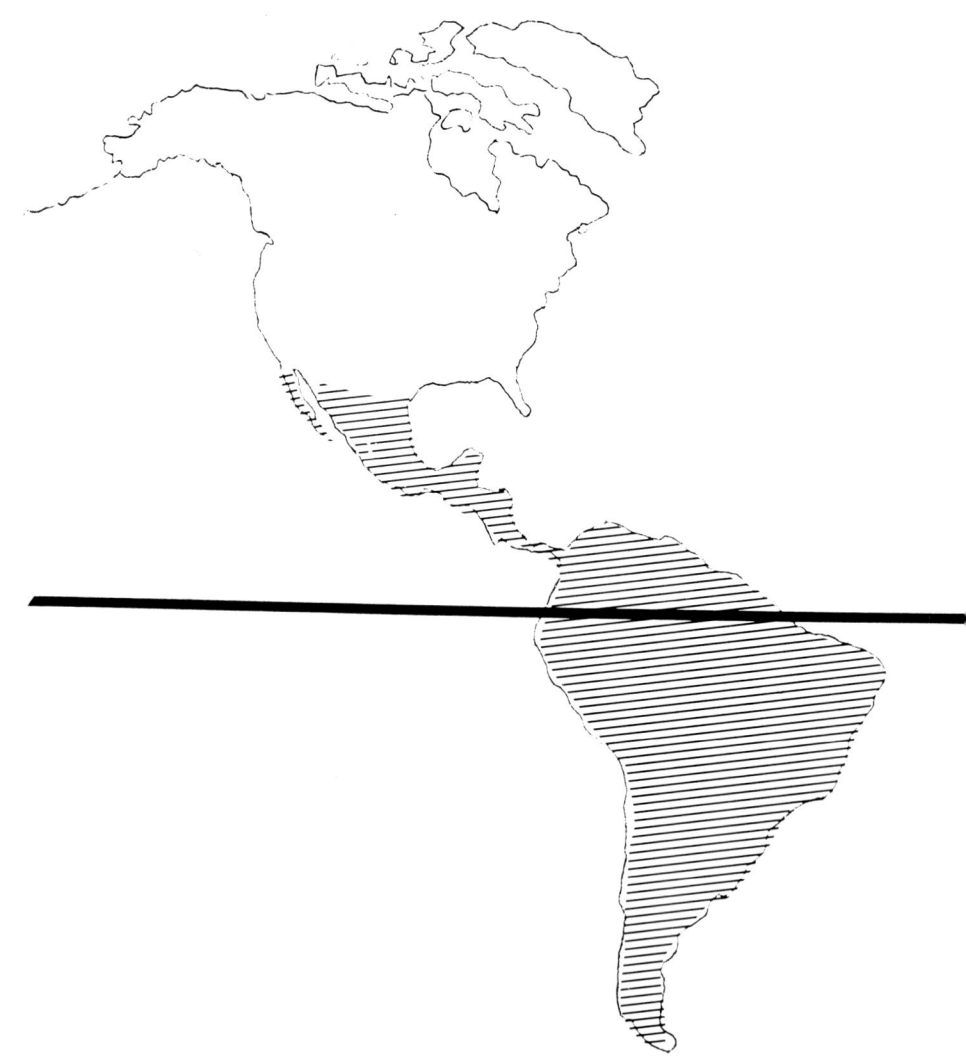

Bikram Garcha

DYNAMICS IN Agriculture
Africa, and Latin America

Edited by
Robert D. Stevens

The Iowa State University Press / Ames

For Nan, Sam, Amelia, Edmund, and Bill

ROBERT D. STEVENS is Professor, Department of Agricultural Economics, Michigan State University, East Lansing, Michigan. He received the Ph.D. degree in agricultural economics from Cornell University in 1959. His research and teaching have focused on accelerating agricultural development in low-income nations. His work has included assignments in Peru, Lebanon, South Vietnam, and Bangladesh. Professor Stevens has published numerous papers on agricultural development and is coeditor of *Rural Development in Bangladesh and Pakistan*.

© 1977 The Iowa State University Press
Ames, Iowa 50010. All rights reserved

Composed and printed by
The Iowa State University Press

No part of this publication may be reproduced, stored in a retrieval system, or transmitted in any form or by any means—electronic, mechanical, photocopying, recording, or otherwise—without the prior written permission of the publisher.

First edition, 1977

Library of Congress Cataloging in Publication Data
Stevens, Robert Dale, 1927–
    Tradition and dynamics in small-farm agriculture.

    Includes bibliographies and index.
    1. Underdeveloped areas—Agriculture—Addresses, essays, lectures.   2. Underdeveloped areas—Peasantry—Addresses, essays, lectures.   I. Title.
HD1417.S68   338.1′09172′4   77-5348
ISBN 0-8138-0055-2

Contents

Preface   vii

Part 1 • Introduction, 1

1   Transformation of Traditional Agriculture: Theory and Empirical Findings
      Robert D. Stevens   3

2   Population and Affluence: Growing Pressures on World Food Resources
      Lester R. Brown   25

Part 2 • Traditional Agriculture, 55

3   Economic Rationality of Traditional Hausa Dryland Farmers in the North of Nigeria
      David W. Norman   63

4   Factors Limiting Change on Traditional Small Farms in Southern Brazil
      Norman Rask   92

5   Constraints on Cattle and Buffalo Production in a Northeastern Thai Village
      A. John DeBoer and Delane E. Welsch   115

Part 3 • Dynamics of Small-Farm Agriculture, 143

6   Farmer Response to High-Yielding Wheat in Pakistan's Punjab
      Jerry B. Eckert   149

7   A Venezuelan Agrarian Reform Settlement: Problems and Prospects
      William C. Thiesenhusen   177

8   Changes in Ejidal Farming in Northwest Mexico's Modernized Agriculture: The Quechehueca Collective, 1938–1968
      Donald K. Freebairn   210

Part 4 • Accelerating Production on Small Farms, 235

9 Policies and Programs for Small-Farm Development
  Robert D. Stevens 237

Index 257

Preface

THE often intractable problems of increasing food production on the 100 million small farms in the developing nations of Asia, Africa, and Latin America are the subject of this work. These farms contain a majority of the rural citizens in low-income nations of the third world.

This volume has one general goal and three specific objectives. Most generally, the aim is to increase understanding of the usually risky and uncertain complex technical, economic, and social decisions faced by small farmers in developing nations as they attempt to increase food production. The specific objectives are (1) to illustrate in depth the nature of the low-income trap of farmers in largely traditional agriculture; (2) to provide detailed examples of development strategies that have led to major increases in production and employment on small farms; and (3) to outline major thrusts for government policies and programs that will accelerate small-farm income growth in developing nations. The objectives are met by providing two introductory chapters that set the stage, followed by six in-depth economic studies representative of small farms in the low-income world of Asia, Africa, and Latin America. Three of these studies examine largely traditional agriculture and three analyze major changes in small-farm agriculture. A final chapter focuses on government policy and programs for small-farm agricultural development.

Four recent world economic trends have greatly increased international focus on the role of small farms in national development. First, growing income disparities have been observed in rural areas of developing nations, as many national agricultural development programs have resulted in relatively rapid growth on large commercially oriented farms and little change on smaller farms. As the governments of most developing nations are unable, for administrative and political reasons, to redistribute income through fiscal means from high-income groups to rural lower-income people, increasing production on small farms is a primary route for improving national income distribution. Second, in rural areas where unemployment is endemic, numerous studies have shown that sufficient off-farm employment opportunities are unlikely to become available in the coming decade, due to a combination of rapid population growth and low rates of growth in employment in the service and particularly the industrial sectors of developing nations. Third, rising food prices and global foodgrain scarcities since the beginning of 1973 have drawn attention to the role that the myriad of small farmers throughout the world might play in food production. A fourth trend has been increasing energy costs for agricultural production, contributed to by recent sharp rises in petroleum prices and subsequent increases in the cost of nitrogen fertilizers. A specific result of these trends was the convening of the FAO World Food Congress in November 1974. The four trends have made clear that solutions to national problems of food supply, income growth, and employment depend on achieving increased productivity and job opportunities on the vast numbers of small farms throughout the developing world.[1]

The remarks made in 1972 by Robert S. McNamara, president of the World Bank, and the ensuing Sector Policy Paper on Rural Development illustrate the heightened concern about progress on small farms:

> Without rapid progress in smallholder agriculture throughout the developing world, there is little hope either of achieving long-term stable economic growth or of significantly reducing the levels of absolute poverty.
> The fact is that very little has been done over the past two decades specifically designed to increase the productivity of subsistence agriculture.[2]

Earlier, in 1969, Wharton in summarizing the conclusions of a major seminar on subsistence and peasant agriculture emphasized the need for more detailed analysis of the economics of small farming systems.

> The primary focus of research requirements in this area concerns the issue of whether "subsistence man" is also "economic man" and whether the economic behavior of subsistence farmers has any basic general properties.
> A great deal more knowledge is required on exactly how peasant and subsistence economic systems operate and change. . . . A great deal more is needed on the exact course and direction of change as well as the forces that influenced the changes and that inhibited them.[3]

Major educational challenges in clarifying the problems of small farmers became apparent to the author from two kinds of experience: in overseas teaching and research in low-income rural areas of Asia and Latin America, and in conducting an introductory agricultural development course for domestic and international students at the advanced undergradute and graduate levels in the United States. The challenge included providing reading material that would elucidate classroom discussions of economic theory of small farms drawn from available texts.[4] Effective teaching also required helping those interested in aiding small farmers to discard wrong or irrelevant ideas about farming in developing nations as a necessary prerequisite for problem solving and action.

An inevitable difficulty for many persons interested in development has been their lack of detailed knowledge of the low-income agricultures of Asia, Africa, and Latin America. Available materials had a number

PREFACE

of drawbacks. In many studies, sufficient detail could be obtained only in long monographs, usually on one community, in which economic analysis tended to become hidden.[5] The many shorter articles in journals with incisive economic analysis lacked sufficient background data and detailed information to give adequate orientation to a problem situation.

In a review of published works, some books were found to contain intensive studies from different parts of one nation or geographic region.[6] Three collections of studies were found with global scope.[7] These studies, however, provide relatively little economic analysis. A final group of works, with wide geographic scope, was limited to a particular professional focus with little material on agricultural enterprises and farming systems.[8] Hence, no work that met the identified educational challenges was found.

In undertaking the development of this volume, four criteria for the case studies were established: (1) detailed economic analysis, (2) studies representative of farms in an area, (3) focus on important general problems in the development of small farms, and (4) studies geographically and culturally representative of small farms in Asia, Africa, and Latin America (see Fig. P.1).

Although contributions of all the social, physical, and biological sciences are needed in the resolution of the varied and often intractable

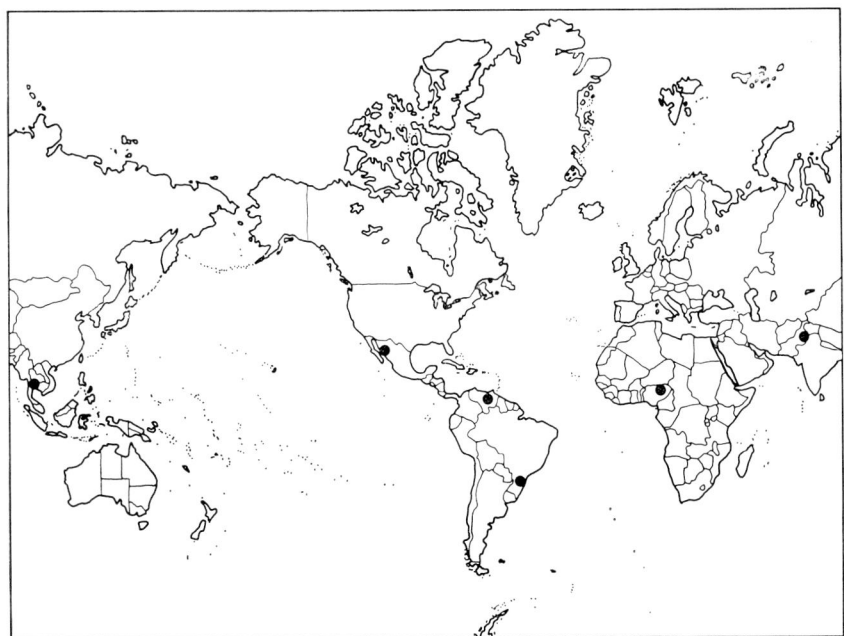

Fig. P.1. World map showing the location of the economic studies of farming.

problems of small farms, studies were chosen that employ economic analysis primarily, as it is a core discipline required for the solution of agricultural production and employment problems on peasant farms. The specific economic tools employed in these studies include budgeting, production function analysis, linear programming, factor analysis, and benefit cost analysis.

Authors were asked to prepare original chapter-length analyses based on their research. The task set was to provide first-hand examples of traditional agriculture and agricultural change in different resource situations and cultural environments. They were to illustrate at the micro, or village level, the interaction of the three major groups of variables affecting agricultural production, resource endowments, level of technology, and the institutional and cultural framework.

The intellectual hazards of case studies are recognized. Although great care was used in selecting the studies, six cannot be representative of the population of small farms in three continents. However, to meet the objectives of this volume, the advantages of the case study approach outweighed its shortcomings.

Each author represented in this volume has conducted important empirical investigations in the low-income world and is intimately familiar with the farms analyzed. The authors are part of a small group of uniquely qualified, mature professionals who have carried out sophisticated detailed field research on peasant farms in the developing world. The studies are representative of farm level research carried out in the low-income world in the last decade.

Each chapter includes a brief geographical and cultural orientation to the area and society studied, detailed information about typical peasant farms and agricultural activities, and sections focused on particular theses or interrelationships. The chapters contain examples of rigorous microeconomic analysis of interest to economists. However, with other audiences in mind, the material has been written so that individuals from other disciplinary backgrounds will find most of the arguments understandable and useful. These materials have been used successfully by students with a wide variety of professional specialties.

The particular needs of two groups of readers have been kept in mind. One group consists of students of the social and agricultural sciences from the relatively developed urbanized world. These readers, whether from more developed nations or the cities of developing countries, often have had little opportunity to gain detailed knowledge of agriculture at home or abroad. For the development of useful analytical skills, this group needs knowledge of how resources and technology interact with traditional institutional and cultural environments so as to affect farmer decision making. A second group of readers is composed of practitioners, some of whom have had considerable personal experience with their own agriculture or who through Peace Corps experience or other deep immersion in a particular low-income agriculture have in-depth knowledge of a peasant farming area. Other practitioners have had responsibilities in government or private business and foundations for programs and policies affecting the opportunities of small farmers. These readers benefit by testing their knowledge and their hypotheses about development gained in one setting against experience in other areas.

Although the agricultural development problems of a particular nation or area may seem unique due to specific resource and cultural characteristics, a central hypothesis of this work is that effective general strategies for increasing agricultural production, income, and employment on peasant farms are similar throughout the world. An Ethiopian, for example, may wonder what he can learn from Latin American agricultural development. Upon deeper analysis he may find that the varying results of land tenure reforms in Latin America are of great value in finding solutions to his own farm tenure problems. Hence, the studies in this volume provide further evidence for rejecting the view forwarded by some that "western economics" is not useful in solving the economic problems of the third world.[9]

The first part of the manuscript sets the stage for the detailed studies. Chapter 1 presents central elements of an economic model of traditional agriculture and of the agricultural transformation process essential for better understanding of the individual studies. Chapter 2, "Population and Affluence: Growing Pressures on World Food Resources," places these studies in the perspective of the early years of the green revolution. The second part of the manuscript focuses on economic decision making by peasants in largely traditional institutional and cultural environments where little technological change is occurring. Three studies offer evidence of traditional peasants' economic rationality supporting Schultz's central hypothesis of the efficiency of traditional agriculture. In the third part, three detailed analyses of particular kinds of policies and programs aimed at increasing production are provided. In Chapter 6 the response of small farmers to new economic opportunities opened up by an accelerated wheat improvement program in a little-modified institutional and cultural environment is examined. The next two chapters delve deeply into how two kinds of major institutional change undertaken to aid in transforming traditional peasant farming into science-based agriculture worked out in practice. In Part 4, the final chapter specifies policies and programs required to accelerate development on small farms.

For instructional purposes, this text was designed for use in advanced undergraduate and beginning graduate courses as a companion to standard texts in economic and agricultural development, economic anthropology, sociology of developing nations, geography, and in technical agricultural fields such as agronomy and agricultural engineering. The use of case material can establish in class a fruitful dialogue by confronting general theories of social and economic growth with the details of particular developmental situations.

A gradually forming plan for this book was nudged into an active phase by Philip Warnken. My colleagues have provided aid and counsel in the development of the book, particularly Professors Carl K. Eicher and Lawrence W. Witt. I wish also to thank many others who have contributed by reviewing manuscripts and in other ways, including J. H. Atkinson, Derek Byerlee, Robert Deans, Ramon Fernandez, Darrell Fienup, Douglas D. Headley, J. A. Hoefer, Lane Holdcroft, Shao-er Ong, Harold Riley, Vernon Sorenson, Warren Vincent, and E. H. Wittwer.

Support for the research and writing has come from the Michigan Agricultural Experiment Station and from a 211d grant to the Department of Agricultural Economics by the U.S. Agency of International Development.

Editorial aid from Addiann Hinds and Sandra Clark; secretarial assistance from Diane Hutchinson, Julia McKay, Jill Versace, Denise Wootan, and Mabel Buonodono; and the drawing of many of the figures by Natalia Maxwell were greatly appreciated.

NOTES

1. The World Food Congress noted the particular problems of small farmers: *Assessment of the World Food Situation—Present and Future*, Rome, Nov. 1974, United Nations, E/CONF. 65/3 p. 120; and *World Food Conference —Note by the Secretary-General* (Report of the Conference), United Nations, Economic and Social Council, E/5587, 22 Nov., 1974, p. 31.
2. Robert S. McNamara. Address to the Board of Governors, Nairobi, Kenya, Sept. 1972. International Bank for Reconstruction and Development (World Bank, Washington, D.C., p. 14, and World Bank, *Rural Development*, Washington, D.C., Feb. 1975.
3. Clifton R. Wharton, Jr., ed. *Subsistence Agriculture and Economic Development*, Aldine Publishing Co., 1969, p. 461.
4. *Transforming Traditional Agriculture* by T. W. Schultz, Yale Univ. Press, 1964; *The Economics of Agricultural Development* by J. W. Mellor, Cornell Univ. Press, 1967; *Subsistence Agriculture and Economic Development* edited by Clifton R. Wharton, Jr., Aldine Publishing Co., 1969; *Agriculture in Economic Development* edited by C. Eicher and L. Witt, McGraw-Hill Book Co., 1964; *Agricultural Development* by Y. Hayami and V. W. Ruttan, Johns Hopkins Univ. Press, 1971; *Economic Development of Tropical Agriculture* edited by W. W. McPherson, Univ. of Florida Press, 1968; *Agricultural Development and Economic Growth*, edited by H. M. Southworth and B. F. Johnston, Cornell Univ. Press, 1967; *Getting Agriculture Moving* by A. T. Mosher, Praeger, 1966; *Creating a Progressive Rural Structure* by A. T. Mosher, Agricultural Development Council, Inc., 1969; *Agriculture in Development Theory* edited by Lloyd G. Reynolds, Yale Univ. Press, 1975, *Agricultural and Structural Transformation* by B. F. Johnston and Peter Kilby, Oxford Univ. Press, 1975; and *The New Economics of Growth* by J. W. Mellor, Cornell Univ. Press, 1976, to list only the most outstanding.
5. A long list of economic studies of farming communities in low-income nations was compiled in developing this volume.
6. These include *Developing Rural India* by J. W. Mellor et al., Cornell Univ. Press, 1968; *Smallholder Farming and Smallholder Development in Tanzania* edited by Hans Ruthenberg, Weltforum Verlag, Munchen, 1968; *African Food Production Systems: Cases and Theories* edited by Peter F. M. McLaughlin, Johns Hopkins Univ. Press, 1970; for Asia, *Opportunity and*

PREFACE   xiii

  Response—Case Studies in Economic Development edited by T. Scarlett
  Epstein and David H. Penny, Hurst and Co., 1972; and *The Design of
  Rural Development—Lessons from Africa* by Uma Lele, Johns Hopkins Univ.
  Press, 1975.
7. *Contemporary Change in Traditional Societies* edited by H. Steward, Univ.
  of Illinois Press, 1967; *Tribal and Peasant Economies—Readings in Economic Anthropology* edited by George Dalton, Natural History Press, 1967;
  *Economic Development and Social Change—The Modernization of Village
  Communities* edited by George Dalton, Natural History Press, 1971.
8. For example, *Capital, Saving, and Credit in Peasant Societies* edited by
  Raymond Firth and B. S. Yamey, Aldine Publishers, 1964; *Land Development and Colonization in Latin America* edited by Craig L. Dozier, Praeger,
  1969; John H. Cleave, *African Farmers: Labor Use in the Development of
  Smallholder Agriculture*, Praeger, 1974; and G. F. Patrick, L. J. Brainard,
  and F. W. Obermiller, eds., *Small Farm Agriculture: Studies in Developing
  Nations*, Agr. Exp. Sta. Bull. No. 101, Purdue Univ., Sept. 1975.
9. See for example, Polly Hill, "A Plea for Indigenous Economics: The West
  African Example," *Economic Development and Cultural Change* 15 (7, Oct.
  1966): 10–20. A more general review of these issues may be found in George
  Dalton, "Theoretical Issues in Economic Anthropology," *Current Anthropology* 10 (1, Feb. 1969): 63–80, reprinted in *Economic Development and
  Social Change* edited by George Dalton, Natural History Press, 1971, pp.
  178–225.

PART 1
Introduction

CHAPTER 1

Transformation of Traditional Agriculture: Theory and Empirical Findings

ROBERT D. STEVENS

IN the second half of the twentieth century, millions of small farms in Asia, Africa, and Latin America began to experience a revolutionary agricultural transformation. Before 1950 most farming in low-income developing nations was carried out in traditional ways. Small farmers had placed emphasis on assuring subsistence food production by minimizing risks of failure. Yields were low and fairly dependable but usually could not be raised appreciably. Opening new land or gradually increasing the intensity of land use permitted sufficient growth in production to meet the slow expansion of food demand, which increased about proportionately to the population growth rate of under 1.3% per year in most low-income nations.

By the year 2000, population growth rates will probably have begun to decline from the very high 2.5 to 3% rates experienced in a large number of developing nations in the second half of the twentieth century. Also by then most small farmers in the world will have begun using some new kinds of farming technology, developed through the application of the biological, chemical, and mechanical sciences to agriculture.

By 1975 the "green revolution" of human history had had mixed impact in developing nations. The "green revolution" is defined here as the period in which modern science and technology began to have major impact on agriculture and resulted in large continuing increases in land and labor productivity. In South Asia, it may be said to have begun in 1967 with the first large-scale planting of high-yielding wheat and rice varieties in India and Pakistan. The impact of the green revolution had varied from record-setting agricultural growth in limited areas, often on irrigated lands, to little or no impact in other areas, particularly in drier, unirrigated regions. In areas where growth occurred, small farms often were bypassed. This volume explores the reasons for the varied impact to date of the green revolution on small farms in developing nations and points to government policies and programs required to accelerate agricultural production on small farms of the third world.

Since 1950, due to rapid increases in population growth rates in most developing nations and to strong growth in per capita income in a large number of more developed nations, great increases in the demand for food and agricultural products have occurred. In Chapter 2 Lester Brown analyzes these growing pressures on world food resources. His conclusions demonstrate the urgency of aiding small farmers throughout the third world to more rapidly increase agricultural production. Brown's chapter also provides the international setting for the central policy focus of this work.

For the purposes of this book, small farms are defined as family farms, the physical size being relative to the farming area. Generally the lower three-fourths of the distribution of size of operating farm units can be classified as small farms in low-income nations. In areas with a very highly skewed distribution of operating units, the proportion that can be labeled small farms may be even larger. In some instances the term "peasant farm" is used in this book as a synonym for small farm.

The central problems of this work focus on what actions by governments of the developing world will best help small farmers to participate in the scientific revolution in world agriculture that began over a century ago in industrialized nations. There are many questions. Some focus on the limitations provided by the technical and economic environment faced by peasant farmers. For example, is the new agricultural technology that is needed to increase production in particular locations actually available for small farms? Or must appropriate new agricultural technology that will be economically productive in these locations be developed? Is the technology locally available in sufficient quantities in the form of such items as new seeds, fertilizer, pesticides, and mechanical equipment? Has the available new technology been demonstrated on typical peasant farms so that farmers know the details of the costs, management practices, and additional returns obtained, as well as about any risks and other possible problems related to working the new technology into the whole farming system? How profitable is the new technology? Are there community and social problems related to new agricultural practices? In some peasant farming areas, it is impractical for a few farms to change their practices because community social patterns limit employing new patterns of water or other resource use.

Other questions involve social constraints and the ways small farmers make decisions. To what extent is an individual farmer in a particular culture permitted to make decisions about his crop and livestock practices? If certain decisions are open to him, what factors influence his decisions? Does he follow tradition "irrationally" due to social or other pressures in the face of new opportunities? Or is he "economically rational"? How necessary are literacy and "education" for use of new agricultural technology? To what extent may the values that a peasant holds about the good life prevent him from undertaking new agricultural activities that could clearly increase his income? Does he desire increased agricultural income? In seeking answers to these and many other questions, the analysis in this book draws on economic and social science theory and on detailed empirical studies of peasant farming behavior.

In this chapter, elements of economic theory of traditional agriculture and of agricultural development are presented. The six detailed case studies in this volume provide empirical tests of this theory and the major hypotheses about small-farm agriculture presented below.

FOUR MAJOR HYPOTHESES AND ASSOCIATED ACTION PROGRAMS FOR CHANGE IN SMALL-FARM AGRICULTURE. Questions about increasing production on small farms can be highlighted in the form of hypotheses. Four major hypotheses and associated action programs that point to important issues among theorists and development practitioners have flourished. The need for determining the validity of these hypotheses is underlined by the long history of failures in major national and international development programs. Large amounts of scarce human and material resources have often been wasted through attempts to carry out irrelevant agricultural programs intended to help small farmers to increase production. These hypotheses point to major theoretical issues examined in the following detailed case studies.

HYPOTHESIS I: SMALL FARMERS ARE POOR DECISION MAKERS. This hypothesis assumes that productive alternative agricultural production opportunities are available to traditional small farmers but that they do not make the right decisions about these new opportunities; they are poor decision makers, or foolish, or lazy. The conclusion is that extension services, community development programs, and other forms of educational and management help are needed to improve farmers' production decisions. This hypothesis, for example, underlay much of the work of the community development programs in Pakistan and in India in the 1950s involving primarily the injection of educated personnel into rural farming areas. After some years of experience, many community development programs were terminated and governments shifted away from heavy emphasis on extension work as the primary method to increase production. Recent works review the extensive literature dealing with this subject [24, 26].

HYPOTHESIS II: SMALL FARMERS LACK CAPITAL. Observations that moneylenders charge high interest rates of 30 to 60% to small farmers in developing nations lend credence to the thesis that capital is scarce in traditional peasant farming areas. A strategy to combat capital shortages has been to develop new institutions to channel credit to peasants. Many examples of this strategy exist in Asia, Africa, and Latin America for increasing agricultural output among small farmers through cooperative credit programs and subsidized government-supervised credit institutions. Large numbers of these programs, however, have resulted in low repayment rates, often ranging from 20 to 70% and, in some cases, little increase in agricultural production. Hence, credit programs for peasant farmers often simply provided windfall gifts for a few years. Other government credit programs have served only large farmers who profited greatly from the low interest rates.

HYPOTHESIS III: SMALL FARMERS WOULD BECOME MORE PRODUCTIVE ON LARGER-SCALE FARMS. This hypothesis assumes that larger scale, perhaps in the form of collective or corporation farms, would lead to greater agricultural productivity. This hypothesis springs from the theory of economies of scale and from the successful factory systems of industrial production. It assumes that small farm size is a major brake on increased agricultural output. The Soviet Union, Eastern European nations, and Cuba have used this thesis as a partial reason for establishing large farming units in agriculture. Large-scale corporation and plantation farms that operate in different locations in other parts of the world have demonstrated that at least under certain conditions large-scale agriculture can be highly productive. However, many projects for large-scale farming in the developing nations have failed. Although data on these unsuccessful projects are often nonexistent or hard to obtain, some are available [4, 16].

HYPOTHESIS IV: SMALL FARMERS IN LOW-INCOME SOCIETIES ARE TRAPPED IN A TECHNICAL AND ECONOMIC EQUILIBRIUM. This hypothesis implies that traditional peasant farmers are generally good decision makers, given their knowledge and resources; hence, reallocation of their resources would not appreciably increase income. It also assumes that the economic returns to investment in peasant agriculture are low. The development strategy under this hypothesis focuses upon making economic, social, technical, and institutional changes so that more profitable economic opportunities become available to small farmers. The hypothesis directs particular focus on the development of locally tested new agricultural technology that is more productive and provides significantly higher returns to investment in agriculture. This hypothesis leads to policies for strengthening national agricultural research capacities, the setting up of international agricultural research institutes, and activities to insure the availability of new agricultural inputs to farmers.

The eight international agricultural research institutes are examples of this thrust. Extended discussion of the economics of smallholder decision making and a review of studies on the supply response of African smallholders are found in Helleiner [11].

Evidence on the validity of these partly contradictory hypotheses is found both in economic theory and detailed empirical research. The remaining part of this introductory chapter reviews central elements of economic theory of traditional peasant agriculture and of agricultural development. In so doing, the empirical findings of the later chapters are related to central questions of theory of agricultural development.

AGRICULTURAL DEVELOPMENT: THEORY AND EMPIRICAL FINDINGS. Since 1950 six major texts on the theory of agricultural development have been published: *Transforming Traditional Agriculture,* by T. W. Schultz (1964); *The Economics of Agricultural Development,* by John W. Mellor (1966); *Agricultural Development: An International Perspective,* by Yujiro Hayami and Vernon W. Ruttan (1971); *Agriculture and Structural Transformation: Economic Strategies in Late-Developing Countries,* by Bruce F. Johnston and Peter Kilby (1975); *Agriculture in Development Theory,* edited by Lloyd B. Reynolds (1976); and *The New Economics of Growth,* by John W. Mellor (1976). In 1967 Mellor proposed that "a useful economic theory of agricultural development includes three interrelated parts depicting: (I) the role of agriculture in economic development; (II) the economic nature of traditional agriculture; and (III) the economic process of modernization of agriculture" [21]. The analyses undertaken in this volume provide evidence impinging on the second and third parts of agricultural development theory as set out by Mellor.

Elements of a Model of Traditional Agriculture. Focus on two theoretical concepts and one major empirical finding illuminates the core of the model of traditional agriculture.

1. *Little Change in Technical, Social, and Economic Variables.* The central thesis about traditional agriculture is that so little change has occurred in the significant technical, social, and economic variables that traditional small farms can be characterized as essentially in a state of equilibrium in both factor and product markets where supply and demand curves interact. According to Schultz,

the critical conditions underlying this type of equilibrium, either historically, or in the future, are as follows: 1) the state of the arts remains constant, 2) the state of preference and motives for holding and acquiring sources of income remains constant, and 3) both of these states remain constant long enough for marginal preferences and motives for acquiring agricultural factors as sources of income to arrive at an equilibrium with the marginal productivity of these sources viewed as an investment in permanent income streams and with net savings approaching zero [19].

The "state of the arts" refers to all technology and nature of the resources used in agriculture, including seeds and fertilizer, as well as traditional knowledge of planting times, crop and livestock management practices, processing, and sales activities. Knowledge of traditional technology has been carried down through the generations orally or by demonstration. It was based on keen local trial and error observations, uninformed by the sciences of chemistry, biology, or physics; hence supply curves tend to remain stable. "The state of preferences and motives for holding and acquiring sources of income" refers to the thesis that slow cultural change has occurred in most low-income societies in religious beliefs, traditional cultural activities, and local institutional arrangements. As a result, the preferences and incentives for economic activity have changed little. Thus the pattern of demand for all items has generally remained unchanged from generation to generation.

2. *Equilibrium in Supply and Demand and Allocative Efficiency.* If little or no change has occurred in previous time periods in the supply of factors affecting agricultural production and in the demand for agricultural products, farmers have had the opportunity to adjust the allocation of their resources to achieve optimum return from farming at acceptable risks.

Essential to understanding this theory of an economic optimum in farming are the marginal concepts of production economics included in many introductory texts [5, 18, 25]. Production economics theory demonstrates that when a farmer equates his marginal costs and marginal returns in all production and more generally in all human activities, he reaches an equilibrium in which no changes will increase his income or in general terms his level of satisfaction. Hence, if there are no ways for small farmers to increase their net income by reallocating the use of their resources of land, labor, and capital, these farmers can be said to be economically efficient. Under these circumstances, traditional farmers are seen to be doing the best they can, given their personal characteristics and their technical, cultural, and institutional environment.

A number of careful empirical tests of the allocative efficiency of traditional agriculture have been carried out in the last decade [7, 12, 14, 27, 28, 29, 30]. These studies, as well as the two tests reported by Norman in Chapter 3, provide mounting evidence in support of the hypothesis of the economic efficiency of traditional agriculture. Further evidence is provided in the study of small farms in southern Brazil (Chapter 4) and in the analysis of a northeastern Thailand village with its rare focus on livestock instead of crop production (Chapter 5). Although a few significant changes had commenced in these two farming areas, considerable evidence of equilibrium conditions in most enterprises was documented in still largely traditional agricultural areas. Norman's analysis is of particular interest for no previous tests were available of the applicability of the Schultz theory of traditional agriculture to western African conditions.

Three major policy implications follow from this model of traditional agriculture. First, both theory and empirical studies indicate that although small farmers are often illiterate in traditional agricultural environments, they are rational, i.e., they use the knowledge they have and apply it to their farming operations. Hence, if small farmers observe that a change in production practice would likely increase net income, they would make such a change with appropriate discounts for weather and uncertainty. The concept of traditional farming does not preclude experimentation with changes in practices. Traditional farmers are not "foolish" in the sense that they do not make changes that appear to increase their well-being.

A second implication of the theory of traditional agriculture is that all available agricultural technology is being used by farmers. Hence, no new technology that would increase net income is known to them.

A third point is that efficient allocation in traditional agriculture may result in changes in production on individual farms as more or less resources become available for use on that farm. For example, gradual increases in production on a farm may occur as more family labor becomes available, or a decline in production may result as soil exhaustion or other factors not under the farmer's control reduce output.

3. *Low Productivity and Slow Growth.* The theory of traditional agriculture discussed above is based on the concept of an economic equilibrium. But at what levels of productivity is the economic equilibrium maintained? Empirical studies conclusively document the low productivity of traditional agriculture.

Productivity can be estimated by partial productivity measures such as output per unit of land (yield) or production per unit of labor or by total productivity measures, including estimates of all the resources used in relation to output. Partial productivity measures show that in spite of long days of hard labor and keen observation traditional farmers have low productivity. Data on yields (land productivity) in traditional agriculture as compared with modern agriculture show this (Table 1.1).

Use of total productivity measures leads to the same conclusion. One such measure is the rate of return on the investment from all resources used. If traditional agriculture were highly productive, empirical studies would show a high rate of return on investment. Empirical studies indicate the opposite. DeBoer and Welsch (Chapter 5), for example, estimated an 8 to 11% rate of return on investment in livestock in a Thai village. National development planners consider this a low rate of

TABLE 1.1. Maize, rice, wheat, potatoes, and sugar yields in traditional and modern agriculture

	Traditional Agriculture			Modern Agriculture		
	Year	Metric tons per ha	Bushels per acre	Year	Metric tons per ha	Bushels per acre
Maize (corn)[a]						
Brazil	1960–64	1.3	21			
India	1960–64	1.0	16			
Mexico	1960–64	1.0	16			
N. Carolina, U.S.A.	1900	0.8	13	1967	4.5	72
Michigan, U.S.A.				1970–72	5.0	81
Wheat[a]						
India	1960–64	0.8	12			
Turkey	1960–64	1.1	16			
China–Mainland	1960–64	0.8	12			
Mexico	1945	0.8	11	1972	2.6	39
United States				1972	2.2	33
Potatoes[a]						
India	1972	9.8	146			
Philippines	1972	6.5	96			
Venezuela	1972	8.5	126			
Colombia	1972	12.3	183			
Kenya	1972	3.9	58			
United States				1972	26	393
W. Germany				1972	30	445
Netherlands				1972	38	563
Japan				1972	24	362

	Year	Metric tons per ha	Pounds per acre	Year	Metric tons per ha	Pounds per acre
Rice[a] (unhulled)						
Brazil	1960–64	1.8	1,421			
India	1960–64	1.7	1,356			
Indonesia	1960–64	2.0	1,627			
United States				1972	5.3	4,330
Japan				1972	5.6	4,580
Sugar[b]						
India	1972	48	42,800			
Zaire	1972	30	26,800			
Colombia	1972	50	44,600			
United States				1973	78	69,600
Japan				1973	57	50,900
Spain				1973	72	64,300

[a] U.S. Department of Agriculture, *Agricultural Statistics*.
[b] *Food and Agriculture Organization Production Yearbook*, 1974.

return as they usually estimate the opportunity cost of capital above 12% and seek investment in agricultural projects with much higher returns. When allocative efficiency and low productivity are coupled with small farm size, in Schultz's succinct phrase, traditional farmers can be described as "efficient but poor" [19].

The concept of traditional peasant farming presented here is consistent with the history of world agriculture. Until after the middle of the twentieth century, traditional agricultural practices dominated much of Asia, Africa, and Latin America. Centuries of trial and error in agriculture produced relatively stable agrarian systems. Many of these agricultural systems were capable of maintaining human cultures at levels of consumption sufficient to prevent usual variations in weather conditions from seriously reducing population numbers. Traditional agriculture permitted the occasional flowering of the major kingdoms and empires of history. Agricultural breakthroughs occurred from time to time due to significant changes that upset the prevailing economic equilibrium in agriculture and opened new economic opportunities. These once-over changes due to internal invention, the adoption of new crops, or the development of new markets abroad through changes in trade and transportation, to mention a few, set off a new round of adjustments that led to new technical, social, and economic equilibriums.

Economic theory of traditional agriculture and empirical studies support the hypothesis that traditional peasant farmers are caught in a technical and economic equilibrium trap. Hence, in general, small farmers in a traditional agriculture can do little to increase their agricultural productivity or income. Acceptance of this hypothesis leads to focusing on the kinds of technical, economic, and institutional changes that could aid farmers in changing from the use of time-tested traditional agricultural knowledge and inputs to scientific ways of farming using the new, much more highly productive inputs produced in other sectors of the economy. The means for transforming traditional agriculture come from outside agricultural villages.

Economics of the Agricultural Transformation. By setting out an economic model of traditional agriculture in the previous section, false views of small farms in low-income nations were pruned away, making possible clear focus upon the two major sources of increased productivity in farming: technological change and institutional innovation. Both kinds of change make possible more productive use of resources so that production functions are shifted upward, i.e., the same resources produce more product. There is general professional agreement about the requirement for technical change in the transformation of small-farm agriculture. However, the nature and importance of institutional change remain controversial. The chapters in Part III of this volume concentrate on analysis of technical and institutional change in agriculture.

Schultz focused sharply on technical change as the source of increased farm productivity. He stated, "The particular new factors of production that are required in making this transformation are presently in a large box labeled 'technological change.' It will be necessary to remove them from this box, sort them, and find ways of making them available and acceptable to farmers . . ."[19].

The more recent Hayami and Ruttan "induced development model" builds on the Schultz theory developing "an explanation of the mechanism by which a society chooses an optimum path of technological change in agriculture" [9]. This theory advances four interrelated mechanisms as critical elements of agricultural development: induced innovation in the private sector, induced innovation in the public sector, induced institutional change, and dynamic sequences in the development process.

Induced innovation in the private sector proposes that farmers and other entrepreneurs in private business respond to changes in production opportunities opened up by new, more productive technology and by changes in relative prices. Examples of "induced innovation" by peasant farmers in response to new economic opportunities are provided in Chapters 6 and 7.

Induced innovation in the public sector sets forth the thesis that actions in the public sector by government officials, and particularly scientists in experiment stations, attempt to alleviate resource scarcities by carrying out research and government programs that make possible increased agricultural output while conserving resources. Analysis of induced innovation in the public sector is outside the scope of this volume.

The authors also propose that induced institutional innovation results as changes are made in the organizations and institutions of society in response to changes in prices, technology, and other variables in order to take fuller advantage of the new technology. Other professionals remain skeptical of the induced institutional innovation model, pointing to the large number of long-standing institutional rigidities in many developing nations that cause artificial constraints on resource use, resulting in slower growth [1]. Institutional innovation is a central topic of Chapters 7 and 8 .

In outlining the causes of the agricultural transformation, three topics parallel to those in the previous section are now examined: dynamics in agricultural technology, successive adjustments to changes in supply and demand, and increasing farm production. Four additional topics are considered: values and institutions in agricultural change, limited scale economies, greater employment, and the complex interrelated nature of the agricultural transformation. The agricultural transformation is defined to include both the shift to science-based agricultural technology and associated changes resulting in the increasing integration of agriculture into a dynamic economy.

1. *Dynamics in Agricultural Technology.* Changes in agricultural technology are obtained through the application of the whole range of modern science and technology to agricultural production processes. This fundamental process is the source of increased agricultural productivity, the production of more products with less resources. Some of the most dramatic recent technological improvements have been achieved by employing the science of genetics to produce high-yielding wheat, rice, and maize (corn) varieties by the International Agricultural Research Centers. The first two centers were the International Rice Research Institute (IRRI), Los Banos, Philippines, and the International Maize and Wheat Improvement Center (CIMMYT), Mexico City, Mexico. Six additional international research institutes have been founded more recently: the International Center of Tropical Agriculture (CIAT), Cali, Colombia; the International Institute of Tropical Agriculture (IITA), Ibadan, Nigeria; the International Crops Research Institute for the Semi-Arid Tropics (ICRISAT), Hyderabad, India; the International Potato Center, (CIP), Peru; the International Laboratory for Research on Animal Diseases (ILRAD), Nairobi, Kenya; and the International Livestock Centre for Africa (ILCA), Ethiopia. A ninth center, the International Center for Agricultural Research in Dry Areas (ICARDA), is expected to be set up in the Middle East.

In many low-income nations, large increases in yields have already been achieved with these new, more productive seeds, thereby reducing the cost of producing each unit of product. Under some conditions, single items of new technology, such as new seeds, can significantly increase yields with few other changes required, as was shown by Rochin [23]. However, employing cost-reducing new technology generally requires changes in related agricultural practices, including appropriate timing, the use of chemical fertilizers and pesticides, and new cultivation and moisture control practices.

In the process of adopting new technology, the source of agricultural inputs shifts from within peasant villages to external suppliers (Fig. 1.1). The shift to externally produced inputs occurs because the new science-based inputs are more productive and profitable (higher-yielding seeds, better plows, more effective pesticides, etc.) or because the new inputs are available in larger quantities from external sources such as plant nutrients from chemical sources and credit at lower cost through loans from banks. In this way, small farmers become increasingly dependent on the rest of the economy. The shift to market-oriented farming will be associated with greater productivity in some enterprises and a reduction in the number of enterprises on the farm. In a restatement of Adam Smith's thesis about specialization and the division of labor, "The mechanism of economic progress in farming is the

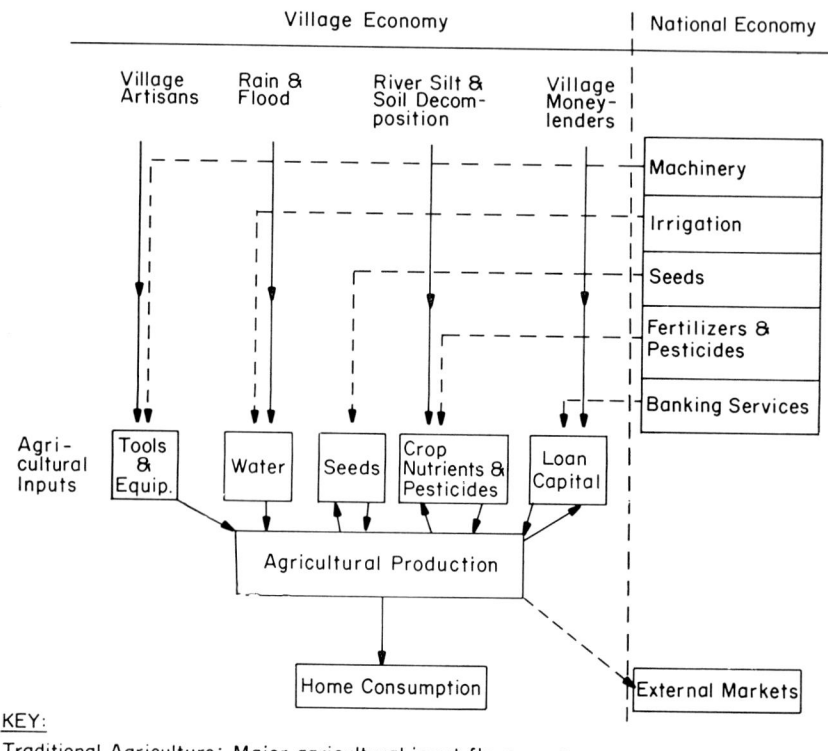

Fig. 1.1. Changes in flows of inputs and products during the agricultural transformation.

same one that operates in every other sector of the economy. The mechanism is *specialization"* [13]. The new inputs are generally produced in industrial plants or experiment stations, parts of the economy outside the small-farm agricultural sector. Thiesenhusen's study (Chapter 7) includes examples of the problems encountered in setting up new input supply systems for a new settlement.

2. *Successive Adjustments to Changes in Supply and Demand.* The agricultural transformation is characterized by continuously changing disequilibriums in demand and supply conditions in both agricultural input (factor) markets and agricultural product markets. On the product demand side, major changes include opening up overseas markets, improvements in transportation (road building, lower trucking rates, etc.), and reduction in many other marketing costs between the farm gate and the consumer. The result is higher prices to farmers or greater quantities of agricultural products sold at given market prices. Thus

farmers are faced in a dynamic agriculture with the task of continuously evaluating and incorporating the opportunities available into their farming operations. In these circumstances at any particular time, all the opportunities cannot be incorporated. Hence, a reallocation of resources could increase income. We conclude, therefore, that due to the difficulties of continuously adjusting in the dynamic, rapidly changing economic and technical environment, modern farmers may be said to be economically less efficient in the allocation of their resources than farmers in traditional agriculture.

3. *Continuously Increasing Farm Production.* Farmers in dynamic agriculture, in contrast to farmers in traditional agriculture, continue to increase farm output by incorporation of new higher productivity technology. Yields per acre in modern agriculture range anywhere from twice to more than 5 times as large as in traditional agriculture (Table 1.1). Productivity per hour of agricultural labor and net farm income have risen to very high levels in developed nations. An example of the growth of agricultural productivity is presented by Hayami and Ruttan for Japan (Fig. 1.2). But more significantly, in a dynamic agriculture levels of agricultural productivity can be expected to continue to increase as an ongoing stream of new scientific discoveries is incorporated in agricultural production.

4. *Values and Institutions in Agricultural Change.* The extent to which the values embedded in social systems may inhibit positive responses to new economic opportunities associated with changes in the demand for agricultural products, in the supply of agricultural inputs, or in the availability of new, more productive agricultural technology, has been little researched. Many suggest that peasant and tribal views of the good life may be important in reducing local demand for agricultural products and, hence, reduce responses to economic opportunities in agriculture. Some examples of these stand out. One clear example of the interaction of values with agricultural production comes from the Amish farmers of Pennsylvania who do not believe in the use of power farm machinery. Hence, in terms of labor productivity, they continue as an island of low-productivity, animal-powered agriculture surrounded by higher-productivity tractor agriculture. In African cultures, including some in Zaire, traditions in which the women do the crop farming inhibit available male labor from participating in agricultural production. Some of the literature on these issues has been summarized by Dalton [6].

The rate of response of small farmers to changes in the relative prices of agricultural products and farm input costs has been examined and found to be generally positive and often as high as for farmers in developed nations. Summaries of the large literature on this subject have been made by Behrman [2] and Helleiner [11].

In Chapter 6 Eckert provides an example of rapid response by

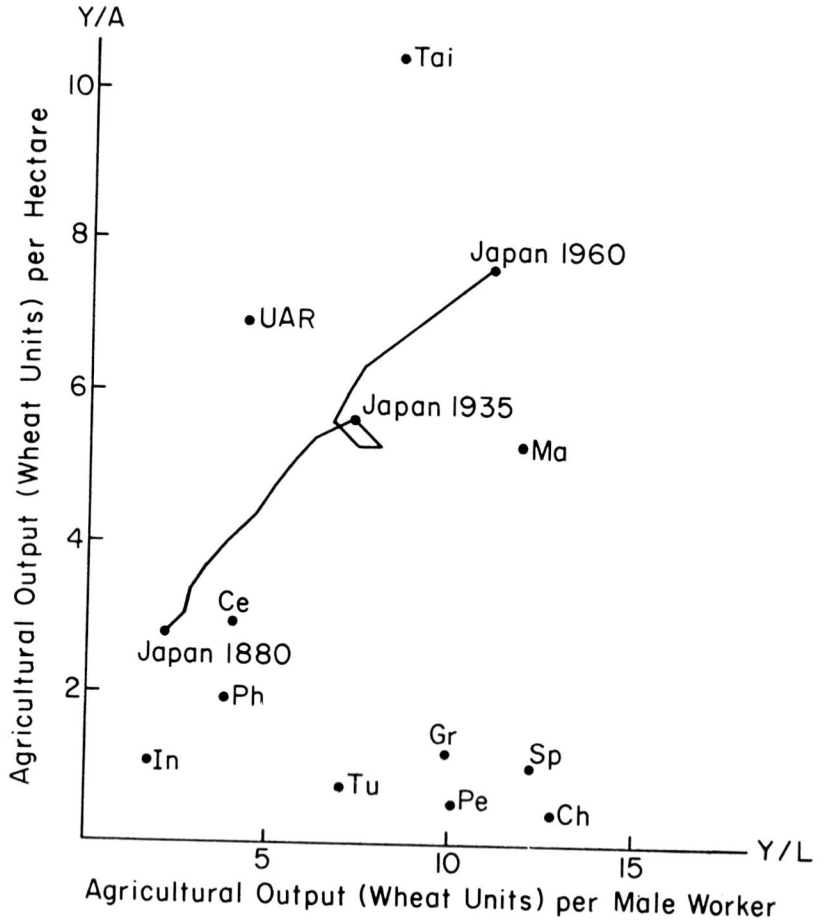

Fig. 1.2. Historical growth path of agricultural productivity in Japan, 1880–1960, with 1960 observations of agricultural productivity in other nations. (From Y. Hayami [10].) Tai = Taiwan; UAR = United Arab Republic; Ma = Mauritius; Ce = Ceylon; It = Italy; Ph = Philippines; In = India; Gr = Greece; Sp = Spain; Tu = Turkey; Pe = Peru; Ch = Chile.

small farmers to new economic opportunities. He analyzes the changes farmers made in the Punjab of Pakistan in response to the availability of new, more profitable wheat varieties. Whether significant additional response would occur as a result of changes in cultural values about the holding and use of resources is uncertain.

Modifications in institutional arrangements are associated with changes in demand and supply and the major shift to external sources of inputs. In almost all cases, organizations for producing and distributing new inputs to farmers hardly exist in traditional agriculture. The shift to new sources of inputs results in the elaboration of a large number of new or modified institutions.

Hayami and Ruttan hypothesize that the mechanism through which these institutional changes are fostered is "induced institutional innovation." "We further hypothesize that the institutions that govern the use of technology or the 'mode' of production can also be induced to change in order to enable both individuals and society to take fuller advantage of new technological opportunities under favorable market conditions" [9]. To date, little research has been focused on testing this hypothesis.

However, many professionals judge improved institutional arrangements are crucial to assure an accelerated flow of new, more productive inputs to farmers throughout the countryside. Although in the early stages of an agricultural transformation some of the new, more productive agricultural technology may be imported from the international agricultural research institutes or from other nations, additional acceleration of agricultural productivity depends on the further development of effective domestic research organizations to produce a continuous stream of locally adapted agricultural technology.

Chapters 7 and 8 provide detailed examples of the working out of major institutional changes in agriculture. In these cases, great changes were made in the control of land. In Thiesenhusen's study of a Venezuelan agrarian reform settlement, farmers were allocated land, while in Freebairn's study in northwest Mexico, land was allocated and farmed collectively. Institutional change is integral to carrying out changes in the supply and demand conditions leading to agricultural development. The way institutional changes influence agricultural development remains little understood and a major professional challenge.

5. *Limited Scale Economies.* Questions about economies of scale in small-farm agriculture arise often as economic theory suggests they may be present and industrial factory production demonstrates great increases in productivity with increased scale. However, empirical studies in agriculture undertaken to explore the relationship between size of farm and productivity in developing nations have often shown an inverse relation (Fig. 1.3). Greater intensity of input use and better husbandry appear to be the causes of larger output per unit of land on small farms.

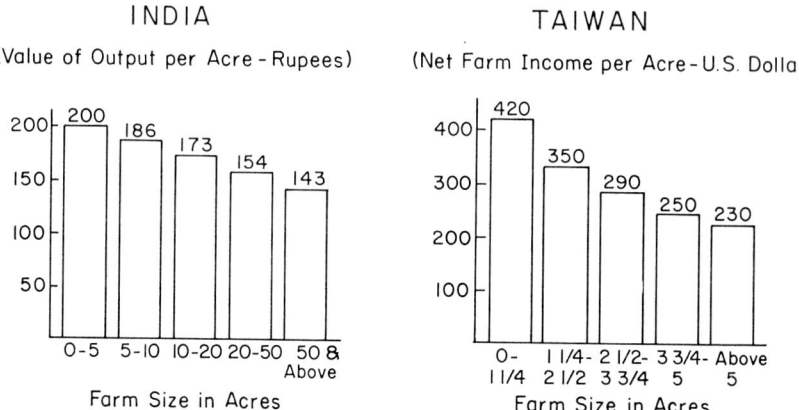
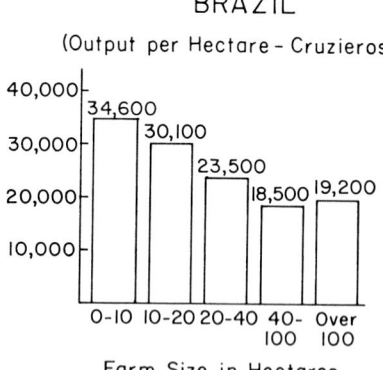

Fig. 1.3. Farm size and production per unit of land in developing nations. (From R. Christensen and L. Schmid.)

The little data available on collective and state farms of the USSR and on similar large farms in Eastern Europe have generally shown lower land and labor productivity than on the smaller individually operated farms in Western Europe. In conclusion, empirical studies do not support a general hypothesis that large farms are now more productive or likely to be in low-income nations in the foreseeable future. Berry [3] provides considerable additional data.

6. *Greater Employment.* A direct consequence of the shift to scientific agriculture and associated increases in yields and cropping intensity is a large increase in demand for labor in most areas. More agricultural operations have to be carried out over the year or in a given time period and the total volume of crop products increases. However, under

some conditions of distorted relative prices of labor and capital (subsidies for mechanization, etc.) or of particular technological breakthroughs such as the cotton picker, considerable labor displacement can occur. Hence, developing nations need to be alert to possible major displacement of agricultural labor by machinery from time to time in some agricultural areas in order to take actions to slow the change or aid the shift of agricultural labor to new jobs. Inaction could result in considerable social and political unrest in affected areas. A recent extended discussion on employment was edited by Edwards [8].

Evidence from small-farm agricultural areas in many parts of the world has demonstrated that the increasing intensity of agricultural production per unit of land associated with the agricultural transformation usually results in considerable increases in employment. Eckert, for example, reported that landless laborers found increased employment and income due to the greater harvests of the high-yielding wheat (Chapter 6). He also pointed out that greater amounts of irrigation permitted more double cropping, further increasing the demand for labor. Both the Venezuelan settlement project and the Mexican collective farm analyzed in this volume illustrate greatly increased use of labor per unit of land as more modern agricultural inputs such as irrigation water and fertilizer were applied on previously unused or extensively cropped areas. A recent estimate for rice areas such as the Philippines shows that for labor on high-yielding rice varieties "the most likely approximation of additional requirements is of the order of 30–50 percent" [20]. Earlier analyses based on a comparison of rice farming in Japan and West Bengal indicated that over longer periods of time labor utilization per acre can rise more than three times on small farms as science-based agriculture replaces traditional farming [15].

7. *The Complex Interrelated Nature of the Agricultural Transformation.* The agricultural transformation consists of a shift from largely unchanging social, economic, and technical farming conditions employing the arts of traditional agriculture to a continuously changing agriculture based on a flow of new science-based agricultural inputs of industrial origin. Three dimensions of the immense complexity of this transformation need emphasis.

First, detailed studies of farming in developing nations have shown the intricate complexity of traditional farming systems. Many of these complex interrelationships in traditional agriculture are illustrated in this volume. Two examples are of particular interest. In the village of Dan Mahawayi in the north of Nigeria, Norman describes the complicated mixed cropping patterns in which a number of crops are planted in a field at the same time. His formal economic analysis supports the hypothesis that these cropping practices based on the traditional art of agriculture produce the highest income for these farmers consistent with reduced risk. In the traditional Thai village analyzed by DeBoer and

Welsch, the complex interrelationships of crop and livestock production are shown.

Second, emphasis is needed on the complexity of changes required by farmers in shifting to new, externally produced, science-based inputs. In some instances, the new agricultural input can be substituted easily in existing agricultural systems. Under these circumstances farmers need only careful observation of field demonstrations to convince them to try the new technology. Eckert's study, showing rapid increases in wheat yield in Pakistan due to new seeds and fertilizer, is an outstanding example of this type of new technology. Typical peasant characteristics such as low levels of literacy (19% literate) in 1961, according to United Nations data, did not prevent these farmers from increasing production greatly. However, as different kinds of new technology become available at a faster rate in later phases of the green revolution, their integration into agricultural systems requires many more adjustments. Hence, as more new inputs are combined in production, knowledge of basic chemical, biological, and management principles applied to animals, plants, and soils becomes more necessary to accelerate farm productivity.

Third, these complicated interrelationships point to the growing need for more agricultural extension work as the number of decisions required of farmers increases. In the equilibrium conditions of traditional agriculture, there is little helpful advice extension workers can provide. However, when new agricultural technology becomes available, the usefulness of some form of agricultural extension is an almost universal conclusion. A standard extension model, with agents visiting farmers and setting up demonstrations on farmers' fields, is often established. However, a more recently tested model drawing on village leadership may better fit some of the cultural and resource conditions of present-day low-income nations. Raper [17] and Stevens [22] provide details on this model.

CONCLUSION. Greatly increased demand for food and agricultural products came about in the second half of the twentieth century due to two major factors: acceleration in population growth rates in low-income developing nations, and strong increases in demand for agricultural products in developed nations due to continued growth in per capita income. Recent world food scarcities and high food prices emphasize the need to increase production on the more than 100 million small farms in Asia, Africa, and Latin America.

Because of current high rates of population growth, high densities of population on much of the good agricultural land of developing nations, and limited off-farm job opportunities, there is little scope in many nations for augmenting the amount of land per farm. Therefore, increasing the intensity of production on a limited land base is essential for higher income in most areas. The transformation of agriculture holds promise of doubling and quadrupling net income on small farms, particularly in irrigated and higher rainfall areas.

Although recent increases in energy and fertilizer costs have raised the prices of many new agricultural inputs, their productivity is so great that these investments remain highly profitable in most areas.

The conclusions that emerge from this chapter on the theory of the agricultural transformation and the empirical chapters that follow provide knowledge of how small farmers may be aided to contribute significantly to increasing world agricultural production.

The outline of theory offered points to the following major strategies for accelerating agricultural production on small farms in developing nations. The central focus of strategy is to upset the technical and economic equilibrium faced by small farmers so as to increase opportunities for greater income. Three major thrusts of action exist, the first two somewhat limited.

The first thrust attempts to increase farm product prices or the quantities of products demanded at given prices leading small farmers to increase output. Particular actions to achieve this objective include judicious government use of farm product price supports, reduction in transportation costs through roadbuilding and other activities, and any number of actions to reduce costs in product marketing systems.

A second thrust focuses on assuring availability and reducing the cost of agricultural inputs to small farmers. Development of effectively operating modern input supply systems is a complex process, often with considerable government involvement and the setting up of numbers of new input supply institutions ranging from central government agricultural development corporations to local cooperatives supplying farm credit and to new local businesses. The increases in output possible on small farms from the use of these two thrusts, while large in some cases, in general remain limited, due to the use of essentially unchanged agricultural technology.

Hence, the third and most fundamental thrust is to develop and make available new, more productive agricultural technology locally adapted to small-farm conditions. The most dramatic recent examples of this thrust are provided by high-yielding wheat, rice, and maize (corn) seeds that in some cases have doubled production with little change in other resource use. When a flow of continuously more productive agricultural technology is established for small farmers and this is coupled with better farm input supply systems and improvements in agricultural product marketing, the complex transformation of small-farm agriculture is under way.

The three thrusts of action relate in the following ways to the four hypotheses set out earlier. The theory of the agricultural transformation presented depends on the assumption of the responsiveness of small farmers to new, more profitable economic opportunities and, hence, that small farmers are reasonably good economic decision makers. Chapter 3 in particular and other parts of this volume further test this hypothesis.

The application of agricultural development theory to the hypothesis that capital shortages prevent small farmers from increasing agricultural output clarifies this question. In the theory of traditional agriculture, increasing the supply of capital generally has little effect on low productivity agriculture in equilibrium. However, in the agricultural transformation, as new, more productive agricultural inputs become available from off-farm sources, increased availability of capital for the new, more costly production resources is critical to the rate of use and the resulting production increases.

With respect to the hypothesis of a positive relationship between increased farm size and higher agricultural productivity, in the low-income developing nations theory suggests there may be such a relationship under some circumstances. Much empirical data from developing nations however have shown an inverse relation under present economic and social conditions. Empirical studies in each farming area are necessary to determine what particular economic and technical conditions actually prevail in relation to existing farm sizes and any possible productivity gains from increasing farm size.

The hypothesis that small farmers in low-income nations are trapped in a social and economic equilibrium underlies the theory of traditional agriculture presented. Norman's study (Chapter 3) undertook two formal tests of this theory. A further test is provided in Chapter 5. These analyses and other research support the hypothesis.

Finally, theory of agricultural development aids in gaining long-run perspective. Throughout history major technical changes in agriculture have occurred as a result of accidental introductions of crops and livestock from abroad or due to chance introductions by conquerors, colonial administrators, or merchants, or through occasional significant local inventions. Today, nations cannot depend on hit or miss introductions and inventions. Continuous growth in agricultural productivity in the low-income nations is dependent on scientific advance in the laboratories and experiment stations, the production and distribution of new locally productive technological inputs, and continuing complex changes by small farmers in their agricultural operations. These technical and institutional changes underlie the gradually accelerating agricultural transformation in developing nations. The transformation of small farms holds forth promise of increasing rural employment opportunities, increasing real income, and moderating rural income disparities.

REFERENCES

1. Beckford, George L. "Strategies of Agricultural Development: Comment." *Food Research Institute Studies,* 1972, pp. 149–54.
2. Behrman, Jere R. *Supply Response in Underdeveloped Agriculture,* Amsterdam: North Holland Publishing Co., 1968.
3. Berry, Albert R. "Cross Country Evidence on Farm Size/Factor Productiv-

ity Relationships," in *Small Farm Agriculture: Studies in Developing Nations,* Agr. Exp. Sta. Bull. No. 101, Purdue Univ., Sept. 1975.
4. Chambers, Robert. *Settlement Schemes in Tropical Africa.* New York: Praeger, 1969.
5. Dall, John P.; Rhodes, V. James; and West, Jerry G. *Economics of Agricultural Production, Markets and Policy,* Homewood, Ill.: R. D. Irwin, 1968.
6. Dalton, George. "Traditional Production in Primitive African Economies," in *Tribal and Peasant Economies,* Garden City, N.Y.: The Natural History Press, 1967.
7. Dillon, John L., and Anderson, J. R. "Allocative Efficiency, Traditional Agriculture and Risk." *American Journal of Agricultural Economics* 53 (Feb. 1971): 26–32.
8. Edwards, Edgar O. *Employment in Developing Nations,* New York: Columbia Univ. Press, 1974.
9. Hayami, Yujiro, and Ruttan, Vernon W. *Agricultural Development: An International Perspective.* Baltimore: Johns Hopkins Univ. Press, 1971.
10. Hayami, Y. *An International Comparison of Agricultural Production and Productivities.* Minnesota Agr. Exp. Sta. Bull. No. 277, 1971.
11. Helleiner, Gerald K. "Smallholder Decision Making: Tropical African Evidence," in Lloyd B. Reynolds (ed.), *Agriculture in Development Theory.* New Haven: Yale Univ. Press, 1975.
12. Hopper, W. David. "Allocation Efficiency in a Traditional Indian Agriculture." *Journal of Farm Economics* 47 (Aug. 1965): 611–24.
13. Johnston, Bruce F., and Kilby, Peter. *Agriculture and Structural Transformation.* London: Oxford Univ. Press, 1975.
14. Massell, Benton F. "Farm Management in Peasant Agriculture: An Empirical Study." *Food Research Institute Studies* 7 (1967): 205–15.
15. Mellor, John W. *The Economics of Agricultural Development.* Ithaca: Cornell Univ. Press, 1966.
16. Nelson, Michael. *The Development of Tropical Lands: Policy Issues in Latin America,* Baltimore: Johns Hopkins Press, 1973.
17. Raper, Arthur F. *Rural Development in Action: The Comprehensive Experiment at Comilla, East Pakistan.* Ithaca: Cornell Univ. Press, 1970.
18. Samuelson, Paul A. *Economics.* New York: McGraw-Hill, latest edition.
19. Schultz, T. W. *Transforming Traditional Agriculture.* New Haven: Yale Univ. Press, 1964.
20. Shaw, Robert d'A. *Jobs and Agricultural Development,* Washington, D.C.: Overseas Development Council, 1970.
21. Southworth, H. M., and Johnston, Bruce R. "Toward a Theory of Agricultural Development," in *Agricultural Development and Economic Growth,* Ithaca: Cornell Univ. Press, 1967.
22. Stevens, Robert D. "Three Rural Development Models for Small Farm Agricultural Areas in Low-Income Nations." *Journal of Developing Areas* 8 (Apr. 1974): 409–20.
23. Stevens, Robert D.; Alavi, Hamza; and Bertocci, Peter J. *Rural Development in Bangladesh and Pakistan.* Honolulu: Univ. Press of Hawaii, 1975, pp. 270–89, "The Adoption and Effects of High-Yielding Wheats on Unirrigated Subsistence Holdings in Pakistan" by R. I. Rochin.
24. U.S. Agency for International Development. *Index of Community Development Publications,* Community Development Reference Service, Office of Development Administration, Bureau for Technical Assistance, CDP–N., Apr. 1970.
25. Vincent, Warren H. *Economics and Management in Agriculture.* Englewood Cliffs, N. J.: Prentice-Hall, 1962.
26. Valsan, E. H. *Community Development Programs and Rural Local Government.* New York: Praeger, 1970.
27. Wolgin, Jerome M. "Resource Allocation and Risk: A Case Study of Small-

holder Agriculture in Kenya." *American Journal of Agricultural Economics* 57 (Nov. 1975): 622–30.
28. Yotopoulos, Pan A. *Allocative Efficiency in Economic Development: A Cross Section Analysis of Epirus Farming.* Athens: Center of Planning and Economics Research, 1968.
29. ———. "On the Efficiency of Resource Utilization in Subsistence Agriculture." *Food Research Institute Studies* 8 (1968): 125–35.
30. Yotopoulos, Pan A., and Lau, Lawrence J. "A Test for Relative Economic Efficiency: Some Further Results." *American Economic Review* 62 (Mar. 1973).

CHAPTER 2

Population and Affluence: Growing Pressures on World Food Resources

LESTER R. BROWN

THE early months of 1973 witnessed a dramatic upsurge in interest in the world food situation, largely in response to global scarcity and rising food prices. Prices for some of the principal food commodities—wheat, rice, feedgrains, and soybeans—soared to historic highs in international markets. Rationing was in effect for at least some foodstuffs in three of the world's four most populous countries: the People's Republic of China, India, and the Soviet Union.

Food was being airlifted into several countries in sub-Sahara Africa during June 1973 to stave off famine. India and Bangladesh faced critical food shortages. The United States was restricting soybean exports in order to bring internal food prices down. Food scarcity was affecting the entire world, rich countries and poor.

The communications media have drawn attention to several factors contributing to the food scarcities of 1973. Among these are the poor rice harvest in Asia, the shortfall in the Soviet wheat crop, and the temporary disappearance of the anchoveta off the coast of Peru for several months in late 1972 and early 1973. But these are short-term factors, and they should not be permitted to obscure other more funda-

LESTER R. BROWN is a Senior Fellow with the Overseas Development Council. From 1963 to 1966 he served as advisor on foreign agricultural policy to the secretary of agriculture. From 1966 to 1969 he was administrator of the International Agricultural Development Service, the technical assistance arm of the U.S. Department of Agriculture. He is the author of *Man, Land and Food* (1963), *Seeds of Change* (1971), *World without Borders* (1972), *By Bread Alone* (1974), and *In the Human Interest* (1976).

Notes: Printed as Development Paper 15, Overseas Development Council, Washington, D.C. Reprinted with permission.

The author gratefully acknowledges the assistance of Erik Eckholm, a colleague at the Overseas Development Council, in the preparation of this manuscript.

mental long-term trends and forces that are altering the nature and dimensions of the world food problem.

During the 1960s the world food problem was perceived as a food/population problem, a race between food and people. At the end of each year observers anxiously compared rates of increase in food production with those of population growth to see if any progress was being made. Throughout most of the decade it was nip and tuck. During the 1970s rapid global population growth continues to generate demand for more food, but, in addition, rising affluence is emerging as a major new claimant on world food resources. Historically, there was only one important source of growth in world demand for food; there are now two.

At the global level, population growth is still the dominant cause of an increasing demand for food. Expanding at about 2% per year, world population will double in little more than a generation. Merely maintaining current per capita consumption levels will therefore require a doubling of food production over the next generation. In demographic terms the world currently divides essentially into two groups of countries: the rich countries that have low or declining rates of population growth, and the poor countries, most of which have rapid rates of population growth. Fully four-fifths of the annual increment in world population of an estimated 70 million occur in the poor countries.

Some of the relatively small poor countries add more to the world's annual population gain than the larger rich ones. Mexico, for example, now contributes more to world population growth than does the United States. The Philippines add more people each year than does Japan. Brazil adds 2.6 million people in a year, while the Soviet Union adds only 2.4 million.

The effect of rising affluence on the world demand for food is perhaps best understood by examining its effect on grain requirements. Grain consumed directly provides 52% of human food energy intake. Consumed indirectly in the form of livestock products, it provides a sizable share of the remainder. In resource terms, grains occupy more than 70% of the world's crop area.

In the poor countries the annual availability of grain per person averages only about 400 pounds per year (Fig. 2.1). Nearly all this small amount must be consumed directly to meet minimum energy needs. Little can be spared for conversion into animal protein.

In the United States and Canada, per capita grain utilization is currently approaching 1 ton per year. Of this total only about 150 pounds are consumed directly in the form of bread, pastries, and breakfast cereals. The remainder is consumed indirectly in the form of meat, milk, and eggs. The agricultural resources—land, water, and fertilizer—required to support an average North American are nearly five times those of the average Indian, Nigerian, or Colombian.

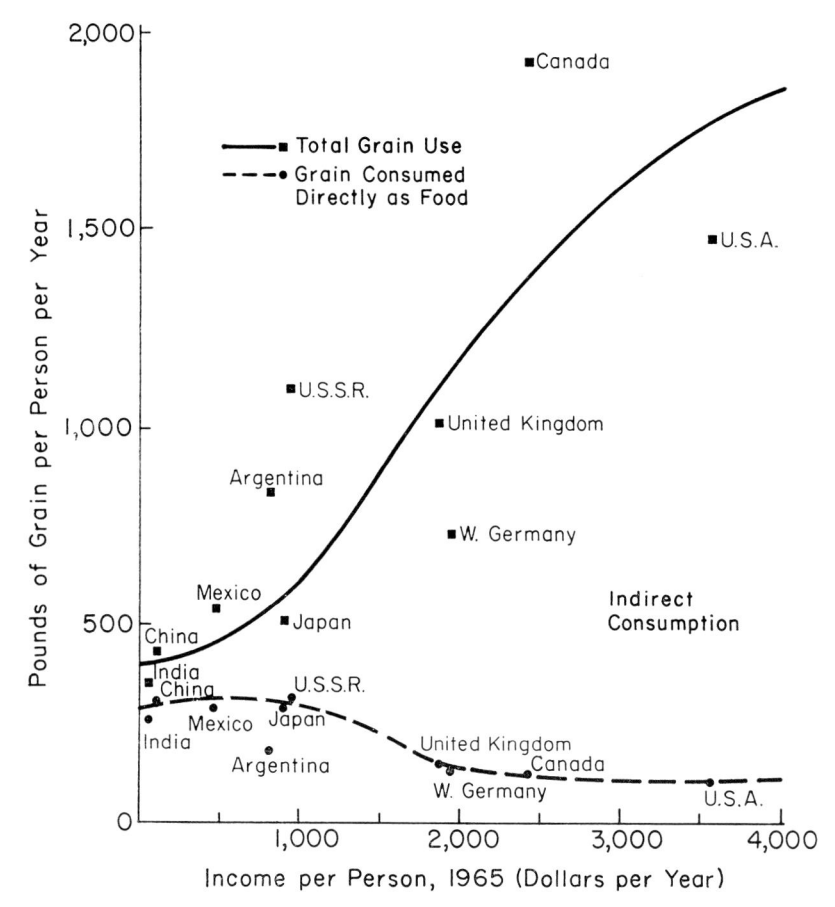

Fig. 2.1. Direct and indirect grain consumption by per capita income, selected countries.

Throughout the world, per capita grain requirements rise with income. The amount of grain consumed directly rises until per capita income approaches $500 per year, whereupon it begins to decline, eventually leveling off at about 150 pounds. The total amount of grain consumed directly and indirectly, however, continues to rise rapidly as per capita income climbs. As yet no nation appears to have reached a level of affluence where its per capita grain requirements have stopped rising.

The impact of rising affluence on the consumption of livestock products is evident in trends in the United States over the past generation. For example, per capita consumption of beef climbed from 55 pounds in 1940 to 117 pounds in 1972, more than doubling. Poultry consumption rose from 18 pounds to 51 pounds during the same period.

There is now a northern tier of industrial countries—beginning with the United Kingdom in the west and including Scandinavia, Western Europe, Eastern Europe, the Soviet Union, and Japan—whose economic advancement and dietary habits more or less approximate those of the United States in 1940. As incomes continue to rise in this group of countries containing some two-thirds of a billion people, a sizable share of the additional income is being converted into demand for livestock products, particularly beef. Many of these countries, such as Japan and those in Western Europe, are densely populated. Others—the Soviet Union, for example—suffer from a scarcity of fresh water. Thus they lack the capacity to satisfy the growth in demand for livestock products entirely from indigenous resources. As a result they are importing increasing amounts of livestock products or of feedgrains and soybeans with which to expand their livestock production.

Throughout the poor countries population growth accounts for most of the year-to-year growth in the demand for food. At best only very limited progress is being made in raising per capita consumption. In the more affluent countries, on the other hand, rising incomes account for most of the growth in the demand for food. In Japan and France, for example, where population is growing at about 1% annually and per capita incomes at several percent, year-to-year growth in the demand for food derives principally from rising affluence.

Wherever population has stopped growing, as in West Germany, rising affluence accounts for all the growth in food consumption. In a country such as India, however, where income rises are scarcely perceptible and population continues to grow rapidly, nearly all the growth in demand derives from population growth. In Brazil, which has both rapid population growth and, in recent years at least, rapid growth in per capita income, both factors loom large in the growth in demand for food.

TECHNOLOGICAL BACKDROP. At the time agriculture evolved 10,000 or more years ago, the earth supported roughly 10 million people, no more than now live in London or Afghanistan. Since then a series of technological innovations has brought about an enormous expansion in the earth's food-producing capacity. Following the discovery of agriculture, food production expanded under the influence of six major technological advances: the use of irrigation, the harnessing of draft animals, the exchange of crops between the Old World and the New World, the development of chemical fertilizers and pesticides, advances in genetics, and the invention of the internal combustion engine.

The earliest of these innovations was irrigation. Water was diverted onto land under cultivation by obstructing the flow of streams and rivers. This intervention in the hydrological cycle, closely associated with the emergence of early civilizations in the Middle East, has greatly boosted the productivity of land. Today close to one-seventh of the world's cropland is irrigated.

About a thousand years after irrigation began, animals were harnessed for tilling the soil. This breakthrough brought about the conversion of grass and hay into a form of energy that could be used to increase the food supply. Using draft animals supplemented limited human muscle power and raised the efficiency of labor to the point where a small segment of the population could be spared from food-producing activities.

The third factor expanding global food production was the exchange of crops set in motion by the linkage of the Old World and the New World. Few people would identify Columbus as a major figure in the effort to increase food supplies, yet his contribution in establishing such a linkage was considerable. One of the most interesting results of this exchange of crops was the discovery that some plants could be grown more successfully in their new environment than in their country of origin. For example, several times more potatoes are produced in Europe, including the Soviet Union, than in the New World where the potato originated.

The use of agricultural chemicals, both to improve soil fertility and to control pests, has been yet another crucial factor in the effort to meet the global demand for food. The early research on chemical fertilizers was undertaken in Germany by Justus von Liebig, who found that the nutrients removed from the soil by farming could be replaced artificially. Although this discovery was made in the 1840s, it did not become commercially important until well into the twentieth century, largely because the presence of frontiers made it possible to continuously bring new land under the plow. Once the frontiers began to disappear, however, farmers turned to fertilizer as the principal means of expanding production.

Then, as man's ability to alter the genetic composition of domesticated species of plants and animals progressed, after the discovery of the principles of genetics, the productivity of these species increased dramatically. Advances in cereal productivity over the past generation have been particularly impressive. Many farmers in the U.S. Midwest now consistently obtain corn yields of 3 tons per acre, making corn the most productive of all the world's grains.

Advances in cereal productivity have at least been matched by those in the livestock and poultry sector. The first domesticated cow probably did not yield more than 600 pounds of milk, barely enough to support a calf until it could forage for itself. In India, milk production remains at about that level today. By contrast, the average cow in the United States last year yielded 10,000 pounds of milk. The holder of the world record is a Maryland cow, Rheinhart's Ballad, which produced 42,000 pounds of milk in a single year. This productive animal could deliver

49 quarts of milk to one's doorstep daily, thus outperforming her early ancestors by a factor of 70 to 1.

In the case of poultry, the first domesticated hens did not lay more than about 15 eggs or one clutch per year. The average American hen produced 227 eggs in 1972. For some time U.S. hens held the world egg-laying title, but a few years ago an industrious Japanese hen set a new record by laying 365 eggs in 365 days. United States agricultural analysts project continuing gains in productivity per cow and hen.

And finally, the development of the internal combustion engine has greatly augmented the available energy resources for expanding the food supply. Today more than half the world's cropland is tilled with mechanical power; the bulk of the remainder is still tilled by animals. Three distinct forms of agriculture exist today, depending on the form of energy used—human muscle power, draft animals, or internal combustion engines. In some areas of the world all three types can be found within a single country. In Colombia, Andean Indians living in mountainous regions practice hand cultivation, family farmers in the lowlands employ draft animals, and the large commercial farmers use tractors.

Achievements in agriculture are impressive. These principal technological advances, coupled with others not discussed here, have increased the earth's food-producing capacity several hundredfold since agriculture began. Despite these advances, hunger remains the daily lot of much of humanity.

Technological advances in agriculture and consequent increases in the food supply have permitted population to increase. Population increases in turn generate pressures for agricultural innovation. Thus trends of expanding food production and growing population have reinforced each other. Population growth continues to absorb all the increases in food production in the great majority of the poor countries, leaving little if any food for upgrading diets.

Expansion of Area or Increased Yield. There are essentially two ways of expanding the world food supply from conventional agriculture. One is to expand the area under cultivation. The other, largely made possible by the advancements in the use of agricultural chemicals and in plant genetics, is to raise output on the existing cultivated area. From the beginning of agriculture until about 1950, expanding the cultivated area was the major means of increasing the world's food supply. Since mid-century, however, raising the yield on the existing cultivated area has accounted for most of the increase. Intensification of cultivation has increased steadily since 1950; during the early 1970s it has accounted for an estimated four-fifths of the annual growth in world food output, far overshadowing expansion of the cultivated area.

The timing of the transition from the area-expanding method of increasing food production to the yield-raising method has been very uneven throughout the world. As population pressures built up in Japan in the late nineteenth and early twentieth centuries, the Japanese were forced to intensify cultivation and were very likely the first people to succeed in making the transition. Ironically, some of the technologies used by the Japanese in attaining a yield-per-acre takeoff, notably the use of chemical fertilizer, were introduced from Europe. Several north European countries in which available farmland was limited were close behind and also successfully completed the transition in the early twentieth century.

In the United States the frontier had vanished just before World War I, but a yield-per-acre takeoff was not achieved until World War II, when economic conditions made the use of the accumulated technologies profitable. During the intervening period, farm output lagged, but land used to produce feed for horses was released for production when tractors began to displace horses after World War I. A second group of industrial countries, including the United Kingdom, Canada, and Australia, also made the area-to-yield transition during the early 1940s, largely as a result of the strong wartime economic incentives to utilize already available technologies to expand production. Interestingly, U.S. corn yields had remained static for nearly a century from the time of the Civil War until the outbreak of World War II.

Some estimates indicate that the world's cultivated area can be doubled. But much of the potentially cultivable land is in the tropics, and recent experience shows that once the protective forest cover is removed from much of this land, it deteriorates rapidly, losing whatever inherent fertility it has. With a few notable exceptions, such as selected areas in the Amazon Basin in Brazil, the world's most productive farmlands are under cultivation. At the global level, the record of the past two decades suggests it is far cheaper and easier to expand the food supply by intensifying cultivation on the existing cropland area than by bringing new land under the plow.

During the first half of the 1960s, food production in the developing countries as a group began to fall behind population growth, bringing rising food prices, growing food scarcity, and increasing dependence on food aid from the United States (Fig. 2.2). The food crisis in these countries that occurred during the early and mid-1960s was brought into sharp focus by the two consecutive monsoon failures in the Indian subcontinent in 1965 and 1966. It was, however, a direct result of the fact that many of these countries had virtually exhausted the supply of new land that could be readily brought under cultivation but had not yet achieved a takeoff in yield per acre. It was in this context that the green revolution—the combination of new cereal technologies and production-oriented economic incentives—came into being.

THE GREEN REVOLUTION. Efforts to modernize agriculture in the poor countries in the 1950s and early 1960s were consistently frustrated. When farmers in these countries attempted to use varieties of corn de-

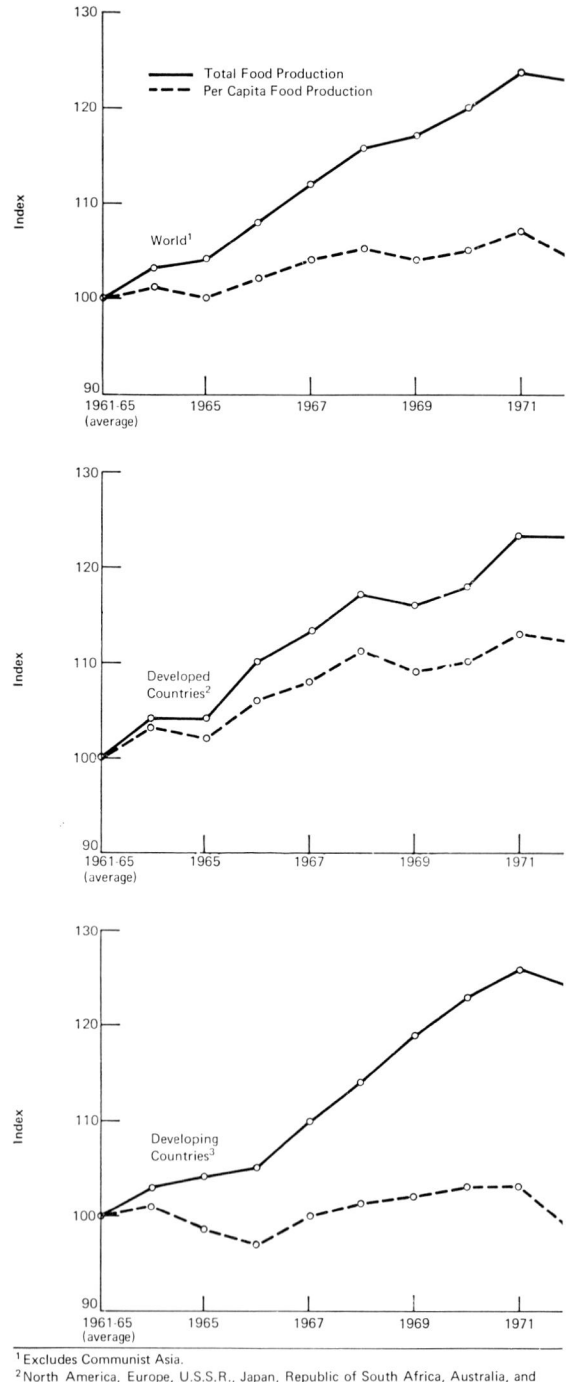

[1] Excludes Communist Asia.
[2] North America, Europe, U.S.S.R., Japan, Republic of South Africa, Australia, and New Zealand.
[3] Latin America, Asia (except Japan and Communist Asia), Africa (except Republic of South Africa).
SOURCE: U.S. Department of Agriculture.

Fig. 2.2. Total and per capita food production, 1961–72.

veloped in Iowa, they often failed to produce any corn at all. Japanese rice varieties were not suited either to local cultural practices or to consumer tastes in India. When fertilizer was applied intensively to local cereal varieties, the yield response was limited and occasionally even negative.

It was against this backdrop of frustration that the high-yielding dwarf wheats were developed by the Rockefeller Foundation team in Mexico. Three unique characteristics of these wheats endeared them to farmers in many countries—their fertilizer responsiveness, lack of photoperiod sensitivity (sensitivity to day length), and early maturity.

When farmers applied more than 40 pounds of nitrogen fertilizer per acre to traditional varieties having tall, thin straw, the wheat often lodged or fell over, causing severe crop losses. By contrast, yields of the short, stiff-strawed dwarf varieties of Mexican wheat would continue to rise with nitrogen applications up to 120 pounds per acre. Given the necessary fertilizer and water and the appropriate management, farmers could easily double the yields of indigenous varieties.

Advantages of New Cereal Varieties. Beyond this, the reduced sensitivity of dwarf varieties to day length permitted them to be moved around the world over a wide range of latitudes, stretching from Mexico, which lies partly in the tropics, to Turkey in the temperate zone. Because the biological clocks of the new wheats were much less sensitive than those of the traditional ones, planting dates were much more flexible.

Another advantageous characteristic of the new wheats was their early maturity. They were ready for harvest within 120 days after planting; the traditional varieties took 150 days or more. This trait, combined with reduced sensitivity to day length, created broad, new opportunities for multiple cropping wherever water supplies were sufficient.

Within a few years after the spectacular breakthrough with wheat in Mexico, the Ford Foundation joined the Rockefeller Foundation to establish the International Rice Research Institute (IRRI) in the Philippines. Its purpose was to attempt to breed a fertilizer-responsive, early-maturing rice capable of wide adaptation—in effect, a counterpart of the high-yielding wheats. With the wheat experience to draw upon, agricultural scientists at IRRI struck pay dirt quickly. Within a few years they released the first of the high-yielding dwarf rices, a variety known as IR-8.

The great advantage of the new seeds was that the developing countries could use quickly the agricultural research that had taken decades to complete in the United States, Japan, and elsewhere. In those areas of the developing countries where there were requisite supplies of water and fertilizer and where price incentives were offered, the spread of the high-yielding varieties of wheat and rice was rapid. Farmers assumed to be bound by tradition were quick to adopt the new seeds when it was obviously profitable for them to do so.

Effects of the Revolution. Early in 1968, the term "green revolution" was coined by William Gaud, administrator of the Agency for International Development, to describe the introduction and rapid spread of the high-yielding wheats and rices. In 1965 land planted with these new varieties in Asia totaled about 200 acres, largely trial and demonstration plots. Thereafter, the acreage spread swiftly as follows:

Year	Acres
1965	200
1966	41,000
1967	4,047,000
1968	16,660,000
1969	31,319,000
1970	43,914,000
1971	50,549,000

The most recent estimate of high-yielding wheats and rices is 101,003,500 acres for 1974–75 in *Development and Spread of High-Yielding Varieties of Wheat and Rice in Less Developed Nations*, by Dana G. Dalrymple, U.S. Department of Agriculture, Foreign Agricultural Economic Dept., No. 95, 1976 (ed.).

Acreage figures for Mexico are not included in the series above since the new seeds had largely displaced traditional varieties before the green revolution became an international phenomenon in the mid-1960s. Among the principal Asian countries to benefit from using the new seeds are India, Pakistan, Turkey, the Philippines, Indonesia, Malaysia, and Ceylon.

During the late 1960s, the Philippines were able to achieve self-sufficiency in rice, ending a half-century of dependence on imported rice. Unfortunately, this situation was not sustained because of a number of factors, including civil unrest, the susceptibility of the new rices to disease, and the failure of the government to continue the essential support of the rice program.

Pakistan greatly increased its wheat production, emerging as a net exporter of grain in recent years. In India, where advances in the new varieties have been concentrated largely in wheat, progress has been encouraging. During a seven-year span from 1965 to 1972, India expanded its wheat production from 11 million tons to 27 million tons, an increase in a major crop unmatched by any other country in history.

One result of this dramatic advance in wheat production in India was the accumulation of unprecedented cereal reserves and the attainment of cereal self-sufficiency in 1972. This eliminated, at least temporarily, the need for imports into a country that only a few years before had been the principal recipient of U.S. food aid. Economic self-sufficiency in cereals—when farmers produce as much as consumers can afford at prevailing prices—is not to be confused with nutritional self-sufficiency, however, which requires much higher levels of productivity and purchasing power.

During late 1971 and in 1972, India was able to use nearly 2 million tons from its own food reserves, initially to feed nearly 10 million Bengali refugees during the civil war in East Pakistan, and later as food aid for Bangladesh. A poor monsoon in 1972 temporarily forced India back into the world market as an importer of grain, but on a much smaller scale—4 million tons—than the massive import of nearly 10 million tons that followed the 1965 monsoon failure.

This is not to suggest that the green revolution has solved the world's food problems, either on a short- or long-term basis. The 1974 drought clearly demonstrated that Indian agriculture is still at the mercy of the vagaries of weather. A second monsoon failure would have seriously disrupted the pattern of progress that has characterized Indian agriculture over the past five years. Worldwide, wheat stocks were down below 30 million tons, the lowest level since 1952, according to the Food and Agriculture Organization.

Assessing the Results. The green revolution can be properly assessed only when we ask what things would have been like in its absence. The grim scenario that this question calls forth lends some of the needed perspective. Increases in cereal production made possible by the new seeds did arrest the deteriorating trend in per capita food production in the developing countries. But although there have been some spectacular localized successes in raising cereal output, relatively little progress has been made in raising the per capita production of cereals among the poor countries as a whole over the past several years.

Many of those involved working closely with the green revolution, including Dr. Norman Borlaug and myself, have stressed from the beginning that the new technologies embodied in the green revolution did not represent a solution to the food problem. Rather we noted that it was a means of buying time, perhaps an additional 15 or 20 years during which the brakes could be applied to population growth. Ultimately the only solution to the food problem will be the curbing of world population growth.

Although several years have passed since the green revolution began, the success stories in national family planning programs in the poor nations are all too few. Among the population giants of Asia, the People's Republic of China appears to be substantially reducing its birthrates; but reductions in India, Indonesia, Pakistan, and Bangladesh are scarcely perceptible. Without a sharply accelerated effort to curb birthrates, the battle to feed Asia's massive and rapidly growing population may yet be lost.

Another question persistently raised concerning the green revolution is: Who benefits from the adoption of these new technologies? The new seeds can be used with equal success by both large- and small-farm owners if the farmers have equal access to the requisite inputs and supporting services. In many countries and locales, however, the owners of large farms have easier access to credit and to technical advisory services than the owners of smaller ones. Where these circumstances prevail, there is a disturbing tendency for the rich farmers to get richer and the poor ones poorer.

But many other factors determine which farmers will benefit from the new seeds. One is the crop they grow. Widely adapted, high-yielding varieties exist only for wheat and rice. Thus, in Mexico, wheat farmers have benefited grandly, but corn farmers, most of them small subsistence farmers, have gained little from technological progress. Likewise, in India the principal beneficiaries of the green revolution are the wheat farmers, since successful adoption of the high-yielding rices has been exceedingly modest by comparison.

Perhaps the most important single factor determining whether a given farmer can use the new seeds is whether or not he has an adequate supply of water. Wheat farmers on the high-rainfall coastal plain of Turkey have benefited enormously from the new seeds, while those on the arid Anatolian Plateau have scarcely been touched.

The impact of green revolution technology on unemployment also is often questioned. If properly managed, this technology can be highly beneficial. The new high-yielding varieties of wheat and rice require much more labor than the traditional varieties they replace. Realizing the full yield potential of the new seeds requires frequent fertilization and irrigation. This in turn requires careful and frequent weeding lest the fertilizer and water be converted into weeds rather than food. Higher yields require more labor at harvest time.

The risk is that farmers profiting from the use of the new seeds will want to invest their profits in Western-style mechanization. This tendency may be aggravated by low, subsidized interest rates on agricultural loans for farm mechanization. Rates that are too low, which is often the case, encourage farmers to substitute machinery for labor rather than to use the maximum amount of labor.

AGRICULTURAL STRESSES ON THE ECOSYSTEM. New signs of agricultural stress on the earth's ecosystem appear almost daily as the growing demand for food presses against our ecosystem's finite capacities. Early interventions were local in effect, but the technological intrusions of modern agriculture often have global consequences. Efforts to expand the food supply, either by expanding the area under cultivation or by intensifying cultivation through the use of agricultural chemicals and irrigation, bring with them troublesome and disturbing ecological consequences.

Accelerating Soil Loss. As livestock herds are increased to meet the growing demands for food and draft power, they graze over ever-larger areas, stripping the land of its natural cover in many parts of the world. This problem is most serious in North Africa, the Middle East, and the Indian subcontinent. And as expanding population increases the need for new agricultural land and for forest products for fuel—particularly in the poor nations—the countryside is being steadily denuded of trees.

Nature requires centuries to create the earth's thin mantle of life-sustaining topsoil; people can destroy it in a few years. Stripped of its original cover of grass and trees, much of the earth's land surface is vulnerable to erosion by wind and rain. In poor countries, millions of acres of these unproductive lands are abandoned each year by rural people who are forced to go to the already overcrowded cities. Furthermore, deforestation in such countries as India and Pakistan is forcing people to use cow dung for fuel, depriving the land of a natural source of fertility.

As the demand for food expands, more and more land that is too steep or too dry to sustain cultivation is being brought under the plow. In the poor countries, where most of the level land is already cultivated, farmers are moving up the hillsides. Accelerated erosion is the result.

Irrigation Problems. In West Pakistan the recently completed $600 million Mangla irrigation reservoir, which originally had a life expectancy of 100 years, is now expected to be nearly filled with silt in half that time. The clearing of steep slopes for farming, progressive deforestation, and overgrazing in the reservoir's watershed are responsible for its declining life expectancy.

Efforts to expand the area of farmland in one locale is reducing the water for irrigation in another. Farmers moving up the hillsides in Java are causing irrigation canals to silt at an alarming rate.

Damming the Nile at Aswan expanded the irrigated area for producing cereals but largely eliminated the annual deposits of rich alluvial silt on fields in the Nile Valley, forcing farmers to rely more on chemical fertilizers. In addition, interrupting the flow of nutrients into the Nile estuary caused a precipitous decline in the fish catch there. Intensive farming in the Philippines with chemical fertilizers is expanding the rice supply but causing freshwater lakes and streams to eutrophy, destroying fish and depriving local villagers of their principal source of animal protein.

One of the most costly and tragic side effects of the spread of modern irrigation in Egypt and other river valleys in Africa, Asia, and northeastern South America is the great increase in the incidence of schistosomiasis. This debilitating intestinal and urinary disease, produced by the parasitic larvae of a blood fluke that burrows into the flesh of those working in water-covered fields, affects a sizable number of the Egyptian people.

The Chinese call this disease "snail fever" and are waging an all-out campaign against it. Unfortunately, schistosomiasis is environmentally induced by conditions created by the human race. The incidence of the disease is rising rapidly as the world's large rivers are harnessed for irrigation. Schistosomiasis is estimated to afflict 250 million people, or 1 out of 14 people living today. It surpasses malaria, which is declining, as the world's more prevalent infectious disease.

The virgin-lands project in the Soviet Union, which was launched in the late 1950s, involved plowing up an estimated 100 million acres of drylands. Only after the land was plowed was it realized that much of it lacked sufficient precipitation to sustain continuous cultivation. Eventually some of the land was returned to grass but not before it became known as the drylands fiasco.

A historic example of the effects of human abuse of the soil is all too visible in North Africa, once the fertile granary of the Roman Empire and now largely a desert or near-desert whose people are fed with the aid of food imports from the United States. Once-productive land was eroded by continuous cropping and overgrazing until much of it would no longer sustain agriculture. Irrigation systems silted, depriving land of the water needed for cultivation. Similar situations are being created in semiarid parts of Asia, such as western India, that are experiencing a rapid buildup of population during this century.

Eutrophication. Efforts to intensify agricultural yields also have adverse environmental consequences. If the effect of chemical fertilizer could be confined to agriculture, it would be fine; but unfortunately it cannot. The water runoff from agricultural land carries chemical fertilizer with it, raising the nutrient content of streams and lakes throughout the world, causing them to eutrophy.

Thousands of freshwater lakes are threatened throughout North America and Europe and increasingly in many poor countries where fertilizer use is beginning to climb. Filipino villagers are finding that rising fertilizer use in rice paddies is resulting in the eutrophication of local lakes and ponds, depriving them of fish, a traditional source of animal protein. No one has calculated the cost to humanity of losing these freshwater lakes, but it is staggering.

Counting the Costs. The preceding analysis shows that the market price of food represents only one of the costs associated with its production. Unfortunately, there is no complete inventory of what it would cost to expand the world food supply continuously to meet the ever-increasing needs. There is no calculation of the tradeoff between increases in population and improvements in diet, a choice that is being forced on human beings as they press against the finite limits of the ecosystem.

An unwillingness to tolerate some of the environmental costs of indefinitely expanding the food supply is beginning to translate into constraints on food production. Many countries have banned or seriously limited the use of DDT, dieldrin, and other chlorinated hydrocarbons, a group of cheap, highly effective pesticides. In some parts of the world, conservationists are objecting to the construction of new irrigation reservoirs.

In the United States, a growing number of local and state governments are banning the use of phosphates in detergents because of eutrophication. It may be only a matter of time until the use of phosphate fertilizer is regulated in some communities. The conflicts between economic efficiency and ecological soundness are myriad. DDT is a potent, low-cost pesticide, but it threatens some species of wildlife with extinction. Chemical fertilizer is far cheaper than organic fertilizer, but runoff is a more serious problem; and beef finished in large commercial feedlots is cheaper than that finished in family-farm feedlots, but waste disposal is much more difficult.

We do not know how many species of birds, fish, and mammals must be sacrificed to achieve a 5% increase in the world's food supply. We do know that as the number of people in the world goes up, the number of extant species goes down. Over time, willingness to pay all the costs for expanding the world food supply surely will diminish.

WORLD FISHERY PROSPECTS. Until recently, the oceans were viewed as an almost limitless source of protein, either in the form of fish or algae. The outlook today, however, contrasts sharply with that of five years ago because world fisheries are in serious trouble, largely because of overfishing.

From 1950 to 1968, the world fish catch reached a new record each year, tripling from 21 million to 63 million tons. The average annual increase in the catch of nearly 5% (far exceeding the annual rate of world population growth) greatly increased the average supply of marine protein per person. Then suddenly, in 1969, the long period of sustained growth was interrupted by a decline in the catch, which has been fluctuating rather unpredictably, while the amount of time and money expended to bring in the catch continues to rise every year. Many marine biologists now feel that the global catch of table-grade fish is at or near the maximum sustainable level. A large number of the 30 or so leading species of commercial-grade fish may currently be overfished; that is, stocks will not sustain even the current level of catch.

International Conflicts. These new and disturbing trends, at a time when the world demand for protein is soaring, have intensified competition in world fisheries. In the North Atlantic, Great Britain and Iceland are in continuous conflict over the fishery resources off the coast of Iceland. The Icelandic economy is closely tied to its fisheries, as evidenced by two devaluations of the krona following two poor fishing years in 1967 and 1968. Aware of this dependence on fishing, Iceland has extended its offshore limits to 50 miles to prevent British ships from depleting its offshore fishery resources.

Soviet fishing trawlers operating just beyond the 12-mile offshore limits along the East Coast of the United States exploited fisheries that American fishermen formerly considered their exclusive domain. To relieve this recent threat the United States extended its offshore limits to 200 miles to prevent the demise of its once vigorous fishing industry. In the North Pacific, the Soviet and Japanese fishing fleets find themselves in direct competition with each other. United States fishermen off the West Coast face stiff competition from Soviet, Japanese, and Korean trawlers. Off the Western Coast of Latin America, the United States is in continual conflict with Peru and Ecuador. During a recent 12-month period Ecuador seized 56 U.S. fishing trawlers found within its unilaterally imposed 200-mile off-shore limit, fining them a total of $2.3 million.

Importance of Fish as Protein. World fishery resources represent an important source of protein. The 1971 catch of 69 million tons amounted to nearly 40 pounds (liveweight) per person throughout the world. Of this catch roughly 60% was table-grade fish, the remainder consisting of inferior species used for manufacturing fish meal, which in turn is used in poultry and hog feed in the industrial countries. For Americans, fish are important in the diet, but direct consumption averages only about 14 pounds per year, compared with 50 pounds of poultry, 73 pounds of pork, and 117 pounds of beef. These data on direct consumption understate the importance of fish in the diet since a significant share of the poultry and pork consumed are produced with fish meal.

In two of the world's more populous countries, Japan and the Soviet Union, fish are significant as a direct source of protein in the national diet. As population pressure built up in Japan during the late nineteenth and early twentieth centuries, the Japanese were forced to turn to the oceans for their animal protein, using their very limited land resources to produce rice to meet minimal food energy needs. As a result, the Japanese evolved a "fish and rice" diet. Fish consumption per person in Japan totals 70 pounds per year, the highest of any major country.

The Soviet Union, experiencing difficulties in expanding its livestock industry at a satisfactory rate, has also turned to the oceans during the past 15 years for much of its animal protein. It has invested heavily not only in fishing fleets, but also in floating fish-processing factories and sophisticated fishing technologies that enable those fleets to fish extensively throughout the world. The direct consumption of fish by the average Soviet consumer is probably at least double that of his American counterpart. Accordingly, as growth in the world catch of table-grade fish slows, and as some important species begin to decline from overfishing, the Soviet and Japanese populations are particularly vulnerable. If they find themselves increasingly unable to meet protein needs from oceanic resources, they may be forced to offset this decline by substantially stepping up imports of feedgrains and soybeans to expand their indigenous livestock production.

Aquaculture. In examining world fishery prospects, the possibility of aquaculture, or fish farming, must always be considered. There have been local successes in various forms of aquaculture in both fresh water and salt water in a number of countries throughout the world, including Norway, Germany, Israel, the Soviet Union, China, Japan, Australia, and the United States. United States aquaculture has become important for two species of fish—catfish and trout. The combined production of these two, which is expanding steadily, now amounts to several ounces per person per year in the United States. But because of many unresolved technical problems there is no immediate prospect that fish farming will be able to provide more than a small percentage of the world's fish supplies, at most. This is not to rule out the possibility a decade or so hence of sufficient expansion in this activity to enable it to become an important global source of protein. Active research programs continue in a large number of countries.

U.S. AGRICULTURE AND WORLD FOOD NEEDS. Over the past generation the United States has achieved a unique position as a supplier of food to the rest of the world. Before World War II, both Latin America (particularly Argentina) and North America (including Canada) were major exporters of grain. During the late 1930s, net grain exports from each of these continents averaged about 5 million tons per year. Since then, however, the failure of most Latin American countries to reform and modernize agriculture and the unprecedented population growth in the region have largely eliminated the net export surplus.

With a few exceptions Latin American countries are now food importers. Over the past three decades, North America has emerged as the world's breadbasket. Australia, the only other net exporter of importance, exports about one-sixth as much grain as North America.

The period since World War II has been characterized by excess capacity in world agriculture, much of it concentrated in the United States. Immediately following the war the United States made a unilateral decision to use its impressive food-producing capacity, which was expanded vastly in response to wartime demands, to intervene anywhere in the world whenever famine threatened. During the quarter century since then, the United States has been remarkably successful in staving off famine, even when one-fifth of the exportable U.S. wheat crop was required during 1966 and 1967 to feed some 60 million Indians over a two-year period.

Downward Trend for Grain Reserves. In many ways the world was fortunate to have, in effect, two major food reserves during this period. One was in the form of grain reserves in the principal exporting countries and the other in the form of cropland idled under farm programs, virtually all of it in the United States.

Grain reserves, including substantial quantities of both foodgrains and feedgrains, are most commonly measured in terms of carryover stocks—the amount in storage at the time the new crop begins to come in. World carryover stocks are concentrated in a few of the principal exporting countries—namely the United States, Canada, Australia, and Argentina.

Since 1960, world grain reserves have fluctuated from a high of 155 million metric tons to a low of about 100 million metric tons (Fig. 2.3). When reserves drop to 100 million tons, severe shortages and strong upward price pressures develop. Although 100 million tons appear to be an enormous quantity of grain, they represent a mere 8% of annual world grain consumption, an uncomfortably small working reserve and a perilously thin buffer against the vagaries of weather or plant diseases. As world consumption expands, so should the size of working reserves; but the trend over the past decade has been for reserves to dwindle while consumption has climbed.

In addition, one-seventh of U.S. cropland, or roughly 50 million acres out of 350 million acres, has been idled for the past dozen years or so (Fig. 2.4). Though not as quickly available as the grain reserves, most of this acreage can be brought back into production within 12 to 18 months once the decision is made to do so.

In recent years the need to draw down grain reserves and to dip into the reserve of idled cropland has occurred with increasing frequency. This first happened during the food crisis years of 1966 and 1967 when world grain reserves were reduced to a dangerously low

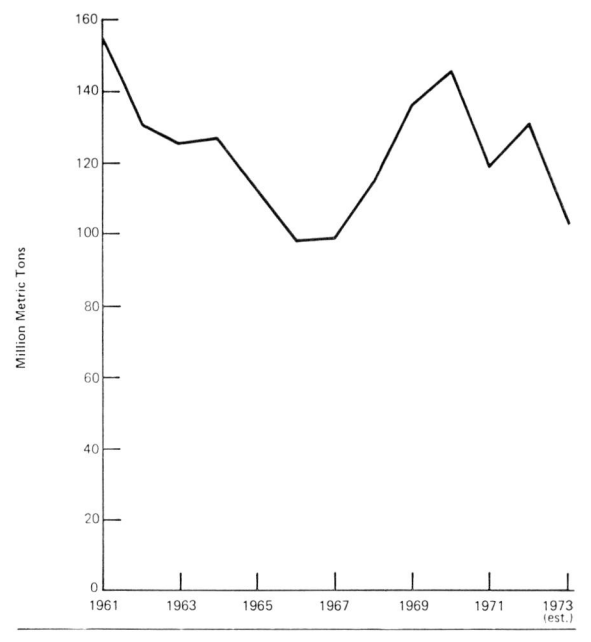

Fig. 2.3. Total grain stocks in principal exporting countries, 1961–73.

level and the United States brought back into production a small portion of the 50 million idle acres. Again, in 1971, as a result of the corn blight, the United States both drew down its grain reserves and brought another portion of the idled acreage back into production. In 1973, in response to growing food scarcities, world grain reserves once more declined, and the United States dipped into its idled cropland, but to a much greater degree than on either of the two previous occasions. Government decisions in early 1973 permitted all but a small fraction of the idled cropland to come back into production.

Since the end of World War II until recently, world prices for the principal temperate zone farm commodities such as wheat, feedgrains, and soybeans have been remarkably stable. In part, this is because throughout much of this period world prices have rested on the commodity support level in the United States. Since world food reserves may become chronically low and the idled crop acreage in the United States may decline sharply or even disappear entirely in the years ahead, there is the prospect of very volatile world prices for the important food commodities. Indeed, in 1974 (ed.) prices of most principal foodstuffs soared to historic highs. This situation could be made far more serious by a prolonged drought of several years like those that have

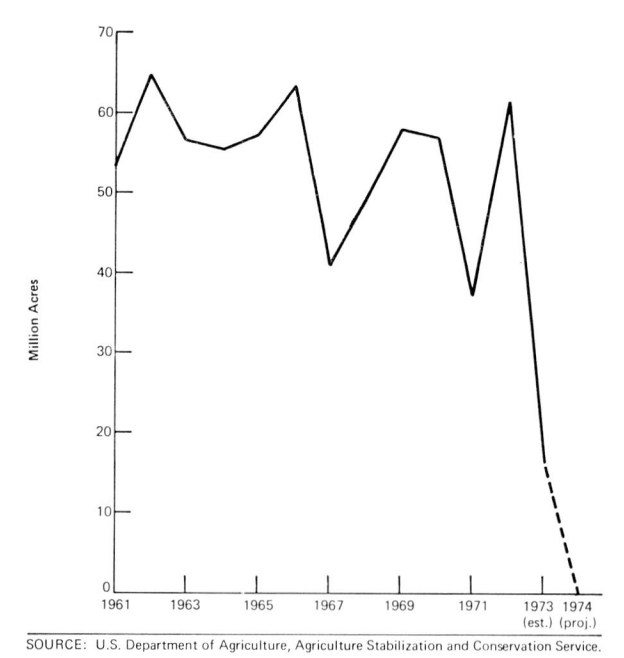

Fig. 2.4. U.S. cropland acreage withheld from production under government programs, 1961–74.

occurred roughly every 20 years in the United States, most recently during the 1950s.

CONSTRAINTS ON EXPANDING THE WORLD FOOD SUPPLY. The prospects for expanding the food supply depend on a wide range of economic, ecological, and technological factors. The traditional approach to increasing production—expanding the area under cultivation—has only limited scope for the future. Indeed some parts of the world face a net reduction in agricultural land because of the growth in competing uses, such as industrial development, recreation, transportation, and residential development. Few countries have well-defined land-use policies that protect agricultural land from other uses. In the United States, farmland has been used indiscriminately for other purposes with little thought to the possible long-term consequences.

Some more densely populated countries, such as Japan and several in Western Europe, have been experiencing a reduction in the land used for crop production for the past few decades. This trend is continuing and may well accelerate. Other parts of the world, including particularly the Indian subcontinent, the Middle East, North Africa, the Caribbean, Central America, and the Andean countries, are losing disturbingly large acreages of cropland each year because of severe erosion.

The area of land available for food production is important, but perhaps even more important in the future will be the availability of water for agricultural purposes. In many regions of the world, fertile agricultural land is available if water can be found to make it produce. Yet most of the rivers that lend themselves to damming and to irrigation have already been developed. Future efforts to expand freshwater supplies for agricultural purposes will increasingly focus on such techniques as the diversion of rivers (as in the Soviet Union), desalting sea water, and the manipulation of rainfall patterns to increase the share of rain falling over moisture-deficient agricultural areas.

The need for capital inputs, particularly in the form of chemical fertilizers and pesticides, is projected to grow at an unprecedented rate over the remainder of this century. If the U.N. medium population projection materializes by the end of the century (giving the world a population of 6.5 billion), far more than a doubling in the use of chemical fertilizer would be required, and the eutrophication of freshwater lakes and streams would become a far more serious problem than it is today.

One of the disturbing questions associated with future gains in agricultural production is the extent to which the trend of rising per acre yields of cereals in the more advanced countries can be sustained. In some countries increases in per acre yields are beginning to slow down, and the capital investments required for each additional increase may now start to climb sharply. In agriculturally advanced countries, such as Japan, the Netherlands, and the United States, the cost per increment of yield per acre for some crops is rising. For example, raising rice yields in Japan from the current 5,000 pounds per acre to 6,000 pounds could be very costly. Raising yields of corn in the United States from 90 to 100 bushels per acre requires a much larger quantity of nitrogen than was needed to raise yields from 50 to 60 bushels.

What impact the energy crisis will have on food production costs and trends remains to be seen. With a substantial rise in the cost of energy, farmers engaged in high-energy agriculture, as in the United States, will tend to use less, thus perhaps reducing future production increases below current expectations. For other inputs used in modern agriculture—nitrogen fertilizer, for example—the rising cost of energy can be important. In part, this is because one of the principal raw materials for the synthesis of nitrogen fertilizer is natural gas, and in part, because one of the dominant costs in manufacturing nitrogen fertilizer is energy.

Constraints on Protein Production. In looking ahead one must be particularly concerned about the difficulties in expanding the supply of world protein to meet the projected rapid growth in demand, which is now being fueled both by population growth and rising affluence. At present people are faced with technological and other constraints in increasing the supply of three principal sources of protein.

The first—fish—is constrained, in the short run at least, by natural or ecological limitations. In an unmanaged state, the world's oceans produce only a certain amount of fish each year. The recent falloff in the growth in the world fish catch indicates the existing catch is pressing against the limits for some species. It does not augur well for the future.

A second important source of protein is beef. Here two constraints are operative. Agricultural scientists have not been able to devise any commercially viable means of getting more than one calf per cow per year. For every animal that goes into the beef production process, one adult must be fed and otherwise maintained for a full year. There does not appear to be any prospect of an imminent breakthrough on this front.

The other constraint on beef production is that the grazing capacity of much of the world's pastureland is now almost fully utilized. This is true, for example, in most of the U.S. Great Plains area, in East Africa, and in parts of Australia. Most of the industrial countries in which beef consumption is expanding rapidly, from Ireland through the Soviet Union and Japan, are unable to meet all the growth in demand from indigenous resources. Either some of the beef or the feedgrains and soybeans to produce it must be imported.

A third potentially serious constraint on efforts to expand supplies of high-quality protein is the inability of scientists to achieve a breakthrough in per acre yields of soybeans. Soybeans are a major source of high-quality protein for livestock and poultry throughout much of the world and are consumed directly as food by perhaps a billion people throughout densely populated East Asia. The economic importance of soybeans is indicated by the fact that they have become the leading export product of the United States, surpassing export sales of wheat, corn, and high-technology items such as electronic computers and jet aircraft.

In the United States, which now produces three-fourths of the world's soybean crop and supplies more than 90% of all soybeans entering the world market, soybean yields per acre have increased by about 1% per year since 1950; corn yields, on the other hand, have increased by nearly 4% per year. One reason soybean yields have not climbed very rapidly is that the soybean, being a legume with a built-in nitrogen supply, is not very responsive to nitrogen fertilizer. The way the United States produces more soybeans is by planting more soybean acreage. Close to 85% of the dramatic fourfold increase in the U.S. soybean crop since 1950 has come from expanding the area devoted to it. As long as there was ample idled cropland available, this did not pose a problem, but if this cropland reserve continues to diminish or disappears entirely it could create serious global supply problems.

Although there are substantial opportunities for expanding the world's protein supply, it now seems likely that the supply of animal protein will lag behind growth in demand for some time to come, resulting in significantly higher prices for livestock products during the remainder of the 1970s than prevailed during the 1960s. The world protein market may be transformed from a buyer's market to a seller's market, much as the world energy market has been transformed over the past few years.

ALLEVIATING PRESSURES OF POPULATION GROWTH AND RISING AFFLUENCE. In this decade the overriding objective of a global food strategy in an increasingly interdependent world should be the elimination of hunger and malnutrition among that large segment of humanity whose food supply simply is inadequate. To be successful, such a strategy must be designed to alter existing trends in food production and population growth while seeking a more equitable distribution of food supplies both among and within societies.

Reducing Population Growth. The prospect of an emerging chronic global scarcity of food as a result of growing pressures on available food resources underlines the need to reduce and eventually halt population growth in as short a period of time as possible. One can conceive of this occurring in the industrial countries as a result of current demographic trends. In the United States, attitudes toward childbearing have changed dramatically in recent years, and U.S. fertility has fallen below the replacement level of 2.1 children. If the recent precipitous decline in the U.S. birthrate continues, and this is a big if, it will bring U.S. population growth to a halt by 1980. Despite this voluntary movement toward zero population growth, however, there has been no official U.S. statement of population policy—even while the United States is urging other nations to drastically reduce their birthrates.

Three European countries—East Germany, Luxembourg, and West Germany—have stabilized their populations within the past few years. Indeed the growth of the German-speaking population of Europe—90 million people who live in East Germany, Berlin, West Germany, Austria, and part of Switzerland—has very nearly ceased. Although this is a beginning toward reaching the goal of reducing or halting world population growth, it unfortunately is only a beginning in a world containing 3.8 billion people.

Many other European countries have relatively low birthrates and appear to be moving toward zero population growth. These countries— including Hungary, Scandinavia, and the United Kingdom—plus the Soviet Union and Japan, could easily achieve a zero rate of population growth within the next decade or so, particularly if both policymakers and the people put their minds to it.

In the poor countries, however, it is much more difficult to reduce growth rates within an acceptable time frame, at least as things are going now. For one thing, the historical record indicates that birthrates do not usually decline in the absence of a certain improvement in well-being—an assured food supply, a reduced infant mortality rate, literacy, and at least rudimentary health services—which provides the basic motivation for smaller families. (See William Rich, *Smaller Families Through Social and Economic Progress*, Overseas Development Council, Monograph No. 7 [Washington, D.C.: Jan. 1973].)

Attacking Global Poverty. In short, it may well be in the self-interest of affluent societies, such as the United States, to launch an attack on global poverty, not only to narrow the economic gap between rich and poor nations but also to meet the basic social needs of people throughout the world in an effort to provide incentives for lowering birthrates. Population-induced pressures on the global food supply will continue to increase if substantial economic and social progress is not made. Populations that double every 24 years—as many are doing in poor nations—multiply 16-fold in scarcely three generations.

Although the costs of promoting economic and social progress cannot be accurately predicted, there is reason to believe they might be less than imagined. UNESCO estimates show, for example, that in a developing country the cost of making a person literate is about $8—slightly less for an adult, slightly more for a school-age youngster. Given a billion illiterates in the world, universal literacy would require an outlay of $8 billion. If the funds could be mobilized and were spread over five years, the cost would come to $1.6 billion a year. If the costs were allocated among the principal industrial countries, each would have to put out only a few hundred million dollars a year.

Similarly, the cost of providing a minimum nutritional diet for most of the human race may be less than commonly thought. In some ways the Chinese experience is instructive. Development efforts in that country have had a strong social focus, with overall economic growth rates being secondary in importance. Despite an unimpressive economic growth rate averaging below 4% yearly, the Chinese approach has apparently been successful in providing adequate nutrition and near-universal literacy, even though incomes per person average only about $140 a year. And birthrates are declining steadily.

Following World War II, the U.S. government decided it would share its food resources whenever famine threatened anywhere in the world. As a result the world has been spared famine caused by natural disasters. Given the level of affluence that exists in many nations today, the time is ripe to take another positive step forward, recognizing that it is both necessary and humane to provide people with a diet that at least meets minimum nutritional needs. In effect, better nutrition could mean lower birthrates by decreasing infant and child mortality and thus reducing the number of pregnancies required to assure the desired number of surviving children in families in poor nations. (In *Population Bulletin* No. 1, 1973, Alan Berg has discussed in detail the relationship between poor nutrition and high fertility.)

Altering Consumption Patterns. As the world shrinks under the impact of advancing communications and transportation technologies and the continuing integration of national economies into a single global economy, the contrast in food consumption levels between rich and poor countries sharpens. As indicated earlier, those living in the poor countries are sustained on 400 pounds or less of grain a year, while those in the wealthier ones require nearly a ton of grain. It is difficult to envisage a situation in which all the human race could progressively increase per capita claims on the earth's food-producing resources until everyone reached the level now enjoyed by the average North American. Thus thought should be given to how diets could be simplified in the wealthy nations to reduce per capita claims on the earth's scarce resources of land and water. What are the possibilities of substituting less costly, more efficient forms of protein for, say, beef?

Consumption patterns in the United States suggest that there are two broad approaches to reducing per capita resource requirements for food. One is to substitute vegetable oils for animal fat; the other is to substitute vegetable protein for animal protein.

Over the past three decades, vegetable oils have been extensively replacing animal fats in the American diet. In 1940, for example, the average American consumed 17 pounds of butter and 2 pounds of margarine. By 1971 the average American was consuming 11 pounds of margarine and 5 pounds of butter. Lard has been almost pushed off supermarket shelves by the hydrogenated vegetable shortenings. At least 65% of the whipped toppings and more than 35% of the coffee whiteners in the United States today are of nondairy origin. This pervasive trend has economic, ecological, and nutritional advantages. It reduces both per capita food costs and per capita claims on agricultural resources, and it reduces the intake of saturated animal fats now widely believed to be a factor contributing to heart disease.

The widespread substitution of vegetable oils for animal fats in the U.S. diet over the past generation has reduced per capita claims on agricultural resources, but this has been more than offset by the simultaneous increase in beef consumption from 55 to 117 pounds. Stimulated by sharp rises in meat prices in late 1972 and early 1973, attention is now focusing on the substitution of high-quality vegetable protein for animal protein. Technology for the substitution of vegetable for animal proteins has made considerable progress, mainly in the area of soya-based meat substitutes. The development of a technique for spinning soya protein into fibers, duplicating the spinning of synthetic textile fibers, permits the close emulation of the fibrous qualities of meat. Food technologists can now compress soya fibers into meat form and, with the appropriate flavoring and coloring, come up with reasonable substitutes for beef, pork, and poultry. With livestock protein, particularly beef, becoming more costly, this technique is likely to gain a strong commercial foothold in the near future.

The first major meat product for which substitution is succeeding commercially is bacon. The soya-based substitute looks and tastes like bacon, and, while the extent of substitution for bacon is still small, it is growing. The substitute product has the advantage of being high in protein, low in fat, and storable without refrigeration.

The greatest single area of protein substitution promises to be the use of vegetable protein to augment meat proteins in ground meats. Soya protein "extenders," as they are known, are being added to a variety of processed and ground meat products, frequently improving flavor, cooking qualities, and nutrition as well as reducing prices. Soya protein extenders are already widely used in institutions throughout the United States, and limited supermarket sales to the public have also begun.

Although the average American already consumes nearly 1 ton of grain per year, either directly or indirectly, indications are that this could climb even higher in the years ahead. Projections of the U.S. Department of Agriculture show per capita beef consumption reaching 140 pounds by 1985, but a continuing rise in the cost of beef could alter this trend downward as consumers seek more economic substitutes. If the substitution of high-quality vegetable protein becomes as widespread as that of vegetable oils for animal fats, it is not inconceivable that, in the United States, per capita claims on agricultural resources could eventually begin to decline. A combination of convergent economic and ecological forces and health considerations could lead in this direction.

SOME IMMEDIATE STEPS. In addition to the actions designed to ameliorate long-term pressures on food resources caused by population growth and rising affluence, the circumstances of the mid-1970s also argue for some specific actions to offset immediate pressures. If, as this analysis suggests, the world is moving from a situation of chronic excess agricultural production capacity to one of chronic scarcity, particularly of protein, a reassessment of the world food production potential may be in order. International competition for available food supplies could become much more intense than any previously experienced.

World Food Reserve System. These new circumstances call for serious consideration of the creation of an internationally agreed system of food reserves as a means of maintaining some order and stability in the world food economy. Just as the U.S. dollar can no longer serve as the foundation of the international monetary system, U.S. agriculture may no longer have sufficient excess capacity to ensure reasonable stability in the world market for food. A world reserve could be built up in times of relative abundance and drawn down in times of acute scarcity. In effect, the cushion that surplus American agricultural capacity has provided for a generation would be provided at least partially by a world food bank.

An important first step would be international adoption of the concept of "minimum world food security" proposed in early 1973 by A. H. Boerma, Director General of the U.N. Food and Agriculture Organization (FAO). Under the FAO plan all governments—exporters and importers—would be asked to hold certain minimum levels of food stocks to meet international emergencies. The governments of participating countries would consult regularly to review the food situation, judge the adequacy of existing stocks, and recommend necessary actions. International agencies such as the World Bank, the International Monetary Fund, and the FAO would help poor countries to establish and maintain the reserve stocks necessary for self-protection against crop failures.

Any system of global food reserves, whether a single, centrally managed food bank or the proposed FAO plan of coordinated national reserve policies, would provide a measure of stability in the world food economy that would be in the self-interest of all nations. The world community also, of course, has a basic humanitarian interest in ensuring that famine does not occur in the densely populated low-income countries following a poor crop year—an assurance the affluent nations may be less able to provide in the future if the current system of autonomous, nationally oriented planning is allowed to continue without modification.

Cooperative Approach to Fisheries. A close examination of the extent of overfishing and stock depletion in many of the world's fisheries underlines the urgency of evolving a cooperative global approach to the management of oceanic fisheries. Failure to do this will result in a continuing depletion of stocks, a reduction in catch, and soaring seafood prices that will make those of the early 1970s seem modest by comparison. Prices of some table fish could double within the next few years. In the absence of cooperation, world fishery resources would dwindle in the same way the world catch of whales has over the past two decades. It is in this context that all nations have a direct interest in the success of the United Nations Law of the Sea. Among other things, there is a need to incorporate institutional mechanisms for cooperatively managing global fishery resources.

Potential of the Poor Countries. One of the most immediate means of expanding the food supply is to return all of the idled U.S. cropland to production. Over the longer run, however, the greatest opportunities lie in the developing countries, where the world's greatest reservoir of unexploited food potential is located.

In those countries having the appropriate economic incentives, fertilizer, water, and other required agricultural inputs, the introduction of new wheat and rice varieties has increased production. The jump in per acre yields in developing countries appears dramatic largely because their yields traditionally have been so low relative to the potential. But today rice yields per acre in India and Nigeria still are only one-third those of Japan; corn yields in Thailand and Brazil are less than one-third those of the United States. Large increases in food supply are possible in these countries at far less cost than in agriculturally advanced nations if farmers are given the necessary economic incentives and the requisite inputs.

When global food scarcity exists and the capacity of the international community to respond to food emergencies has diminished, a convincing case can be made for strengthened support of agricultural development in such populous food-short countries as Bangladesh, India, Indonesia, and Nigeria. India and the United States, for example, have about the same crop area with many similar characteristics. If India's yield levels equaled those of the United States, its current annual cereal production would be 230 million metric tons rather than the present total of approximately 100 million tons. If rice farmers in Bangladesh attained Japanese yield levels, rice production would jump fourfold from 10 million to 40 million tons. Brazil, by doubling its present cultivated area, could produce an additional 22 million tons of grain even if its currently low yield levels were not improved.

A bipartisan legislative proposal was introduced in the U.S. Congress in 1973 that restructured the U.S. Agency for International Development to focus more sharply on solving the problems of the poor majority. An increase in the Agency's support for agricultural and rural development was implemented in the following years. This thrust capitalizes on the unique capacity of the United States to lead an enlarged effort to expand the world's food supply and to spur rural development. This stratagem enables the United States to respond to the most devastating consequences of population growth—widespread malnutrition and the threat of famine— by strengthening support for modernizing the processes and structure of agriculture in the developing world and to provide more effective support for health and education services that reach the poores majority and thereby increase the motivation for limiting family size.

Concentrating efforts on expanding food production in the poor countries reduces upward pressure on world food prices, creates additional employment in countries where continuously rising unemployment poses a serious threat to political stability, raises income and improves nutrition for the poorest portion of humanity (the people living in rural areas of the developing countries), and increases motivation for smaller families. If these efforts succeed, the countries most afflicted by population growth would simultaneously gain both additional time in which to cope more effectively with the demographic components of hunger and additional help with their efforts to stabilize population growth.

The urgency of the food problem is underscored by increasingly frequent reports of starvation in sub-Sahara Africa and of food riots in Asia. Solving the problem is a complex task—one that requires thoughtful analysis and determined action by both rich and poor nations. Assuring adequate food supplies at reasonable prices within individual countries may now be possible only through international cooperation. The disappearance of surplus food stocks and the return of idled cropland to production has removed the cushions that once existed as partial insurance against catastrophe. (In 1975 Brown pointed out that the worldwide food shortages of recent years, assumed to be temporary, could become more or less chronic. Lester R. Brown, "The World Food Prospect," *Science* 190 [Dec. 1975]: 1053–59, ed.)

REFERENCES

1. Allaby, Michael. *The World Food Problem: Can We Solve It?* London: Tom Stacy, 1972.
2. Berg, Alan. *The Nutrition Factor: Its Role in National Development.* Washington, D.C.: Brookings Institution, 1973.
3. Brown, Lester R. "Human Food Production as a Process in the Biosphere." *Scientific American* 223 (3, Sept. 1970): 160–70.
4. ———. *Seeds of Change: The Green Revolution and Development in the 1970s.* New York: Praeger, 1970.
5. ———. *World Without Borders.* New York: Random House, 1972.
6. Ehrlich, Paul R., and Ehrlich, Anne H. *Population, Resources, Environment: Issues in Human Ecology.* 2d ed. San Francisco: W. H. Freeman & Co., 1972.
7. Food and Agriculture Organization of the United Nations. *State of Food and Agriculture, 1972.* Rome, 1972.
8. *Food: Readings from Scientific American.* San Francisco: W. H. Freeman & Co., 1973.
9. Holt, S. J. "The Food Resources of the Ocean." *Scientific American* 221 (3, Sept. 1969): 178–94.
10. Idyll, C. P. "The Anchovy Crisis." *Scientific American* 228 (6, June 1973): 22–29.
11. Katz, Robert. *A Giant in the Earth.* New York: Stein and Day, 1973.
12. Poleman, Thomas T., and Freebairn, Donald K. (eds.). *Food, Population, and Employment: The Impact of the Green Revolution.* New York: Praeger, 1973.

PART 2
Traditional Agriculture

THE OBJECTIVE of this section containing three studies, one each from Asia, Africa, and Latin America, is to demonstrate the interacting economic, technical, and social causes of the low-income trap of farmers in largely traditional agriculture.

An underlying question of this section is, Do these studies exhibit the central elements of the model of traditional agriculture presented in Chapter 2? How much change in technical, social, and economic variables is occurring? Do equilibrium conditions in the supply and demand for agricultural resources and products appear to be present, resulting in allocative efficiency? What levels of productivity are estimated for these largely traditional agricultures? Additional questions focus on what methodologies were used to explore these issues. What specific hypotheses were set out in each study and how were they tested?

These cases also provide detailed illustrations of the nature of three very different traditional agricultures in the north of Nigeria, in southern Brazil, and in northeastern Thailand. In doing this the economic realities of traditional agriculture come forth, which contrast with the false beliefs and myths held by many about farming in developing nations. These false beliefs about agriculture in low-income nations include the views that larger farms are more productive; that traditional farmers are not rational—they tend to be foolish and lazy; that new, more productive farming practices are available if the farmers would only use them; that farmers would improve their farming if they took the advice of extension workers;

and that traditional farmers need more credit to better their farming.

Among these cases, the purest example of an agriculture that exhibits little significant change in technical, social, or economic variables is the study by Norman of Hausa dryland farmers in a village in the north of Nigeria. In southern Brazil, Rask found little technical change had occurred in three of the five agricultural enterprises studied. (An enterprise is a crop or livestock production process, in this case, maize [corn], soybean and tobacco crops, and hog and milk production.) On these farms the vertically integrated tobacco enterprise using some modern inputs presented an instructive contrast to the traditional practices employed in other agricultural enterprises. The study of cattle and buffalo production in a village in northeastern Thailand by DeBoer and Welsch shows how the complex constraints of a traditional crop production system limited attempts to increase animal production. This study highlights the intricate nature of crop and livestock interrelationships in traditional village agriculture and points to the need for appreciable modifications in village resource use if cattle and buffalo production are to break out of the existing equilibrium.

The allocative efficiency of farmers in these largely traditional agricultures was tested rigorously by employing different econometric methodologies. In Nigeria two tests supported the hypothesis of economic equilibrium. (For discussion of economic equilibrium, see Chapter 1.) In the first test, the majority of the Cobb-Douglas production function estimates had marginal productivities of land and labor, which were not significantly different from the prices (costs) of these resources, implying equilibrium in these markets. In the linear programming test, the increase in income, which might be obtained by reallocating resources, was found small under the technical, social, and economic conditions prevailing, demonstrating efficient allocation by these traditional farmers. Analysis of farm enterprises by Rask in southern Brazil showed that, except possibly in the case of the hog enterprise, few profitable new investments in agricultural technology were currently available for these farms, given current prices. In the village in Thailand, production function analysis by DeBoer and Welsch of crop enterprises provided mixed results. But the analysis gave the important result that the marginal value productivity of labor was very close to the average wage of hired labor, supporting the hypothesis of equilibrium in the labor market.

The three cases also provide data showing that the productivity of traditional agriculture is low, whether measured in terms of yields (output per acre), of net income to farmers, or of rates of return on investment. The low yields of the major crops in the three farming areas compared with typical yields for these crops in modern agriculture are illustrated by the rice yield of 1.2 metric tons per hectare (1,070 lb per acre) in the northeast Thai village (Chapter 5, Table 5.8) compared with modern rice yields of some 4 metric tons per acre (Chapter 1, Table 1.2), a sorghum grain yield of 701 lb per acre (785 kg per hectare) in the village in the north of Nigeria (Chapter 3, Table 3.7) compared with modern U.S. yields of more than 2,800 lb per acre (3,100 kg per hectare) (U.S. Department of Agriculture, *Agricultural Statistics, 1974*, Washington, D.C.: USGPO, 1975, p. 51), and a maize (corn) yield of 1.2 metric tons per hectare (19 bushels/acre) on the small farms in southern Brazil (Chapter 4) compared with 4.5 tons or more per hectare in the United States (Chapter 1, Table 1.2). These maize yields, it should be noted, were low even on the relatively large small farms in southern Brazil (mean size 24 hectares or 59 acres).

The low farm wage rates and net incomes in these farming areas are shown in Table PII.1. The unique estimates obtained by DeBoer and Welsch of the rate of return from investment in cattle and buffalo production in a Thai village also demonstrate the low productivity in traditional agriculture. Their estimated rates ranged from 8 to 11%, appreciably below the 12 to 15% generally used by planners as the minimum opportunity cost for public investment and considerably below the 20 to 30% internal rate of return sought by project planners and the private sector for high return investments.

Each of the following three studies has placed particular emphasis on certain aspects of the largely traditional agriculture examined. In the study of farms in the north of Nigeria an extraordinary opportunity was present to test the rationality of producing a mixture of crops on the same piece of land—a predominant planting pattern in this area. Did this practice, little used in modern agricul-

TABLE PII.1. Farm wages and net incomes per year in traditional and modern agriculture

	Year	Farm Wages per Day	Net Family Income per Person for Farm Residents	Net Income per Farm from Farming
Traditional Agriculture				
North of Nigeria (Norman, Ch 3, Table 3.8)	1966	$0.30	$ 35	$ 292
Nigeria[a]	1959	0.50		
Small farms in Southern Brazil (Rask, Ch 4, Table 4.3)	1969		200	1,000
Northeast Thailand (DeBoer & Welsch, Ch 5)	1970	0.49		
Modern Agriculture[a]				
Japan	1968	3.34		
France	1968	2.92		
United States	1968	9.30	1,180 (from farm sources) 2,220 (from all sources)	4,957[b]

[a] *FAO 1970 Production Yearbook* farm wage estimates not available for Thailand, Brazil, or Nigeria in 1966.
[b] U.S. Department of Agriculture, *Agricultural Statistics*, 1970, p. 477.

ture, provide the highest returns to farmers in terms of security and profit maximization goals? Critical tests were undertaken that showed the traditional mixed cropping pattern was more rational in relation to peasant farmers' goals than sole (single) crops.

Norman concludes however that the availability in the future of much more productive agricultural technology for sole (single) crop farming could result in a divergence between the security and profit maximization goals of these farmers. This study was also able to analyze the influence of location and population density on farm size, cropping system, and the amount and kinds of off-farm activities through comparison of data from three villages at different distances from the nearest city.

In carrying out this research, Norman provided one of the first rigorous tests in Africa of the Schultzian hypothesis that product and factor equilibrium tends to prevail in traditional agriculture. (This hypothesis of equilibrium in traditional agriculture is discussed in Chapter 1.) Under these conditions there is little opportunity for farmers to increase income through a reallocation of their resources. The solution to their problem is to obtain new, more highly productive agricultural technology, such as new seeds, chemical fertilizers, and pesticides.

Rask's objective was to identify technical and institutional factors limiting change in southern Brazil on traditional small farms, which averaged 24 hectares (59 acres), in view of the great changes and increases in productivity that had occurred in nearby regions of southern Brazil on large farms, which averaged 133 hectares (328 acres). The small farms examined over a four-year period were found to exhibit large amounts of production for home consumption, large numbers of farm enterprises per farm, and low levels of technology. These interrelated factors contributed to both low productivity and meager returns from farming as well as little growth in production.

In examining why little new technology had been adopted on these small farms, Rask analyzed the productivity of the five major enterprises—maize (corn), soybeans, hogs, dairy, and tobacco—and made estimates of farm income in 1965 and 1969. He found that these small farmers perceived relatively little economic advantage to be gained by using the inputs and new technology that were available. Sixty percent of the farmers, for example, judged there would be no increase in returns from the use of additional fertilizer.

The specific factors causing these views were identified as uncertain agricultural product prices, lack of knowledge of the productivity effects of new technology, and lack of credit availability. Although some low-cost new inputs had been used, failure to employ more expensive related inputs deprived farmers of the additional complementary product obtainable when, for example, low-cost high-yielding seed is combined with high-cost fertilizer to assure an input package producing the highest net returns.

The study determined that many of the institutional changes made by government for the agriculture of southern Brazil had aided the wheat and beef enterprises in the large-farm areas. Significant change had occurred in the small-farm area in only two enterprises over the four-year period, which served to further elucidate the prevailing problems. In the case of tobacco, vertically integrated companies supplied high productivity inputs and insured prices through contracts, contributing to high adoption rates of new technology. In the case of District III, where wheat was grown, increased use of inputs was associated with government credit policies providing a low price for fertilizer in wheat production and a guaranteed high price for wheat, a policy that greatly benefited the large-farm areas. Two additional findings of particular interest were related to the institutional structure of the small farms. First, in the small-farm area no relation was found between size of farm and productivity per acre—no economies of scale under the existing operating conditions. However, a second finding showed more use of new technology among the larger small farms.

The Rask study demonstrates that the theory of traditional agriculture in equilibrium is also a useful framework for analyzing farms consisting of traditional animal-powered agriculture of European origin and having relatively large resources as compared to the much smaller farms in most regions of Africa and Asia.

The unique examination of village cattle and buffalo production in northeastern Thailand by DeBoer and Welsch sought to determine the potential for increased meat production in Thai villages in view of rapidly increasing demand for beef and buffalo meat in Thailand. Relatively little increase in cattle and buffalo production was found however, leading to the central research questions about the nature of the constraints and whether they could be removed. This situation prevailed despite at least two major advantages for this village in increasing meat production—proximity to a major all-weather road and the presence nearby of a livestock experiment station with improved breeds. One constraint suggested by theory of traditional agriculture relates to the profitability of cattle and buffalo production. If the returns to the allocation of resources to these livestock enterprises were low, little incentive would be provided villagers to expand production. Through the accumulation of details of the resources used and the amounts of products and services produced in these animal enterprises, benefit-cost analysis was carried out that showed 8 to 11% rates of return on investment. Hence, although evidence was found of the incorporation of improved cattle breeding stock, this technological change was not sufficient to provide really high-return investment opportunities to farmers in cattle production under the existing village conditions.

Possible constraints to increased livestock production were explored by focusing on the crop-livestock interrelationships in the village production system. Animals provide draft power and manure as well as meat, while consuming large volumes of vegetable products, including crop by-products and forage crops, which in some cases were found competitive in resource use with human food crops or village export crops. In analyzing these relationships, the study provides unique insight into specific constraints controlling livestock reproduction and growth under traditional village conditions. They include the timing of the annual pasturing of the village livestock herd, the sources of fodder and other feed available, and the lack of additional land resources for fodder production that the village presently requires for food production. This analysis of the complex crop-livestock interrelationships demonstrates the difficulty in many traditional villages of altering one part of the agricultural system without significant changes in other parts of the system.

CHAPTER 3

Economic Rationality of Traditional Hausa Dryland Farmers in the North of Nigeria

DAVID W. NORMAN

ALTHOUGH much has been written about traditional agriculture [12, 25, 26], relatively few detailed microeconomic studies have been undertaken to test theory and to develop guides for policymakers and change agents in different regions of developing nations. The central premise of this chapter is that detailed understanding of present production processes and decision behavior in traditional agriculture in each socioeconomic region can be of paramount importance in determining the relevance, practicality, and potential success of proposed changes and innovations in agriculture.

This case study proposes to:

1. Describe traditional farming in the Zaria area in terms of inputs, products produced, and income.
2. Examine the influence of present conditions, i.e., location and population density, on type and intensity of economic activity.
3. Undertake empirical tests of profit and security goals of farmers in a traditional setting.
4. Derive from the descriptions and analyses some implications for introducing change.

Much of the area farmed by the Hausa and settled Fulani in the northern part of Nigeria lies in the Sudan and Guinea ecological

DAVID W. NORMAN is Associate Professor, Department of Economics, Kansas State University. He conducted economic studies in the north of Nigeria from 1965 to 1976 and was head of the Rural Economy Research Unit, Ahmadu Bello University, Zaria, Nigeria.
Note: The constructive criticisms of E. Simmons, H. Hays, the Publications Committee of I.A.R., R. D. Stevens, Carl K. Eicher, and an anonymous reviewer are gratefully acknowledged.

zones [10]. The case study presented here examines the dryland farming practices and production of Moslem farmers in the Zaria area, which is situated in the northern part of the Guinea zone. Through the empirical description and analysis of the reasons for the present farming activities, an attempt is made to suggest factors that would need to be taken into account if change to a less traditionally oriented system of agriculture were to be successfully introduced.

The Zaria area is characterized by a predominantly granite basement complex covered by loess. The land is generally a gently undulating plain at an altitude of 2,000 to 3,000 feet (610 to 914 meters) with some broad valleys and isolated hills. Leached ferruginous tropical soils are typical of the upland parts while the valleys are poorly drained hydromorphic soils of clay textures. The mean annual rainfall of about 43 inches, which falls from April to October, results in a severe water deficit during the dry season and a surplus during the rainy season [28]. Mean monthly temperatures fluctuate from 72° F (22° C) in January to 84° F (29° C) in April [17]. The natural vegetation is savanna woodland, which, as a result of human activities, has been replaced largely by parkland. (Most of the information in this paragraph has been supplied by K. Klinkenberg, Head of Soil Survey Section, Institute for Agricultural Research, Ahmadu Bello University, Zaria.)

Agriculture forms the principal means of livelihood for 75% of the working population in the Zaria area. The predominantly illiterate rural population consists of two main segments: the nomadic pastoral Fulani who roam throughout the northern part of Nigeria with their herds of cattle; and the settled, primarily crop farming population of both Hausa and Fulani origins. The settled rural population lives in two distinctive settlement patterns, which can be differentiated on the basis of religion. Those of the Moslem faith tend to settle in villages or well-defined hamlets while non-Moslems are usually found in single residential units often in the more isolated areas.

In undertaking the research, two main criteria were employed in the selection of the survey villages. First, they should differ in ease of communication with Zaria. The underlying basis for adoption of this criterion was the concentric ring theory of von Thunen, reformulated by Schultz [24]. This more sophisticated version, which considers both the factor and product markets, reasons that farmers' incomes will tend to be higher nearer urban areas than those situated farther away, owing to greater efficiency of the factor and product markets. The second criterion was that they should be representative of other villages in the same general location.

The three Moslem villages selected for study were: (1) Hanwa, which borders on Zaria itself; (2) Doka, which is situated about 25 miles (40 kilometers) from Zaria on the main Kano to Zaria road; and (3) Dan Mahawayi, which is located about 20 miles (32 kilometers) from Zaria, the last seven miles of road being motorable only during the dry season.

The field work initially involved a detailed census of about 800 people in each village, providing a frame of farming families from which the samples could be drawn. A simple random sampling procedure was used to obtain a sample of 104 farms for intensive study: 42 in Dan Mahawayi, 44 in Doka, and 18 in Hanwa. Aerial photographs were used to delineate field boundaries through personal visits to each field farmed by individuals included in the population census. Each of the families in the sample chosen for intensive study was interviewed twice weekly during the survey year to obtain detailed day-to-day information on farm inputs (i.e., labor, land, seeds, fertilizer, tools, and animals), output, and details on marketing, off-farm activities of family members, etc. Further details on the methodology of this research are discussed elsewhere [20, 21].

In the fulfillment of the first objective in this chapter, the discussion is largely limited to the results derived from the sample of 42 farming families in the village of Dan Mahawayi. In this analysis, the families were split into small and large farm groups: 19 farming families with less than 1.5 acres (0.61 hectares) per farm family member and 23 farming families with 1.5 or more acres per member, a stratification suggested by Clayton [3]. To fulfill objectives two and three, data from the 62 additional farming families in the other two villages were also included in the analysis. The data presented here pertain to the period April 1966 to March 1967.

TRADITIONAL FARMING IN DAN MAHAWAYI VILLAGE

Background. The village area of Dan Mahawayi had a total population of about 1,300 inhabitants. The village itself is reputed to have been founded about 150 years ago by a pagan, although it is now Moslem in faith. During the laying of the Gusau to Zaria railway in 1929, the Emir of Zaria compelled villagers to help in its construction. As a result many fled into nearby Katsina Province and never returned.

The village head, as in most villages in Hausaland, wields a great deal of influence, being responsible for collecting taxes on behalf of the local authority, allocating vacant land, witnessing other land transactions, and mediating disputes. There was little evidence of significant change in the village, relative inaccessibility being a major contributing factor. Although the market, which operated on Thursdays and Sundays, was a focal point for the surrounding rural area, no extension worker or primary school was in the village during the survey year. Provision of inorganic fertilizer, seed treatment dressing, and cash crop purchasing was undertaken in a seemingly haphazard fashion by unofficial middlemen who often sold fertilizer at prices higher than the official prices and purchased cash crops at lower prices than those officially set by the marketing board.

Resource Availability and Use

Land Distribution and Types of Land. Land in Dan Mahawayi, as in all of Nigeria, was traditionally a communal asset. Consequently, individuals had only usufructuary rights to use the land for certain time periods. However, in spite of this and the low population density in the village area, there was a high degree of inequality in the distribution of use rights to farmland. Fifty percent of the farmers farmed only 22% of the land farmed, rather than the 50% they would farm under conditions of perfect equality. The extent of this inequality is indicated by the average of 5.5 acres (2.2 hectares) among the 19 small farms in contrast to the average of 17.2 acres (6.7 hectares) among the 23 larger farms. For the village as a whole, the average size of farm was almost 12 acres (4.8 hectares). The range was from 0.6 to 53.6 acres (0.2 to 21.7 hectares).

The farms tended to be fragmented and consisted of an average of almost seven fields, which varied in size from less than 0.1 to almost 19 acres (7.7 hectares). Fragmentation tends to be accentuated by the practice of dividing each field among the male heirs on the death of the fam-

TABLE 3.1. The Hausa farm family and its land resources: Dan Mahawayi and the three study villages, north of Nigeria, 1967

	Dan Mahawayi			Average for the 104 Farms in the Three Villages	
	Small farms (19)		Large farms (23)		
	(no.)		(no.)		(no.)
Family Characteristics					
Family size[a]	6.9		6.7		8.4
Age of family head	44.6		41.5		43.7
	(%)		(%)		(%)
Type of family					
Iyali (single adult male)	63.2		52.2		57.1
Gandu (more than 1 adult male)	36.8		47.8		42.9
	(acres)	(ha)	(acres)	(ha)	(acres)	(ha)
Land Resources						
Farm size[b]	5.5	2.2	17.2	7.0	9.1	3.7
Type of land						
Upland	5.0	2.0	15.8	6.4	8.1	3.3
Lowland	0.5	0.2	1.4	0.6	1.0	0.4
Farmland per family member	0.8	0.3	2.7	1.1	1.3	0.5
Types of tenure						
	(%)		(%)		(%)	
Inherited or a gift	71.5		82.4		75.2	
More mobile types of tenure such as rented, pledged, purchased	28.5		17.6		24.8	

[a] A family was defined as "those people eating from one pot."
[b] A field was defined as a contiguous piece of land farmed by 1 family. The sum of the acreages of fields left fallow or farmed by members of the family during the survey year constituted the farm.

ily head. Although the bulk of the use rights to the land are inherited, it appears that more modern or "mobile" types of tenure, e.g., loans, pledges, etc., were relatively more important to smaller farmers (Table 3.1).

Two types of farmland can be differentiated: the rain-fed upland fields that supported crops of relatively low value per acre, such as millet, sorghum, groundnuts (peanuts), and cotton; and lowland fields that supported more labor-intensive, higher value per acre crops such as sugarcane.

The possibility of year-round cultivation of the limited amounts of lowland (Table 3.1) should logically induce intensive use of such land. However, two factors appeared to prevent this: lack of labor required for cultivating lowland, due partly to alternative employment opportunities during the dry season; and the relative inaccessibility of the village, which prevented sale of the lowland crops. As a result, about 40% of the lowland was not cultivated (Table 3.2).

TABLE 3.2. **Land use and kinds of crops grown, Dan Mahawayi and the three study villages, north of Nigeria, 1967**

	Dan Mahawayi		Average of the Three Villages
	Small farms	Large farms	
	(%)	(%)	(%)
Proportion Fallow			
Total	13.0	23.4	19.8
Upland	10.3	21.6	19.7
Lowland	37.4	43.6	20.0
Proportion Adjusted Cultivated Acres[a] Devoted to			
Cereals[b]	59.5	49.2	49.3
Grain legumes[c]	23.4	23.8	24.7
Starchy roots and tubers[d]	4.7	6.5	8.2
Vegetables[e]	4.6	2.5	4.1
Sugarcane	2.7	4.1	6.9
Nonfood[f]	5.1	13.9	6.8
Proportion Cultivated Acres Devoted to			
Sole crops	25.8	23.1	23.3
Crop mixtures	74.2	76.9	76.7
	(no.)	(no.)	(no.)
Mixed cropping index[g]	2.5	2.4	2.5

[a] The calculation of adjusted acreage was necessary due to extensive use of mixed crops. To do so the acreage of each crop in the mixture was calculated by dividing the acreage of the crop mixture by the number of crops in the mixture. For example, a 2-acre millet/sorghum mixture was recorded as 1-acre millet and 1-acre sorghum.
[b] Millet, late millet, sorghum, maize (corn), rice, and iburo.
[c] Groundnuts (peanuts), bambarra nuts, and cowpeas.
[d] Cassava (manioc), Irish potatoes, sweet potatoes, yams, and cocoyams.
[e] Okra, onions, pumpkins, pepper, garden egg, and tomatoes.
[f] Henna, cotton, Deccan hemp, tobacco.
[g] The mixed cropping index is designed to measure the degree to which crops are grown in mixtures. The value of the index can vary from 1 for a sole crop to 6, which was the maximum number of crops found in a crop mixture [23].

Labor Availability and Use

FAMILY SIZE AND ORGANIZATION. The size of family varied from 2 to 21 persons with the average of 7 persons. Families can be divided into two types of units: a simple family or *iyali*, which consists of a single married male with his wives and dependent children; and a composite family or *gandu*, which is composed of two or more adult males, usually married, together with their wives and children.

In Dan Mahawayi, simple families were found to be more common than composite families (Table 3.1). Both Goddard [5] and Buntjer [2] have observed that traditionally the composite family was the preferred type. One of the reasons it is no longer most popular lies in the fact that the head of a composite family has considerable authority; he supervises the farming activities on most of the family fields and he is able to tell the family members what and how much work should be done. At the same time he has some obligations; he is responsible for providing food for the family and for paying any taxes due. Although male adults other than the family heads in a composite family have security as far as their food needs are concerned, there has been, according to Buntjer, an increasing tendency to resent the restrictions on freedom of action and behavior. Also, in the composite family young married male adults are not in a position to undertake a management role as far as farming activities are concerned. For these reasons the composite family organization apparently was being superseded by the simple family type *(iyali.)* The rate at which this occurs depends on a number of factors such as availability of farmland, opportunities for off-farm employment, etc.

The increasing popularity of the simple family type has a number of implications important for change in agriculture. First, this change would decrease the average age of the family head—for example, from 48 to 39 years in Dan Mahawayi. According to the managerial effectiveness cycle formulated by Hedges [8], this may, if the risk element attached to most innovations can be minimized, bring about a more favorable attitude toward changing farming methods. For under family farming conditions, in traditional agriculture the bulk of the labor input, the managerial functions, and the control of the production process are vested in the family head. A second implication is that farm size would decline. The average for composite family farms was 17.7 acres (7.2 hectares) compared to 7.1 acres (2.9 hectares) for the simple family type.

TYPES OF WORK ON THE FAMILY FARM. As would be anticipated in a society where a class of landless laborers did not exist in rural areas, most of the work undertaken on the average farm was provided from family sources, although there was some hired labor on large farms (Table 3.3).

In Dan Mahawayi about 71% of the labor on the farm was from

TABLE 3.3. Utilization of family labor, Dan Mahawayi and the three study villages, north of Nigeria, 1967

	Dan Mahawayi		Average of the Three Villages
	Small farms	Large farms	
	(hr)	(hr)	(hr)
Total Adjusted Annual Person-hours[a] of Farm Work	1,036.9	1,912.3	1,753.3
	(%)	(%)	(%)
Source of Farm Work (percent of total person-hours):			
Family: Male adults	77.4	56.4	74.6
Female adults	0.1	0.1	0.4
Older children	10.2	7.4	9.7
Nonfamily	12.3	36.1	15.3
	100.0	100.0	100.0
	(hr)	(hr)	(hr)
Person-hours Worked per Cultivated Acre			
All fields (average)	216.0	144.9	240.2
Upland	194.2	133.7	204.4
Lowland	339.7	526.3	525.2
	(hr)	(hr)	(hr)
Work per Male Adult			
Hours per day worked	4.7	5.0	5.0
	(da)	(da)	(da)
Days worked per year			
On family farm	146.2	136.3	141.1
Off-farm occupations	130.6	117.7	82.8
Total	276.8	254.0	223.9
	(%)	(%)	(%)
Type of Off-farm Work by Male Adults			
Traditional			
Manufacturing[b]	22.6	20.3	19.1
Services[c]	41.4	39.0	31.3
Trading[c]	35.6	34.7	22.3
Modern			
Services[d]	0.4	6.0	27.3
	100.0	100.0	100.0

[a] Older children 7–14 years old = 0.50; male adults 15–64 = 1.00; female adults 15–64 = 0.75; and men and women 65 years old or more = 0.50. The estimate of adjusted hours worked does not include time spent traveling to and from the fields.

[b] Includes blacksmiths, tailors, carpenters, spinning, leather working and making pots, cigarettes, mats and sugar, etc. Average remuneration per day worked was $0.4 (0.14 pounds).

[c] Includes tending own house (fencing, building, thatching, cutting grass and firewood), barbers, butchers, hunting, begging, washermen, public officials, Koranic teachers, etc. Trading can also be classified as a traditional service. Average remuneration per day worked was $0.3 (0.11 pounds).

[d] Includes commission agents, messengers, laborers, night watchman, bicycle repairers, buying agents, etc. Average remuneration per day worked was $0.6 (0.21 pounds).

family sources. Of this, family male adults contributed by far the greatest proportion, 88%. The insignificant participation of women in farm work is related to the Moslem practice of seclusion of wives [26].

Hired labor can take three forms: work paid by the hour, contract work paid by the job, and communal labor, which is often contributed free of charge but may be rewarded with a meal or drink. Work paid by the hour and contract work are more productive and were most common, accounting for 50 and 49%, respectively, of the hired labor.

WORK BY MALE ADULTS. The amount of work individuals will undertake is determined by many factors such as health, nutrition, climate, size of family and farm, subsistence needs, incentives, presence and accessibility of markets, attitude and educational level, availability of financial resources to pay for hired labor, and off-farm employment opportunities. In Dan Mahawayi an average male adult worked about 263 days per year for an average of about five hours per day (Table 3.3). These figures compare closely with those derived by other research workers in West Africa: Luning [13, 14], Kohlhatkar [11], Mann [15], Galleti et al. [4], Guillard [6], and Haswell [7].

Because of the seasonal nature of farming, 47% of the average male adult's time in Dan Mahawayi was spent on off-farm occupations. The degree of emphasis on off-farm occupations appeared to be largely independent of the size of farm (Table 3.3).

Off-farm occupations can be divided into two groups: traditional occupations and modern ones. Traditional occupations are defined here as fairly independent of the developmental process or the kind of work that has been undertaken for many generations. In contrast, jobs in the modern sector are defined as those that have come about directly or indirectly as a result of improved communications and the development of large cities, commercial firms, and governmental bodies. Because of the relative inaccessibility of Dan Mahawayi, off-farm occupations are largely confined to the traditional activities. The isolation has helped in establishing the importance of the Dan Mahawayi market in the locality and in preserving the traditional services and crafts. Because of the presence of the market, trading was an important off-farm occupation. There appeared to be no marked differences between the type of off-farm occupations undertaken by small and large farmers (Table 3.3).

PROBLEMS OF SEASONAL EMPLOYMENT. The seasonal nature of farming in the Zaria area is due to the uneven rainfall distribution. June and July are the busiest months for farming activities (Table 3.4.). In Dan Mahawayi about 55% of the annual use of labor on family farms occurred during the May through August period. Conversely, the four-month period from December to March accounted for less than 16% of the annual farm labor.

TABLE 3.4. Seasonality of farming and off-farm work in Dan Mahawayi, north of Nigeria, 1967

	Distribution of Work on the Farm[a]		Distribution of Work by Male Adults[b]		Weather	Farming Activities
	By family members	By non-family members	On-farm	Off-farm		
	(%)	(%)	(%)	(%)		
April	3.9	1.5	3.3	5.0	Rainy	Planting
May	8.1	2.6	6.0	3.8	Rainy	Planting & weeding
June	11.3	4.5	8.0	3.4	Rainy	Planting & weeding
July	10.6	4.7	7.2	3.5	Rainy	Weeding
August	9.7	3.3	6.7	2.5	Rainy	Weeding
September	7.1	2.9	5.5	2.7	Rainy	Weeding & harvesting
October	5.5	2.0	4.4	2.4	Rainy	Harvesting
November	5.3	1.5	4.2	2.8	Dry	Harvesting
December	3.3	2.2	2.6	4.0	Dry	Harvesting
January	2.2	1.4	1.7	5.4	Dry	Harvesting
February	1.8	0.9	1.6	6.1	Dry	Harvesting
March	2.5	1.2	2.2	5.0	Dry	Harvesting
Subtotal	71.3	28.7	53.4	46.6		
Grand Total	100 || 100				

[a] Of the total of 1,516.3 adjusted person-hours of work performed per family farm, 1,080.8 person-hours were performed by family members and 435.5 by nonfamily members. These hours are here distributed by month in percent.

[b] Of the total of 262.7 days of work performed by adult male members of the farming family, 140.1 were performed on the farm and 122.6 involved off-farm work. This work is here distributed by month in percent.

The amount of labor a family has or hires during the June–July period determines to a large extent the amount of land used and the level of agricultural activity during the rest of the year. The bulk of the farm work in this labor bottleneck period was devoted to cultivating and weeding.

The availability of labor in this period was, therefore, a major restriction on the level of agricultural activity. There are at least three ways of modifying this restriction.

1. Increase the availability of family members for work on the family farm by reducing the time spent on off-farm activities. In Dan Mahawayi a significant inverse relationship was found to exist between the days spent per month by family male adults in family farm work and off-farm employment. Yet, even during the bottleneck period of June and July, about nine days per month or about 31% of an average adult male's working days were spent in off-farm occupations (Table 3.4). It would, therefore, appear that these men could not substitute work on the farm for time devoted to off-farm employment to the extent that it would have been desirable during these months.

The major reason may be that to be reasonably successful in the off-farm occupation during the dry season it was necessary to provide some continuity throughout the year. This is particularly true for occupations that involve regular clientele, e.g., crafts and services such as trading. The importance of this off-farm work was emphasized by the fact that little additional income was obtained from farming activities until after the bottleneck period. Cash and food resources tended to be low at the peak period of farming activities, since most crops were harvested between August and December.

2. Hiring of labor could also reduce this bottleneck. One would expect that since labor is in such demand during the June–July period, it would also be the period when the bulk of nonfamily labor is hired. In fact, recalculation of the data in Table 3.4 shows that 32% of the total person-hour input of nonfamily labor was employed during this period. This is about the same proportion of family member labor used during these two months (31%). A statistical test demonstrated that there is no significant difference in the amount of nonfamily labor used as compared to family labor during this peak period. Thus little additional hired labor appears to be obtained for the June–July period. Rather, hired labor appears to be used throughout the year in a pattern similar to family labor. Two possible reasons why more hired labor is not used during the peak demand period are: (1) there is no class of landless laborers to fill this demand, thus the period hired labor is most in demand is the time when the individuals who could hire out are busiest on their own farms; and (2) the low level of cash resources during this period imposes a restriction on the amount of labor that can be hired by farm families.

An important empirical finding was that the wage rate for nonfamily labor remained almost the same throughout the year. A possible explanation is that during the dry season the decrease in demand for nonfamily labor may be coupled with a decrease in labor supply to maintain wage rates at the level paid during the rainy season. This decrease in labor supply during the dry season could be attributed to the greater desire for leisure resulting from the increased cash reserves obtained from the just completed harvest. This issue is discussed further elsewhere [21].

3. The introduction of improved technology, e.g., animal power and equipment, herbicides, etc., could modify the labor bottleneck. The potential success of this approach depends on many factors, including education of farmers in the use, profitability, and dependability of improved technology and perhaps on the provision of funds to help purchase these new inputs.

Use of Durable Capital in Farming. The two main inputs of traditional agriculture are labor and land. The amount of capital and the proportion of income invested in traditional agriculture are usually low.

Mellor [16] has emphasized that the amount saved and invested in agriculture is a result of the interaction of the capital supply and demand schedules. The position of the supply schedule for investable farm capital depends on such matters as general attitudes toward saving and consumption. The position of the demand schedule for investment of capital in agriculture depends largely on the marginal returns obtained from additional investments. Thus low capital formation in traditional agriculture may not be due to a low capacity for saving but to low returns on investments. Mellor gives two reasons for the low rates of return on investments in agriculture: (1) many forms of capital goods are directly formed from labor, e.g., simple tools, land improvements, etc., so that the returns are low because of the low returns to labor and (2) the low level of technology results in low capital productivity.

In Dan Mahawayi it was not surprising to find that investment in durable farm capital goods, such as livestock, buildings, and equipment, was low (Table 3.5). The dependence on hand tools, together with the absence of farm buildings other than grain stores, resulted in an average

TABLE 3.5. Farm capital and cash expenses for farm production, three villages, north of Nigeria, 1967

	Dan Mahawayi				Average of the Three Villages (104)	
	Small farms (19)		Large farms (23)			
	(U.S. dollars)	(Nigerian pounds)	(U.S. dollars)	(Nigerian pounds)	(U.S. dollars)	(Nigerian pounds)
Inventory Value of Durable Capital April 1966						
Livestock	7.80	2.78	22.60	8.07	21.90	7.82
Buildings, tools, and equipment	6.10	2.17	6.80	2.43	6.20	2.21
Total	13.90	4.95	29.40	10.50	28.10	10.03
Estimated Cost of Using Capital April 1966–March 1967						
Durable	2.90	1.04	8.90	3.18	5.80	2.07
Nondurable						
Seed	8.30	2.96	31.30	11.17	19.60	7.00
Fertilizer	3.40	1.21	4.80	1.71	5.10	1.82
Total	14.60	5.21	45.00	16.06	30.50	10.89
Total Cash Expenses	19.30	6.89	74.09	26.45	35.70	12.74
	(%)		(%)		(%)	
Use of Cash Expenses						
Land	6.7		6.0		4.9	
Hiring labor	49.3		68.5		57.9	
Capital goods						
Durable	27.2		12.9		20.6	
Nondurable	16.3		11.7		14.6	
Marketing costs	0.5		0.9		2.0	
Total	100.0		100.0		100.0	

inventory value of investment in these items of only U.S. $6.50 (2.3 pounds) per farm on the 42 farms. The relative significance of investment in livestock, i.e., mainly chickens, sheep, and goats and a few guinea fowl, donkeys, and horses, occurred in spite of the fact that livestock did not play an important role in the farming activities and incomes of most households. However, they did provide a form of investment that could readily be translated into cash.

The low level of use of nondurable capital such as seed and fertilizer was to some extent influenced by the seasonality of farming, which has been emphasized in the preceding section. It was noted that during the June–July peak period in farm activities, cash resources tended to be at their lowest level. The same problem pertained somewhat less acutely to the two months immediately prior to this, April and May, when most of the main crops were being planted. This was the time when the demand for nondurable capital was greatest. As a result, little inorganic fertilizer was used, less than U.S. $0.37 (0.13 pounds) per family farm. Some organic manure was obtained through contract with nomadic Fulani cattle owners. In this arrangement the manure produced on the fields by the cattle was usually considered sufficient payment for the Fulani right to graze their cattle on the postharvest crop residues. An attempt was also made to maintain fertility through fallowing.

Seed, which apart from cotton was unimproved, was saved from the previous year's harvest or purchased, sometimes with borrowed money. Such money was borrowed from local moneylenders and traders who charged high interest rates.

Credit was a severe problem. Since land was a communal asset, farmers had little collateral and commercial institutions had not been willing to consider giving rural credit. Government agencies had suffered heavy losses in channeling loans through cooperatives and were doing little in the field of credit. In a study in the northern part of Nigeria, Vigo [27] found that less than one-third of the farmers were free from debt. Almost 50% of the credit was borrowed from traders whose effective annual rates of interest were from 50 to 90%. Finally, a most sobering finding arising from the study was that over 80% of the credit was used for consumption purposes.

Cash Outlays for Production. Cash expenses are used to obtain the services of inputs either on a temporary basis, e.g., renting, pledging, or leasing land; hiring labor; purchasing seeds, fertilizer, etc., or on a more permanent basis, such as purchasing the usufructuary rights to land and for equipment.

Farm cash expenses in Dan Mahawayi amounted to an average of U.S. $49.20 (17.56 pounds) per family, U.S. $19.30 (6.89 pounds) for the small farms, and U.S. $74.09 (26.45 pounds) for the large farms (Table 3.5). As would be expected in an area where the right to land was usually inherited, only 6% of total cash expenses was spent on obtaining the rights to use additional land. Not surprisingly, an average of 65% of the cash expenses or reward in kind valued in money terms was incurred in hiring nonfamily labor. The cost of the extra hired labor accounted for most of the difference in cash expenses of small and large farms. With respect to the nondurable capital goods, seed and fertilizer accounted for an average of 10% of the cash expenses per family. The importance of sources of supply other than the marketplace has been emphasized earlier. Costs of marketing, 1% of total farm cash expenses, were relatively insignificant, both because of the low proportion of total production sold and because of the operation of middlemen or traders who purchased products directly from farmers and arranged for transport to market.

Land and Labor Relationships. The amount of the labor used per acre by farmers was expected to be inversely related to the number of cultivated acres on the farm. Although the use of nonfamily labor increased with an increase in the size of family farm, analysis of this relationship shows the increase was not sufficient to offset the decline in the total person-hour input per acre (Fig. 3.1). The results also indicate that the labor input per acre on upland was considerably less than on lowland.

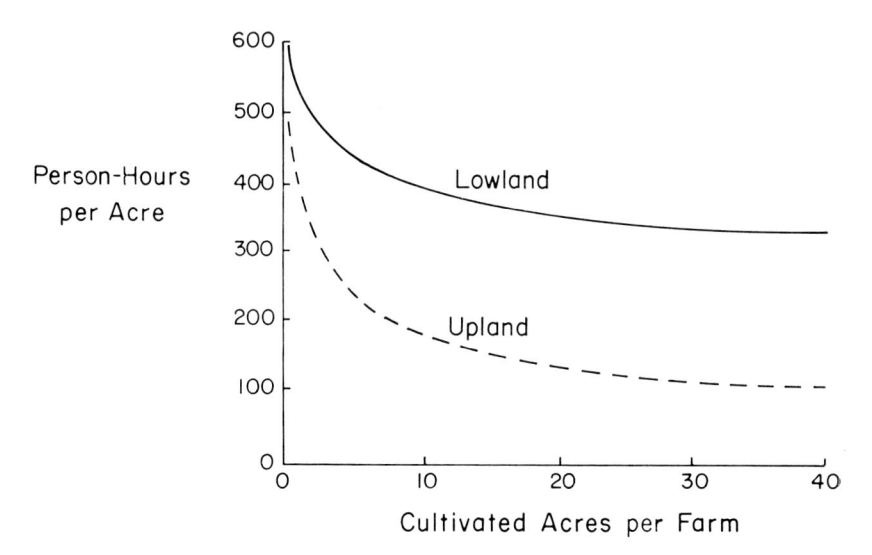

Fig. 3.1. Relationship between labor used and the number of cultivated acres per farm: Three villages in the north of Nigeria, 1966. Estimated from functions of form log Y = $a + b$ log X. The functions include the farmers surveyed in all three villages, i.e., $n = 105$. Mean farm size was 9.1 acres (3.7 hectares).

TABLE 3.6. Marginal value products of land and labor on small and large farms in Dan Mahawayi, north of Nigeria, 1967 (U.S. dollars)

Variable	Small Farms	Large Farms
Per acre of cultivated upland	16.81	8.42
Per acre of cultivated lowland	46.19	31.87
Per person-hour of family labor	0.07	0.10
Per person-hour of nonfamily labor	0.04	0.05

Note: Small and large farms were the same as those defined in Table 3.1. The marginal value productivities were estimated from the following Cobb-Douglas production function:
$$Y = 37.3600\ X_1^{0.2724}\ X_2^{0.0665}\ X_3^{0.2067}\ X_4^{0.0585}\ X_5^{0.2179}\ X_6^{0.0803}$$
$$Sy_x = 0.1529$$
$$R = 0.8987$$
$$n = 104$$
Where:
Y = gross income from crop production (Sh)
X_1 = cultivated *gona* acres (upland)
X_2 = cultivated *fadama* acres (lowland)
X_3 = person-hours of family labor devoted to work on the family farm
X_4 = person-hours of nonfamily labor hired for work on the family farm
X_5 = imputed expenditure on nondurable capital (Sh)
X_6 = depreciation of durable capital (Sh)
The values of X_3, X_4, X_5, and X_6 were held at the means for the average farm in Dan Mahawayi.

The estimation of marginal value productivities of labor and land under different circumstances is important in searching for ways to obtain greater output. A Cobb-Douglas production function analysis indicated that the marginal productivity of upland was less than lowland (Table 3.6). Also, the marginal productivity of labor was found to be greater on the large farms due, as expected, to greater acreage available per unit of labor.

Crop Production and Family Income

Cropping Practices and Yields. The crops grown in any area are determined by physical, social, and economic considerations. Water, temperature, and soil conditions are the main determinants of the physical ability of crops to grow. Nevertheless, although the physical determinants may be favorable as far as growth of a particular crop is concerned, social and economic factors such as personal tastes, tradition, prices, ease of transport, and marketing board activities may bring about cropping patterns very different from those physically possible.

About half the total adjusted cultivated acres were devoted to the cereals, which provided the basic diet (Table 3.7). Because of their greater productive capacity, larger farmers supplemented their grain crops with greater quantities of nonfood cash crops, primarily cotton. Grain legumes comprised the other main crop class that occupied a prominent place in terms of acreage in the survey area.

Millet, sorghum, and cowpeas were the most important food crops,

TABLE 3.7. Acres and yields of food and cash crops, three villages, north of Nigeria, 1967

	Dan Mahawayi Adjusted acres 42 sample farms		Total of the Three Villages					
			Adjusted acres 104 sample farms		Yields			
		Acres grown sole		Acres grown sole	Sole crop (single crop)		Mixed crop	
	Total		Total					
	(acres)	(%)	(acres)	(%)	(lb/ acre)	(kg/ha)	(lb/ acre)	(kg/ha)
Crop								
Millet	64.4	0.0	139.8	0.2	...	...	318	356
Sorghum	122.8	40.9	232.8	30.7	701	785	537	601
Cowpeas	47.5	3.0	98.8	2.3	...	...	105	118
Groundnuts	46.0	15.9	94.6	17.3	524	587	391	437
Sugarcane	14.8	98.8	57.6	97.7	12,316	13,793	...	...
Cotton	45.9	19.2	65.2	26.4	190	213	159	178
Food Crops[a]	270.4	20.1	568.7	17.8				
Cash Crops[b]	123.9	22.5[c]	249.6	23.9[c]				
Total Cultivated Acres	394.3		818.3					
Fallow Acres	106.1		225.2					
Total Acres	500.4	23.7	1,043.5	24.9				

[a] Food crops are defined as those food crops in which less than 50% of total production is usually sold, i.e., millet, late millet, sorghum, maize, iburo, bambarra nuts, cowpeas, cassava, sweet potatoes, yams, cocoyams, okra, pumpkin, and garden egg. The entry also includes two very minor nonfood crops, henna and Deccan hemp.
[b] Cash crops are defined as crops in which more than 50% of total production is usually sold, i.e., rice, groundnuts, Irish potatoes, onions, peppers, tomatoes, sugarcane, cotton, and tobacco.
[c] Excluding sugarcane.

accounting for almost 60% of the total adjusted cultivated acreage, while groundnuts, sugarcane, and cotton constituted the main cash crops and accounted for a further 27% of the total adjusted cultivated acreage (Table 3.7).

Of the total of 21 crops grown by the farmers in Dan Mahawayi, many were grown in mixtures rather than in pure stands (sole crops), a practice termed "mixed cropping." These crops may be intertilled on the same field for short periods or for the whole crop season. The importance of mixed cropping is indicated by the fact that only about 24% of the total cultivated acreage was devoted to sole crops (pure stands) (Table 3.7). Mixed cropping of 2 crops proved to be the most common pattern of cultivation, although occasionally as many as 6 crops were found in a mixture. In Dan Mahawayi, 77 different crop combinations were identified during the survey, but 60% of the acres devoted to mixtures were accounted for by only 7 different crop mixtures. (For details, see Table 3.10.) A millet-sorghum combination was by far the most important mixture, accounting for about 27% of the area devoted to crop mixtures. Grain legumes, starchy roots and tubers, and vege-

Millet and Sorghum Crop Mixture

—X— — —X— — —X— — —X— — —X—

O   O

—X— — —X— — —X— — —X— — —X—

Millet, Sorghum, Groundnut, and Cowpea Crop Mixture

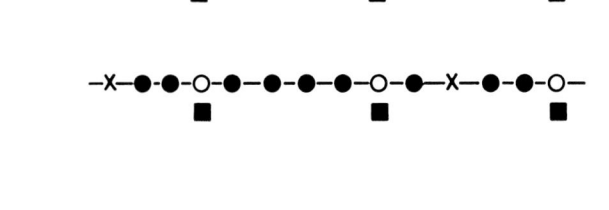

—X—●-●-O-●-●-●-●-O-●—X—●-●-O—
     ■   ■   ■

—X—●-●-O-●-●-●-●-O-●—X—●-●-O—
     ■   ■   ■

Key

Ridge	— — —
Millet	o
Sorghum	x
Groundnuts	●
Cowpeas	■

0   3   6 feet

SCALE

Fig. 3.2. Usual spatial arrangements of two common upland crop mixtures in the north of Nigeria, 1966.

tables were mostly grown in mixtures, while sugarcane was invariably planted as a sole crop.

For each crop mixture, many different spatial arrangements are possible. However, it was found in this village as in much of the northern part of Nigeria that certain arrangements were most popular for each crop mixture (Fig. 3.2). On uplands, crops were usually planted on ridges three feet apart while on lowlands they were planted on the flat.

Reasons for these mixed cropping practices include making maximum use of the land and obtaining maximum return from past labor involved in preparing and ridging the land. In the case of millet and cowpeas it would appear reasonable to grow them in mixtures since millet was harvested in the middle of the growing season, during the first half of August, while cowpeas were not planted until well after the beginning of the rainy season in the second half of July. It also seems reasonable that sugarcane, which produces tall plants with dense foliage, be planted at high population densities in pure stands.

Growing crops in mixtures provides a good example of a practice about which modern agricultural scientists have little knowledge. Most technology in more developed nations relates to pure stands of crops. A detailed comparison of crops grown as sole stands and in mixtures under indigenous technological conditions is given later in this chapter. Under indigenous conditions yields of crops are low (Table 3.7). Improved varieties are seldom used and the application of fertilizer is minimal.

Family Income. The average total income for the 42 farms in Dan Mahawayi was estimated at U.S. $287 (102 pounds) per family, which includes net farm income and off-farm income. Considerable difference between the two farm-size groups is illustrated in Table 3.8, with large farmers earning more than twice as much as small farmers.

The bulk of the income from farming was derived from crop production with only small contributions by livestock. The average percentage of crops sold for cash was about 40%; the remainder was consumed or used for seed. Off-farm sources of income were significant, amounting to an average of 24% of total income. In the case of smaller farmers, the reliance on income from such sources was higher, 34%.

For most families incomes were low. Because of this, savings were very limited and the ability to overcome adverse circumstances was therefore severely curtailed. This is likely to result in a quest for security and a conservative attitude to change.

TABLE 3.8. Composition of farm and family income, three villages, north of Nigeria, 1967

Income	Dan Mahawayi Small farms (19) (U.S. dollars)	(Nigerian pounds)	Large farms (23) (U.S. dollars)	(Nigerian pounds)	Average of the Three Villages (U.S. dollars)	(Nigerian pounds)
Crop income	137.30	49.01	385.40	137.59	263.60	94.10
Livestock income	3.80	1.36	6.60	2.35	3.80	1.36
Gross Farm Income	141.10	50.37	392.00	139.94	267.40	95.46
Costs of Production	21.80	7.78	91.20	32.56	45.90	16.38
Net Farm Income	119.30	42.59	300.80	107.38	221.50	79.08
Off-Farm Income	61.40	21.92	73.70	26.31	70.70	25.24
Total Family Income	180.70	64.51	374.50	133.69	292.20	104.32
Net Farm Income per acre	21.70	7.75	17.50	6.25	24.30	8.68
Total Income per resident	26.20	9.35	55.90	19.96	34.80	12.42

INFLUENCE OF LOCATION AND POPULATION DENSITY ON ECONOMIC ACTIVITIES: A COMPARISON OF THREE VILLAGES. Location, which influences accessibility, and population density both affect the economic life of traditional societies. The literature abounds with discussions as to how agriculture is influenced by these two factors [1, 18, 24]. These factors affect agricultural development and influence the availability of off-farm income sources and the necessity of seeking them. Although the three villages reflect differences in location or accessibility and in population density, these factors were associated (Table 3.9).

Effects on Farm Size and Cropping System. As expected, the average size of farms decreased with an increase in population density (Table 3.9). Somewhat less obvious was a concomitant decrease in the variation in the size of farm. The coefficient of variation of size of farm declined

TABLE 3.9. Effect of population density and accessibility on economic activities in the three villages, north of Nigeria, 1967

	Dan Mahawayi	Doka	Hanwa
Accessibility	Poor	Good	Very Good
Population density per square mile	81	396	709
Farmland per resident (acres)	1.9	1.3	0.6
Average farm size (acres)	11.9	9.8	5.5
	(%)	(%)	(%)
Proportion of land fallow			
Total	21.2	26.8	2.6
Upland	19.2	28.5	2.8
Lowland	42.1	12.4	1.0
Proportion of more mobile types of tenure[a]	19.0	6.4	68.5
Inputs per cultivated acre			
Labor (person-hours)	161.6	227.0	393.5
Organic fertilizer (tons)[b]	0.4	0.5	1.5
Inorganic fertilizer (dollars)	0.10	0.10	0.10
Net farm income per acre (dollars)	18.40	23.70	38.90
	(%)	(%)	(%)
Proportion of income obtained off farm	23.8	12.4	34.2
Proportion of different types of off-farm work done by male adults			
	(%)	(%)	(%)
Traditional			
Manufacturing	21.3	29.3	11.3
Services	40.0	27.2	20.9
Trading	35.0	24.7	3.4
Modern			
Services	3.7	18.8	64.4
	100.0	100.0	100.0

[a] The rest of the land was either inherited or received as a gift.
[b] 2,240 pounds (1,016 kilograms).

from 88.4 in Dan Mahawayi to 70.2 in Hanwa. There are a number of ways population density could influence land distribution. For example, the high demand for land in the most densely populated village, Hanwa, could cause greater equity in land distribution. The opportunity cost of leaving land fallow in such an area is relatively high and farmers are encouraged to surrender their usufructuary rights. In Hanwa the result has been that since additional income can be obtained from renting, pledging, and leasing of land, only 2.6% of the farmland has been left fallow (Table 3.9). It is of significance also that the more mobile types of tenure predominated in Hanwa compared with the two other less densely populated survey villages.

As a result of the decrease in the average size of farm with increase in population density, land was farmed more intensively. Organic fertilizer and labor inputs were increased per acre, resulting in a greater net farm income per acre. However, with further increases in population density, an upper limit would be reached in the return per acre under indigenous technological conditions. The only hope of substantially raising this return per acre ceiling is through introduction of improved technology, including much greater use of inorganic fertilizer, improved seeds, seed treatments, and irrigation, or by substantially changing the farming system to grow higher value crops such as vegetables.

Accessibility can be of considerable influence in determining the types of products produced [19, 24]. Because Dan Mahawayi's location was relatively unfavorable with respect to transportation, farmers tended to leave the lowland fallow, although in more accessible areas it was in great demand. Sugarcane, which could be grown more extensively in the Dan Mahawayi lowland, has a low money value per unit weight and its transport costs were high. This partially accounts for the fact that only 12% of the lowland in Doka was left fallow compared with 42% in the more inaccessible, labor-scarce village of Dan Mahawayi (Table 3.9). The concentration in Doka on the highly remunerative but labor-intensive sugarcane resulted in a correspondingly high percentage of upland being left fallow.

Effects on Amount and Kind of Off-Farm Activities. It could be hypothesized that as population density increases and land becomes more limiting in relation to labor, greater reliance would be placed on off-farm sources of income. Apart from the special case in Doka where sugarcane cultivation was a substitute for off-farm employment, there is some support for this hypothesis (Table 3.9). As the population density increases, such employment is more likely to be undertaken throughout the year rather than confined to the dry season.

The types of opportunities for income from off-farm sources depend to some extent on a village's location or accessibility. Because Hanwa was close to Zaria, men appeared to prefer to obtain employment in the modern sector, which was generally more remunerative than work in the traditional sector. As noted, the relative inaccessibility of Dan Mahawayi precluded employment opportunities in the modern sector. This, together with the presence of an area market, encouraged activities in the traditional sector in Dan Mahawayi. In Doka, employment opportunities in the modern sector were also very limited. However, accessibility to a main road encouraged farmers to concentrate on growing the remunerative sugarcane rather than relying on the less certain sources of income provided from off-farm activities, particularly in the traditional sector.

EMPIRICAL ANALYSIS OF SECURITY AND PROFIT MAXIMIZATION GOALS IN A TRADITIONAL SETTING. Previous sections have detailed the characteristics of farming in the survey area and the influence of accessibility and population density on economic activities. We now focus on certain other influences on economic activity, namely, the farmers' perceptions of their economic situation as exemplified in the goals they adopt.

Family goals have considerable influence on the decisions and actions taken in the farm business and on the family view of the suitability and acceptability of innovative agricultural technology. Two goals are examined here: security and profit maximization. The concept of the security is defined as minimizing risk. More specifically, security is the desire to provide enough food for home consumption, with surplus resources devoted to crops for sale in the market.

Some indication of risk aversion strategy is shown by the following survey information: (1) the average family grew a diverse group of eight crops, thus reducing risks of disease incidence and total crop failure; (2) about 70% of the total adjusted cultivated acreage was devoted to food crops, including particularly millet, sorghum, and cowpeas (almost all farmers grew these crops, indicating the high value placed on assuring the family food supply); and (3) food crops tended to be planted nearer the residential area. More attention was paid to the nearby upland fields usually devoted to food crop mixtures such as millet-sorghum. At more intermediate distances, legumes mixed with cereals such as millet-sorghum-groundnuts-cowpeas tended to dominate. The most distant fields included mixtures emphasizing cash crops such as the cotton-cowpeas-sweet potato mixture.

A pervasive characteristic of all the farmers studied, regardless of size of farm, location, and population pressure factors, was their practice of using crop mixtures in which a number of crops were intermingled in the same field. This practice was, therefore, examined in some detail for consistency with the two goals of security and profit maximization.

Rationality of Mixed Cropping. The objective of this section is to examine the economic and social nature of the practice of mixed cropping. If attempts are to be made to encourage dryland farmers to shift from traditional hand cultivation based primarily on mixed crops to more technologically advanced cultivation methods involving sole crops, it will be useful to understand better the economic relationships facing the individual farmer and his perception of these relationships. After considering the farmers' reasons for mixed cropping, data are presented comparing the returns and variability of sole and mixed crops. Finally, a formal test of the economic rationality of mixed cropping is undertaken.

Reasons Given by Farmers for Mixed Cropping. Family heads were asked why they prefer mixed crops to sole crops. Answers to the open-ended questions should be interpreted with caution. The reasons tended to fall into four broad categories: tradition, the need to maximize return from the most limiting factor, the need for security, and the beneficial effect of legumes on other crops.

Reasons of tradition were consistent and overlapping with the expressed need to maximize return from the most limiting factor and the need for security. Farmers' explanations that mixed cropping was a way of maximizing their return to their most limiting factor suggested they considered there was a relationship between land security and mixed cropping. However, through correlation analysis, the degree of mixed cropping actually practiced in the survey villages was found to be largely independent of the land-labor relationship.

Security motivation and the beneficial effects of interplanted legumes have obvious rational bases that some farmers articulated in their responses. Mixed cropping leads to security through diversification of crops. This is an insurance-type strategy. Mixing legumes with other crops provides an implicit rotation within each year rather than a year-to-year rotation.

Returns to Sole and Mixed Crops. Empirical data on the returns to sole and mixed crops provide support to farmers' preferences for mixed crops. The physical yields per acre for each crop were found to be lower when a crop was grown in mixtures rather than as sole stands (Table 3.7). Possible reasons for this include competition with other crops in the mixture for water, light, and nutrients, and the lower population density of an individual crop when planted in mixtures. However, to obtain a full picture of the yield of mixed crops, the production from each separate crop must be combined in value terms per acre and per person-hour.

1. GROSS RETURNS PER ACRE. Although the yields of individual crops were lower when grown in mixtures, the decrease was more than offset by the other crops present in the mixture. Consequently, the average gross return per acre on upland for crop mixtures was U.S. $34.80 (12.42 pounds) or almost 62% higher than from sole crops (Table 3.10). However, the average gross return per acre from sugarcane, the main crop grown on lowland, was much higher than any type of crop grown on upland.

2. GROSS RETURN PER PERSON-HOUR. In terms of total annual person-hour input, the average gross return for sole crops and crop mixtures was about the same (U.S. $0.10 to U.S. $0.20). However, since labor was only truly limiting during the June–July peak period, a more valid ratio is the average gross return per person-hour input during June and July. Using this ratio, the return on upland was higher for crop mixtures (U.S. $0.50) than for sole crops (U.S. $0.40), in spite of the fact that the labor inputs tended to be higher in the case of crop mixtures. The return to June–July labor on lowland sugarcane, was, however, considerably higher (U.S. $1.80). This estimated return is due, to a considerable extent, to the fact that sugarcane on lowland has a different set of monthly labor requirements. Labor required for sugarcane during June–July was relatively low.

TABLE 3.10. Labor inputs, gross and net returns per acre of sole and mixed crops, three villages, north of Nigeria, 1967 (dollars)

Type of Land	Number of Crops in Mixture	Person-hour Input per Acre Annual	June/July	Acre	Gross Return per Unit Input Annual (person-hours)	June/July	Net Return per Acre Cost of labor not included	Cost of all labor included
		(person-hours)	(person-hours)	(dollars)	(dollars)	(dollars)	(dollars)	(dollars)
Upland	Average–sole[a]	146.6	49.5	21.50	0.10	0.40	20.80	10.40
	Two[b]	235.6	60.7	33.70	0.10	0.60	33.00	16.20
	Three[c]	225.3	61.1	32.20	0.10	0.50	30.80	14.70
	Four[d]	271.1	90.3	47.70	0.20	0.50	45.20	25.80
	Average–mixed	237.3	63.9	34.80	0.10	0.50	33.70	16.80
	Average–Upland crops	218.7	60.9	32.00	0.10	0.50	31.00	15.40
Lowland	Sole crop of sugarcane	525.6	66.8	120.70	0.20	1.80	91.00	53.40

Note: Gross and net returns estimates from survey data, appropriately weighted [20].
[a] Sorghum, groundnuts, and cotton.
[b] Millet-sorghum, sorghum-groundnuts, and cotton-cowpeas.
[c] Millet-sorghum-groundnuts, millet-sorghum-cowpeas, and cotton-cowpeas-sweet potatoes.
[d] Millet-sorghum-groundnuts-cowpeas.

3. NET RETURN PER ACRE. In assessing the net return or profitability of enterprises in a traditional society, numerous problems arise concerning the cost of inputs, as many of the inputs are provided by the family and are not purchased. To attempt to solve this problem, two measures of net return are given. They indicate that, in general, the profitability per acre of upland crop mixtures was about 60% higher than that from sole crops (Table 3.10). For example, if the cost of all labor, including unpaid family labor, is included, the average net return from mixed crops was U.S. $16.80 (5.60 pounds) per acre as compared with U.S. $10.40 (3.71 pounds) for sole crops. However, sugarcane grown on lowland was much more profitable than any crop enterprise produced on upland.

Variability of Returns from Sole and Mixed Crops. Focusing on the goal of security, a primitive test can be made to determine whether the practice of mixed cropping is consistent with this goal by comparing the relative variation in gross return per unit of input between crop mixtures and sole crops. Lower figures for crop mixtures would imply there is less risk or more certainty of return than can be expected from sole stands. The results of the analysis support the hypothesis that mixed cropping increases security of income (Table 3.11). For example, the coefficient of variation of gross return per acre for all sole crops, 16.30, is considerably larger than the coefficient for all crop mixtures, 9.50.

Production Function Test of the Rationality of Mixed Cropping. A formal test of the economic rationality of mixed cropping can be made using a Cobb-Douglas production function. This test determines whether the crop data collected from farmers are consistent with profit maximization. To do this, Cobb-Douglas production functions were calculated for each crop to obtain estimates of the marginal productivities of the inputs used, particularly land and labor. The test consists of comparing

TABLE 3.11. Comparison of variability in the gross return of sole and mixed crops grown on upland, three villages, north of Nigeria, 1967

	Per Acre		Per Person-Hour	
	Average gross return[a]	Coefficient of variation	Average gross return[a]	Coefficient of variation
	(dollars)		*(dollars)*	
All sole crops included	25.33	6.90	0.17	16.30
All crop mixtures included	35.00	6.40	0.14	9.50
Average of 3 sole crops[b]	19.57	21.40	0.15	28.20
Average of 7 mixed crops[b]	28.32	17.20	0.14	23.50

Note: Estimates obtained from survey enterprise accounts.
[a] The figures in these rows differ slightly from those in Table 3.10 because sample sizes used in the calculations were often different and no weighting system was used in the calculation.
[b] This is the average of the average figures obtained for each specified crop or crop mixture

TABLE 3.12. Marginal value productivities of land and labor resources, three villages, north of Nigeria, 1967

	Labor (per person-hour)		Land (per acre)	
	Sole	Mixed	Sole	Mixed
One function for sole crops and one for mixed crops	—0.01[a]	0.07	15.90	7.67
Average for the functions of all individual crop enterprises	0.01	0.03	11.76	13.18
Number of times MVPs from individual crops differed significantly from opportunity costs	1 out of 3	1 out of 7	0 out of 3	0 out of 7

Note: The complete results and a more detailed discussion of their limitations are given elsewhere [20].
[a] Significantly different from zero at the 5% level.

the calculated marginal productivity of the resources with the prices of the resources or their opportunity costs recorded during the survey.

The majority of Cobb-Douglas functions gave estimates of marginal productivities for labor and land that were not significantly different from the observed prices (cost of the resources) (Table 3.12). Thus, for example, in the case of sole crops, in only one out of three tests was the estimated marginal value productivity of labor significantly different from the cost of labor (wage rate). These tests confirm the notion implied in Table 3.10 that, under the conditions existing in the survey area, profits were maximized when a large proportion of the crops were grown in mixtures rather than as sole stands.

In conclusion, this analysis supports the hypothesis that the practice of mixed cropping under indigenous technological, sociological, and economic conditions is consistent with the goals of security and profit maximization.

Rationality of Farm Resource Use—A Linear Programming Test. The preceding empirical analysis indicates the rationality of mixed cropping under indigenous conditions. A further test was undertaken using linear programming to determine whether by reallocating their resources these Hausa farmers could have improved their welfare in terms of their goals. For the purposes of this test a combined profit and security goal was incorporated by setting a goal of profit maximization subject to the security constraint of sufficient food for family needs.

The details of the resources used, products actually produced, and the income received from crop production by the average farmer in the three villages are given in the first column of Table 3.13. With these data a profit-maximizing linear programming model was used to test whether reallocation of existing resources could increase income appreciably, given the constraints that family food needs must be satisfied and

TABLE 3.13. Comparison of actual crop income with a linear program estimate of possible income resulting from reallocation of resources, three villages, north of Nigeria, 1967

	Actual (Average for 104 Farms)	Linear Programming Model
	(acres)	*(acres)*
Total Acres Available		
Upland	8.1	8.1
Lowland	1.0	1.0
	(acres)	*(acres)*
Cultivated Upland		
Sole crops	1.2	0.9
Crop mixtures	5.3	4.7
Cultivated Lowland	0.8	0.5
Fallow		
Upland	1.6	2.5
Lowland	0.2	0.5
Adjusted Acres of Crops Grown		
Millet	1.3	1.5
Sorghum	2.0	2.5
Groundnuts	0.9	1.3
Cowpeas	0.9	0.3
Sweet potatoes	0.3	. . .
Cotton	0.5	. . .
Sugarcane	0.5	0.5
Others	0.9	. . .
	(person-hours)	*(person-hours)*
Labor Used (person-hours)		
Family	1,485.0	1,274.8
Nonfamily	268.3	268.3
Total	1,753.3	1,543.1
	(dollars)	*(dollars)*
Net Income from Crop Production		
Including seed and fertilizer costs only	238.90	259.90
Including nonfamily labor costs also	218.20	239.20
Including family labor	103.90	141.00
Are food needs satisfied?	Yes	Yes

that upland, lowland, and monthly labor devoted to crop production not be greater than current levels.

With a reallocation of resources, if the cost of family labor is not included, the programming results suggest that income might have been increased 13% to U.S. $239.20 (85.39 pounds) (Table 3.13, column 2). This is accomplished in two ways: concentrating more on the production of millet, sorghum, and groundnuts and eliminating sweet potatoes, cotton, and other minor crops. This change appears to be a trade-off between an increase in income and a reduction in security through reduced crop diversification.

Thus, when allowances are made for individual farm variations and the degree of uncertainty facing farmers in their actual farming operations, the potential increase in income to be obtained from reallocating resources is not very high under the technological, sociological, and economic conditions prevailing. This test confirms the earlier conclusion that families were, in general, allocating resources in a manner consistent with the goal of profit maximization.

IMPLICATIONS FOR BRINGING ABOUT CHANGES IN A TRADITIONAL SETTING. Much literature has been devoted to the discussion of the profit maximization [9, 25] and security goals [12] in traditional agriculture. This research has examined both hypotheses and found that farmers' practices were consistent with both goals. The growing of crop mixtures provides an outstanding example of a practice meeting both the profit-maximization and security criteria.

However, there is no assurance these goals would continue to be consistent with each other if a change in the existing conditions were to occur. For example, if improved technology resulted in the greatly increased profitability of crops grown as sole stands rather than in mixtures, the two goals could move into conflict. The relatively low incomes of farmers seriously hamper their ability to shoulder much risk. This implies that adoption of new technology will be much greater if, in addition to proved increased profitability, the risk or standard deviation in returns of the improved technology is the same or preferably less than traditional technology. Wharton [29] has emphasized even though innovation can be proved objectively to result in higher profitability and lower standard deviation, the critical factor in ascertaining its possible adoption are farmers' subjective evaluations of these characteristics. The fact that these two evaluations of profitability and risk can greatly differ highlights the valuable role extension workers can play in aiding change that will increase farm income at acceptable risk levels.

There are two ways that incomes can be increased when resources are limiting: by reallocating the resources currently committed to production, or by increasing inputs particularly of an improved nature, such as chemical fertilizer, seed, and insecticides. The results of the studies of Hausa farmers have shown that under the current technological, sociological, and economic conditions, the potential for increasing income through reallocation of resources was very limited.

The primary limiting resource was found to be the labor available during the peak labor demand months of June and July. This labor determined the amount of land a family can cultivate. Under existing conditions some land was left fallow. Further analysis reported elsewhere [22] indicated there was relatively little scope for increasing income even with some increase in labor availability. Thus a primary focus must be on increasing productivity of labor, particularly in the peak months, through the use of improved inputs obtained from applied agricultural research.

In carrying out applied agricultural research to evaluate returns from new agricultural inputs, the criterion of maximum profitability should be supplemented with the objective of minimizing the standard deviation of the returns to reduce risk to the farmer. Knowledge of the standard deviation of the returns can be obtained by testing new seeds and other new technology under conditions experienced by farmers. This can be accomplished by laying out test plots on farmers' fields with all operations undertaken by the farmer.

Emphasis should be given to exploring the adaptability and usefulness of new technology when combined in indigenous cropping patterns including, particularly, crop mixtures. These tests are especially important for food crops, because farmers are less willing to take risks in the growing of food crops. An important question relates to the possibility of overcoming labor bottlenecks in weeding during June and July through the use of herbicides, small mechanical power tools, or other intermediate technology.

An effective extension service is vital in accelerating the adoption of production-increasing innovations on farms. There appears to be considerable merit in concentrating the limited extension services in a few specific locations where there is potential for development so there may be a critical minimum frequency of contacts between farmers and extension personnel. The aim of extension personnel should be to reduce the divergence between farmers' subjective perception and objective reality with respect to the profitability and standard deviation of the innovation concerned. This is usually most effectively accomplished through demonstrations carried out on farmers' fields. The closer the demonstration is to the farmer's actual conditions, the more likely he is to accept new technology.

In conclusion, this study has found that new technology appears to be the most important tool for increasing output. To assure its availability, emphasis must also be placed on continuing improvement in the rural infrastructure including roads, the marketing system, and so forth. The availability of new inputs such as fertilizer and sprays at the right price and at the right time depends on improved rural communications and marketing.

REFERENCES

1. Boserup, E. *The Conditions of Agricultural Growth: The Economics of Agrarian Change under Population Pressure.* London: Allen and Unwin, 1965.
2. Buntjer, B. J. "The Changing Structure of the *Gandu*," in M. J. Mortimore (ed.), *A West African Savannah City and Its Environs.* Occasional Paper No. 4, Zaria, Department of Geography, Ahmadu Bello University, 1970, pp. 157–69.
3. Clayton, E. S. *Agrarian Development in Peasant Economies.* London: Pergamon Press, 1964.
4. Galleti, R.; Baldwin, K. D. S.; and Dino, I. O. *Nigerian Cocoa Farmers.* London: Oxford Univ. Press, 1956.

5. Goddard, A. D. "Are Hausa-Fulani Family Structures Breaking Up?" *Samaru Agricultural Newsletter* 11 (June 1969): 34–47.
6. Guillard, J. "Essai de Mesure de l'Activite d'un Paysan Africain: le Toupouri." *Agronomie Tropicale* 13 (1958): 415–28.
7. Haswell, H. R. "The Changing Pattern of Economic Activity in a Gambia Village." *Department of Technical Co-operation, Overseas Research Publication No. 2.* London: HMSO, 1963.
8. Hedges, T. R. *Farm Management Decisions.* Englewood Cliffs: Prentice-Hall, 1963.
9. Hopper, W. D. "Allocation Efficiency in a Traditional Indian Agriculture." *Journal of Farm Economics* 47 (Aug. 1965): 611–24.
10. Keay, R. W. J. *An Outline of Nigerian Vegetation.* Lagos: Federal Government Printer, 1959.
11. Kohlhatkar, V. Y. *F.A.O. Socio-Economic Survey of Peasant Agriculture in Makarfi, Ako, Mallam Madari, and Ibeto Districts in Northern Nigeria.* Kaduna: Northern Region Ministry of Agriculture, 1965 (Mimeographed).
12. Lipton, M. A. "The Theory of the Optimizing Peasant." *Journal of Development Studies* 4 (Apr. 1968): 327–51.
13. Luning, H. A. *An Agro-Economic Survey in Katsina Province.* Kaduna: Government Printer, 1963.
14. ———. "The Measurement of Labour Productivity: A Case Study." *Netherlands Journal of Agricultural Science* 12 (1964): 281–90.
15. Mann, W. S. *Farm Management Report of Makarfi District, Zaria Province.* Kaduna: Northern Region Ministry of Agriculture, 1967 (Mimeographed).
16. Mellor, J. W. "Toward a Theory of Agricultural Development," in Herman R. Southworth and Bruce F. Johnston (eds.), *Agricultural Development and Economic Growth.* Ithaca: Cornell Univ. Press, 1967.
17. Ministry of Economic Planning. *Statistical Yearbook, 1964.* Kaduna: Government Printer, 1965.
18. Newman, P. C.; Gayer, A. D.; and Spencer, M. H. *Source Readings in Economic Thought.* New York: V. W. Norton, 1954.
19. Norman, D. W. "An Economic Study of Three Villages in Zaria Province. 1. Land and Labour Relationships." *Samaru Miscellaneous Paper No. 19.* Zaria: Institute for Agricultural Research, Ahmadu Bello Univ., 1967.
20. ———. "An Economic Study of Three Villages in Zaria Province. 2. An Input-Output Study, Vol. 1 Text." *Samaru Miscellaneous Paper No. 37.* Zaria: Institute for Agricultural Research, Ahmadu Bello Univ., 1972.
21. ———. "An Economic Study of Three Villages in Zaria Province: 3 Maps." *Samaru Miscellaneous Paper No. 23,* Zaria: Institute for Agricultural Research, Ahmadu Bello Univ., 1967.
22. ———. "Initiating Change in Traditional Agriculture." Invited paper read at a symposium on the Role of Agriculture in the Post-War Economic Development of Nigeria. *Proceedings of the Agricultural Society of Nigeria* 7 (1970): 6–14. Also in *Agricultural Economics Bulletin for Africa* 13 (June 1971): 31–52.
23. ———. "Intercropping of Annual Crops under Indigenous Conditions in the Northern Part of Nigeria." Invited paper presented at a conference on Factors of Agricultural Growth in West Africa organized by ISSER at Legon, Ghana, 1971.
24. Schultz, T. W. "A Framework for Land Economics: The Long View." *Journal of Farm Economics* 33 (1951): 204–15.
25. ———. *Transforming Traditional Agriculture.* New Haven: Yale Univ. Press, 1964.

26. Smith, M. G. The Economy of Hausa Communities of Zaria. *Colonial Research Studies No. 16.* London: HMSO, 1955.
27. Vigo, A. H. S. *A Survey of Agricultural Credit in the Northern Region of Nigeria.* Kaduna: Ministry of Agriculture, 1965 (Mimeographed).
28. Walters, M. W. "Observations on the Rainfall at the Institute for Agricultural Research, Samaru, Northern Nigeria." *Samaru Miscellaneous Paper No. 15,* Zaria: Institute for Agricultural Research, Ahmadu Bello Univ., 1967.
29. Wharton, C. R., Jr. "Risk, Uncertainty and the Subsistence Farmer." Paper read at Joint Session, American Economic Association and Association for Comparative Economics, Chicago, Dec. 1968 (Mimeographed).

CHAPTER 4

Factors Limiting Change on Traditional Small Farms in Southern Brazil

NORMAN RASK

SMALL FARMERS participated little in the rapid technological change occurring in the mid 1960s in southern Brazil. Similar experiences have occurred throughout the developing world where surges in technological innovation often have been accompanied by substantial disparity in the speed and magnitude of change among different types and sizes of farms and among regions. A major reason is the variation in conditions by locality. In Brazil great regional variations occur since this large country extends from the equator south into the temperate zone. The resulting agricultural systems, ranging from tropical to semitemperate, give rise to substantial regional variations in the applicability of currently available technology.

Among the geographic regions of Brazil, the most dramatic use of technology and changes in agricultural productivity occurred in southern Brazil, the region of this study. However, considerable disparity resulted between the large farms, which made dramatic changes in production practices, and the neighboring small-farm areas containing two-thirds of the rural population, which have changed slowly. The differences in rates of change between large-farm and small-farm areas appeared to be influenced by geographic factors and historical settlement patterns. They were also affected by government growth policies that tended to favor the development and introduction of new technology on large farms.

The purpose of this study was to analyze the economics of tradi-

NORMAN RASK is Professor in the Department of Agricultural Economics and Rural Sociology at Ohio State University. He conducted research in Brazil from 1963 to 1974 and was Research Director of a 5-year Capital Formation study in Brazil.

Note: The research on which this chapter is based was supported in part by the United States Agency for International Development. Field research was conducted by the Institutes of Economic Studies and Research at the Federal Universities of Rio Grande do Sul and Santa Catarina. The usual disclaimers apply.

tional small farms in southern Brazil to explain their slow rates of agricultural growth in a region where large farms made dramatic progress. The analysis sought to identify the factors that limited small farmers' responses. In doing so it focused on three clusters of factors: (1) the nature of available technology, (2) the structure of agriculture (size of farms), and (3) the composition and orientation of the institutions serving agriculture. A similar categorization of factors was made by Gotsch [5] in his excellent treatment of the dynamics of technological change at the community level. The three clusters of factors are defined as follows:

Technology. It comes in many forms: mechanical, biochemical, labor-saving, or managerial. Technology is often crop or task specific. In the case of mechanical technology, the size of farm operation is important. Thus the form in which technology is developed and made available to farmers often determines which farm group can best use it.

Structural factors. In agriculture, the size of farm is a major structural variable. The distribution of farm sizes may range from a high-peaked unimodal pattern in which farms are relatively uniform in size to a bimodal pattern in which significant numbers of farms are found at both extremes of the size continuum. Farm size has implications for the amount and composition of production inputs. Many forms of mechanical technology, for example, can be economically employed only on large farms. Enterprise choice and combination are additional structural characteristics that influence the use of agricultural technology.

Institutions. A third cluster of factors that shape development and the use of new technology are institutional. Institutions can have a significant impact on the rate and direction of technological change in agriculture; these impacts can range from influence on the allocation of resources, to public research, to policies that encourage or discourage the use of specific forms of technology. Credit and price policies are two additional examples of important institutional factors that affect technological change.

The next section of this chapter provides background information on the agriculture of southern Brazil and relates the clusters of factors discussed above to the conditions in the state of Rio Grande do Sul in the 1960s. A later section provides an in-depth study of Lajeado municipio (county), which is representative of the small farms of the region.

AGRICULTURE IN RIO GRANDE DO SUL. Two major farm groups are represented in Rio Grande do Sul. The large farm group is characterized by medium and large cattle and wheat farms. These farms by the mid 1960s had made substantial use of modern technology, agricultural credit, and enterprise specialization with a concomitant increase in output and farm income. The small-farm group presents a sharp contrast to the large cattle and wheat farms. In particular, the small farmers lagged behind in the adoption of new technology. Although they included only about one-fourth of the land area of Rio Grande do Sul, they were considerably more important in terms of people, since these 375,000 farms included over two-thirds of the farm households in the state. The small farming areas are characterized by rugged mountainous terrain with many diversified farms using traditional forms of cultivation. Continued subdivision of farm units has further restricted the ability of small farmers to adopt modern technology and to generate sufficient incomes.

The small farmers are descendants of European settlers who came to Brazil during the 1800s. These farmers were considered traditional because they lagged behind while significant changes in technology use, productivity, and economic growth occurred in adjacent areas and in the Brazilian economy as a whole. For example, participation rates for large farms in the use of various forms of crop technology were generally more than twice as great as on small farms (Table 4.1). Intensity of land use as measured by crop expense per cultivated hectare was tenfold greater on larger farms. In addition, the percentage of farmers who participated in the credit markets and the intensity of credit use were both substantially less in the small-farm area. The limited advances

TABLE 4.1. Use of advanced technology in small and large farm regions of southern Brazil, 622 sample farms, 1969

Technological Practice	Small-Farm Region	Large-Farm Region
Number of Farms	375	247
Number of Ha[a] per Farm		
Total	24	133
Cultivated	9	83
Technological Practices	(% of farms using)	
Soil analysis	7	55
Fertilizer	37	94
Lime	16	44
Improved seed	62	95
Insecticide	44	88
Herbicide	8	24
Intensity of Practice Use	(1969 dollar equivalents)	
Operating expenses/cultivated ha[a]	$28	$64
Crop expenses/cultivated ha[a]	3	33
Credit Use		
Number using (%)	55%	84%
Value per cultivated ha[a]	$24	$70

Note: The sample of small farms was taken from three counties in southern Brazil—Lajeado in the state of Rio Grande do Sul and Concordia and Timbo in the state of Santa Catarina. The sample of large farms was taken from two counties in the state of Rio Grande do Sul—Carazinho and Nao-Me-Toque.

[a] One ha = 2.47 acres.

that had been made by the small farmers were generally in areas of technology requiring very little cash outlay.

Geographic Regions and Settlement Patterns. Rio Grande do Sul, the southernmost state in the nation, is bordered on the east by the Atlantic Ocean, on the south by Uruguay, on the west by Argentina, and on the north by other states of Brazil (Fig. 4.1). It is located in the temperate zone of the southern hemisphere at about 30° latitude. Altitude variations coupled with favorable latitude have allowed most tropical and temperate climate crops to be grown in close proximity.

An important geographical feature of this area of Brazil is an escarpment at an altitude of approximately 900 meters (3,000 feet) above sea level (Fig. 4.1). This escarpment is the beginning of a great plateau that is inclined away from the sea toward the west. The tilt of the plateau has resulted in almost no major river systems on the east coast of southern Brazil. Rivers beginning near the escarpment, only a few miles from the sea, flow hundreds of miles west and south before entering the Atlantic Ocean as part of the Platte River system in Argentina.

Two low-level plains contrast with the high plateau. One is a narrow coastal plain along the Atlantic. The other is an interior open rangeland area in the southern half of the state of Rio Grande do Sul.

A fourth geographical area is a hilly mountainous region connecting the escarpment to the low-level plains.

Each of these areas is characterized by distinctive soil, topography, vegetation, and climate conditions, which have resulted in different patterns of settlement and systems of agriculture.

Cattle and Wheat Regions. The open plains of the plateau were the first areas settled for agricultural purposes in southern Brazil (Fig. 4.1). Large estates were established for the production of beef cattle. Agricultural production remains predominantly range livestock on medium to large farms; however a partial transition to highly mechanized wheat and soybean production has been taking place. Due to the transitional nature of present-day agriculture in this locale, systems of farming run the gamut from traditional to the most modern. The introduction of tractors for the cultivation of wheatland has also led to the use of these machines for establishment of improved pastures.

A national emphasis on mechanical technology and on research for development of crop varieties and the cultural practices that accompany mechanical technology has favored large farmers. Credit and price support policies have also focused on the crops grown on these large farms, reinforcing the mechanization advantages.

The lowland plain of the southern half of the state of Rio Grande

Fig. 4.1. Geographic regions and type of farming regions, state of Rio Grande do Sul, Brazil.

do Sul is open grassland, which, like the high plateau, was settled by Spanish and Portuguese settlers interested in raising cattle. Both sheep and cattle are raised on large farms using traditional ranching practices. Some wheat is produced here; however, climatic conditions for this crop are less favorable than on the plateau. Some irrigated rice is produced along the principal waterways. Farms are relatively large, generally ranging in size from several hundred to several thousand hectares.

Small-Farm Regions. There are two major regions of small-farm agriculture; one is located in the hilly mountainous area at the edge of the escarpment, commonly called the "Encosta Inferior do Nordeste," and the other in the interior of the plateau, or "Alto Uruguai" (Fig. 4.1). The Encosta Inferior do Nordeste, which extends from the coastal plain and lowland plains to the high escarpment, is composed of a series of very steep hills and valleys. The municipio of Lajeado is located in this region. The rapid increase in elevation results in substantial annual rainfall. The natural vegetation consists of a deciduous tropical forest. The soils are relatively fertile but, because of topography, do not lend themselves well to intensive cultivation or mechanization.

The region was settled by European immigrants in the middle 1800s and later. Many people still retain their mother tongue, principally German and Italian. The immigrants were settled on small farms of 25 to 30 hectares (62 to 74 acres). Most of the potentially tillable land has been cleared and is under cultivation. Farm subdivision has resulted in a sharp increase in the number of small farms.

Agricultural production is carried on for both subsistence and market purposes. In this mixed farming, at the time of the study, maize (corn) and beans were the most important crops and hogs the most important livestock enterprise. In areas close to major cities, substantial amounts of dairy products were produced.

The Alto Uruguai region of small-farm agriculture is located in the mountainous areas of the high plateau. Where the rivers are cut very deeply into the plateau, climatic, topographic, and settlement patterns are found similar to those of the other small-farm region discussed above. The interior mountainous region was settled in the early 1900s by second- and third-generation descendants of German, Italian, and other European immigrants moving from the coastal mountain range into the interior valleys. The types of agricultural production found in the interior valleys are similar to those of the coastal mountain range.

In summary, the agriculture of the regions of Rio Grande do Sul is a result of district geographic and climatic factors and is partly dependent on the settlement patterns. Three commercially important types of farming can be identified. First, in the open area on the high plateau and on the low grassland area, extensive cattle and sheep grazing occurs on large farms. Within these same areas, some farms undergoing a technological revolution in the use of modern agricultural inputs make up a second type of farming, focused on mechanized cash grain production. The third type of farm is in the mountain regions and is characterized by mixed farming with a predominance of maize and hogs on medium and small farms. The disparity in levels of farm income between the third type of farm and the other two types has been accentuated by the differential impact of technological change. Among the small farmers, small size of operation and enterprise diversification have contributed to the complexity of incorporating new technology in their farming practices. Often the technology available in Brazil was not appropriate for small farmers (large-scale mechanical technology, for example).

CHARACTERISTICS OF SMALL FARMS IN RIO GRANDE DO SUL.

The number of farms in Rio Grande do Sul has increased dramatically. During the decade 1950–60, farm numbers increased by one-third, while the number of farms of less than 10 hectares (25 acres) doubled. Estimates of the total number of farms in 1970 show an even greater increase during the last decade (45%). The increase in farm numbers and the greater concentrations of farms in smaller size categories indicate the growing importance of small-farm agriculture in southern Brazil, particularly in view of the very large number of people involved.

The purpose of this section is to present an overview of the general characteristics of the small farms in southern Brazil. While displaying considerable variability, small farms do have certain general characteristics that set them apart from the larger, more commercial farms of adjoining regions. While the discussion is limited to one state, the small-farm situation described here is common to each of the three southern states of Brazil. Problems associated with small-farm agriculture can be found throughout Brazil; however, the physical and economic setting in other areas is somewhat different. (A series of farm and community level studies carried out by the Institute of Economic Studies and Research [IEPE] of the Federal University of Rio Grande do Sul serve as a basis for this presentation of small-farm agriculture in Rio Grande do Sul [1, 2, 8, 14, 15, 18, 19].)

The general characteristics of small-farm agriculture were the following:

1. *Farm ownership*—The small farms were usually owned by the person operating the farm business. Studies in the small-farm regions indicated that about 97% of the farmers owned the property they worked. In some areas the number was nearer 90%, partly because of the incidence of tobacco farming in which a sharecrop system was common. Also, about 15% of the farmers rented some additional land to enlarge their farm operation.

2. *Farm size*—The number of hectares operated varied from 1 to over 50 (123 acres). A majority of the farms, however, had from 10 to

25 hectares (25 to 62 acres). Farms with less than 25 hectares constituted almost three-quarters of all farms in the region. Cropland normally occupied from one-third to more than one-half the total land operated.

3. *Labor supply and utilization*—The labor supply was drawn almost totally from members of the immediate family. In some cases, small amounts of seasonal labor were employed during periods of peak labor requirements. The incidence of full-time employed labor was very rare. On most farms the supply of family labor was in excess of that needed to perform the productive farm operations. In addition to being in abundant supply, family labor had little alternative use other than farm employment. Farm labor available averaged from two to more than three person-equivalents per farm.

The contrast between available family labor and the amount of productive labor needed to operate the farms was very apparent, especially on the smaller farms. For example, the farms under 15 hectares (37 acres) had about twice as much labor available as they could productively utilize. Farms under 5 hectares (12 acres) had from three to four times more labor than needed [15]. Crop production accounted for the greatest use of labor (60 to 70%).

4. *Crop and livestock diversification*—Although the farms were small, many types of livestock and crops were found on each farm. For instance, almost all farms had milk animals, poultry, and hogs, and raised a variety of crops for sale and for use by animals or the family. Maize (corn) was the principal crop grown and normally occupied from one-half to two-thirds of the cultivated acreage. It was used mainly as feed for hogs, which constituted the principal livestock enterprise and source of cash income. Other cash crops, with regional variations, included soybeans, wheat, tobacco, and black beans. Commercial dairy herds were located near urban centers; however, on the typical farm, dairy product sales were seasonal and consisted of surplus supplies above family consumption needs.

5. *Productivity levels*—Levels of both crop and livestock productivity demonstrated two important points: (1) they were generally very low, and (2) the difference between the high-level producers and the average was very great, often achieving a magnitude of two or three. In one study [9], the high 10% of the farms in maize production achieved yields over 3,000 kilograms per hectare (48 bushels/acre), while the average for all farms was about 1,200 kilograms per hectare (19 bushels/acre). Wheat and soybean yields were similar, with average production levels of 1,000 and 1,200 kilograms per hectare (13 and 16 bushels/acre), respectively. In milk production the high 10% achieved levels twice as high as the average. In hog production, when the more efficient farms (high 10%) were compared with the average, the number of market hogs raised each year from one sow was three times as high, and the average age for selling fat hogs was less than half that of the average group.

6. *Home consumption*—A significant portion of annual livestock

and crop production is consumed by the farm family. On the larger farms studied, an average of 20 to 30% of total production was consumed at home, whereas on the very small farms this percentage approached 80.

7. *Power sources*—Agricultural operations were performed largely by hand methods with limited animal power. The incidence of tractors or modern land preparation, cultivation, or harvest equipment was very small. Often dairy animals served as work animals.

8. *Modern technology*—The use of hand methods to perform farm operations was one indication that modern technology had not come to these farms. Other indications were limited use of modern inputs such as fertilizer, hybrid seeds, and seed inoculation, and the lack of modern sanitary and feeding practices in livestock enterprises. This lack of modern technology resulted in generally low levels of productivity in the crop and livestock enterprises and in substantial differences between these low averages and the results obtained by the few farmers who employed improved methods.

9. *Low incomes*—The resulting economic performance was very low as measured by farm income. Enterprise diversification inhibited the benefits of specialization. This, combined with little use of modern methods and a small land base, resulted in low levels of productivity per acre or animal. Thus the possibility for a large volume of production, already hampered by small farm size, was further reduced by the low levels of production per unit. When the abundant and, in most cases, excessive labor force (even with hand methods of work) is added to the picture, the small volume of production is further diluted when considered on a per capita basis.

In the large farm areas of Rio Grande do Sul, a more favorable situation existed throughout the 1960s. Guaranteed prices for wheat, favorable credit policies for wheat production costs, and machinery acquisitions created an environment that stimulated massive changes in the use of technology and enterprise combinations. These policies resulted in tremendous increases in output and farm income and increased wheat production from 10 to 50% of Brazil's domestic consumption needs in eight years. Small farmers shared only marginally in these government incentive programs.

The above description generally typifies the major characteristics of the small farmer. The remainder of this study is devoted to an in-depth analysis of one municipio (county), Lajeado, within the Encosta Inferior do Nordeste small-farm region. Ninety-one farmers in three districts of Lajeado were interviewed in 1965 and again in 1969. As noted, this was a period in which significant gains in the use of technology and credit were being experienced by adjoining farm regions in Brazil. The small-farm region unfortunately did not share much in this change.

ENTERPRISE PRODUCTIVITY AND FARM INCOME IN THE MUNICIPIO OF LAJEADO.

The municipio of Lajeado is located near the center of the state of Rio Grande do Sul. The topography of the area is varied but generally mountainous. There is a central river valley bordering Lajeado on the east. In the extreme northern part, the mountains blend into the high plateau. Altitude variations range from 30 meters (approximately 100 feet) to more than 600 meters (1,968 feet) above sea level. Many of the farms are located on very steep slopes. The soils are generally lateritic, developed from a basalt base. They are highly acid (about 5.0 pH), low in phosphorus, and high in potassium. Aluminum toxicity reduces yield potential in most areas, while erosion is a problem, especially on steeper slopes. Annual precipitation averages 48 inches, with good seasonal distribution. Light frost may occur occasionally at night during the months of June through August.

The original colony was established by German immigrants in 1836. A smaller, more recent Italian settlement is located in the northern part of the municipio. The immigrants were originally settled on farms of about 25 hectares (62 acres) in size. The process of population growth and subdivision of property has resulted in a gradual decline in size. In 1969 there were more than 6,500 small farms in Lajeado and more than 50% contained less than 15 hectares (37 acres) [8]. The major enterprises were maize (corn), soybeans, tobacco, hogs, and dairy products.

Two distinctly different institutional frameworks served the agriculture of the municipio. One, related to the production of tobacco and tobacco products, was composed of a vertically integrated industry with one dominant company acting as a price leader. The other framework included all other agricultural enterprises and displayed the more typical situation of a variety of institutions serving farm people. In the case of tobacco, the companies buying tobacco from the farmers also supplied the necessary purchased inputs such as seed, fertilizer, insecticides, fungicides, small implements, and curing barns. With little exception, these items were advanced to the farmer and their cost subtracted from the value of his crop at the end of the season. In addition, the companies furnished technical consultants who instructed farmers on proper methods of growing tobacco.

For other agricultural enterprises, a variety of institutions served farmers. ASCAR, an autonomous extension service supported with federal funds, maintained an office in Lajeado and employed two agents, a man and a woman, to instruct farm people in proper farming methods and to disseminate other information of general help to the agricultural community. The state government also maintained an agricultural extension office with an agronomist and a rural technician.

There were several banks and other financial institutions that loaned money to farmers; the most important for the small farmer was the Bank of Brazil. For farm inputs, the county government purchased some items such as hybrid maize, fertilizer, some types of feed, and medical supplies for resale to small farmers. These items were sold at cost, with a small charge to cover handling costs (about 10%).

There was one slaughterhouse that purchased most of the hogs and sold hog feed. Dairy products were mostly marketed privately by producers or consumed at home. The rest were sold to local distributing or processing plants, hospitals, and similar establishments.

For this study farmers were interviewed in three of the eight districts of Lajeado. The three districts represented different market and resource situations. District I is located along the river valley, has superior soils and topography, and includes the county seat. District II is located in the foothills of the mountains. It has relatively good access to markets. Topography and soil conditions are, however, less favorable than in District I. District III is situated at the higher elevations near the edge of the plateau. This area is extremely mountainous, with poor soil. Consequently, farms need to be considerably larger to provide enough tillable land to support a farm family. A major all-weather highway completed in 1969 now links the plateau area of Rio Grande do Sul with the state capital. This road passes close to but does not pass through each of the three districts. Districts I and II, with previous access to markets, did not evidence major adjustments following completion of the road. However, changes in the pattern of agriculture and employment were already evident in 1969 in District III due to improved access.

Technology and Productivity Levels of the Five Principal Farm Enterprises. Farming in Lajeado included a variety of farm enterprises. Five principal enterprises were selected for detailed analysis: maize (corn), soybeans, hogs, dairy cows, and tobacco.

Maize. Maize accounted for more acreage than any other crop (Table 4.2). It was a multipurpose crop, serving as the principal feed for fattening hogs on the more advanced farms and as a household staple used as flour for bread. Maize was also sold or purchased, depending on the manner in which the farm operator combined his farm enterprises.

Until recently the common system of maize production used very little advanced technology. Traditionally, a white variety was used because it was better for household use as flour. Recently, improved varieties of field maize have been introduced on some farms. Use of fertilizer on maize was practically nonexistent. The common method of planting was to place 3 to 5 seeds in a hill and space the hills about a meter and one-half apart (four and one-half feet). Often other crops such as pumpkins, black beans, soybeans, or cassava were planted between the hills of maize. This mixing of crops was more common on the smaller farms. For example, in Districts I and II, over 90% of the

TABLE 4.2. Farm characteristics, ninety-one farms, Lajeado, Rio Grande do Sul, Brazil, 1969

Farm Characteristics	District I		District II		District III	
Number of Farms	28		30		33	
	(ha)	(acres)	(ha)	(acres)	(ha)	(acres)
Land Use						
Cultivated	7.8	19.3	6.7	16.5	7.7	19.0
Pasture	2.0	4.9	3.7	9.1	9.4	23.2
Other	5.6	13.8	4.3	10.6	14.3	35.3
Total operated	15.4	38.0	14.7	36.2	31.4	77.5
Cropping Pattern						
Maize (corn)	3.4	8.4	2.8	6.9	3.7	9.1
Soybeans	2.7	6.7	1.9	4.7	0.4	1.0
Wheat	0.1	0.2	0.1	0.2	1.7	4.2
Cassava	0.8	2.0	1.1	2.7	0.5	1.2
Tobacco	0.3	0.7	0.3	0.7	0.9	2.2
Other	0.5	1.2	0.5	1.2	0.5	1.2
Total	7.8	19.2	6.7	16.4	7.7	18.9
Livestock Numbers						
Cattle	9		11		11	
Hogs	22		25		17	
Poultry	54		48		52	
Draft animals[a]	2.6		1.9		3.0	
Labor Supply (person-equivalents)[b]						
Family	2.7		2.7		3.0	
Hired	0.1		0.1		0.1	
Total	2.8		2.8		3.1	
No. of People Residing on Farm	5.0		4.8		7.5	
Years of Schooling Completed by Farm Operator (% of total)						
0	4		2		30	
1–2	7		6		18	
3–5	89		92		52	
	100		100		100	

[a] In many instances, dairy animals served a dual role as both dairy and work animals. Therefore, this value is somewhat underestimated.
[b] A person-equivalent is defined as 300 days of productive labor available on the farm and is determined by age and sex for family members.

farms followed this practice. On the larger farms of District III, over 60% planted companion crops with maize. Planting occurs during the months of August, September, and October. When the crop is mature, the farmer passes through the field and breaks each maize plant below the lowest ear. This is done so the ear will be pointed downward and thus prevent the penetration of water inside the husk. The maize is harvested from March to June, depending on needs, storage facilities, and time available. Although little fertilizer was used in maize production by the small farmers, experimental results demonstrated that of the major crops it was the most responsive to increased fertilization [6]. Uncertain prices, especially during harvest season, may have been responsible for farmer reluctance to fertilize maize.

On most farms, storage facilities were not adequate. Therefore, when hogs were kept, the harvest period served as a hog-fattening period and after the maize was consumed the hogs were marketed. If the maize was produced for sale, it was generally sold at harvest. This practice apparently caused a 30 to 50% drop in price soon after harvest. Maize prices then recovered gradually after the end of the harvest in July and reached a peak in February.

Soybeans. Soybeans were the second most important crop grown, based on land use. On most farms they were the principal source of cash income from crop sales. The systems of planting involved an intertilling of soybeans with maize as the principal crop. Planting was in October and November, using the same implements for both maize and soybeans. Harvest was generally in May, at which time most of the crop was marketed. Some farmers inoculated soybeans, almost none used fertilizer.

On a broader scale, soybeans represent a potentially important export crop as world demand for vegetable oils increases. Within Brazil, a shift from heavy reliance on animal fat to a greater use of vegetable oils has also increased the prospects for this crop. These strong internal and export demands make soybeans an attractive cash enterprise for small farmers. To compete successfully for limited land resources, however, yields must be increased significantly. Some genetic improvement has been achieved and major efforts are now under way to make substantial improvements through a coordinated genetic and cultural practice research program.

Hogs. Hogs are found on more than 90% of the farms in Lajeado. They are the most important single source of cash income and an important part of the meat consumed in the farm home. Fifty percent of the annual commercial slaughter is processed during the four-month period of June through September. Another 30% is slaughtered in October, November, and December. The remaining 20% is processed during the five months of January through May. The price drops about 10% during the heavy slaughter period of June through September. Until recently there had been very little price incentive for the meat-type hog. A discount on price was made when the weight of the hog was outside 80 to 140 kilograms.

The enterprise was originally established on the basis of a fat-type hog. The Duroc Jersey and other new breeds are gaining increasing approval among the more advanced farmers. This resulted from two factors: a shift in national market demand toward greater use of vegetable oils and lean meat, and the faster growth rate and better feed conversion ratio of the new meat-type breeds.

Sows generally had one litter per year on the farms studied, usually in the summer months of January to March. The litters were small and the mortality rate was high. Considerable variation among farmers occurred. For example, about 30% weaned fewer than five pigs per sow each year. Only 15% weaned more than ten. The timing of reproduction was tied closely to the seasonality of feed production, because maize was harvested in April, May, and June. With little available storage, the maize was fed out and the hogs marketed. In the period before their few months of fattening, the hogs subsisted on cassava, sweet potatoes, pumpkins, and pasture. Often many of these ingredients were mixed and cooked before being fed, a process called "lavagem."

The principal problems limiting the productivity of this enterprise were health, sanitation, feeding, and breeding. Health and sanitation were the most important problems, and severely limited any potential benefits from better feeding and breeding. The State Department of Statistics estimated a 20% mortality in the hog herd each year. Some veterinarians working in the field placed the estimate as high as 30%. The greatest loss occurred prior to weaning. Poor care of the young pigs, dirty pens, exposure to wind and rain, and a general lack of health management were the principal causes of death.

Other than the fattening period, hogs were not fed maize and in general were not well fed. Balanced rations were used only by a few farmers. The feeding method, with the fat-type hog and late marketing, resulted in a wasteful feed conversion ratio of six or seven units of feed for every unit of animal weight gain.

Much of the necessary technology for improved swine production was available locally and was used by the better farmers. It was mostly a matter of using a series of management techniques, many of which were not high cost. Failure to use these techniques reflected a lack of management capability or of sufficient information to adequately understand the returns that might be obtained from use of the improved technology.

Dairy cows. Milk production was a secondary enterprise on most farms in Lajeado. While dairy cows were commonly found (92% of the farms had at least one cow), the average number of cows per farm was only 3.3. When specialized dairy farming was found, it occurred near several major market outlets. Lack of good all-weather roads and suitable transportation and cooling facilities limited the production of milk for fluid sales to the proximity of the markets. For example, while most farms had dairy animals, only 30% sold dairy products. Thus most dairy production was for home use, and sales were generally the result of seasonal overproduction that could not be consumed at home. (A study of dairy farms in a neighboring municipio found the specialized farms were situated around a major city [14]. This small group of dairy farms averaged 11.5 cows per farm and in general was more technologically advanced than the average producer. The differences in the dairy enterprises noted between the commercial group of dairy farms and other small farms were substantial. For example, the average annual production per cow was more than two times as great on the commercial farms near the city. Furthermore, the price received for the milk was from 50 to more than 100% greater. This difference reflected (1) lower transportation costs, (2) a greater percentage of fluid milk sales, and (3) the assimilation of some market and distributing functions by the farmer located near the city.)

With the marked regionality of commercial milk production, the possibilities for dairy expansion would be limited largely to the existing commercial milk production areas. Expansion of commercial milk production into the interior of the municipio would have to await the development of new market outlets.

The principal limiting factor in milk production was proper feeding. Native grasses do not provide year-round feed and few farmers provided more than the minimum requirements for animal life during the winter period.

Tobacco. Tobacco occupied a special position in the agricultural life of Lajeado and when viewed in a time perspective presents an unusual paradox. For the very small farmers who did not have enough land to produce other crops to support their families, it was the principal income-generating enterprise and the only crop alternative. Intensive tobacco farming, however, has contributed to the gradual decline in farm size. As population pressure increases and new land becomes more difficult to find, it is easy for farmers to divide their properties among their sons and, with the cultivation of tobacco, each can maintain an economic unit. The development of share cropping, especially in tobacco, also has permitted further intensification of people on the land.

Tobacco has unique features that have given rise to the present system of production. First, it has heavy labor and low land requirements. Tobacco has not lent itself to mechanization. It requires hand labor and constant attention throughout all phases of planting, growing, harvesting, and curing. Furthermore, the diverse operations are ideally suited to a family labor supply as some tasks are better or at least equally well performed by children, such as the first harvesting of bottom leaves of the plants.

A few norms have been established with regard to a family tobacco farm. A curing barn capable of handling the normal production from 1.6 hectares (4.0 acres) of tobacco was considered the appropriate size unit for a family of five or six people. When a property had two or more curing barns, each was typically handled by separate families. This was the basis for the "parceiro" or share-cropping arrangement in which a landowner furnished the land for growing tobacco, the curing shed, a small house, enough other land for producing food for home consumption, and often some animal power. The annual inputs were supplied on credit by the tobacco company. The landowner and parceiro divided the profits, usually on a 50–50 basis.

The tobacco companies were vertically integrated, manufacturing and selling finished tobacco products. On the production side, they provided all inputs and services except land, labor, and animal power, including a very systematic management service. Payment for the inputs was deducted from the value of the crop at harvest time. The company controlled the basic production process to ensure that certain types and qualities of needed tobacco in specified amounts were available to make their finished products. By controlling production they were able to specify the variety of tobacco a particular farmer grew, and through their management service they guided the planters to produce the qualities necessary for their particular blends.

The organization was efficient and the costs of inputs to the farmer appeared minimal. The system, however, was not without drawbacks. Agronomists admit that on the various soils of the region several different types of fertilizer should be used. However, for convenience, tobacco companies bought only one type. The rigid control of all phases of the production process left little room for effective experimentation. A general attitude of noncooperation between company agronomists and the extension agencies dampened the opportunity for new ideas to penetrate the established system of work. Finally, much of the management decision making was based on the questions of how much, what kind, and what quality of tobacco the company wanted and not on the economic well-being of the producer.

Farming Returns. The major enterprises considered above were included in various combinations on the small farms in Lajeado. Livestock, particularly hogs, were the principal source of cash income (Table 4.3). Among the crops, soybeans and tobacco were major sources of cash income. Maize, the crop occupying the most acreage was almost totally consumed within the farm (less than 1% of total production was marketed). Tobacco was relatively more important on farms in District III. Nonfarm income was of little importance in 1965. However, it increased sharply by 1969, especially in District III, where it accounted for about one-fourth of total cash income.

Among the expense categories, livestock expenses were the largest single item. This reflects the importance of the hog enterprise. Capital expenditures increased greatly in District III during 1969. Cash living expenses were quite uniform for each area and account for about one-half the total farm and family expenditures.

It is difficult to evaluate the changes in income levels between 1965 and 1969, since inflation rates of 20 to 40% were encountered during this period. However, when the monetary values are expressed in terms of constant 1969 dollars, it appears that modest gains were experienced in family income. Similarly, the cash requirement for family living went up slightly while the value of home-produced consumption items declined.

TABLE 4.3. Cash flow and income measures, Lajeado, Rio Grande do Sul, Brazil, 1965 and 1969

	District					
Cash or	1965			1969		
Income Category	I	II	III	I	II	III
	(1969 dollar equivalents)					
Receipts						
Hogs	$450	$285	$137	$343	$334	$163
Other livestock	169	176	90	237	284	168
Wheat	1	4	9	0	5	80
Soybeans	110	76	9	153	111	15
Tobacco	28	65	152	82	57	125
Other crops	7	15	99	19	16	41
Other farm receipts	51	56	15	49	30	33
Total farm receipts	$816	$677	$511	$883	$837	$625
Capital sales	46	0	0	91	45	26
Nonfarm income	55	5	24	189	114	237
TOTAL CASH RECEIPTS	$917	$682	$535	$1,163	$996	$888
New credit	35	51	80	148	76	156
Expenses						
Crop costs	19	29	49	43	18	35
Livestock costs	181	99	147	157	123	66
Other operating costs	83	67	69	127	91	99
Total operating costs	$283	$195	$265	$327	$232	$200
Capital purchases	215	121	9	261	159	325
Loan payments (principal)	40	2	14	42	42	11
Cash living expenses	415	453	462	500	479	484
Income Measures						
Inventory change	30	22	66	−55	78	−9
Depreciation	107	24	8	34	21	16
Perquisites	289	283	358	244	196	287
Gross farm output	1,031	880	825	921	972	812
Net family cash income	634	487	270	836	764	688
Net family income	846	768	686	991	1,017	950
Net family income per person residing on farm				198	254	126

The substantial changes noted in District III, including an increased emphasis on wheat and tobacco, a tenfold increase in nonfarm income, and expanded agricultural credit and capital improvements, all point to major adjustments in the economic life of this area. These changes probably resulted from increased opportunities presented by the construction of a major farm-to-market, all-weather highway passing close to the area. Both wheat and tobacco are market crops requiring purchased inputs and market outlets. Improved transportation facilities also opened up employment opportunities in neighboring cities. The new road increased economic opportunities available to the farm people and it appears they quickly took advantage of them.

INTERACTION OF TECHNOLOGY, FARM SIZE, AND THE INSTITUTIONAL SETTING. The preceding sections have described small-farm agriculture in Lajeado. These farms were generally representative of small-farmer problems in southern Brazil. Since these farmers did not share equally in the expanding use of new technology, we now consider some of the factors responsible. In explaining differences in the use of technology and farm growth, the interaction of three sets of factors—the form of available technology, the size of agricultural producing units into which it is introduced, and the institutional setting—constitutes a useful framework for analysis.

Effect of Farm Size on Productivity and Use of Technology. Farms in Lajeado were considered small within the context of all farming in Brazil. However, there was considerable size variation among these farms, ranging from 1 (2.5 acres) to over 50 hectares (124 acres). For purposes of this analysis, the most meaningful measure of size is the number of hectares productively utilized. A concept of land equivalents is used to separate the 91 farms studied into three groups. One land equivalent is equal to 1 hectare (2.5 acres) of cultivated land or 3 hectares (7.4 acres) of natural pasture. Farms with less than 10 land equivalents were placed in the first group, those with from 10.0 to 19.9 land equivalents in the second group, and those with more than 20 in the last group.

If the three farm-size groups are examined, there is little evidence of economies or diseconomies of size (Table 4.4). That is, larger farms did not have greater productivity per cultivated acre than smaller farms.

TABLE 4.4. Farm size comparisons, Lajeado, Rio Grande do Sul, Brazil, 1969

Characteristics	Farm-Size Groups (land equivalents)[a]					
	under 10		10 to 19.9		20 and over	
Number of Observations	13		43		35	
	(ha)	(acres)	(ha)	(acres)	(ha)	(acres)
Land Operated	7.2	17.8	15.1	37.3	33.3	82.2
Land Cultivated	3.4	8.4	6.4	15.8	12.1	29.6
Income						
Gross output	$358	(105)[b]	$754	(118)	$1,276	(106)
Cash income	158	(46)	445	(70)	722	(60)
Farm income	256	(75)	547	(85)	1,011	(84)
Family consumption of farm products:	$158		$232		$289	
as % of gross output	44		31		23	
Person-equivalents of Family Labor	2.0		2.4		3.4	
Percent of Farms Using:						
Fertilizer	23		42		60	
Insecticides	77		65		49	
Improved seed	46		81		74	
Credit	46		44		46	

[a] One land equivalent is equal to 1 ha of cultivated land or 3 ha of natural pasture.
[b] Expressed in 1969 dollar equivalents. ( ) indicates values on a per cultivated ha basis.

Gross output and farm income measures on a per cultivated hectare basis are relatively constant for each size group. The smaller farms were, however, more subsistence oriented in that they consumed a larger proportion (44%) of their farm production than did the larger farms (23%).

Significant differences also were apparent in the use of modern technology. Improved seed and fertilizer use was much less prevalent on the small farms. While differences in cropping patterns could be partly responsible for this, it is apparent that technology had been adopted more rapidly on larger farms within the small-farm region. Relatively constant levels of productivity between farm-size groups would indicate either that modern technology was compensating for poorer land or that increased intensity of technology use had not yet had sufficient effect to cause substantial increases in yield.

Institutional Setting and the Selective Use of Improved Technology. Technological change among small farmers has been very selective. For example, fertilizer use did not increase in Districts I and II during the period of study. However, it more than doubled in District III (Table 4.5). A close analysis of the data demonstrated that fertilizer was used primarily on two crops—tobacco and wheat. In 1969 both crops showed substantial increases in crop acreages in District III. Hence dramatic increase in fertilizer use occurred there. The most significant point, however, is that each of these crops had special institutional arrangements that encourage use of modern inputs. For tobacco, the purchasing companies provided the necessary inputs, including fertilizer. In the case of wheat, the government provided special low-interest credit for production expenses associated with wheat growing and guaranteed a high support price for wheat.

Fertilizer is a major component of the crop technology package with new high-yielding seeds, and conditions must be favorable for its use if small farmers are to maximize returns from this technology. Farm-

TABLE 4.5. Change in the use of selected technologies, Lajeado, Rio Grande do Sul, Brazil, 1965–69

Technology	District I	II	III
	(% of Farms Using)		
1965			
Fertilizer	25	27	30
Improved seed	21	23	24
Insecticides	46	47	30
1969			
Fertilizer	32	23	64
Improved seed	75	70	76
Insecticides	71	53	58

ers, however, were willing (or able) to purchase fertilizer only when additional financial resources were made available to them either through company financing (tobacco) or special credit and price programs (wheat). This experience gives additional support to the key roles of institutional factors such as availability of credit and stable prices at adequate levels as important prerequisites for significant increases in the use of output-increasing technology on small farms.

Other components of crop technology also illustrate selective adoption and point to the importance of institutional factors. The elements of technology selected were low cost. In District III these included the use of insecticides, which increased about 50%, and the use of improved seed, which increased threefold. Similar increases in improved seed use were experienced in Districts I and II. For livestock enterprises, inexpensive technologies were also accepted, but little use of high-cost technology such as a balanced ration was apparent.

This selective process of accepting only those components of crop technology having a low cash outlay has serious implications for farm productivity. In many situations the high returns from technological change come only with the use of a package of new inputs requiring appreciable cash outlay. For example, Sorensen [17] showed that hog farmers in these small-farm regions of Brazil obtained only low returns to the adoption of individual practices. However, use of the appropriate package of new inputs resulted in substantial differences in income.

Farmer Perception of Factors Influencing Selective Technological Change. An alternative way of examining the interaction of factors in the adoption of new technology is to consider farmers' perceptions of important technological changes they have incorporated.

The farmers of Lajeado were asked in 1969 what important changes in practices or techniques had been made on their farm operations during the past five years. A total of 70 changes were reported on 47 of the 91 farms. The remaining farmers felt that no significant changes had been made during the five-year period. Of the changes noted, improved seed accounted for the most changes (20%); others were vaccination of livestock (14%), use of fertilizer (12%), and improved breed (10%). The total number of changes was equally divided between livestock and crop practices. Low-cost forms of technology were mentioned most often. The farmer's perception of changes made closely followed the empirical results of the detailed farm survey comparing 1965 and 1969.

Of particular interest were farmers' reasons for not using more high-cost technology such as fertilizer. Three general areas of concern emerged from this unstructured question. The most important response was about the economics of fertilizer use. Sixty percent of the farmers felt it was not profitable to use (more) fertilizer. Reasons given included the high cost of fertilizer, low potential increase in yields, and noneconomic return. One-fifth of the farmers reported capital constraints to the increased use of fertilizer and 10% listed lack of knowledge about fertilizer use as the most important deterrent.

CONCLUSIONS. The following generalizations may be made about the three clusters of factors affecting the growth of farm income in the state of Rio Grande do Sul, Brazil.

1. *Farm Size and Enterprise Combinations.* The different regions of the state presented a great contrast in size of farm and farm enterprise combinations. In the mid-1960s the two areas of small farms contained two-thirds of the farm population and had an average of 24 hectares (59.3 acres) per farm, of which 9 hectares (22.2 acres) were cultivated. Mixed farming predominated, with maize, beans, and hogs being the most important enterprises. Other regions of the state were divided into large cattle, sheep, and wheat farms containing an average of 133 hectares (328 acres), of which 83 hectares (205 acres) were cultivated. This contrasting structure of farming was the result of a number of major long-term influences, including resource conditions and settlement patterns, conditions bound to lead to different responses to new technology. The study showed that the small farmers of Rio Grande do Sul were not keeping pace with the general rates of increase in farm production experienced by larger farms in adjacent areas. Small size, significant quantities of subsistence production, enterprise diversification, and low levels of technology use were causes of slow growth.

2. *Technology.* Much of the new agricultural technology that became available in southern Brazil was in a form appropriate for mechanization on large farms. As a result, the adoption of new agricultural technology occurred more rapidly on the large cattle, sheep, and wheat farms. Access to credit markets and assured product prices, especially for wheat, further encouraged its use on these farms. A certain amount of the new technology, particularly in biological and chemical forms such as new seeds, fertilizer, and pesticides, was more easily divisible. Some of this technology became available to small farms and proved profitable. While many small farmers made modest advances in the use of low-cost technology, other forms of more expensive technology such as investments in fertilizer and improved rations were limited to a few farms, and even then to selected enterprises. In general, the small farmer perceived little economic incentive to employ these more expensive practices. The failure to use these expensive forms of technology not only deprived farm operators of their direct effect on output but also diminished their complementary effect on other forms of technology such as improved seed. Thus on many small farms the complementary gains of the "production package effects" were not realized, and significant productivity growth was foregone.

3. *Institutions.* National and local institutions and policies were

focused largely on encouraging the production of wheat and cattle through the allocation of research resources to these enterprises and the provision of credit and price supports for wheat. Hence the large cattle and wheat farms benefited considerably. Some small farmers were able to respond to the credit and price policies relating to wheat. In tobacco where vertically integrated companies supplied inputs and assured prices, small farmers increased output rapidly. In contrast, output did not increase very much in the two major crops of the small farmer, maize and soybeans, due to the increased risk associated with a lack of credit and no price supports. Hence it would appear that additional credit and assured prices for a wider range of agricultural products could greatly accelerate the growth of small farms as risk aversion is a major influence on small farmer decision making. Evidence was also found of a lack of an effective extension effort in profitable new technology and management knowledge in hog production for small farms.

A more general conclusion points to the challenge of redirecting the focus of government support for technological development so that small farmers may more equally participate in the technological revolution in agriculture. In the past, national policy emphasis on mechanical technology and associated crop inputs and outputs has provided proportionately large gains to the larger farms. A redirection of technology policy would include greatly increased support for the development of appropriate forms of profitable small-farm technology and greater attention to assure that the necessary information channels are open to small farmers so they may judge the profitability of the new technologies. A particular example of insufficient communication flows to small farmers appears to be present in livestock practices. If small farmers are to share in the increasing levels of productivity and income made possible through new agricultural technology, they must receive sufficient information so that on-farm trials of new technology may have reasonable chances for success.

REFERENCES

1. Fachel, Jose Fraga. *Adocao de Praticas Agricolas Numa Area Sul-Riograndense.* Universidade do Rio Grande do Sul, Teses de Conclusao dos Cursos de Especializacao em Economia e Sociologia Rural, No. 2, 1966.
2. Fliegel, F. C., and Oliveira, F. C. *Receptividade a Ideias Novas e Exodo Rural Numa Area Colonial.* Estudos e Trabalhos No. 14, Bulletin, Instituto de Estudos e Pesquisas Economicas, Universidade do Rio Grande do Sul, Porto Alegre, Brasil, 1963.
3. Gastal, Edmundo Araujo, and Duarte, Jayme A. C. *Estudo de Administracao Rural em Pelotas, Rio Grande do Sul.* Brasil. Instituto Inter-Americano de Ciencias Agricolas, Zona Sur de la O.E.A., Montevideo, Uruguay, Apr. 1961.
4. Gastal, Edmundo Araujo, and Mario, Olinto C. *Estudo de Administracao Rural em Ibiruba, Rio Grande do Sul.* Programma Cooperativo de Extensao Rural–ASCAR, Porto Alegre, Brasil, May 1965.
5. Gotsch, Carl H. "Technical Change and the Distribution of Income in Rural Areas." *American Journal of Agricultural Economics* 54 (2, May 1972).

6. Knight, Peter T. *Brazilian Agricultural Technology and Trade: A Study of Five Commodities.* New York: Praeger Publishers, 1971.
7. Mosher, Arthur T. *Getting Agriculture Moving.* New York: Frederick A. Praeger, 1966.
8. Poli, Joao Batista E. H. *Descricao e Analises das Rendas em Ralacao ao Uso de Emprestimos em Pequenas Propriedadas Rurais; Lajeado.* Universidade do Rio Grande do Sul, Teses de Conclusao dos Cursos de Especializacao em Economia e Sociologia Rural, No. 6, Porto Alegre, Brasil, 1967.
9. Rask, Norman. "Farm Size and Income: An Economic Study of Small-Farm Agriculture in Southern Brazil." Unpublished Ph.D. dissertation, Univ. of Wisconsin, Madison, 1964.
10. ———. "An Analysis of Capital Formation and Utilization in Less Developed Countries." Terminal report for research project, ESO Paper No. 4, Department of Agricultural Economics and Rural Sociology, Ohio State Univ., 1969.
11. ———. "The Impact of Selective Credit and Price Policies on Use of New Inputs." *Development Digest* 9 (2, Apr. 1971).
12. Rask, Norman, and Meyer, Richard L. "Credito Agricola e Subsidios a Producao como Instrumentos para o Desenvolvimento da Agricultura Brasileiro." *Revisto Brasileira de Economia,* No. 1/73 (Jan.–March 1973) Rio de Janeiro, Brazil, 1973.
13. Reichert, Alan K., and Rask, Norman. "Distributional Problems of an Expanding Agricultural Credit Supply: The Case of Southern Brazil." *Occasional Paper No. 83,* Department of Agricultural Economics and Rural Sociology, Ohio State Univ., June 1972.
14. Richter, Humberto V. *Producao de Leite em Santa Cruz do Sul.* Universidade do Rio Grande do Sul, Teses de Conclusao dos Cursos de Especializacao em Economia e Sociologia Rural, No. 4, 1967.
15. Sa', Jose Itamario. "Utilizacao da Mao de Obra e Niveis de Renda em Pequenas Propriendades Rurais." Universidade do Rio Grande do Sul, Teses de Pos-Graduacao, Porto Alegre, Brasil, 1965.
16. Simeonidis, Haralambos. "Net Farm Income and Potential for Capital Accumulation on Livestock Farms: Rio Grande do Sul, Brazil." Unpublished M.S. thesis, Ohio State Univ., 1967.
17. Sorenson, Donald M. "Capital Productivity and Management Performance in Small-Farm Agriculture in Southern Brazil." Ph.D. dissertation, Department of Agricultural Economics and Rural Sociology, Ohio State Univ., 1968.
18. Souza, Eli de Moraes, and Buse, Rueben. *Relacao do Tamanho da Propriendade Rural com sua Organizacao, Produtividade e Rende na Area da Antiga Santa Rosa—Rio Grande do Sul, Brasil.* Universidade do Rio Grande do Sul, Estudos e Trabalhos Mimeografados, No. 6, Porto Alegre, Brasil, 1969.
19. Sturm, Alzemiro El. *O Efeito do Isolamento na Difusao das Praticas Agricolas em Santa Cruz do Sul, Brasil,* Universidade do Rio Grande do Sul, Estudos e Trabalhos Mimeografados, No. 7, Porto Alegre, Brasil, 1969.

CHAPTER 5

Constraints on Cattle and Buffalo Production in a Northeastern Thai Village

A. JOHN DE BOER &
DELANE E. WELSCH

INTRODUCTION AND BACKGROUND. In the face of growing food grain supplies in some less developed countries, increasing interest is being shown in the improvement of nutritional levels in these areas through the production of larger quantities of animal protein. This study concentrates on one aspect of this problem: the role of village-based bovine (cattle and buffalo) production systems in meeting this challenge.

The general objectives of this study of bovine production in a Thai village were to determine the extent to which changes were occurring in cattle and buffalo production and to assess the constraints on increased production. The specific questions were: Why has expansion of bovine numbers lagged behind virtually every indicator of Thai economic growth? What characteristics inherent in village animal production systems act as restraints on improved performance? And particularly, are there important crop-livestock interrelationships that must be taken into account? Of what magnitude are the economic returns provided by bovines? What economic inefficiencies, if any, in the allocation of village resources suggest opportunities for increased production? What does the future hold for these village-based bovine production systems?

A. JOHN DE BOER is Lecturer in Agricultural Economics, Department of Agriculture, University of Queensland, St. Lucia, Brisbane, Australia. He received his Ph.D. from the University of Minnesota in 1972. His research in livestock production in Asia began in 1969.
DELANE E. WELSCH is Professor, Department of Agricultural and Applied Economics, University of Minnesota. He was Agricultural Economist, Rockefeller Foundation, Bangkok, Thailand, 1967–1976.

Prior to analyzing these questions, material is first presented providing background knowledge of changes in the Thai economy. Examination of technical and economic characteristics of the crop-livestock production system in Non Som Boon village follows. The final sections analyze resource use in crop production and the returns to bovine production.

Changes in the Thai Economy. The kingdom of Thailand consists of an area of about 550,000 square kilometers, is approximately the size of France or Texas, lies in the center of the Indochinese peninsula, and is both similar to and strikingly different from most other developing countries. The population in 1970 was estimated at 37 million, growing at 3.2% per year. It was predominantly rural (80%), with most of the agricultural production undertaken by small-scale family farms. Production technology was largely traditional, with men and animals the chief sources of power. Very few inputs are purchased, and low yields in crop and livestock enterprises prevail. In common with most other Asian countries, rice dominates production and consumption activities. Thailand differs, however, in always having been a food-surplus country. It has been a major rice exporter since the mid-1800s. The person-land ratio has always been low, so that even small peasant farms are fairly large by Asian standards (4 or 5 hectares [10 or 12 acres]). Economic growth has been rapid and steady, exceeding 8% per year during the 1960s. Growth in agricultural output during this period has averaged over 5% per year. Major sources of agricultural growth have been rapid clearing and settling of new land and the adoption of new crops, mostly for export. Agricultural exports have soared, leading to the observation that Thailand is one of a number of developing areas in which agricultural exports have been the "engine of growth."

Rapid growth, however, has brought problems. Urban incomes have been growing much more rapidly than rural incomes. Within rural areas the differences in the rates of growth between regions have been sharp. Northeastern Thailand has been the most laggard in income growth. Rural welfare is similar to levels existing earlier. Increasing urbanization, although less rapid and accompanied by much less rural-urban migration and unemployment than in other countries, has resulted in changing consumption patterns and shifting demands for agricultural production.

Total private consumption expenditure over the past decade has been growing at 7.2% per year and private consumption expenditure on food at 5.4% per year. Although empirical estimates of income elasticities of demand for specific commodities in Thailand are not available, there is little reason to believe that they are very different from other developing countries in Southeast Asia. Thus the income elasticity of demand for meat is probably about 1.0. In fact, the growth in demand

TABLE 5.1. Relative importance of meat sources, meat prices, and animal inventory in Thailand

Meat Source	% Total Weekly Family Expenditures[a]	Average Annual Wholesale Price (baht/kg)[b] 1957	1960	1966	Total Animals on Farms: Thailand (000,000)[c] 1957	1960	1966
	(%)				(no.)	(no.)	(no.)
Pig	21.5	14.44	11.55	13.50	3.7	4.2	4.0
Chicken	5.2	16.58	13.02	15.55	23.9	24.0	35.3
Beef	4.8	12.50	12.36	17.28	10.9[d]	11.9[d]	12.0[d]

[a] *1969 Household Food Expenditure Survey, Bangkok-Thonburi.* National Statistical Office, Office of the Prime Minister.
[b] For 1966 these prices in U.S. dollars per pound at the official exchange rate were pork $0.30, chicken $0.34, and beef $0.51. Department of Commercial Intelligence, Ministry of Economic Affairs, *Retail Prices and Consumer Price Index for Bangkok and Thonburi Markets.*
[c] *Agricultural Statistics of Thailand, 1967 Edition,* Division of Agricultural Economics, Office of the Under-Secretary of State, Ministry of Agriculture, Bangkok.
[d] Sum of cattle and buffalo.

for meat may be higher in Thailand because there are no religious or cultural taboos against meat consumption.

The aggregate livestock sector had grown at only 3% per year during the 1960s. From 1957 to 1966 cattle and buffalo numbers increased by only 0.34 and 1.48% per year (Table 5.1). Why the respective annual Bangkok wholesale meat prices increased by only 1.34 and 1.61% can only be speculated upon. The use of new technology in pig and chicken production, which has been rapidly and widely adopted, may have taken the pressure off cattle and buffalo meat prices. Relative price relationships between the major groups of meat have shown some changes, particularly with a rise in beef prices after 1962. As beef (cattle and buffalo) represented only 4.8% of food expenditures in 1969, other meats may have been substituted for it.

The persistently slow growth in the bovine portion of the livestock economy led to this detailed field study of cattle and buffalo production in three villages, in widely different physiographic regions, during 1970–71 (Fig. 5.1). The northeastern village, Non Som Boon, was selected for analysis in this chapter.

Characteristics and Utilization of Cattle and Buffalo in Thailand. The two types of domesticated buffalo are the swamp buffalo and the river buffalo. Swamp buffalo are distributed throughout southern China, southern Asia, the Philippines, Indonesia, and parts of the Indian subcontinent. River buffalo are found mainly in India, Pakistan, Egypt, the Middle East, and southern Europe [8]. The present family of swamp and river buffalo *(Bos bubalis)* is descended from the wild buffalo *(Bos arni),* a native of Southeast Asia. At the present time only swamp buffalo

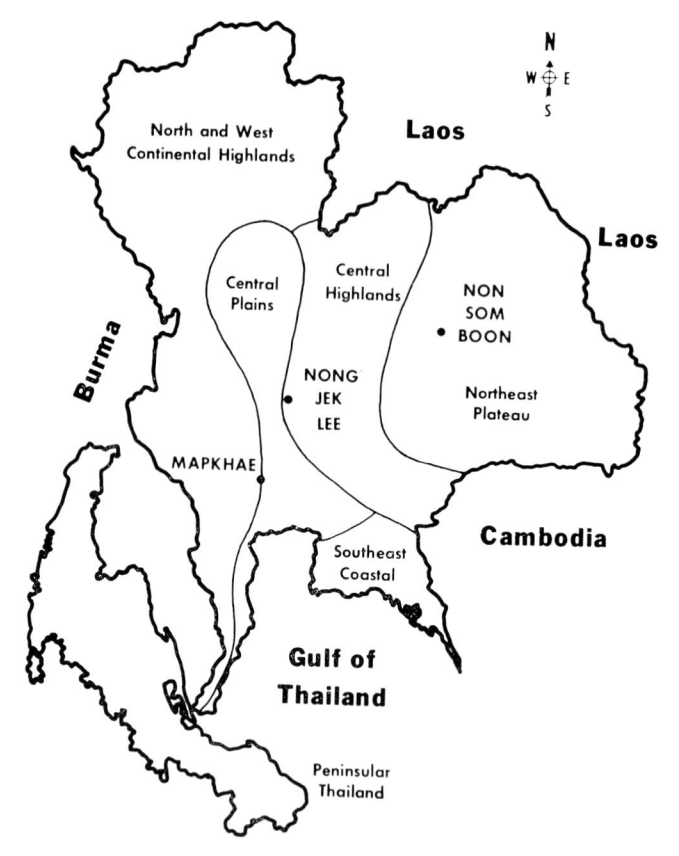

Fig. 5.1. Physiographic regions of Thailand with the locations of the three study villages.

are found in Thailand. Their average weight is 500 kilograms (1,100 pounds) for the males and 400 kilograms (880 pounds) for females, and dressing percentages range from 35 to 48% [2, 17]. Sexual maturity is reached at about three years of age under village conditions. Although several breeds of river buffalo are commercial milk producers, the swamp buffalo cows found in Thailand are barely able to sustain their calves [2, 15]. This has not been important in Thailand, because cow's milk is not consumed in the villages and only very limited quantities are used in urban areas. Although buffalo have slow reproduction rates, slow maturity, a long gestation period (325 to 330 days), short periods in heat, and difficulty in heat detection, all contributing to low turnover rates, buffalo do have the advantage of being able to utilize lower quality roughages [7]. This ability has been important in traditional production situations, where only weeds and grass are available in the rainy season and only rice straw in the dry season.

The origin of native cattle in Thailand is unclear. Great heterogeneity is found in characteristics such as size of hump, length and erectness of ear, color, dewlap, navel, and animal size. Mason classifies them as zebu in breed and originating in northern Malaysia [8]. Rouse describes them as nondescript, humped animals [11]. The influence of American Brahman bloodlines is now pronounced in certain areas. The composition of Thai cattle is perhaps best described as a mixture of zebu *(Bos indicus)* and shorthorn *(Bos brachyeeros)* types [17]. Weights of native cattle seldom exceed 350 kilograms (760 pounds), but dressing percentage is higher than for buffalo, averaging about 55% [1].

The location of cattle and buffalo in Thailand varies greatly. Areas that produce only rice, in flooded or inundated conditions in the rainy season, tend to have concentrations of buffalo, such as the Chao Phya delta and river valleys. Areas producing mostly upland crops tend to have more cattle. Areas producing both rice and upland crops generally have a mixture of cattle and buffalo, although specific villages can be found that prefer cattle while in nearby villages buffalo predominate. Both buffalo and cattle also play different roles in various areas and villages within these areas. In some places, the major role of bovines is to provide power, while in other areas breeding for sale is the major role. Still other village herds fill roles of both, providing power to cultivate the village fields and reproduction of enough animals so that there is a surplus for sale outside the villages. Although in a few cases, the young surplus animals go directly to slaughter, the usual case is for young animals to go into power herds, with only old or cull animals being slaughtered for meat.

The traditional, pre-World War II, crop-bovine farming system in Thailand was not necessarily a static system, but changes in it were slow and could be described as follows:

1. Population growth expanded steadily but slowly, with limited rural to urban migration.

2. Farm size remained static since the increasing population was able to clear and settle new areas, expanding the area in rice roughly in proportion to the increase in the population.

3. Draft animal requirements increased at the same rate as the rice area cultivated.

4. The growing bovine population needed to provide the increasing number of draft animals required also resulted in proportional increase in cull animals, which were slaughtered for meat, thus increasing meat supplies at the same rate as population.

But this static or rolling-equilibrium situation underwent a change during the 1950s and 1960s. Greatly improved human health conditions resulted in a rapid spurt in population growth. Pressures for increased economic growth led to urbanization increasing at a faster rate than population. The higher urban incomes also changed the pattern of demand for meat. In rural areas, at the same time, expansion of rice areas slowed. Upland crop areas, however, expanded rapidly, with quite different power requirements. In some areas, large four-wheel tractors were introduced to plow both the dry upland soils and the heavy delta soils during the dry season. Within this context of change, we examine in detail crop and livestock production in Non Som Boon village.

CROP AND BOVINE PRODUCTION IN NON SOM BOON VILLAGE

Brief Description of the Village. Non Som Boon is a typical northeastern Thai village in most aspects. It lies in the Northeast Plateau physiographic region of Thailand. Topography in this region is gently undulating in the upland areas and flat in the river bottoms. The region is separated from the rest of Thailand by the Central Highlands, and the rivers drain eastward into the Mekong River system. For centuries the steep hills and dense, malaria-infested jungles of the Central Highlands presented a severe barrier to movement of people and products from the Northeast to the rest of the kingdom, so the inhabitants of the Northeast lived in isolation during much of the year. Year-round communication was possible only after construction of the railway from Bangkok to Korat in 1904. But the people still essentially lived in a subsistence economy until the early 1950s, when the first all-weather road, called the Friendship Highway, was opened. Since that time, several provincial capitals have emerged as commercial centers, and farmers have gradually entered the market economy. Kenaf, a fiber crop grown in upland rain-fed conditions and used as a substitute for jute in gunny bags and carpet backing, was introduced after World War II. It has provided an attractive source of cash income. The heavy buildup of military bases in conjunction with the war in Vietnam also provided a source of off-farm income for farmers and their families and substantially raised their expectations with respect to income and consumer goods.

Although the low-humic gley and gray podzolic soils dominating this area are generally poor, this village is fortunate in having 30% alluvial soils. The upland areas are sandy and well leached but appear to be somewhat above average in fertility as measured by crop yields. Natural vegetation consisted of Dipterocarp forest, but most uncultivated land is now in savannah and shrub regrowth. The normal monsoonal rainfall pattern includes onset in April or May and a slight decrease in rains in late June or early August but increasing again so that September is the highest rainfall month. By the end of October the rains have practically ceased. Eighty-seven percent of the rain falls in the May-to-October period. Annual rainfall varies a great deal from the mean of 1,240 mm (49 inches), as does the onset of the rains.

Location of the village with respect to the provincial capital and transportation routes is shown in Figure 5.2. Village land extends west

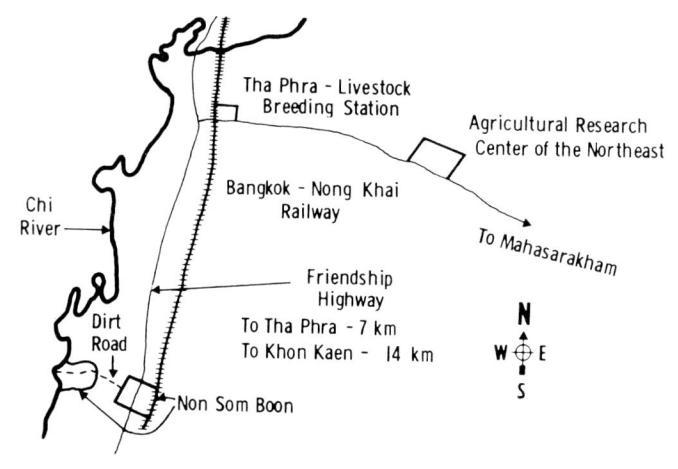

5 / Livestock Production in a Thai Village / *A. J. DeBoer, D. E. Welsch* 121

Fig. 5.2. Location of Non Som Boon Village, Thailand.

to the Chi River lowlands and across the major north-south highway to the railroad tracks. Land use of the village is shown in Figure 5.3. The houses are arranged in the nuclear pattern typical of the Northeast.

The village is near two major commercial centers. Khon Kaen, the provincial capital, is 14 kilometers north and Baan Phai, a major commodity assembly and shipment center, is 30 kilometers south. A Department of Agriculture Livestock Development Station is seven kilometers away and the Northeast Agricultural Center is also near. The proximity of the village to the highway and the improved livestock center have been key influences on the availability of new technologies that

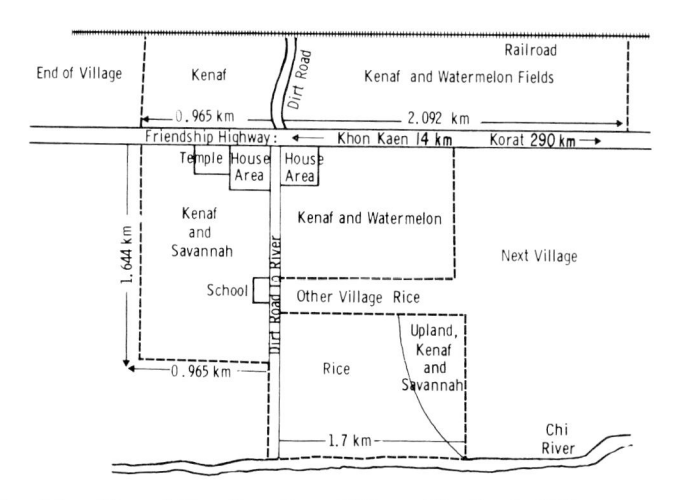

Fig. 5.3. Map of Non Som Boon Village, Thailand, 1971.

have altered the traditional livestock system. Thus Non Som Boon was a good location for a study of these changes.

Although income data for village households were not collected, it became evident that a moderate amount of income was earned outside the village in nonagricultural activities and that the value of subsistence and handicraft activities carried out within the village contributed substantially to villagers' welfare. The central location provided easy transportation to commercial centers. The two government-sponsored agricultural establishments also provided permanent and casual employment for a limited number of villagers. Mat weaving from immature kenaf fiber was widespread, with the mats moving to markets at the local town. Tobacco, kapok, bananas, papaya, chickens, and pigs also complemented the major agricultural activities and, at times, provided small amounts of cash income.

Interrelationships in the Village Resource Allocation System. The patterns of village resource flows are now discussed as an introduction to the village farming system. The relationships between people, land, and bovines are indicated in Figure 5.4. Although for purposes of analysis, the crop and livestock components are discussed separately, Figure 5.4 indicates the numerous interactions in both producing and using bovines in Non Som Boon.

In examining this diagram, the reader should keep in mind the process of agricultural modernization. It is useful to view this process as a spectrum, with purely subsistence farmers on one end and highly productive, commercialized farmers on the other end. With respect to inputs and products, the subsistence farmer, by definition, buys few agricultural inputs and consumes most of his output. He is almost totally self-sufficient. At the other extreme, the highly commercialized farmer buys nearly 100% of his inputs and sells nearly 100% of his production. The farmers in Non Som Boon, only a generation ago, were pretty much at the subsistence end of the spectrum. Today, with respect to kenaf and watermelon, they have moved a considerable distance toward the commercial end of the scale in disposal of the output but not as far in regard to inputs. Rice, the main activity, still is operated as a subsistence activity.

For purposes of this study, the village production system may be described as consisting of three resource categories: land (X_1), labor (X_2), and capital (X_3). These are combined to produce five major products: food and fiber crops (Y_1), fodder production (excluding grain) (Y_2), meat (Y_3), draft power (Y_4), and grazing (Y_5). These five products can be further divided into three categories. Food and fiber crops and meat are the final products consumed within the village or sold outside. Fodder production (used in bovine production) and draft

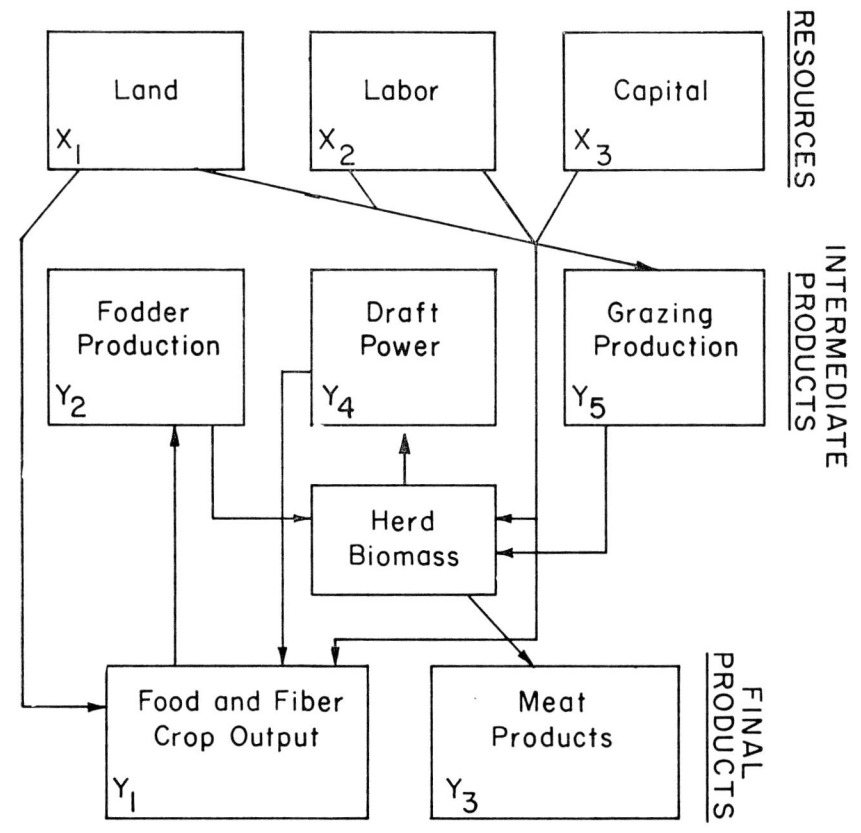

Fig. 5.4. Interrelationships in the allocation of resources and the production of intermediate and final products in Non Som Boon Village, Thailand, 1971.

power (used in crop production) are intermediate products, i.e., intermediate in the sense that they are not consumed directly but instead become an input into a subsequent production activity. Food and fiber and fodder are joint products; their production occurs in relatively rigid proportions. Meat and draft power are also joint products, as one cannot be produced without the other, but the farmer has more choice in choosing the proportion of each produced.

Changes in Crop and Livestock Technology. Changes in crop and livestock technology have come from three major sources. The proximity of the village to Friendship Highway has had a number of interrelated effects. Transportation and communication became very much less costly, while labor and land costs increased. Second, the Livestock Breeding Center has been a major factor in the introduction of new livestock technology into the village. Third, since the late 1950s Non Som Boon has participated in the rapid expansion of upland crops in the Northeast, particularly kenaf, but also with scattered areas of watermelon. The result of these developments has been increased cash incomes and, of particular interest to our study, a sustained demand for draft animal power.

The major specific change in crop production technology consisted of a complete substitution of mechanical energy (in the form of trucks) for animal energy (in the form of ox-drawn carts) for the major hauling activities. Several factors provided impetus for this transition:

1. Trucks become technically feasible as the all-weather highway and feeder road in the village guaranteed that trucks could be used year round.

2. A major time restraint was alleviated by custom hiring of local trucks. This restraint occurred when farmers became faced with the prospect of hauling one crop while harvesting another.

3. Considerable distances were often involved in transporting kenaf to the river for retting and the subsequent hauling of the dried fiber to the Tha Phra market (see Figs. 5.2 and 5.3). (Retting is the process of separating kenaf fibers from the stalk by soaking. The mature plant is submerged in water ten to fourteen days until the outer, fibrous layer slips off the stalk. The fiber is then washed, dried, and bundled.)

4. The opportunity cost of using oxen for cart pulling increased as the introduction of new technology in cattle breeding increased returns in the latter enterprise.

Thus the traditional Thai cattle cart has disappeared from Non Som Boon as have the oxen that pulled it. Some of the resources formerly required to maintain oxen now go into the production of breeding stock.

Improvements in bovine production technology have concentrated on improved breeding stock through the introduction of Brahman bloodlines in 1957 [1]. The only other break with traditional production methods was a yearly visit by the government veterinarian for vaccinations. This service was widespread, however, and does not set this village apart from others. The source of economic gain has been the production and sale of crossbred cattle that, for a variety of reasons, command premium prices. Thus the objectives of holding cattle have become oriented toward the production of offspring for breeding and sale.

No parallel changes have occurred for buffalo, however. For a variety of reasons, tractor substitution for buffalo draft power has been very limited in northeastern Thailand and has not taken place in Non Som Boon. In fact, increased draft power requirements of upland crops have bolstered the position of buffalo as providers of village draft power.

TABLE 5.2. Crop combinations of 26 sample farms, Non Som Boon, Thailand, 1970-71

Crop Combinations	Kenaf only	Rice, Kenaf	Rice, Kenaf, Watermelon
Number of Farmers	1	15	10

Crop Production Practices. Cropping patterns in the village are fairly simple (Table 5.2). Every farmer in the village grew kenaf as a cash crop. Forty-two of the 52 village farmers grew glutinous rice, all of which was home consumed. Of the sample of 26 farmers used for detailed analysis, 10 grew watermelons as a cash crop. Cropping patterns are generally the crop-fallow system for upland crops; however, watermelon is occasionally double cropped. Kenaf cannot be double cropped because of its extended growing period. Lowland rice was never double cropped.

Rice fields on the lower terraces usually have adequate water for transplanting and are planted every year. The fields on the upper terraces near the houses are transplanted only if rainfall is adequate, otherwise they are left fallow. Often rainfall is sufficient to plant only part of these fields, with the remainder of each field left fallow.

Because of low rice yields and low rice prices during the study year, rice, which was planted on 45% of the area farmed by the sample farmers, produced only 18% of the total value of crop production (Table 5.3). In comparison, kenaf, with 47% of the area planted, accounted for 70% of the value of production. Distribution of village planted area among the three crops has been relatively stable over the past five years, with watermelon expanding rapidly during the past two years (Table 5.4). Average total cultivated area per sample farmer was 28 rai (4.48 hectares [11.0 acres]).

Rice production activities at the time of the study began in June with the plowing and sowing of nursery beds. Initial plowing of the main fields commenced in July and August when the soil was sufficiently wet. Buffalo were used for all field work in this village. Both males and females were used and work rotation of animals was common, one working in the morning and another in the afternoon.

TABLE 5.3. Planted area, percent of planted area and gross value, by crop, of 26 sample farms, Non Som Boon, Thailand, 1970-71

	Rice	Kenaf	Watermelon	Total
Area (in rai)	322	336	62	720
% of Total Area	44.72	46.67	8.61	100
% of Gross Value	18.21	69.97	12.12	100

Note: 6.25 rai = 1 hectare; 2.5 rai = 1 acre.

TABLE 5.4. Planted area of major crops, 1966-70: All village farms in Non Som Boon, Thailand (rai)

Year	Rice	Kenaf	Watermelon[a]	Total Cropped Area
1966	573	531	0	1,104
1967	573	550	0	1,123
1968	571	577	5	1,153
1969	574	557	37	1,168
1970	563	591	66	1,220
% of 1970	46.15	48.44	5.41	100

Note: 6.25 rai =1 hectare; 2.5 rai = 1 acre.
[a] Watermelon totals are sum of early and late crops.

The second plowing, followed by harrowing, started as soon as the soil was soft enough to puddle. Transplanting started in late July or August, depending on the depth of standing water, and was completed in September. All fields with enough water were transplanted, while fields without standing water were left fallow and were grazed if access was available. Weeding and water control work after transplanting were not common, and fertilizing and spraying were not carried out.

Harvesting occurred from October to late November when the rice was mature, depending on the planting date and variety. But on no field was harvesting complete before December. As each field was harvested, the rice was gathered and bound into bundles. The bundles were then carried by hand to a central threshing floor in the field serving a group of farmers. There the bundles were stacked until all fields were harvested.

Threshing was done by hand. Northeastern Thai customs prohibit rice threshing by animals or women. To thresh the grain the bundles were held firmly between two sticks bound by thongs at one end and slapped on the pile of threshed paddy. Threshed paddy was transported by truck to the household storage sheds. Depending on the size of the crop, one or two trips were made from the threshing floor to the sheds. The paddy was unloaded by using five-gallon cans. The remaining space in the truck bed was loaded with rice straw to be stacked at the houses. The use of trucks accelerated the harvesting sequence and permitted cheap hauling of the bulky rice straw. Kenaf cutting commenced as soon as the rice and straw were stored.

Kenaf production procedures were similar for all sampled farmers. Field preparation preceded that of rice. The same tillage implements were used. The initial plowing was followed by broadcast seeding and then a light harrowing to cover the seeds. Plowing began in April or early May and was finished before June. Broadcasting and harrowing followed immediately. When the plants reached 4 to 6 inches in height, hand cultivation and thinning began and continued through July. This was the last input until cutting began following the completion of rice harvest in November and December.

Cutting began when the plants turned red, seed pods had fully formed, and the leaves had fallen. The stalks were cut individually, bound into bundles of twenty to thirty, and stood in piles in the field. The kenaf was then loaded onto trucks by the farmer and exchange labor for transfer to the river bluffs. Retting was done exclusively at the Chi River, giving these villagers a quality advantage in that fresh water was continuously available, since the stagnant water available in most northeastern villages reduces fiber quality.

Retting proceeded in batches, with the size of the batch depending on the family and hired labor available, but most batches were about one truckload. Retting consisted of carrying bundles to the river, lashing the bundles together to make a raft, and immersing the raft by piling dirt on top of it. After ten to fourteen days, the raft was brought to the surface and hauled to shore for fiber separation. The fiber from a bundle of stalks was gathered in one hand and simultaneously pulled upward and off the core. The fiber was then folded and put in the river to soak until the batch was finished. After soaking, the small fiber bundles were washed in the river and hung to dry on bamboo drying racks for two days. Finally, the fiber was folded and tied into 200-kilogram bundles to await sale.

Watermelons were grown in two seasons. The early season was from April to June and the late season from September to December. Three farmers grew two crops in 1970. The other seven grew only the late-season crop. Melons required purchased inputs consisting of seeds, spray, fertilizer, and hired labor. Tractors were not used for plowing in Non Som Boon as the fields were small but were used in neighboring villages for the plowing of larger melon fields. Plowing for the early melon crop began in April. The soil was still dry, but melons were grown on sandy soils so buffalo plowing was possible. The planting and fertilizing were done in May. Initial fertilizing often included applications of buffalo manure, which was the only instance in which animal manure was used in the village. After the plants were large enough, hand hoeing and spraying began. The first crop was ready by June. Melons were harvested by the farmer for sale at his home or sold unharvested in the field.

The second crop of watermelons was planted in October. Plowing was done during slack periods throughout the summer for the double-crop farmers. Farmers who produced only one crop of watermelons began planting in September and October and did not fertilize. Planting was followed by cultivation and spraying in October and November. Harvest began early in December. Most late-crop melons were sold unharvested in the field.

Bovine Production Practices. Forty-nine of the 52 farmers in Non Som Boon owned buffalo; the 3 who did not rented or borrowed buffalo to use for draft power in crop production. Most farmers owned 1, 2, or

3 buffalo, with a few owning 4 or 5, and 2 farmers owned 6 head each. In contrast, only 10 farmers owned cattle, and although the average number owned was 4.7, the number owned by individual farmers ranged from 2 to 10 head. Apparent reasons for the limited cattle numbers were: (1) resource restrictions in the form of a large number of buffalo on a heavily cropped village area (feed restriction), and (2) the large capital costs for starting a cattle enterprise because of the high prices for Brahman crossbred cattle in the area.

Compared to noncattle owners, farmers with cattle had similar economic characteristics with the exception of total crop value produced: this averaged 5,700 baht ($251) per farm for noncattle households and 8,500 baht ($374) for cattle-owning households. Since cropland holdings were about equal (28.0 rai [4.5 hectares or 11.2 acres] for noncattle households versus 30.7 rai [4.9 hectares or 12.3 acres] for cattle holders), this would indicate cattle owners grew a larger proportion of high-value crops and/or obtained better yields. The average buffalo per household was 2.5 for noncattle holders and for cattle holders. The total amount of capital invested in crop production facilities was also of the same magnitude for the two groups. Given the homogeneous nature of the households within the village, no striking features highlight those farmers that have gone into cattle production with the exception of a higher gross value of crop production, a proportion of which would most likely be available for cattle investment purposes.

Since cattle were not used for draft purposes in Non Som Boon, all 10 cattle owners were producing for sale, i.e., the cattle herds were exclusively for breeding purposes. On the other hand, buffalo were kept primarily to provide power (see Tables 5.5, 5.6, and 5.7).

In this analysis of the bovine herds in Non Som Boon, three functional groups were distinguished: young calves kept in the herd (0 to 2 years); young animals growing toward maturity and available for sale or for herd replacement (2 to 4 years); and mature animals capable of power or reproduction or both. A breeding herd, producing animals for sale, will have a high proportion of mature females and young animals in the 0 to 2 and 2 to 4 age categories. A herd kept for draft will have a high proportion of mature males. Increases in a herd kept for breeding can come from births in the herd itself, while increases in a strict power herd must be by purchases from outside the herd. The distribution by age shows most buffalo were of mature working age while nearly one-half the cattle were young animals (Table 5.6).

TABLE 5.5. Beginning numerical inventory of bovines in Non Som Boon, Thailand, 1970

Total No. Farmers	Animal Type	No. with That Type	Total Animals	Total Males	Total Females	Biomass (kg)	Total Herd Biomass (kg)
52	Cattle	10	47	15	32	9,373	58,330
	Buffalo	49	125	70	55	48,957	

TABLE 5.6. Beginning biomass inventory by functional groups of bovines in Non Som Boon, Thailand, 1970 (kg)

Animal Type	Male Age 0–2	Male Age 2–4	Male Age Mature	Female Age 0–2	Female Age 2–4	Female Age Mature	Total Age 0–2	Total Age 2–4	Total Age Mature	Grand Total
Cattle	1,125	1,050	675	133[a]	1,680	4,710	1,258	2,730	5,385	9,373
Buffalo	2,312	3,862	23,148	1,125	2,858	15,652	3,437	6,720	38,800	48,957

Note: 1 kilogram (kg) = 2.2 pounds.
[a] A large number of female calves were sold during the 1969 dry season; the males were retained for future sale.

TABLE 5.7. Increases and decreases in bovine herd over one year in Non Som Boon, Thailand, 1970–71

	Beginning Inventory	Herd Increases Transactions Purchase	Rent in	Gift, loan	Biological Births	Animal growth	Herd Decreases Transactions Sales	Gift, loan	Rent out	Theft	Natural death	Net change	Ending Inventory
Numerical													
Cattle	47	4	0	0	18	...	14	0	0	0	0	+8	55
Buffalo	125	20	2	8	28	...	36	5	1	0	2	+14	139
Biomass (kg)													
Cattle	9,373	840	0	0	2,210	805	2,142	0	0	0	0	+1,713	11,086
Buffalo	48,957	9,108	1,028	4,102	4,348	2,896	14,304	2,063	514	0	351	+4,250	53,207

Note: 1 kilogram (kg) = 2.2 pounds.

Sources of increase in the herd show that for buffalo the number of purchases, gifts, and rented animals was greater than the number of births. So the aggregate buffalo herd of the village could not be called strictly a power herd, because some females gave birth. It was essentially a power herd, however, as the number of births was not enough to offset sale of aged and cull animals, and additional buffalo had to be brought from outside the village to maintain the size of the aggregate village herd.

Cattle and buffalo birthrates over the study year were 69% and 65%, respectively. These were calculated as the total number of live births divided by the total number of females capable of reproduction over a one-year period. Sharp seasonality in cattle births was evident. Sixty-seven percent of all cattle births were over the three-month period October–December. Sixty-eight percent of the buffalo births were during the three-month period November–January. This seasonality of births was found to depend on the crop production system. Calves born during this three-month period must have been conceived during the preceding three-month period of January–March. As soon as crops were planted, all animals were herded individually, or in very small groups, to avoid trampling the plants and avoid crop damage in general. After harvest of the major crops, a larger number of animals, owned by several farmers, were combined into a herd and allowed to graze on crop residues and weeds on the harvested fields. It was then that the noncastrated males could circulate and breed. This particular calving seasonality seemed favorable. In the winter (November–February), temperatures are moderate, plenty of feed in the form of crop residues is available, and although the rains have stopped, the extremely dry conditions have not yet started. After March, all three factors are unfavorable for both calves and their mothers. Another study in nearby villages indicated that mature animals lost 10 to 15% of their body weight during the January–April period [12].

In addition to cropland, there was some permanent pasture available in the village for communal grazing by all village animals. Although the total land area in Non Som Boon was 4,310 rai (690 hectares or 1,722 acres), only 117 rai (27.2 hectares or 68 acres) were in savannah fields suitable for permanent pasture near the village. Other permanent pasture was near the Chi River and in savannah areas interspersed throughout the areas of upland cropping. For postharvest grazing, 563 rai (90 hectares or 225 acres) of rice fields were available as well as a portion of the 3,288 rai (527 hectares or 1,320 acres) of upland fields. Some of the upland areas were not utilized, due to their distance from the household area.

Figure 5.5 shows the seasonality of the cropland area available for grazing on the 26 sample farms. The area available is probably understated because complete grazing records could not be obtained, and more area than shown in the figure is probably available during the

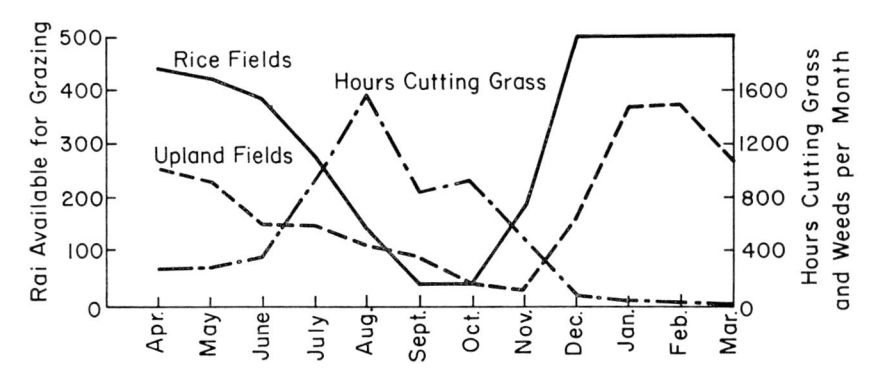

Fig. 5.5. Monthly availability of grazing areas and hours of fodder cutting for supplemental bovine feedings, Non Som Boon, Thailand, 1970–71.

December–March period. If one assumes that the total village area was available during this period, it would amount to 35 rai (5.6 hectares or 14 acres) per animal. Carrying capacity drops rapidly as the rains start and crops are planted, reaching a low of about 2 rai (0.32 hectares or 0.80 acres) per mature animal equivalent. As less land became available, animal owners spent up to 200 person-hours per month cutting grass and weeds in the cropped areas and hand carrying it to their animals. If any rice straw was left over from the dry season, it also was fed to the animals.

Other labor used in caring for the bovines was herding, with village children doing most of this. Herding labor per month corresponded closely to area available for grazing shown in Figure 5.5. The peak was during harvest because animals grazing on newly harvested fields had to be kept out of areas not yet harvested. High levels of herding labor continued even after harvest when communal grazing was available. The lack of fences, threat of theft, distance to water and wallows (buffalo need a daily wallow to maintain their health), and high incidence of calving during this period required individual attention to the animals by each of the farmers' children, even though all village animals were grazing together.

RESOURCE USE IN CROP PRODUCTION. Two objectives are reached by examining resource use in crop production. The first is to obtain evidence on the economic efficiency with which villagers were allocating their crop production resources, and in particular to estimate the efficiency of the villagers' adjustments to using resources in the relatively new upland crops, kenaf and watermelon. If villagers appear to be relatively responsive "economic persons" in the use of resources for crop production, the estimated marginal productivities of resources used in

2 / TRADITIONAL AGRICULTURE

TABLE 5.8. Summary of costs and yield of three major crops, Non Som Boon, Thailand, 1970-71

Item	Unit	Rice	Kenaf	Watermelon
No. of Farmers	no.	25	26	10
Area Planted per Farmer				
Planting Crop	rai[d]	12.9	12.9	6.2
Per Rai Values			per rai[d]	
Yield	kg	185[e]	152[f]	
	no.			883
Crop Value	baht[a]	95	347	331
Labor	hr	88.4	141.9	51.3[b]
Animal Power	hr	13.9	9.3	16.7
Cash Costs	baht[a]	5.5	9.0	93.1
Crop Capital Charge	baht[a]	6.0	0.9	0.3
Land Rent[c]	baht[a]	42.7	40.0	50.0

[a] 1 baht = U.S. $0.0486 (20.6 baht = U.S. $1.00) in 1970.
[b] Melons were sold in the field so labor requirements were less than if the farmers did the harvesting.
[c] Since the farmers own their land, a well-developed land rental market was not operating. However, farmers readily placed rental values on land since a limited number of parcels became available for rental each year through illness of farmers or farmers taking temporary jobs.
[d] 1 hectare = 6.25 rai; 1 acre = 2.5 rai.
[e] 1,160 kg per hectare or 1,020 lb per acre.
[f] 950 kg per hectare or 835 lb per acre.

crop production could aid in setting shadow prices or opportunity costs for the use of these resources in bovine production. Thus the second objective of this section was to obtain estimates of the marginal productivity of the use of labor, capital, and bovine plowing in crop production. These estimates are important as labor is a major cost in bovine production and bovine plowing is a major product of bovine enterprises.

The average levels of crop input costs and production per rai in Non Som Boon during the 1970-71 crop season are shown in Table 5.8. Rice yields were a little above 1 metric ton per hectare (1,160 kilograms or 1,020 pounds per acre), well below the general annual average for the village (due to a poor rice year) and slightly below the average yield for the Northeast. Kenaf yields, in kilograms of washed and dried fiber, were above average for the Northeast. Melon yields, in number of melons, do not take into account size and quality differences.

Major differences among crops in levels of inputs are apparent. Labor use was heaviest on kenaf because, in addition to thinning and hoeing, retting is a labor-intensive process. Watermelons required heavy inputs of animal power because the fields were plowed several times before planting. Cash (purchased) inputs were minor for rice and kenaf but heavy for watermelons, for which seed, fertilizer, and insecticide were purchased.

Four important issues related to estimating crop budgets and profits for crops produced by farmers are illustrated in Table 5.9. One issue

TABLE 5.9. Crop budgets and profits with daily wage charged for labor, Non Som Boon, Thailand, 1970-71

Crop and Unit	Rice Baht[d]	%	Kenaf Baht[d]	%	Watermelon[a] Baht[d]	%
Land at Rental Value	42.69	20.69	40.01	15.69	50.00	19.41
Labor at Baht 1.25 per Hour	110.48	53.55	177.38	69.54	64.09	24.88
Draft Power at Baht 3 per Hour	41.67	20.20	27.78	10.89	50.04	19.43
Cash Costs	5.47	2.65	8.99	3.52	93.10	36.15
Crop Capital Charge	6.01	2.91	0.90	0.36	0.33	0.13
Total Cost per Rai	205.32	100	255.06	100	257.56	100
Total Revenue per Rai	95.24	...	346.62	...	330.77	...
Profit per Rai	−111.08	...	91.56	...	73.21	...
Total Cost per Kg[b]	1.11	...	1.68	...	0.29	...
Price per Kg[b]	0.51	...	2.28	...	0.37	...
Profit per Kg[b]	−0.60[c]	...	0.60	...	0.08	...

[a] Data include early and late watermelon crops.
[b] Per melon for watermelons.
[c] The rice yield this year was below average and the rice price also was depressed well below historical levels due to several years of average and large crops. Under these conditions and with the wage rate and rent assumed in this calculation, losses in the rice production enterprise were estimated. As over 80% of the rice was consumed within the village, rice price fluctuations were of much less importance for these villagers' welfare.
[d] 1 baht = U.S. $0.0486 (20.6 baht = U.S. $1.00) in 1970.

relates to the difficulty of interpreting the accounts when all inputs are priced at the actual cost of purchased inputs or at the opportunity costs assumed for the inputs. With these imputed prices rice production shows a large loss. A major factor in this result relates to the usual problems of the *imputed* opportunity costs used for the farmers' own land, labor, and draft power. As rice is a subsistence crop, to make secure the family food supply many farmers would willingly take lower returns (lower imputed costs in the accounts) on their resources or accept higher costs per kilogram of home-produced rice. A second factor in this result is that no value was assigned to the by-products of the rice crop utilized by the bovines such as rice stubble, volunteer rice, or weeds, all of which were grazed. This forage, plus the straw left at the farmstead after threshing, provides a major source of nutrition for the bovines during the dry season. Although quantitative measures of these products are not possible, they are valuable for buffalo production and maintenance. Kenaf and watermelon fields, however, provide practically no grazing, even on weeds, during the dry season.

A second issue relates to the unimportance of staple food prices for subsistence farmers. Rice is the staple food of most Thai farmers, including those in this village. Over 80% of the rice produced was consumed in the village. The 52 farmers averaged 10.8 rai (1.7 hectares or 4.3 acres) each, which with the low average yield of 185 kilograms per rai obtained in this year produced about 2,000 kilograms of paddy or 1,200 kilograms (2,640 pounds) of milled rice per family (60% conversion rate from paddy to milled basis). Using an average family size of 8 persons gives 150 kilograms (330 pounds) per person, which is the average rice consumption in Thailand. The Non Som Boon farmers thus appear to have succeeded in producing sufficient food for their subsistence needs even in a poor rice year and the price of rice had little effect on this outcome.

Third, one could argue that only out-of-pocket cash costs should be charged to the rice enterprise. If this were done, then "profit" per rai from rice would be equal to kenaf and higher than watermelon even in a bad year.

Fourth, another approach would be to include land rental value (as an opportunity cost), exclude draft power cost (assuming the value of the unaccounted for crop residues compensate for animal power used), and exclude a direct labor charge but instead calculate the residual as returns to labor. This set of calculations gives a return of 0.46 baht ($0.02) per hour of labor, or 3.68 baht ($0.18) per eight-hour day. Although this is considerably below the going wage rate in the area (10 baht [$0.49] per day), it is doubtful that alternative employment could be found for all the labor used in rice production in the village.

A resource productivity analysis was also carried out using crop production functions. (For a summary of the procedure and interpretation of results, see Welsch [16]. For further results applied to Non Som Boon, see DeBoer [5].) Estimation of individual crop production functions provided coefficients that were positive and significant for the most part. Labor productivities were low with the exception of watermelons, being 0.1 to 0.54 for rice and kenaf, respectively, and 2.7 for watermelon. The figures indicate, for example, that an hour of additional labor would return only 0.1 baht in additional output if it is used in rice production but 2.7 baht if used in watermelon production. A similar pattern of lower-value productivity in the rice enterprise emerged for draft power and capital inputs. These results fit with a natural lag in shifting resource use from rice, a subsistence crop, to the nonsubsistence crops, kenaf and watermelon. Undoubtedly, the excessive input use on rice also reflects a hedge against the risk of crop failure in the staple crop. Finally, productivities of cash cost inputs were also high, probably reflecting a general shortage of cash in the village.

Problems arose while attempting to estimate individual crop production relationships as other crops were simultaneously being produced with the same resources. Hence, constraints arose more often in the use of one or more factors of production. For example, an analysis of the value of draft animals must include their contribution to all enterprises. A solution was to develop a whole farm production function. Inputs on each farm were aggregated over all crops and outputs were aggregated by total value. Using these data, individual input resource productivities were calculated. These production functions indicated the productivity of the inputs used over all crops produced.

The function giving the most plausible results was of the Cobb-Douglas form (variables linear in logarithms), with inputs per rai as independent variables, gross value produced per rai (V/L) as the dependent variable, and total planted area also entering as an independent variable indicating scale effects. (Details of the results using various production functions are provided in DeBoer [5]). The estimated function was:

$$\frac{V}{L} = 13.27 \; \frac{N^{0.579}}{L} \; \frac{A^{0.016}}{L} \; \frac{C^{0.078}}{L} \; \frac{R^{-0.167}}{L} \; L^{0.145} \qquad R^2 = 0.55843$$

The estimated production function coefficients in this equation show that labor (N/L) and planted area (L) had large, positive, production coefficients while draft power (A/L) and cash (C/L) were much less important in explaining total value of production per acre. The rent variable (R/L) was negatively correlated with the dependent variable. This was not surprising as a well-developed land rental market was not present and rice land, producing a low gross value per rai in the 1970–71 crop year, had rather high rental values assigned to it by the farmers. Cash cost, taken over all crops, assumed the form of a lumpy input, with most farmers paying a flat fee for truck hire, the major cash cost for the majority of farmers.

The small size of the draft power coefficient (it was not statistically different from 0) is more difficult to explain. One possible reason is that draft animal tillage reached diminishing returns quickly and further tillage added little or nothing to yields and therefore to value produced per unit of area. Thus draft power in this village could be considered essentially a fixed input per unit of area. These results suggest that a minimum level of draft power was necessary for land preparation but additional increments added very little to output, at least during the survey year. The most plausible reason seems to be that, for the major crops, value produced per rai and animal inputs were negatively correlated. The value of kenaf produced per rai was 346.62 baht ($16.90), yet a rai of kenaf required, on the average, only 9.26 hours of animal team power. Rice, on the other hand, produced but 95.24 baht ($4.62) per rai, yet required an average of 13.89 hours of team power input. Thus the relationship between value produced and animal inputs would be insignificant or negative.

A test for efficiency of resource allocation was also made. In this test, if cost-minimizing behavior by the farmer was assumed and no resource constraints were considered, each factor would be used up to the point at which the marginal value productivity (MVP) of that resource equals its marginal factor cost (MFC), or the price of the resource. The average price of the input in the village was used as the MFC. If input restrictions are ignored, a ratio of one indicates the farmer has

TABLE 5.10. Aggregated Cobb-Douglas crop production function, Non Som Boon, Thailand, 1970–71

Variable	MVP/MFC	Significance Level[a]
Planted Area (L)	0.744	0.001
Labor (N)	0.940	0.01
Draft Power (A)	0.106	0.001[b]
Cash Cost (C)	1.487	0.001
Land Rent (R)	−0.979	0.99

[a] Significance level here refers to the probability the required production coefficient (required to equate MVP and MFC) is not equal to the coefficient actually estimated.
[b] As the coefficient used to compute the MVP was not significant, the significance level should be used with caution.

allocated the resource so its returns are just paying for its additional cost. A ratio less than one implies excess use of the resource and a ratio greater than one indicates a constraint on the resource preventing optimal levels of use. The ratios and their corresponding statistical significance levels are shown in Table 5.10.

These comparisons of the MVP of resources used in crop production with estimates of the costs of the resources provided mixed results. MVP of labor obtained from the production function analysis was 1.175 baht ($0.06) per hour, which was close to the average going rate for hired labor of 1.25 baht per hour, giving a ratio close to one (0.940). The marginal value productivity of draft power was only 0.318 baht per hour, about one-tenth of the rental rate per hour (3.00) given as ratio of 0.106. For use in calculating bovine returns in the following section, it was decided that the rental rate was more accurate. Capital charges were found to be nonsignificant in production function estimates and, therefore, these were dropped from the analysis. The interest rates on medium term agricultural loans were the rates used for comparison with the computed rates of return to bovine production.

RETURNS TO BOVINE PRODUCTION. In examining the reasons why cattle and buffalo production had not expanded more rapidly, estimates of the returns to investment in these enterprises are useful. Low returns to investment would help explain low rates of increase in bovine numbers; high rates would raise questions as to why the farmers were not responding to profitable investment opportunities. In this section a benefit cost framework is used to estimate the returns to bovine production.

The nature of the production and utilization processes suggested a rate of return approach to enterprise evaluation rather than a simple profit maximization framework [10]. This is because the animals have a nonproductive period (birth to maturity) when their contribution, measured as a net cash flow, is negative, then upon reaching maturity

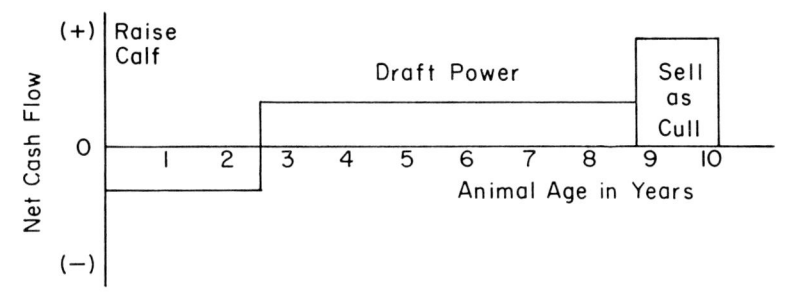

5 / Livestock Production in a Thai Village / A. J. DeBoer, D. E. Welsch

Fig. 5.6. Changes in net cash flow over the life of a work animal.

the animal produces a stream of positive net cash flows and, when culled, provides a lump sum of money (Fig. 5.6). The costs and returns over the life of the bovine enterprises are represented as net cash flows (returns minus costs) during each time period. Thus the flow is negative until the animal contributes more in returns than costs.

The returns to the bovine enterprises are composed of the animals' contributions to crop production activities, the breeding of animals and resultant sale of offspring, and the sale of cull animals.

The internal rate of return was used to estimate profitability as it allows direct comparison with alternative investments and interest rates and does not require the selection of a social discount rate. The formula for this measure is

$$\sum_{t=0}^{n} \frac{1}{(1+i)^n} F_n = 0$$

where
n = number of years for which the internal rate of return is relevant
F_n = net cash flow in year n
i = an internally calculated rate of interest that makes the discounted present value of the flow of costs equal to the discounted present value of the flow of returns at a point in time.

Calculation of discount rates that equalize the areas above and below the zero net cash flow line requires a yearly accounting of costs and benefits. Data were collected on initial animal costs, yearly labor costs, a charge on livestock production facilities, yearly returns for the enterprise in question, and final sale prices. (Land costs were not included, due to the residual nature of grazing and the zero opportunity cost of grazing during the dry season since irrigation was unavailable. If substantial changes in crop enterprise technology should occur, this assumption might no longer be valid.)

Costs were calculated from data on labor and capital inputs in

TABLE 5.11. Costs and returns per year in bovine enterprises, Non Som Boon, Thailand, 1970-71

	Labor Use per Animal (person-hours)		
	Herding labor	Grass and weed cutting	Total
At Mean Herd Size	785	31	816
Per Additional Animal[a]	52.0	8.9	60.9

	Cattle		Buffalo	
	bahts	dollars	bahts	dollars
	Costs per Animal			
Wage Bill[b]	479	23.28	479	23.28
Capital Facilities	42	2.04	42	2.04
Total Cost per Head per Year	521	25.32	521	25.32
Purchase Price of Male Replacement	1,940	94.28	1,600	77.76
Purchase Price of Female Replacement	1,740	84.56	1,170	56.86
Calf Cost	300	14.58	300	14.58
	Returns per Animal			
Draft Power[c]	...	...	700	34.02
Breeding Returns per Cow per Year	836	40.62	673	32.71
Sale Price of Cull Male	1,200	58.32	1,890	91.85
Sale Price of Cull Female	1,410	68.53	1,440	69.98

[a] This is the marginal labor required in adding a calf to the herd.
[b] Total hours of labor times an assumed one-half the marginal value product of labor used in crop production. 1.175 baht/2 = 0.588 baht
[c] Average total hours of draft animals times the hourly rental rate of 3.00 baht per hour.

bovine production (Table 5.11). All initial animal costs were assumed to equal 300 baht ($14.60) at weaning age. Revenues for animal breeding were estimated by computing a net value per calf raised to maturity and multiplying this figure by the birthrate for the animal class under consideration. This gives the average yearly revenue contribution of a cow. Sale and purchase prices were those prevailing in the village. The total time under consideration in a weaning to slaughter enterprise was eleven years. Dual purpose (draft plus breeding) animals were assumed to work four years and breed six years. All animals began producing revenue during their fourth year.

The results of this analysis permit examination of the herd adjustments brought about by the changes in technology (Table 5.12). First, enterprises have adjusted to the point where specialized breeding herds are the prevailing form of cattle enterprise (refer to the discussion of herd composition and herd use and to Tables 5.5 to 5.7). A similar trend toward specialization of water buffalo for exclusive use as draft animals has not occurred. The dual purpose female buffalo appeared to be the most profitable form of bovine investment by a small margin. Specialization in this enterprise, however, is prevented by several factors. First, the limited size of land holdings restricts animal power requirements, so expansion of draft animal numbers is limited. Second, farmers prefer

TABLE 5.12. Internal rates of return for cattle and buffalo enterprises in Non Som Boon, Thailand, 1970-71

Type	Sex	Enterprise	Rate of Return
Cattle	Female	Raised from birth to 4, bred from 4 to 11, sold at end of 11 years as cull.	8.2%
Buffalo	Male	Raised from birth to 4, used as draft from 4 to 11, sold at end of 11 years as cull.	6.1%
Buffalo	Female[a]	Raised from birth to 4, used as draft from 4 to 8, used as breeding from 4 to 11, sold at the end of 11 years as cull.	10.9%

[a] Assumes power returns = one-half that of male draft animals.

having one or more males available for draft purposes to avoid problems that arise if their buffalo cows become pregnant or give birth during a peak draft power demand period.

The cattle breeding enterprise appeared more profitable than the traditional male buffalo draft enterprise. Returns to cattle breeding should continue to rise as each succeeding generation of offspring has higher proportions of Brahman blood and thus commands higher prices.

The rates of return in Table 5.12 are comparable to prevailing commercial lending rates of 12% and are close to the 9% rate of return estimated by the Asian Development Bank for a major cattle improvement project [3]. These estimated rates are substantially greater than the 3 to 5% range obtained in other studies of traditional agriculture [13, 14].

SUMMARY AND CONCLUSIONS. Some of the reasons bovine meat production has not expanded more rapidly in Thailand are now clear. The analysis of bovine production in Non Som Boon has indicated that it is difficult to alter one part of the interrelated crop-bovine production system without changing other parts. Hence, increases in bovine output from Thai villages will depend on changes in both crop technology and bovine production technology. Changes in only one area are not likely to be enough. For example, farmers were prevented from taking full advantage of the performance potential of the Brahman crossbreeds because inadequate nutrition was being provided by the crop production system. The study shows, however, that farmers were apparently using their herds quite efficiently, given existing levels of technology.

To be successful, efforts to promote change must be based on an understanding of the interrelations of the whole crop-livestock system. This system in Non Som Boon village in northeastern Thailand was found to have the following characteristics. First, bovine returns take several forms and increasing one type of revenue stream (increasing breeding cows) decreases another revenue stream (fewer males available for draft), given the fixed capacity of the village to support a bovine herd. Second, nutritional constraints were found to be determined by the land resources of the entire village, not of individual farmers. Nutrition was found to be a function of the amounts and types of crops grown that provided by-product fodder in the form of crop residues and various periods of grazing harvested fields. Third, grazing improvement programs as distinct enterprises did not appear profitable unless grazing could be integrated with existing crop production methods. Communal grazing and high capital costs of fencing made grazing investments by individuals irrational [4]. Communal grazing also makes investment in improved animal health measures irrational for the individual farmer. A village or regional approach is required. Fourth, the analysis indicated that there did not appear to be any major sources of economic inefficiencies in the allocation of production resources in 1970–71 that could be tapped to increase animal populations at the current levels of technology in Non Som Boon.

Rapid advances in crop technologies in the northeast that would alter the system have not generally occurred. One exception is the widespread use of tractors for plowing in some areas, but not in Non Som Boon. Tractor use does not appear to have increased overall crop productivity but has simply decreased draft power requirements. In addition, analysis in other villages indicated that, to date, tractors have not decreased draft animal numbers significantly [5].

The impact of new technologies generally associated with the green revolution was minimal in Non Som Boon in 1970–71 and indications are that their impact will be gradual. Given this background of relatively slow technical change in the food and fiber sector in Non Som Boon, it should not be surprising that bovine production technology is also still at very low levels.

The longer-run future for bovine production in Thai villages is not clear. The answer depends partly on the progress of the Thai economy as a whole. In a situation of rapid and sustained growth in the general economy and in agriculture, cattle numbers are likely to increase at the expense of the buffalo population. This is because technical relationships dictate that more breeding animals can be supported on a given resource base with cattle than with buffalo because of size differences. In addition, the breeding performance of cattle can be increased more rapidly than buffalo because of mating characteristics. Expected relative price changes also favor cattle for cattle meat commands higher prices in the Thai market and the differential seems likely to widen with increasing income levels. Finally, both existing production technologies and those likely to be developed soon are primarily for cattle, not buffalo.

If, on the other hand, Thai agriculture and the Thai economy enter a period of stagnation, then the reverse could occur. Buffalo are very efficient animals under present village patterns of use. Without significant change in the rural sector, the buffalo will be very difficult to dislodge. For, as this study shows, the returns to investments in female buffalo are somewhat higher than in other bovine enterprises.

REFERENCES
1. Brooks, E. R. *A Pasture and Forage Program for Thailand.* Agency for International Development, USOM, Bangkok, 1961.
2. Buranamus, P. A Survey of the Buffalo in Thailand. Monograph. Kasetsart Univ., Bangkok, 1963.
3. "Cattle Industry Lags Behind." *Financial Post* 3 (6, 1972), Bangkok.
4. Crump, D. K. *Is Cattle Raising Profitable? An Evaluation of Three Strategies for Development of Beef Cattle Production.* Unpublished manuscript, Faculty of Agriculture, Khon Kaen Univ., May 1972.
5. DeBoer, A. J. "Technical and Economic Constraints on Bovine Production in Three Villages in Thailand." Unpublished Ph.D. dissertation, Univ. of Minnesota, Apr. 1972.
6. Ingraham, J. C. *Economic Change in Thailand, 1850–1970.* Stanford: Stanford Univ. Press, 1972.
7. MacGregor, R. "The Domestic Buffalo." *Veterinary Record* 53:443–50.
8. Mason, I. L. *A World Dictionary of Livestock Breeds, Types, and Varieties.* Technical Commission No. 8, Commonwealth Bureau of Animal Breeding and Genetics, Edinburgh, 1969.
9. National Economic Development Board. *National Income of Thailand: 1960–1968.* Government of Thailand, Bangkok, 1971.
10. Peterson, W. L. "The Returns to Investment in Agricultural Research in the United States." Univ. of Minnesota Department of Agricultural and Applied Economics Staff Paper Series No. P.69-5, St. Paul, 1969.
11. Rouse, J. E. *World Cattle.* Vol. 2. Norman: Univ. of Oklahoma Press, 1969.
12. Rufener, W. R. "Cattle and Water Buffalo, Production in Villages of Northeast Thailand." Unpublished Ph.D. dissertation, Univ. of Illinois, Sept. 1971.
13. Schultz, T. W. *Transforming Traditional Agriculture.* New Haven: Yale Univ. Press, 1964.
14. Sethuraman, S. V. "Long Run Demand for Draft Animals in Indian Agriculture." Unpublished Ph.D. dissertation, Univ. of Chicago, Mar. 1970.
15. Singh, H., and Parmerkar, Y. M. *Some Basic Facts about Cattle Wealth and Allied Matters.* New Delhi: Central Council of Gosamuardhaua, 1966.
16. Welsch, D. E. "Response to Economic Incentive by Abakaliki Rice Farmers in Eastern Nigeria." *Journal of Farm Economics* 47 (Nov. 1965): 900–914.
17. Williamson, S., and Payne, J. A. *An Introduction to Animal Husbandry in the Tropics.* London: Longmans, Green and Co., 1959.

PART 3

Dynamics of Small-Farm Agriculture

THE PURPOSE of Part III is to analyze the causes of change in agriculture and the sources of agricultural growth. Illustrations of the seven theoretical and empirical issues in the economics of the transformation of traditional agriculture set forth in Chapter 1 are provided in the following three case studies. Questions related to the seven issues are: (1) How did changes in agricultural technology come about? Where and by whom was the new technology produced? (2) What evidence of successive adjustments to changing supply and demand conditions in both factor (agricultural input) and agricultural product markets was observed? (3) What increases in production occurred and what were the prospects for future growth? (4) What changes in values and institutions were reported and how did they affect agricultural production? (5) Was higher farm productivity related to greater farm size? (6) How was employment on farms influenced by the changes in agricultural production and technology? (7) To what extent were the complex interrelationships in the agricultural transformation process illustrated?

Dynamics, or change, in agriculture is achieved through the use of more productive agricultural innovations or new technology obtained by local development or, more usually, importation. Rapid change in technology in agriculture today requires the establishment of a flow onto farms of new science-based inputs, such as high-yielding seeds, chemical fertilizer, pesticides, and machinery. The Eckert study (Chapter 6) is a classic analysis of a dynamic change in agriculture. At the time of the study a wave of the green revolution was passing through Pakistan's Punjab. Eckert shows that the introduction of a short-strawed wheat from Mexico and increased use of chemical fertilizer resulted in a doubling of yields as compared with traditional varieties. On a national basis, a 30% increase in wheat production took place over a four-year period, an increase that broke historical records in South Asia for rapid growth in national agricultural production.

On the Venezuelan land settlement project (Chapter 7), new crops and crop production systems, including four-wheel tractor technology, were introduced through the leadership of a group of settlers and through government extension efforts. In northwest Mexico (Chapter 8) the increases in production came about through the shift to irrigation farming technology and the accelerated use of new off-farm inputs, including chemical fertilizers, pesticides, and agricultural machinery, all facilitated by government credit.

Each of the three cases explores the adjustments made by farmers to changes in supply and demand conditions in both factor and product markets. The response of farmers to the new investment opportunities opened by the Accelerated Wheat Improvement Program in Pakistan is documented in detail by Eckert. With increased supplies of new inputs on the Venezuelan land reform project, including highly subsidized tractors, the more experienced settlers were able to increase considerably the land under cultivation to meet demand conditions in certain product markets to which they had access. Adjustments to changes in supply and demand conditions in the Mexican collective ejido farm are documented by the shifting proportions of different crops produced in response to changing input supply conditions and product demand.

Illustrations of imperfect allocative efficiency in developing agricultures abound in these cases. (Farmers with "imperfect allocative efficiency" have opportunities to reallocate their resource use to appreciably increase income.) The most rigorously documented case is the conclusion by Eckert that the farmers in Pakistan's Punjab could have profited by increasing further their levels of nitrogen application on the new high-yielding dwarf wheats. The Venezuelan study reports a large number of examples of changes in prices and technology. Because of the relatively few years of settlement, the farmers had had little opportunity to adjust to these changes.

The opportunities for greater income appeared related to the number and kind of weeding of corn, corn-sesame rotations, the use of postemergence herbicide, the use of backpack spraying, alternative uses of water pumps, and the solution to marketing problems for vegetables. In northwest Mexico, the large-scale irrigated collective farming case illustrates continuing adjustment to changes from 1937 to 1968, as more irrigated land became available, product and factor prices changed, and two divisions of the farm occurred.

All three cases illustrate continuously increasing farm production. However, in the case of the Venezuelan settlement project, uncertainty surrounded the amount of increases in production that would occur in the future due to lack of clarity about government plans and policies for the project.

The ways in which values and institutions interact in the agricultural transformation are exceedingly complex and little understood. The Hayami and Ruttan induced development model proposes that institutional change is induced by individuals perceiving new economic opportunities that could be secured by institutional modifications. In the Pakistan Punjab little change in values and institutional conditions were apparently required for the rapid adoption by farmers of high-yielding wheat technology. However, Ekert concludes that the rapid acceptance of dwarf wheat was leading to changes in values and modifications of the institutionalized relations between tenant and landlord, between artisans and landlords, and between farmers and product markets. The interactions between major institutional change and production increases are central themes of Chapters 7 and 8. The evolution of the development of an agricultural settlement in Venezuela documents the complex leadership and changing organizational arrangements usually involved in the setting up of new institutional arrangements aimed at accelerating agricultural production. In the case of the collective farm in northwest Mexico, Freebairn's analysis illuminates some of the achievements and failures of an important new type of agricultural institution, the ejido.

Scale economies leading to higher productivity on larger farms, which might underlie the technical relations in agriculture, were not found in the following three studies. In Pakistan's Punjab the seed and fertilizer technology for wheat was easily devisable for any size farm. The median operating unit of 2.6 hectares (6.5 acres) in Sahiwal District participated fully in adopting the new varieties, although small farmers were about a year behind in adoption rates due to various other factors. In the Venezuelan land settlement program, few of the settlers had been able to develop their full 6-hectare (14.8-acre) allotment by the end of the sixth year of settlement. Hence, significant scale issues related to the 6-hectare limit had not arisen. In the collective farming experience reported in Chapter 8, the two divisions of the collective farm that greatly reduced the scale of operations suggest that the original scale was too large to provide the greatest income to the members, or, at least that the members who withdrew saw little potential loss from division to the relatively small individually operated units of about 14 hectares (35 acres).

The complex nature of the agricultural transformation process is illustrated in many ways in these three chapters. The study in Pakistan points to the impact of the new wheat varieties on marketing institutions and upon interpersonal relationships in traditional villages. The Venezuelan agrarian reform study shows the unexpected occurrence of a highly skewed distribution of income on a settlement in which land was divided evenly. The study also concluded that a new type of leadership may be required for the further development of the settlement, now that the establishment phase had been completed. The analysis of collective farming in northwest Mexico demonstrates that the productive farming operations providing relatively high income and growth to its members did not succeed in satisfying many of the members, leading 142 of the original 183 families to withdraw from the collective ejido. These families chose to undertake individual operation of farmlands after some years of experience with collective farming.

Each of these studies provides in-depth analysis of particular dimensions of the agricultural transformation. The Eckert study focuses on the underlying economics of farmers' response to high-yielding varieties of wheat in an area having good environmental conditions for irrigated wheat and accessible water. The history of this spectacular program that distributed high-yielding wheat seeds and chemical fertilizer is outlined, illuminating the roles of the contributing organizations: the government of Pakistan, the International Center for Maize and Wheat Improvement (CIMMYT), the Ford Foundation, and the large and small farmers. The increase in wheat production at the national and farm levels is documented, with detailed analysis of adoption patterns and the fertilizer

3 / DYNAMICS OF SMALL-FARM AGRICULTURE 147

and water use adjustments undertaken by farmers in response to the new high-return investment opportunity provided by the improved wheat varieties. The implications for government policy changes of the adoption of the new wheat varieties, particularly with respect to chemical fertilizer supply and subsidies, are indicated. The analysis concludes by examining the wider impact of the adoption of the new wheats on marketing institutions, goals of government wheat policy, and traditional village relationships. Knowledge of the details of this major success of the green revolution is instructive for other traditional agricultural areas where rapid increases in agricultural production are sought.

New agricultural settlements on largely unoccupied land will continue to be undertaken in certain areas as part of the dynamics of agriculture. The detailed study of a Venezuelan Agrarian Reform Settlement by Thiesenhusen presents a rare view into settlement processes and some unexpected outcomes. The study provides a summary history of the founding of the settlement and the roles of important figures, as well as the sometimes confusing government actions impinging on the project. Examination of the use of land, labor, farm capital, and credit illuminates the production activities carried out and the numerous problems faced. The study indicated that much of the land lay idle during parts of the year when it could have been cultivated, associated with considerable unemployment. Also, although land was allocated relatively equally to families on the settlement, a highly skewed income distribution occurred. In exploring the factors associated with settler success, the importance of an intensive cropping pattern and the use of yield-increasing inputs became apparent. The policy implications point to the critical importance of assuring the necessary flow of inputs and technology into settlements and of adequate market outlets.

Intensive examination of the development over thirty years of a form of collective or cooperative farm in the particular form of a Mexican ejido provides an example of a major approach to agricultural transformation. The study in northwest Mexico is of one of the collective farms founded throughout Mexico following the Mexican Revolution and the Constitution of 1917. By 1969 almost three million Mexicans had received rights to land under ejido legislation. Many of the farmers receiving land decided to operate their land in groups through a collective management system. Other farmers who received land opted for individual operation. This study focuses on a collective farming ejido that had very good economic performance. In this particular area, a relatively large amount of irrigated land was allocated per ejido family (14 hectares or 35 acres by 1941); hence, relatively high levels of income could be expected and collective or other types of organization could be projected to prosper. Since many reform and revolutionary governments assume that group farming will lead to greater prosperity for small farmers, the outcome of the Mexican experience with ejido collective farms is of particular interest.

This study provides some of the Mexican experience and places the ejidal farming sector in the perspective of the Mexican national economy in which the private farm sector has remained dominant in terms of agricultural output but has employed less of the farm labor. The study shows that the collective management of the ejido succeeded in producing yields comparable with private and other farms in the valley. Given the large amounts of land per member, a relatively high income was produced per member. Despite this success, the original ejido founded in 1937 divided twice, leaving in 1957 only 41 members in the cooperative farming organization. This outcome is representative of trends in ejidos in many parts of Mexico, including the poorer agricultural areas. The loss of membership in the collective farming ejidos suggests that difficulties in human relations and economic incentives may inhibit continued productive operation of these farms.

An unexpected result of ejido development in this area was found in this study. Although the original intention of the Mexican land reform, of which the ejido was the central mechanism, was to provide land to the tillers, by 1969 a high proportion of the labor on the collective studied was being supplied by wage laborers employed from outside the collective.

Freebairn is led to the conclusion that Mexico faces major decisions about the future of the ejidos. Through various actions, the government could support and strengthen the ejidal farm sector with its ability to employ large amounts of labor or it could decide to let the sector wither, leading to accelerated transfers of population to urban areas and increased agricultural production on private commercial farms. The study documents an era in Mexican rural land reform dynamics and concludes that new problems now face the Mexican nation in which the ejidal sector could play a significant part, depending, however, on more general trends of politics and national development.

CHAPTER 6

Farmer Response to High-Yielding Wheat in Pakistan's Punjab

JERRY B. ECKERT

THIS CHAPTER examines farmer response to a wheat improvement program. The program, undertaken in Pakistan[1] between 1965 and 1970, was a major agricultural development success in the low-income world at the time. During this program, high-yielding wheats were adopted faster and more completely in Pakistan than in any other country. From 1965 to 1970, production of the nation's two most important cereals, wheat and rice, rose by 61%. Considering that these cereals constituted more than 80% of the foodgrains consumed and more than 60% of the total caloric value of the diet, one can assert that improved cereal technology had a greater impact in Pakistan than anywhere else at that time.

Intensive study of the behavior of a sample of farmers in Sahiwal District in Pakistan's Punjab Province who participated in the wheat improvement program provides conclusions that can aid similar programs elsewhere and increase our understanding of the agricultural development process.

The study explores a number of questions affecting agricultural growth. It permits examination of the interactive roles of many factors in spurring growth. It emphasizes the time lags that may sometimes be necessary for the maturation of a developmental effort. Reactions of individual farm managers in a traditional agriculture to a dramatically profitable but nontraditional technology are shown. Farmers' adoption patterns and farming practice adjustments confirm that these farmers are profit responsive. At the same time the data underline the role of uncer-

JERRY B. ECKERT is Assistant Professor, Department of Economics, Colorado State University. His research in Pakistan began in 1968. He has been Agricultural Planning Advisor, Ford Foundation, Pakistan, and a member of the Colorado State University Water Management Research Project Stationed in Islamabad, Pakistan, 1972–1975.

tainty in the peasant farmer's decision making. Close inspection of Pakistan's experience with wheat also identifies limitations in a farmer's ability to extract the greatest productivity from new varieties—limitations that will prove serious as population continues to press on food supply.

The national setting of the accelerated wheat improvement program in Pakistan is considered first. Details of traditional farming practices and evidence of change in agriculture in Sahiwal District are then presented to provide a background for examination of the high-yielding wheat adoption patterns and the resource adjustments made by farmers. Finally, indications of the expanding impact of the new wheats are provided.

NATIONAL SETTING OF THE ACCELERATED WHEAT IMPROVEMENT PROGRAM. In 1970 West Pakistan was classified as an agricultural economy since agriculture contributed some 46% of West Pakistan's gross national product and employed nearly 55% of the labor force. However, in comparison to many developing countries, the economy of West Pakistan was well diversified with strong commercial, industrial, and service sectors.

Rural population is clustered in mud-walled villages. Few families live in isolated houses on their land. Immediate and extended families form the basic units of social organization and provide an important dimension of a great many types of human interaction. It is not uncommon for entire villages to be composed of one or perhaps just a few broadly defined families, each descended from the original landlord or his servants. Village authority is rigidly hierarchical with a concentration of power in the hands of a very few individuals. Authority and status generally have been land based so that the larger farmers tend also to be the hereditary village leaders.

Several unifying forces run through Pakistani society. Most important is the Islamic religion that pervades many facets of life. The nation itself owes its birth and integrity to the desire for a nation wherein Islam could be brought to further fruition without hindrance. Under the 1962 constitution, the state was designated as the Islamic Republic of Pakistan and it legally embodies the teachings and philosophy of Islam as its guiding tenets.

Other unifying threads include many common cultural and historical experiences shared either as Muslims in a united India, dominated politically by the British and culturally by the Hindus, or as residents of a young and struggling nation once independence had been achieved.

Early government activity has contributed to regional unity and has been important in setting the stage for the acceleration of economic growth in Sahiwal District as in the rest of the Punjab. British administrators began work on a railroad in 1861. In the century that followed, a network of roads and railroads was systematically built so that communications today are well developed compared with other developing regions. Systematic economic planning was begun with the First Five-Year Plan in 1955. During this and subsequent plans, the country's planners and policymakers have developed a reasonable expertise at setting goals and mobilizing resources.

Yet at the same time West Pakistan is a large area of diversity and contrast. In 1970 West Pakistan had four provinces: the Sind, Punjab, Baluchistan, and the Northwest Frontier Province. The four provinces plus the mountainous areas classified as tribal territories were all administered from a single capital at Lahore. Five district local languages are spoken along with several dialects and tribal tongues. The language of government has been English.

Perhaps the most striking source of diversity is geographical variation. In the 1,000 miles (1,600 kilometers) from south to north, the land rises from sea level to over 26,000 feet (7,900 meters), receives from 0 to some 60 inches (1,500 mm) of rain, and contains barely inhabitable deserts, arid grazing lands, highly productive irrigated farmlands, and heavily forested mountains. The range of economic and agricultural specialization is equally broad. In sum, Pakistan is a highly diverse country, composed of a number of historically independent units now held together by religion, shared experience, and a central government.

Slow Growth in National Wheat Production. The history of wheat research in the Punjab extends over three-quarters of a century. As early as 1893, foreign varieties were being tested for their local adaptability. Researchers of the Punjab Board of Agriculture isolated pure lines from locally cultivated wheats in 1906 and subsequently began early wheat-breeding experiments using these isolates. From these and later efforts, a succession of improved varieties spread in waves over the land, each being adopted most completely in those areas for which it was best suited. Varieties were periodically imported from abroad and some of them achieved acceptance. Progress was slow, however, and new varieties were only occasionally approved for release. In 1965 the standard "traditional" varieties cultivated in Punjab were C-591 (released in 1934), C-271 and C-273 (1957), and Dirk, which had been imported in 1958. While each of these improved new varieties contained some advantage over its predecessor, they were all long-stemmed varieties that did not respond to heavy doses of chemical fertilizers.

Despite three-quarters of a century of wheat research, national average yields remained essentially static. Whatever increased yield potential the new varieties might have offered was effectively nullified by increased soil salinity, the extension of wheat cultivation to less suitable acreage, and an insufficiently rapid turnover of varieties, which allowed farmers' seed selection practices to degrade the purity and potential of the seed they were growing. The correlation of trends in production and acreage

3 / DYNAMICS OF SMALL-FARM AGRICULTURE

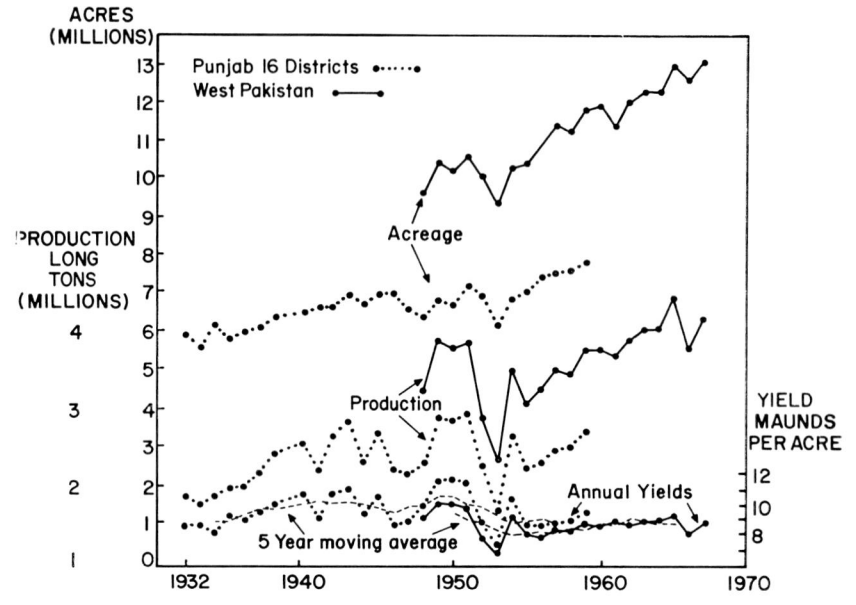

Fig. 6.1. Trends in production, acreage, and yields of wheat for West Pakistan and districts of the former Punjab state that became part of West Pakistan, 1932–68. 1 long ton = 1.016 metric tons; 1 maund of wheat = 82.29 lb or 37.32 kg; 10 maunds of wheat per acre = 13.7 bu/acre or 922 kg/ha.

among the 16 districts of the Punjab before Partition (the term used to refer to the division of the Indian subcontinent into India and Pakistan in 1947) and later of all West Pakistan shows that the gradual growth in wheat production was almost exclusively due to expanded acreage (Fig. 6.1). The dominance of the Punjab in the wheat acreage of West Pakistan is indicated in this figure as are the somewhat higher yield levels that have historically occurred in the Punjab due to the concentration of irrigation in that province.

Wheat production has grown slowly, expanding since 1947 at an average annual rate of only 1.5%. This was inadequate since population has increased more rapidly, perhaps by as much as 3.5% annually [1]. As a consequence, foodgrain deficits appeared in the mid-fifties and grain imports rose until they amounted to more than 15% of total consumption.

Careful interpretation of the gradual rise in planted acreage leads to an important hypothesis about farmers' goals. Wheat acreage rose steadily beginning in the early 1950s. For the period 1946–47 through 1966–67, 86% of the variation in acreage may be explained as a simple linear function of time.[2] Thus an estimated 175,000 additional acres of wheat were planted each year with only modest variations around the trend line. At prevailing yields, the annual addition to production was some 55,000 long tons.[3] This striking parallel between the increase in demand suggested by rural population growth and the estimated increases strongly implies that the nation's wheat growers tended to plant enough additional acreage to feed their families and to meet the usual extended family obligations, provide a small amount for ceremonies and charity, and to repay creditors in kind. This hypothesis suggests that the villages were largely self-sufficient in wheat and that relatively few farmers were engaged in wheat production with marketing it as their primary objective.

Data on imports and urban consumption support this hypothesis. Wheat imports into West Pakistan averaged 1.24 million (long) tons (1.26 million metric tons) annually for the 1964–66 period, 18.6% of total national wheat consumption [3]. During these years the urban population consumed approximately 1.77 million tons annually, thus implying an annual net flow of only 0.53 million tons of wheat from rural to urban areas out of a total production of about 4 million tons.

If cereals had not been available from abroad on concessional terms, rising foodgrain prices in urban areas would have brought forth greater supplies from rural areas. However, this would have required that urban consumers spend a higher proportion of their disposable income on food. As a result, the growth of nonagricultural sectors of the economy and the structural transformation that has resulted in today's fairly balanced economy would have been delayed.

Accelerated Wheat Improvement Program. The urgency of a deteriorating foodgrain balance was made clear to national leaders during the 1965 war with India and the drought that followed during the 1965–66 crop year. In a postwar revision of priorities, foodgrain self-sufficiency became the most important national civilian goal. As a result, an Accelerated Wheat Improvement Program was established, built on expertise from the International Center for Maize and Wheat Improvement (CIMMYT) in Mexico and with financial backing by the Ford Foundation [5]. This program served to coordinate government and private efforts in a concentrated attack on stagnant wheat yields. Under its auspices, policy and institutional changes were wrought, resources and people mobilized, and decisions taken in accordance with an overall implementation plan.

A basic program goal was to improve Pakistan's wheat research enough to make possible a significant increase in the rate of growth of wheat production through improved yields rather than through acreage expansion. By 1965 field trials had shown that wheats developed in Mexico were far superior to local varieties in yield potential. They were accordingly chosen as the technological vehicle for rapid progress. These high-yielding wheats had short stems, hence were labeled dwarf wheats; the terms *dwarf wheat* and *high-yielding wheat* are used interchangeably in this discussion.

The first steps in the research program that followed were: (1) screening the Mexican dwarf material under Pakistan's conditions, (2) stabilizing the best lines, and (3) developing a package of cultural practices that would result in optimum yields with the new varieties. During this period of testing and adaptation, research workers were provided opportunities to earn advanced graduate degrees and were given applied training so they would be qualified scientists when the research program expanded, using the imported wheat varieties.

Evaluation of promising lines under actual farm conditions rather than on experimental stations was believed essential. The method chosen provided the necessary information but, more importantly, it capitalized on the hierarchical social structure of the villages in awakening the farm sector to the dramatic potential of the new varieties. In a series of Micro-Plot Trials and Semi-Commercial Trials, the Mexican wheats and instructions for their cultivation were given to many of the larger farmers. After experimental measurements were taken, the farmer was allowed to keep the seed. The dwarf wheats usually produced two or three times the yields of native strains, creating the incentive for these early cooperators to shift varieties rapidly. The cooperating farmers received the seed, knowledge of the required practices, and knowledge of the high yields in return for their participation, while the research service obtained needed data. Since the cooperators were generally large farmers, they were usually village leaders. Once convinced of the merits of dwarf wheats, they served as change agents within the rural community, transmitting their enthusiasm about the technology. Quite often the second group of adopters in a village were the tenants of the cooperator who were given seed by their landlord and told to grow it. This mandate removed any hesitation the tenant may have had about investing in an untried technique and contributed to the speed with which dwarf wheats were accepted.

A major strategem chosen by agricultural planners was to rely on imports of seed wheat to speed the multiplication process. Pakistan imported 350 tons (356 metric tons) of the initial dwarf varieties in 1965, 50 tons of Mexipak in 1966, and in 1967 concluded the largest single purchase of seed in the history of world agriculture when 41,720 tons (42,388 metric tons) of Mexipak were brought in. In this way seed scarcity ceased to be a limiting factor at least one year earlier than would have been the case without seed imports.

The early effects of the wheat program on national production are summarized in Figure 6.2. The acreage trend is represented by the straight line superimposed on a plot of the acreages through 1966–67. The linear trend function would have forecast an acreage of 13.23 million in 1967–68 (the 95% confidence interval was 12.232 to 14.288). However, total acreage reached 14,785,000 acres (5,985,830 hectares), signifi-

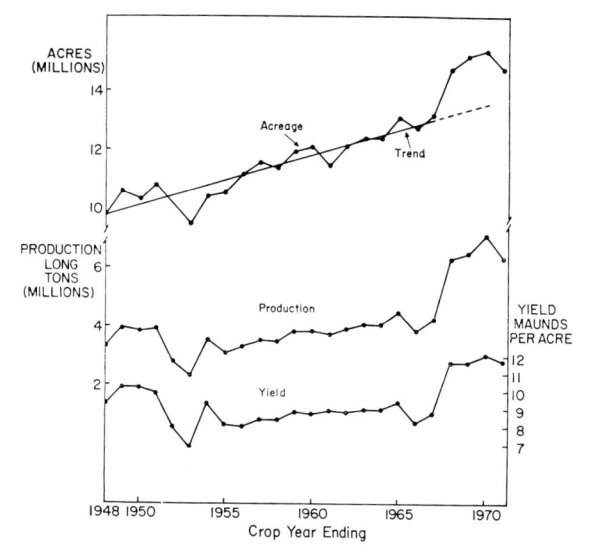

Fig. 6.2. Acreage, production, and yield of wheat in Pakistan, showing changes, 1948–71. 1 long ton = 1.016 metric tons; 1 maund of wheat = 82.29 lb or 37.32 kg; 10 maunds of wheat per acre = 13.7 bu/acre or 922 kg/ha.

cantly exceeding the figure forecast by the trend. The area under dwarf wheat jumped in 1967–68 from 256,000 to 2,365,000, or from 2 to 16% of the total (Table 6.1). Yields, which had averaged only a static 8.78 maunds per acre (809 kg/ha or 12 bu/acre) throughout the previous ten years, rose to an unprecedented 11.63 maunds (1,072 kg/ha or 16 bu/acre) average.

TRADITION AND CHANGE IN FARMING IN SAHIWAL DISTRICT. This section examines the technical, cultural, and institutional environment within which the rapid growth of cereal production oc-

TABLE 6.1. Dwarf wheat as a proportion of total wheat acreage, West Pakistan, 1965–70

Year	Total Acreage	Dwarf Acreage	Percent of Total
	(000)	*(000)*	*(%)*
1965–66	12,738	12	0.1
1966–67	13,738	250	1.9
1967–68	14,785	2,365	16.0
1968–69	15,221	5,892	38.7
1969–70[a]	15,393	7,129	46.3

Source: Directorate of Statistics, Agriculture Department, Government of West Pakistan (subsequently Government of Punjab).
[a] Second estimate.

curred. Traditional wheat cultivation practices are discussed, emphasizing the relationships between village social groups associated with this productive activity. A subset of irrigation and associated cultivation practices is examined in detail to emphasize the role played by risk aversion in traditional agriculture. This factor is an important influence on adoption of new technology, such as dwarf wheat. Finally, consideration is given to the use by farmers of two nontraditional inputs, tubewell water and chemical fertilizer.

Sahiwal District has served as a microcosm of the irrigated Punjab in many research studies, the present one included. Median farm size in the district is 6.5 acres (2.6 ha), usually in several fragments. Nearly all the cultivated land is irrigated, 75% of it from the canal network, 7% from Persian wells, and 15% from tubewells in 1966–67. In summer, cotton and rice are grown for cash; and maize (corn), sorghum, and millet are grown for food and animal fodder. In winter, physical conditions for the principal crop, wheat, are good with high amounts of solar radiation, low incidence of disease, and controlled water through irrigation. Wheat is grown on 80% of the farms, while clover, rape and mustard, tobacco, fodder mixtures, and vegetables are also part of the crop mix. Sugarcane occupies fields throughout the year, with planting in March and harvest from December through February.

Sahiwal is second only to Lyallpur among the districts of Pakistan when ranked in order of progressiveness. Yet Sahiwal retains a rural character. No major urban complex distorts the structure or functioning of the district's economy. Nor is it close enough to the research institute and the Agricultural University at Lyallpur to cause agricultural practices to be atypical. The district's farmers do show slightly higher fertilizer usage, more tubewells, and a somewhat higher cropping intensity than the national average, yet, in none of these facets could the district be faulted as nonrepresentative.

Traditional Cultivation Practices. Traditional wheat cultivation in Sahiwal District requires almost no purchased inputs and few tools that cannot be obtained in the village. It also involves a number of functional interrelationships between various groups of people—landowners, laborers and artisans, producers, and consumers—which reinforce the integration of the village.

Land is traditionally plowed with a bullock-drawn, iron-tipped wooden plow. After a number of plowings and smoothings with a plank, seed is broadcast before the final plowing and planking. This preparatory labor and sowing is usually done by family members. When extra help is needed it is usually obtained through labor-sharing arrangements with relatives. During the growing season, little attention is given the field except for weeding and irrigation, which also involves family labor. Women and children do the weeding in their spare time and use the weeds for livestock feed. Water inputs are so precious in most areas that their application can be entrusted only to a family member or permanent servant.

Farmers provide manure for their wheat fields if possible and save their own seed from year to year. Most of the tools needed throughout the season are obtained from carpenter and blacksmith families, who have often served the farmer's family for generations. Such inputs do not constitute "purchased inputs" in the normal sense. The artisan family provides a steady supply of services throughout the year in return for payments of grain after each harvest and other occasional considerations. The relationship between landowner and artisan is more that of patron-servant than customer-salesman.

Nonfamily labor is employed for the cutting and winnowing operations of harvest. Farmers often offer these jobs to their artisans who are incompletely employed or to certain other landless families. In compensation, one out of every twenty headloads is paid for cutting and one and one-half units of grain are paid for every forty units winnowed. The farmer's family normally threshes the grain by treading out the grain under the hooves of bullocks. A potter is often called upon to transport grain from the field to the village or to a market for which he receives payment in kind.

Hence, traditional wheat cultivation involves the farm family's own labor under the direct control of the farmer, blacksmiths, and carpenters under the traditional patron-servant relationship in which payments are more or less fixed as a function of acreage, and representatives of other, usually poorer, village groups who are employed for certain harvesting operations in return for a fixed percent of the crop paid in kind. A subsequent section will examine how these relationships have been strained by the new wheats.

Canal Water Development and Adaptations to Water Scarcity. Sahiwal District and most of the best agricultural areas of Pakistan today were settled and opened to farming as part of colonizing programs accompanying the construction of irrigation canals during British rule. Before the development of canal irrigation in the Punjab, an early British traveler described these now lush areas as a "vast desert, glistening with salt." Nomadic herders and a few tribal agriculturalists along the rivers were the only inhabitants. The first modern (inundation) canals for irrigation were begun in the late 1880s. These were followed with diversion dams that captured the waters of the five tributaries of the Indus River and turned them into an extensive system of perennial canals. Subsequent developments included link canals to better distribute river flows and storage reservoirs to capture some of the excess river flow in the summer. Today, Pakistan has nearly 25 million acres of irrigated crops, the world's largest irrigated agricultural area. The spread of the irrigation network permitted intensive farming and a dense settlement pattern. Much of rural Punjab life depends critically upon this irrigation system.

Local allocation of water is a village decision process. Enforcement of allocations is often given to the village religious leader since he is the one person who can be trusted by all when disputes over this most valuable resource develop. A farmer's rights to his turn at receiving water are among his most zealously guarded possessions. While irrigation turns are traded occasionally, sale of water rights separately from the land is prohibited. There is essentially no market and no price for exchanging water flow rights.

Several factors reduce the adequacy of the irrigation system. First, it was originally designed to provide supplemental water, not for the full requirements of farming. Second, the network was established at a time when cropping intensities, acreages planted, and human densities were much less than at present. Steady population growth has necessitated an intensification of agriculture with a consequent reduction in the adequacy of water flow in many areas. In addition, silting of minor distributaries and illegal altering of canal and take-out structure designs have altered the relative distributions so that villages at the end of a channel do not receive their proportional share.

Wheat farmers have made two adaptations to the scarcity of water. First, they save their own seed from year to year, presumably from the field that did the best in each year. During dry years in particular, seed can be selected only from varieties that produced. And given the uncertainty faced by most small farmers, they are moved to select seed that offers the promise of best resistance to drought should it happen again. Yet a seed that resists negative fluctuations in water availability may also be less responsive to positive fluctuations—increased applications—of water. The traditional farmer, facing an inadequate and often uncertain water supply, is likely to have sacrificed some productivity for increased certainty. Such a seed would have a fairly flat production response curve with respect to water in order to ensure that the curve does not drop too rapidly as water inputs are reduced. The native wheats being grown in 1965 had these characteristics as they were the result of many years of farmer selection. They were relatively drought resistant and were only marginally responsive to additional irrigation.

The second adaptation to the scarcity of water relates to the method of sowing. Three traditional methods are widely known: broadcasting, dribbling seed into the furrow behind the plow, and dribbling seed into a funnel tube behind the plow. The latter provides good control of seed depth and line sowing, the dribbled furrow gives some control of seed depth as well as crudely defined rows, while broadcasting followed by a plowing appears to control nothing. A widely known Punjabi saying definitely ranks the two line-sowing methods as better than broadcasting, the latter being designated as a beggar's method. Yet despite their familiarity with this piece of village wisdom, most farmers continue to broadcast seed.

The explanation again is probably one of gaining constancy by sacrificing a small amount of yield. Broadcasting followed by a single plowing distributes the seed fairly evenly over the field and throughout the top six inches of soil. Since the vagaries of temperature, rainfall, and soil structure may prevent seedling emergence from any one particular depth, the vertical dispersal achieved by this method increases the probability of achieving a uniform stand and satisfactory growth. The broadcasting of seed, therefore, appears to be another indigenous technique of reducing yield variability in an environment of incomplete water control, although at some possible reduction in yield.

Tubewell Water and Chemical Fertilizer. Given the reasonably good general infrastructure base and an extensive canal irrigation system, a set of nontraditional agricultural inputs was required by the wheat improvement program that would, when combined with existing resource conditions, constitute the new and highly productive wheat technology. The new inputs were tubewell irrigation water for improved water availability, chemical fertilizer, and the new high-yielding seeds. By 1965 farmers in Sahiwal District were already using some tubewell water and chemical fertilizer.

Tubewells had been used in the Punjab before the creation of Pakistan, but only in limited numbers. Nevertheless, their profitability became gradually established and since the early 1950s increasing numbers were installed. By 1961–62 there were 10,000. Twenty thousand were operating in 1963–64, implying that over one million acres in the Punjab were receiving supplemental water from this source. By 1967–68, over 50,000 had been installed when the annual rate exceeded 9,000 units.

Since water is a major limiting factor in Punjab's agriculture, farmers are exceptionally careful to allocate it to the most profitable use. This is particularly true of water from tubewells, the most expensive source. Before the advent of high-yielding wheat and rice, the cash crops of cotton, sugarcane, and tobacco were the principal recipients of supplemental tubewell water. Only when the new varieties became available could cereals compete economically for the use of tubewell water.

Chemical fertilizer had been introduced in small amounts in 1952. Expansion of fertilizer use can be separated into three periods, each of which was characterized by a different pattern of agricultural growth (Table 6.2).

This pattern of growth in fertilizer sales suggests that fertilizer application was concentrated on the highly remunerative cash crops until 1966–67, as was the case with tubewell water. The use of these resources on cash crops helps explain why the yields of these crops rose while cereal

TABLE 6.2. Three periods of expansion of chemical fertilizer use in West Pakistan

Period	Annual Growth Rate of Fertilizer Sales	Characteristics of Period
1953–54 to 1959–60	4.2%	Growth in agriculture limited largely to acreage expansion.
1959–60 to 1966–67	29.1%	Gradually increasing yields observed for cash crops (cotton, sugarcane, tobacco). Cereals production increases remain a function of acreage only.
1966–67 to 1968–69	46.8%	Dwarf wheat and rice plus improved maize spread. Yields rise rapidly for cereals while cash crops continue steady yield increases.

Source: West Pakistan Agricultural Development Corporation, "The Demand for Fertilizer in West Pakistan," Lahore, Dec. 1968.

yields remained stagnant. With the advent of Mexican wheats and dwarf rice varieties, the cereals were able to return marginal value products to chemical nutrients and water that at least equaled and often exceeded those available from the cash crops. Large-scale application of water and fertilizer to cereals followed, with predictable impact on yields. If the government had not increased the fertilizer supplies enough to meet this new demand, it is likely that cash crop yields would have declined as inputs were bid away from them.

In summary, dwarf wheats were inserted into a rural environment that included a fairly well-developed infrastructure and farming experience with two nontraditional inputs, tubewell water and chemical fertilizer. The addition of cereal varieties with dramatic productive responses completed a technological package of sufficiently high profit potential to elicit eager farmer adoption. Once adopted, this technology placed wheat production on a different production function—one with higher response coefficients and a much higher total potential. Subsequent sections of this chapter examine the dwarf wheat adoption patterns, the economics of the new technology at the micro level, and the types of adjustments made by farm operators.

HIGH-YIELDING WHEAT ADOPTION PATTERNS. The strategy of the introduction process in the accelerated wheat improvement program and the difference in the economic characteristics of small and large farms influenced wheat adoption patterns. The accelerated wheat improvement program strategy sought farm operators as the initial recipients of the dwarf wheat. The farmers who became cooperators usually had larger acreages and had demonstrated competence in wheat production. These men faced few constraints in their farming operations. They were better able to obtain adequate quantities of inputs and to control timing and method of application than the average size farmers. As cooperators they received detailed technical consultation, thereby removing some of the risks of innovation. Since they were able to provide optimum complementary inputs and apply them as recommended, these farmers were capable of realizing the optimum yield potential of dwarf wheats, thus heightening the expected profitability of switching varieties. Furthermore, as large, reputable farmers, these men were better educated and more experienced and presumably could perceive and respond to smaller profit margins than others.

Consequently, the first growers of dwarf wheat were eager adopters who readily planted as much seed as they could obtain. During the first year, low seed rates were recommended to enhance multiplication. The practice continued a second year as farmers sought to spread limited seed over the maximum feasible acreage. In their view, seed supply was the effective constraint and dwarf wheat seed commanded premium prices of as much as 100 rupees per maund compared to 20 rupees ($3.06 per bushel or $0.11 per kilogram) for other types. Thus, because of the way the program was implemented, through large farmers many of the difficulties and delays usually postulated for innovators by communication theorists were easily overcome.

Data show that smaller farmers usually obtained the dwarf seed one season later. In 1966–67, only 250,000 acres of dwarf wheat were planted and the ability of the larger farmers to command scarce resources was evident in its distribution (Table 6.3). These surveys show that innovators in each size grouping committed about one-third of their acreage during their first trial. Those who adopted the following year started with a larger commitment and moved more rapidly toward complete adoption. Observation of others' experiences substituted in part for personal experimentation in removing the uncertainty surrounding the adoption decision.

The smaller farmers had economic characteristics leading to somewhat different approaches to adoption. Risk and uncertainties appear to be of dominant concern, especially where the family food supply was concerned. To commit wheat acreage to an untried and more expensive technology when those same acres must dependably produce a given

TABLE 6.3. Percentages of total wheat acreage committed to dwarf wheat in West Pakistan, 1966–68: Two field surveys

	1966–67	1967–68	1968–68
Large Farmers[a]			
First planted in 1966	34	65	92
First planted in 1967	...	40	84
Smaller Farmers[b]			
First planted in 1967	...	32	74
First planted in 1968	...	...	56

[a] Mostly village leaders and cooperators with Accelerated Wheat Improvement Program.

[b] One-quarter of sample farmed 25 acres (10.1 ha) or more and three-quarters farmed less than 25 acres.

TABLE 6.4. Changes in acreage by wheat type, West Pakistan, 1965-70

Year	Acreage (000) Total wheat	Dwarf wheat	Native wheat
1965-66 (base)	12,738	12	12,726
1966-67	+454	+238	+216
1967-68	+1,593	+2,115	−522
1968-69	+436	+3,527	−3,091
1969-70	−257	+1,237	−1,494

Source: Government of West Pakistan.

amount of one's dietary staple is a decision not lightly taken. Furthermore, the bulk of the rural sector had a tendency to discount the claims of government and outsiders. The only really valid experience is felt to be one's own or that of a trusted villager.

Official data provide evidence for this hypothesis that a secure foodgrain supply is an important farm management goal. In 1966-67 native wheat acreage expanded by 216,000 acres, a figure consistent with the annual trend value for native wheat in Figure 6.2. Dwarf wheat acreage expanded by an additional 238,000 acres (Table 6.4). The fact that there was no interruption of the trend in native varieties even though additional acreages were planted with new seed suggests that total acreage was expanded to allow for experimentation.

The following year, dwarf wheat area increased by more than two million acres, yet only 500,000 acres of this displaced native wheat. Some substitution was occurring, but three-quarters of the new dwarf wheat was being grown on the increment by which acreage had been expanded.

With the crop planted in 1968, large-scale substitution began to occur. Eighty-eight percent of the extra dwarf wheat planted that season replaced traditional varieties. Some farmers began to contract their acreage as they no longer needed to plant extra ground for experimentation. Many farmers shifted completely to the new dwarfs; others, having tried them unsuccessfully, returned to the old wheats. This process of consolidation brought a reduction in total wheat acreage in 1969-70. Acreage remained relatively stable at approximately the 1969-70 level in the following two crop years. The trend factor of 175,000 acres annually would have suggested a 1970-71 area of 13.9 million acres, although confidence limits are wide for an extrapolation four years beyond the base data series. Actual acreage remains 1 million acres in excess of this level indicating that, for many farmers, the new wheats were profitable enough to justify a permanently increased acreage and production for the market in addition to home consumption requirements.

FARM RESOURCE ADJUSTMENTS. The introduction of a new, more productive technology in any production process changes the profitability of associated inputs. Thus additional profits can often be obtained by adding more of the same inputs. In the case of the new, more highly productive dwarf wheats, additional returns to farmers could be expected by adding more fertilizer and water. A major economic question was, therefore, how much additional fertilizer and water should be used with the new wheats to obtain the greatest net income from the acres the farmer has devoted to wheat. This was an important question not only for the indivdual farmer but also for various units of government. The extension service must know what levels of fertilizer and water use to recommend to farmers. The planning department must know the most profitable levels of fertilizer and water use with the new varieties so it can estimate the increases in fertilizer and water supplies needed for the years ahead. Critical associated issues are the amount of fertilizer and pump parts that must be imported and the rate of expansion required of the domestic fertilizer industry. In the next section, focus will be placed on estimating the changes in fertilizer and water use at the farm level that are profitable with the introduction of dwarf wheats in Pakistan.

Adjusting Nitrogen Fertilizer Levels for More Profit. Production economics theory shows that maximum net income to farmers is obtained when the returns obtained from adding another unit of an input are equal to the cost of that unit of input. Applying this theory to the use of fertilizer on wheat in Pakistan's Sahiwal District, a number of researchable questions can be asked. Do farmers producing traditional wheat varieties appear to have adjusted their use of fertilizer to the most profitable levels on the basis of their past experience as hypothesized by Schultz [6]? Have farmers using the new wheats increased their levels of fertilizer use as predicted by production economics theory in order to increase their net income? And, have farmers using the new varieties already reached the highest profit levels of fertilizer use or can they be expected to increase the amount of fertilizer used per acre as they become convinced additional profits may be obtained by further increases?

In 1968 in Pakistan, little information was available to answer these questions. It was known that the dwarf wheat plant types were designed to respond to heavy fertilization. While farmers using traditional varieties usually applied 30 pounds of nitrogen per acre (34 kg/ha), Mexipak dwarf wheat was being tested and selected with nitrogen levels as high as 200 pounds per acre (224 kg/ha). When this variety was released, the accompanying fertilizer recommendation called for 100 pounds per acre (112 kg/ha) of nitrogen and 50 pounds per acre (56 kg/ha) of phosphate. Farmers did find fertilizing Mexipak to be very profitable and expanded their purchases of chemical nutrients. Although nitrogen fertilization of wheat had been studied frequently in Pakistan, most, if not all, of these studies provided only average productivity estimates, with little information on the marginal productivity of fertilizer use. Thus it was not possible to tell whether farmers were currently using optimum amounts of fertilizer and whether they could be expected to increase fertilizer use.

Research was, therefore, undertaken to provide empirical data to help answer the questions posed above. The methodology chosen was to estimate a Cobb-Douglas production function of the form:

$$Y = aX_1^{b_1} X_2^{b_2} \ldots X_n^{b_n}$$

where wheat yield was the dependent variable (Y) and the independent variables (X_i) were bullock-pair-hours of preparatory tillage, seed rate, pounds of nitrogen, pounds of phosphate, number of irrigations, and pounds of farmyard manure. Separate production functions were estimated for dwarf and traditional wheat. Observations were taken from 66 farmers in Sahiwal District who were growing both wheat types in the winter and spring of 1969. Input levels and cultural practices were recorded throughout the season and yields were obtained from sample fields after harvest. Management of the fields and the farm enterprise was left completely to the farmers. The choice of input level and application technique was theirs.

The Cobb-Douglas production functions estimated from the farm survey data provided detailed empirical evidence of the dramatically higher productivity of the Mexican wheats and their much greater response to fertilization on farmers' fields. The calculated marginal physical product curve indicates that, throughout the range of fertilizer application used by farmers on the 1969 wheat crop, the Mexican wheat consistently produced about three times as much additional wheat as the native varieties (i.e., at 40 pounds of nitrogen per acre, the marginal product was 0.051 maunds of wheat for the Mexican varieties as compared with 0.015 for the native varieties) (Fig. 6.3).

The farm survey data substantiated the estimates of the average productivity of nitrogen used by specialists in the accelerated wheat improvement program and by government officials for the food self-sufficiency program. The average grain-nutrient response ratios used for planning purposes were 16:1 for dwarf wheats and 8:1 for native wheats. Similar grain-nutrient response ratios of 17.0:1 and 2.3:1, respectively, were obtained from the production function analysis by setting all inputs at the geometric mean of the observations (Table 6.5). Thus the farm survey research verified the average production response data that have been used in national planning.

The marginal product of nitrogen at the arithmetic average appli-

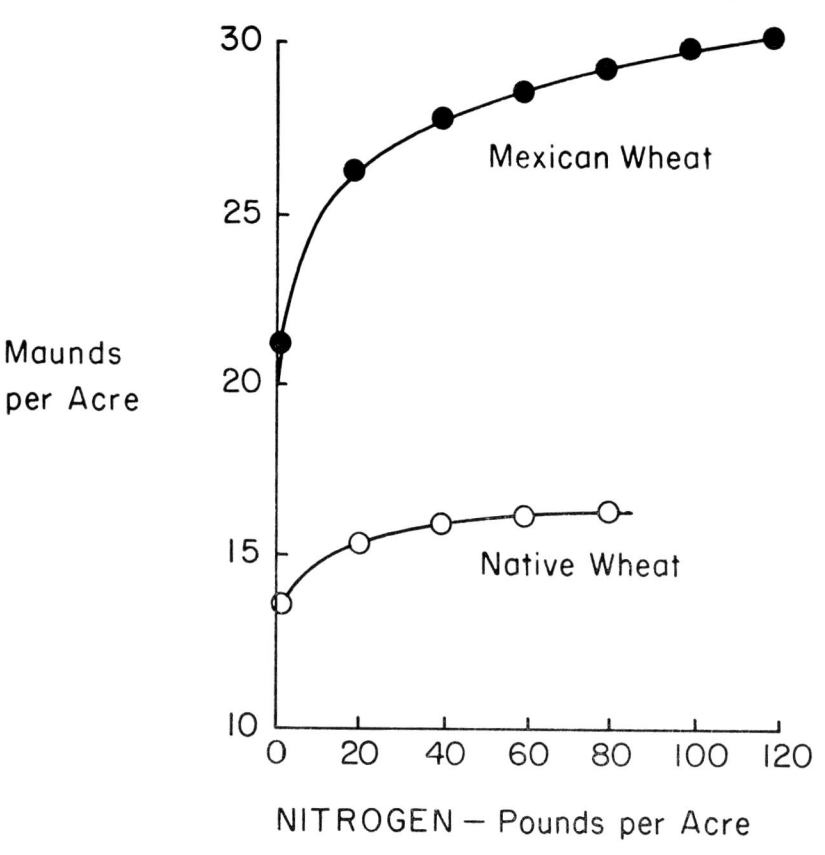

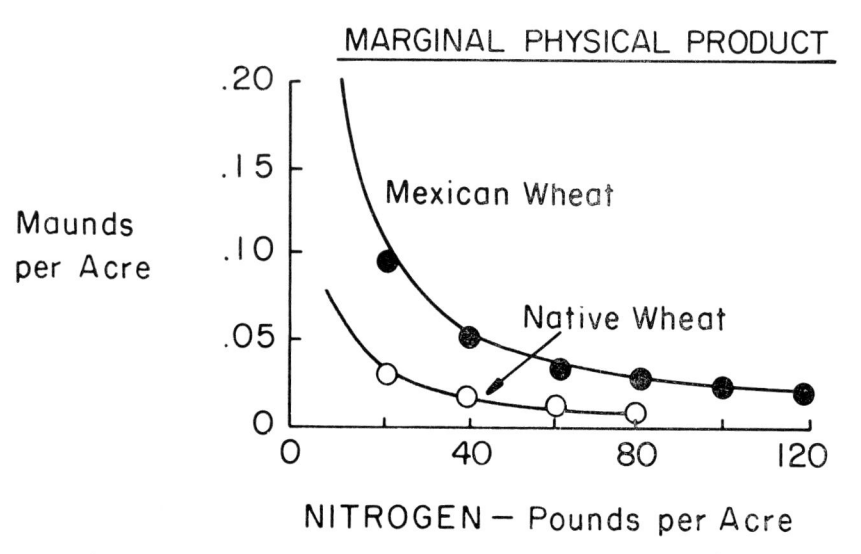

Fig. 6.3. The response of native and Mexican wheat to nitrogen fertilizer, Sahiwal District, Punjab, Pakistan, 1969.

TABLE 6.5. The average and marginal physical products of nitrogen fertilizer on native and dwarf wheat, farm survey, Sahiwal District, Pakistan, 1968–69

	Arithmetic Average Nitrogen Application	Grain Produced per Pound of Nitrogen Fertilizer Average	Marginal
	(lb of N per acre)	(lb)	(lb)
Dwarf	49.5	17.0	5.8
Native	36.8	8.3	3.3

cation of nitrogen was estimated in this analysis at 3.3 pounds of grain for the native varieties and 5.8 for the dwarf varieties (Table 6.5). Three significant points are indicated by this table. First, the arithmetic mean of the observed nitrogen applications on native wheat was 36.8 pounds per acre (41.3 kg/ha), very near the conventional recommendation of 30 pounds. Second, the fact that the arithmetic average application of nitrogen on dwarf wheats (49.5 pounds) was about 12 pounds greater than on native wheats indicated that farmers had begun to adjust their fertilizer practices so that more fertilizer was used on the more responsive dwarf wheats. However, the data also point out that, at the rates of nitrogen application farmers were using, the marginal productivity of nitrogen fertilizer was still almost twice as great on the dwarf varieties as on the native varieties. Thus these farmers had a considerable distance to go in adjusting their levels of input use for highest profit (i.e., when the marginal products of all resources in all uses are equal).

A more detailed test was undertaken to determine whether farmers using native varieties and other traditional technology had achieved an equilibrium or maximum profit position in the use of nitrogen fertilizer. In such a production function test, the marginal value product (MVP) of nitrogen is obtained by multiplying the additional amount of wheat obtained from the unit of nitrogen by the price of wheat for comparison with the cost of the unit of nitrogen. If the MVP of nitrogen is approximately equal to its costs, farmers could be said to have adjusted to economically optimum levels of nitrogen application. Due to more desirable eating qualities, native wheats were valued at 17 rupees per maund ($95.60 per metric ton or $2.60 per bushel) while Mexipak prices were 16 rupees per maund. These were the price expectations at planting time in November 1968.

The estimated MVP obtained by farmers with native wheats was 0.68 rupee (Table 6.6). Note that the MVP was estimated at the calculated geometric mean pounds of fertilizer applied (14.5 pounds). This corresponds to the observed arithmetic mean of 36.8 pounds of nitrogen applied on native wheat on the sample farms. Government had been attempting to standardize the cost of a pound of nitrogen at 0.50 rupee ($0.10 per pound or $0.23 per kg) but had been unsuccessful in the face of shortages. A black market flourished. Most farmers paid 0.32 rupee

TABLE 6.6. The marginal value product of nitrogen fertilization at different levels of fertilizer use and wheat prices, 1969, Sahiwal District, Pakistan (rupees)

Pounds of Nitrogen Applied per Acre	Mexican Wheat Rs 14.00/maund	Rs 16.00/maund	Native Wheat Rs 17.00/maund
10	Rs 2.58	Rs 2.94	Rs 0.97
14.5[a] (native)	...	...	0.68
20	1.36	1.55	0.49
28.4[a] (Mexican)	0.98	1.12	...
30	0.92	1.06	0.32
40	0.71	0.82	0.26
50	0.57	0.66	...
60	0.49	0.56	0.17
70	0.42	0.48	0.15
80	0.38	0.43	0.14
90	0.34	0.38	...
100	0.31	0.35	...
110	0.28	0.32	...
120	0.25	0.29	...

[a] The level of nitrogen application when all inputs are set constant at their geometric means for native and Mexican wheats.

for a bag of urea officially priced at 0.26 rupee. At this price 1 pound of elemental nitrogen cost 0.62 rupee. In addition, a small cost, estimated at not more than 0.02 to 0.05 rupee per pound, was involved in transportation between retail outlet and the farm, bringing the cost delivered to the farm up to between 0.64 and 0.66 rupee.

One may conclude therefore that, in the survey year, Punjabi farmers had equated marginal factor cost (MFC) with MVP when applying nitrogen to native wheat. Chemical fertilizers and the traditional varieties had both been available since 1953, so repeated personal experimentation had given farmers a definition of their high profit point using the combination of the two.

Farmers who adopted new seed and retained the traditional fertilization levels would have had an MVP of nitrogen in excess of 1.55 rupees, considerably greater than the cost of nitrogen. The rational response was to increase fertilizer applications, driving down the marginal value of nitrogen. As large numbers of farmers responded in this way, the price of nitrogen was bid up until a new equilibrium was established.

Due to a decline in the expected price of dwarf wheat during the 1968–69 growing season, an additional question arose as to whether farmers had overfertilized. Sample farmers had applied an arithmetic mean of nearly 50 pounds of nitrogen per acre on Mexipak in the 1968–69 wheat season. In the production function analysis, with an expected price of 16 rupees per maund, the estimated MVP of wheat was 1.12 rupees (Table 6.6). By the time of sale the price of Mexican wheat had declined to 14 rupees, however, providing an MVP of only 0.98 rupee. Nevertheless this was still much greater than the estimated cost of nitrogen at the farm (0.64 to 0.66 rupee), indicating that farmers could have profited by increasing their levels of nitrogen application even though the price of wheat had declined.

The process of striking a new equilibrium through a series of gradual approximations can be viewed in the context of risk aversion. When a near-subsistence farmer seeks to minimize risks, one method he uses is to discount the reported yield productivity of a new, untried technique. Instead of accepting the reported yield of which he is unsure, he plans his operations on the assumption he will have a somewhat lower yield but that it will be a level he is reasonably sure can be achieved. The discounted marginal product reduces expected profits in proportion, and the farm manager makes a smaller investment in inputs as a result. With each successive crop, experience is gained and the actual production function for the technology can be defined with greater certainty. Risk discounting diminishes as knowledge accumulates and farmers increase their utilization of the technique until they have struck a new equilibrium position. Apparently in 1968–69, farm managers were discounting the reported fertilizer responsiveness of Mexipak by about one-third.

The overall effect of farmers' adjustments in the use of nitrogen with the new dwarf wheat varieties has been to greatly increase the demand for nitrogen. The spread of dwarf wheat to over three-fourths of the irrigated wheat acreage has been associated with higher levels of fertilizer use per acre. It also appears from the preceding analysis that farmers were likely to continue to move to higher levels of nitrogen fertilization as they recognized that the marginal returns to wheat fertilization were, in many cases, still much greater than the cost of fertilizer. After some years of experimentation, if no new varieties come along, farmers might define a new fertilizer use equilibrium level at substantially higher nitrogen input levels than used in 1969.

Water Use Adjustments. Regression coefficients were estimated for irrigation water applied to native and Mexican wheat fields. Since data were solicited from farmers who kept no records, the only usable unit of measure was the number of irrigations. An "irrigation" constituted one wetting of the field regardless of the actual acre-inches of water applied, percolation rate, or water-holding capacity of the soil. It is assumed these uncontrolled factors were randomly distributed.

No significant response to irrigation was measured for native wheats within the range of observed treatments. In contrast, dwarf wheat was highly responsive to water applications. The difference reflects the different purposes and goals under which the two types were developed as well as twenty years of farmer reselection of native varieties in an uncertain and inadequately irrigated environment. Indigenous strains were developed on the subcontinent with the goal of widespread adaptability to the region's often underirrigated or rainfed land. Dwarf wheats were bred and selected under more adequate moisture conditions with the goal of maximum responsiveness to inputs, particularly fertilizer. It was hypothesized above that the practice of saving one's own seed when water inputs are inadequately controlled eventually selects a variety that does not reflect moisture variations but instead provides a stable food supply, albeit at low yield levels. The absence of a significant coefficient relating indigenous wheat yields and water inputs is evidence that productivity has been sacrificed to increase the certainty of food supplies. Beyond some minimum level, which was surpassed by most farmers in the sample, native wheats are essentially unresponsive to additional irrigations.

Farmers sampled in 1968–69 averaged 6.5 and 7.5 irrigations, respectively, on native and dwarf varieties—averages that differed from each other at the 99% level of significance. At this level dwarf wheat gave a marginal product of 1.52 maunds per acre (140 kg/ha) the value of which was 21.28 rupees ($4.47 per acre of $9.86 per ha) with wheat priced at 14 rupees per maund.

Under the present pricing system, farmers pay a flat fee for each acre they irrigate from the canal system. The amount varies by crop and assessment district, but it is assessed to each acre receiving canal water, even if irrigated only once. This becomes, in effect, a fixed cost: 16 rupees per wheat acre in the sample area. The farmer may use as much additional water during the season as he can get at a marginal cost of zero per irrigation except for a small imputed cost for family labor used during application.

In view of the calculated MVP of water, it is not surprising that demand far exceeds supply and that tightly controlled rotation systems are needed to distribute water among village farmers. The water received by a given farmer can vary due to several causes, most important of which are the variable adequacy of the distributary for the village(s) served and the possibility of a temporary canal closure occurring during a particular individual's rotation turn. Farmers infrequently received as many as 7 or 8 irrigations for a given field, almost never 10. Since the recorded mean number of applications was 7.5 and observations ranged from 2 to 14, most farmers must turn to other sources, primarily tubewells, for supplementary water.

Purchasing tubewell water from neighbors is an increasingly common practice in Punjab. It is the primary mechanism by which small farmers benefit from this indivisible technology. Common practice is to sell this water by the hour of pump operation. Prices charged and the number of hours needed to irrigate an acre vary, however; the respondents identified an average cost of 10.08 rupees per acre of irrigation. For those few who have only a Persian well for supplemental water, the cost can be estimated at 15.60 rupees per acre of irrigation. (To irrigate one acre with a Persian well requires four pairs of bullocks working twenty-four hours in three-hour shifts. The approximate daily cost of a pair of bullocks is 3.90 rupees.)

At the mean input level, an actual estimated MVP of 21.28 rupees for dwarf wheat compares with marginal costs of nearly zero for canal water, 10.08 rupees for tubewell water, and 15.60 rupees for Persian well water. In all cases there is a strong incentive to expand production through increased water use. One could expect farmers to expand their use of supplemental water until MVP declined to equal cost or until supply limitations arose. Within a limited total supply, water will be reallocated away from unresponsive native wheats toward dwarf wheats where it returns a higher product.

EXPANDING IMPACT OF DWARF WHEAT. The preceding sections examined some of the more significant adjustments made by farm managers as they sought to define new equilibria incorporating dwarf wheat and its associated production techniques. Water and fertilizer, the two inputs whose productivities were most significantly improved by the new seeds, incurred the largest adjustments. These individual changes, aggregated over several million adopters, created disequilibrium situations at several points within the agricultural sector. The speed with which farmers adopted and adjusted to the new technology exacerbated the urgency for adjustments in factor and product markets and in price and procurement policy. The dwarf wheats also were beginning to have an impact on traditional village relationships.

Fertilizer Supply and Pricing Adjustments. To popularize fertilization, the government subsidized the cost of nutrients at the primary distributor levels. Actual subsidy levels varied widely among the different types and sources of fertilizer, with the highest rates applying to ammonium sulfate produced domestically in obsolete plants. Variable subsidies allowed the government to standardize the price of a given nutrient regardless of source, thereby removing one source of confusion for the farmer.

In 1966–67 and 1967–68, the overall fertilizer program included government payment of 34% of the wholesale price. A 46% annual growth rate in nutrient usage had not been anticipated and the government soon found itself unable to maintain its level of subsidy. Preliminary estimates indicated that retaining a 34% subsidy in 1968–69 would have cost nearly 150 million rupees, a total deemed unsupportable. Retail prices were raised accordingly and the final fertilizer program contained a 24% subsidy. Again the bulk of the subsidy went to support inefficient domestic plants using older technology. The prospects of further growth sharply focused planners' attention on the fertilizer supply picture. Among the resultant decisions was a program to expand the capacity and lower costs of the old plants and a decision to authorize construction of a third complex using the latest technology to produce nitrogenous fertilizer. Meanwhile, subsidy payments have been further reduced without further price rises simply because the first two modern urea plants had come into production, replacing imported supplies. These plants are now providing the bulk of the total supply at a cost that does not need subsidization.

Indigenous wheat varieties taxed the soil much less than the new seeds replacing them. Under these less exhausting conditions, some nutrients probably became available in the soil more rapidly than cropping with native wheats removed them. When dwarf wheats arrived, the soil into which they went contained an abundance of several elements including, particularly, phosphates. Their response to nitrogen was thus enhanced by ample supplies of complementary nutrients and a doubling or tripling of yields occurred initially. But farmers fertilized with nitrogen alone. As some of the other nutrients became exhausted, dwarf wheats were increasingly constrained to levels of production that could be supported by the natural annual release of these nutrients. Plants became less able to respond to additions of chemical nitrogen. Crop yields and the apparent nitrogen response declined, contributing to a belief that the seed was deteriorating genetically.

What has emerged from this experience is a strong need for a broader understanding among farmers of plant-soil relationships from which they can implement a more balanced fertilization program. Such understanding will not easily be achieved by farmers who have little or no education, who keep no farm records, and who are basically illiterate. Second-order effects of dwarf wheats will be felt then in the need for more effective extension and soil-testing services. It is also possible, based on earlier response curves, that Pakistan may be producing an unbalanced fertilizer mix relative to crop requirements. Hence a phosphate plant may now be needed.

Changes in Marketing Institutions and Goals. One of the aggregate impacts of the wheat program stemmed from the sheer volume of additional production coming into the market. Severe strains were placed on marketing, handling, and storage mechanisms throughout the irrigated areas. To make their support price effective to all farmers, the government more than doubled the number of procurement points from 184 to 415. These additional outlets, plus some relaxation of delivery requirements, permitted a great many farmers to sell to the government rather than to the traditional commission agents in the produce markets. Commission agents perform the service of selling the farmer's grain for him. They often extend him fertilizer and other inputs on credit and require repayment in grain at harvest. Government procurement rose from nearly zero to over 30% of the marketed crop.

Farmers, through increased marketings, were accumulating additional cash resources and lessening their dependence on commission agents as a source of credit. Both factors contributed to a reduction in demand for commission agents' services, placing them in a more competitive situation. The practice of discounting the price of farmers' produce below official levels abated; input prices were also reduced, particularly as a small price war arose among fertilizer dealers and in other, more subtle ways among commission agents who offered additional services and considerations to retain their clientele. The trend was enhanced by the government's decision, taken in conjunction with the wheat program, to expand private sector involvement in agribusiness, particularly input supply.

One must conclude that in several ways the wheat program contributed to a noticeable decline in the commission agent's authority over the farm sector. The volumes of additional grain entering the system forced an increased pluralism in the produce markets, subsequently leading to increased competition among market firms and somewhat better terms of trade for farmers. Moreover, the change appears to be permanent and to have brought the country closer to having the type of commercially oriented market necessary to sustain a vigorous commercial agriculture.

Within a few years Pakistan moved rapidly from a deficit food-grain position to near self-sufficiency, well before the full potential of the new cereals had been exploited. Faced with limits to domestic consumption, the country's planners in 1969 had already begun to contemplate wheat exports. Several possibilities were considered, including barter and commercial sales by government directly, the use of the services of an international marketing firm under contract to the government, and finally by relaxing the restrictions on private sector trade in grain. The problem was complicated by the fact that until the secession of Bangladesh, Pakistan was receiving large quantities of PL 480 grains for that region and was thus prohibited by treaty from exporting grain. Nevertheless, planners believed they foresaw self-sufficiency throughout the country and hoped that by developing an export outlet they could continue to use the productive potential of dwarf wheat to further fuel agricultural and national growth.

Expert consultant assistance was sought for research into this question. The resulting analysis showed that many factors stood as obstacles, making it difficult, perhaps impossible, for Pakistan to enter the world market in any substantial way [4]. The Mexican dwarf wheat does not command a premium in world trade but is the type most often traded as feed wheat. Production, harvest, and handling practices in Pakistan result in a product that does not meet any but the lowest of the internationally traded grades. Admixtures of various types of dirt, trash, shriveled and broken grains, barley, and other impurities normally result from traditional practices. While acceptable in the local market, these factors effectively prohibit sales abroad. Many of these impurities, once mixed in, are impossible to remove. An additional factor cited was Pakistan's inexperience in cereal exporting. All the country's institutions and facilities were designed to move grain from foreign sources to domestic consumers rather than from local producers to foreign markets. For Pakistan to gain the necessary experience to compete effectively, when it must start with an inferior product in a market that has been dominated by five major exporting nations for decades, appeared next to impossible.

The government accepted the reality of these facts and abandoned its plans to become a wheat exporter. As the Fourth Five-Year Plan was finalized, it contained a revised role for wheat production in the nation's economy. Production targets were set equal to projected national consumption requirements, an approximate growth rate of 5% per annum, with only a small amount used to build a foodgrain reserve. Under these plans, dwarf wheat would allow farmers to produce their families' requirements on fewer acres, permitting more cash crops on the acres released. But total contribution of wheat to gross national product and to the income of the larger, commercial wheat producers was constrained by the extent of internal demand.

Impact on Traditional Village Relationships. One area of change in traditional village relationships induced by the rapid acceptance of dwarf wheat was evident in landlord-tenant relationships. New profit opportunities stirred the interest of the landlords in farming. Furthermore, being one of the early cultivators and growing the crop well became a prestige accomplishment, something highly valued in a prestige-conscious society. Many large farmers began to take a much more direct interest in the management of their fields. In some cases absentee landowners moved back to their farms, investing their managerial talents in agriculture while lessening their involvement in urban pursuits. At least one subtle change in the existing laws was also effected so that tenants could be more easily dismissed from their tenure holdings. Widespread eviction did not occur, however, since social and economic pressures internal to the village tended to reinforce traditional rights and obligations. My extensive visits to villages throughout Punjab in 1968 and 1969 showed only a few landlords attempting overt eviction as a direct result of dwarf wheat technology and in most instances their attempts resulted in prolonged litigation.

A sense of uneasiness among tenants developed, however, which erupted in violence in a few localities. With the inauguration of a new elected government in 1972, the tenancy laws were changed, making tenure more permanent and requiring the landlords to contribute a greater share of farm expenses.[4]

A second area of change resulted in an increased demand for the services of artisans and implement makers serving wheat producers. Many farmers remained traditional in their cultural practices and once their acreage adjustment ceased, their demands for more tools and implements reached a new static equilibrium. Others, however, did commercialize their wheat production activities, relying increasingly on purchased inputs. To the extent that they were now dealing in cash rather than kind, they gained flexibility with respect to where, what, and from whom they bought. Many of them were finding urban-produced goods preferable to village manufactured implements and they spent their money in market towns. Those who did change their cultural practices often adopted a nontraditional tool available only from an urban workshop. Hence, dwarf wheat, by further monetization and by making nontraditional implements and machines profitable, enhanced the trend away from those artisans and craftspersons whose services are related directly to acreage planted. Thus blacksmiths and carpenters, although presently the most prosperous artisans, face an uncertain future. By raising incomes in the village generally, dwarf wheats have resulted in a counterbalancing increase in demand for many things such as consumer items and education. If these goods and services can provide employment for blacksmiths, carpenters, and other village artisans, they can continue to benefit as long as dwarf wheats fuel village economic growth.

Expenditure on transportation, however, shows the highest income elasticity of any type of expenditure by villagers in the Indian subcontinent [7]. Rising incomes will result in a more mobile rural population who will gain access to several nonvillage markets.

The net balance of these forces is unclear. It does seem they will result eventually in an end to the traditional artisan-landlord patronage relationship. It is clear that the process has been accelerated by dwarf wheat.

In another area, landless day laborers often find seasonal agricultural employment in the harvest operations of cutting and winnowing. Payment has traditionally been in kind and on the basis of the amount of grain processed. When it became evident that vastly greater grain quantities would result from the new varieties, some employers attempted to switch to cash payment on an acreage basis in an apparent attempt to keep their wage payments from rising in proportion to yields. Again village social pressures generally succeeded in preventing such a change and most landless laborers found increased employment and income at least during wheat harvest. Both acreage and yield increases resulting from dwarf wheat were initially reflected in the employment of agricultural day laborers. To the extent that these wheats elicit investment in supplementary water, which in turn increases cropping intensity, demand for day labor expanded even further. This is particularly true if multiple cropping leads to a product mix that includes the more labor-intensive fruits, vegetables, and other commodities not easily mechanized.

With respect to mechanization, just as dwarf wheat increased the profitability of fertilizer and water, it also increased the incentive to mechanize certain operations. The economics of mechanical threshing are a function of volume. A given tonnage must be processed each year if the thresher is to be more profitable than traditional bullock-treading methods. Dwarf wheat meant that mechanical threshing could be more profitable for smaller farmers than before. As farmers learn optimum timing and quantities of inputs to combine with the seed, yields will increase further so the farm size needed to justify a mechanical thresher will decline.

In Pakistan's Punjab, where cotton and rice harvests overlap with the wheat harvest, time occasionally serves as a constraint to the amount of wheat planted. To the extent that mechanized tillage and sowing can speed the process, additional acres can be planted. Since land preparation and planting of wheat usually involve only family labor, there is little danger of labor displacement if these operations are mechanized. And additional acreage is likely to employ more labor to complete the harvesting activities—at least initially. The mechanizing of the planting operations may eventually raise production enough to lead to mechanizing harvest activities as well, with some labor displacement in the process.

Our quantitative understanding of the labor dynamics of Punjab farming is not sufficiently well developed to predict the ongoing balance between mechanization and farm employment. One can say only that many of the traditional employer-employee relationships have been strained as the result of the introduction of new wheat varieties and also that labor use by farms as well as the distribution of rural incomes, labor migration, and many other aspects related to rural employment will be adjusting to the new technology and its broader implications for some time to come.

Pakistan's wheat producers are not merely moving from one static equilibrium to another; a more fundamental change is taking place. They are departing from traditional modes of cultivation that were not truly static but did emphasize stability and security and evolved only very slowly. In their place they are adopting techniques more closely linked to many dynamic forces, both rural and urban, agricultural and industrial. Since it is improbable that all these forces will come to a final, unchanging position, it is unrealistic to expect agriculture to ever achieve even the near-equilibrium adjustment it obtained traditionally. Instead, Pakistan's farmers are rapidly entering a highly dynamic environment characterized by continual resource adjustment and requiring sophisticated enterprise management—in short, modern agriculture.

NOTES

1. Since 1972, the word "Pakistan" applies to the area formerly called West Pakistan of the larger nation of the years 1947–71. The former East Pakistan became Bangladesh in Dec. 1971. The term West Pakistan is used in this study when referring to material specifically related to the years 1947–71.

For readers unfamiliar with units of measure used in Pakistan the following table of conversion factors is provided. Some important conversions are also provided in the text.

Conversion Factors

1 pound (lb) = 0.454 kilograms (kg)
1 rupee (Rs) = $0.21 or Rs 4.76 = $1.00
1 maund = 37.33 kg
1 maund = 82.29 lb
1 long ton (2,240 lb) = 1.016 metric tons
1 acre (A) = 0.405 hectare (ha)

2. The equation is: $A = 9555 + 175\ T$ ($R^2 = 0.86$), where A = acres in thousands and T = the number of years elapsing since 1946–47.
3. Annual production increment from 175,000 additional acres at 700 pounds yield per acre. This is about equal to an annual consumption increment from 480,000 additional rural residents each year (a 3.0% growth rate) eating either 15 or 16 ounces of foodgrain daily, three-quarters of which is wheat [3].
4. Chief Martial Law Administrator, Martial Law Regulation No. 115, "Land Reforms Regulation, 1972," Government of Pakistan (Islamabad, 1972).

REFERENCES

1. Bean, Lee L., et al. *Population Projections for Pakistan, 1960–2000*. Monographs in Economics of Development, no. 17. Karachi: Pakistan Institute of Development Economics, 1968.
2. Eckert, Jerry B. "The Impact of Dwarf Wheats on Resource Productivity in West Pakistan's Punjab." Unpublished Ph.D. dissertation, Michigan State Univ., 1970.
3. Hufbauer, G. C. "Cereal Consumption, Production and Prices in West Pakistan." *The Pakistan Development Review* (Summer 1968).
4. Madill, J. W. "Wheat Marketing in Pakistan: An Appraisal of Prospects and Requirements." Islamabad: Ford Foundation, 1969 (Mimeographed).
5. Narvaez, Ignacio. "Accelerated Wheat Improvement Program in West Pakistan." Lahore: Ford Foundation, 1969 (Mimeographed).
6. Schultz, T. W. *Transforming Traditional Agriculture*. New Haven: Yale Univ. Press, 1964.
7. Simon, Sheldon R. In John W. Mellor et al., *Developing Rural India*. Ithaca: Cornell Univ. Press, 1968.

CHAPTER 7

A Venezuelan Agrarian Reform Settlement: Problems and Prospects

WILLIAM C. THIESENHUSEN

THE 1960s brought forth a deluge of polemic on the necessity for agrarian reform in Latin American countries. Unfortunately, there has been a less concerted effort to study what problems new landholders face and how they can be solved. How, in other words, may agrarian reform settlements become "going concerns"? This, I believe, must become a paramount research question in the years ahead.[1] This chapter does not address the debatable issue of "whether Venezuela, in fact, had an agrarian reform in the 1960s" or simply a series of colonization projects. It merely examines in some detail one settlement founded in the early 1960s. Using data gathered in mid-decade, it attempts to determine the difficulties and successes of the settlers. Colonists on the Leonardo Ruiz Pineda settlement (called Ruiz Pineda hereafter) experienced problems that are not unique. Their experience may be generalizable to other agrarian reform or colonization settlements.

WILLIAM C. THIESENHUSEN is Professor of Agricultural Economics and Agricultural Journalism, Land Tenure Center, University of Wisconsin, Madison. His research and teaching in Latin America commenced in 1963 in Chile and has included assignments in Latin America and Asia.
    Note: I would like to thank the Inter-American Committee for Agricultural Development for allowing me to use the data presented herein, which were originally gathered as part of its Venezuelan country study, and the Centro do Estudios del Desarrollo (CENDES) of the Central University of Caracas, the cosponsor. Assistance in the preparation of the first version was rendered by Dr. Luis Ratinoff, former international Codirector of the Venezuela project; Ing. Pompeyo Rios, Codirector; and Ing. Gustavo Pinto Cohen. Acknowledgements are also due to Mr. Lawrence Lynch of the University of Wisconsin, who assisted with much of the tabulation. Peter Dorner, Emily Haney, and Jose Martinez commented on earlier drafts of this study.
    I would also like to thank my collaborators in the first draft of this study, Ing. Ricardo Alezones, Dr. Ramon Pugh, and Dr. John Mathiason. Invaluable editorial help was rendered by Dr. Eric Schearer and Dr. Thomas Carroll, Inter-American Development Bank, and Ms. Jane Knowles, Land Tenure Center. I alone am responsible for errors.

BACKGROUND

Founding of the Settlement. The basis for the Venezuelan land reform was the settlement (or asentamiento) of farmers possessing few resources. The land reform in Venezuela had its political reasons—peasants who are given land tend to become government supporters. But the economic rationale was that peasants who are granted land are able to raise their incomes and general welfare by increasing their production. Some "group farming" agrarian reforms have been attempted in Latin America. In these, advances may be given to settlers so that they can live from day to day. Work is done in common, and field assignments are made by committee; profits at the end of the year are divided according to days worked or by some other convenient coefficient (see Chapter 8 on collective farming in Mexico). Some of these "production cooperatives" were established in Venezula, but this was not the postreform organization of the colony to be described here.

Ruiz Pineda was carved from 10,000 hectares (24,700 acres) of land belonging to the town (municipio) of Barbacoas. Barbacoas, the district seat of Urdaneta in the state of Aragua was a town with a population of 3,150 (1961 census). It is located at the gateway to the Llanos, a region in the "hot country" about 140 kilometers south of Caracas. The municipio acquired its property when, at the founding of the republic, title to Indian land passed to the government.

In 1960 the town ceded 8,000 hectares (19,760 acres) of this territory to the Instituto Agrario Nacional (IAN)—the principal agrarian reform agency of Venezuela—for a settlement that led to the founding of Ruiz Pineda. Unlike the situation in some other parts of the country, there was no real pressure for a settlement in this area of low population density. Indeed, at that time, the land was quite vacant; only 200 hectares (494 acres) had been deforested and worked by 30 farmers. Eight of the farmers were recent (early 1950s) Spanish immigrants from the Canary Islands (islenos) who were given temporary permission by the town council to farm an average of 10 hectares (24.7 acres) per family. Native Venezuelans (criollos) farmed the remaining 120 hectares (296.4 acres) as subsistence holdings, which averaged about 5 hectares (12.4 acres). Except for the fact that shifting agriculture of the "slash and burn" type was quite rare in the area, these subsistence farms were of the traditional type in Venezuela, i.e., tiny farms on which food crops such as maize and beans were grown. Some of these farmers made a small cash rental payment for their plots to the town council.

The crucial person in bringing the reform settlement to Barbacoas was a town councilman who had been an active member of Accion Democratica, the party elected to power with Romulo Betancourt in 1958. He later became president (or secretary general, as this office is usually called in Venezuela) of the local peasant union (sindicato). Although not a farmer himself, he was observant as well as astute, and he came to know a great deal about agriculture in the Barbacoas area. In addition to a sincere belief in the inherent justice of agrarian reform, this man also visualized it as one way of increasing his prestige in the community.

With the help of the other members of the town council, the secretary general of the local sindicato set about transferring all but 2,000 hectares (4,490 acres) of Barbacoas land to the IAN. While this transfer appears on the records as a "donation," in fact, IAN agreed to pay Bs 100,000 (U.S. $22,222) for the largely uncleared property. The town council envisioned the sale of its lands as one way in which some road improvement could be financed in Barbacoas; they had little use for the idle lands from which they collected only a few insignificant rental payments. The 2,000-hectare (4,940-acre) reserve, it was thought, would be ample to take care of the most optimistic town expansion projections.

What the council and IAN did not completely understand at the time was that the town did not have undisputed title to this land. As in so many cases in Venezuela, the survey lines were not defined on the original title drawn up in 1783. Through the years and without deforesting the property, 8 or 9 neighbors whose farms bordered the town property grazed their animals on the land that was about to be sold. When they heard that the land used by their farms—some for generations—was about to be requisitioned for a settlement, they raised a public outcry and initiated a court case. The only land that could be definitely proved as town property was a 930-hectare (2,297-acre) unit, the current size of the land reform settlement. Of this, about 860 hectares (2,124.2 acres) were subsequently cleared and divided into individual farms. About half of this acreage was bottomland along the Guarico River; the remainder was savanna—land at a somewhat higher elevation.

The convergence of three factors thus accounted for the founding of the Ruiz Pineda settlement: the need for IAN to have lands on which to settle new colonists; the availability of town lands in the Barbacoas area; and, most important, the desire of one member of the town council, working through the newly founded sindicato, for local prestige.

Early Development of the Settlement. In 1960 IAN initiated cadastral surveys on the portion of the town land that could be irrefutably transferred. The survey team appraised the land improvements (such as fences, drainage ditches, granaries, shelters) made by the current occupants of the land at Bs 265,115 (U.S. $58,914); this amount was paid to the occupants by the government in 1961. Meanwhile, under the sindicato's direction, the land was split into parcels—all of very nearly 6 hectares (15 acres). Such infrastructural investments as roads, irrigation works, fences, etc., were made by various public agencies under IAN's general supervision and coordination. If the total of the Bs 931,794 (U.S. $207,065) spent for these purposes were divided equally among the 119 settlers who occupied parcels in 1965, it would amount to Bs 7,830

(U.S. $1,740) per family. However, this expense, as well as the stipulated payment for the land, was assumed by the government.

The 8 islenos were asked whether they wanted to leave the settlement or whether they would accept parcels averaging only 6 hectares (15 acres) as replacements for the larger plots they were farming. Their decision was to remain in the settlement since they would be paid for the fixed capital improvements they had made (which were largely destroyed by later subdivision) and they would receive title to their plots. The islenos reasoned that with firm title and without fear of eviction they could plant higher value orchard crops than formerly; hence, their acceptance of less land would not necessarily mean a reduction in net income. Besides, they had little desire to set out anew to relocate themselves. Seven of the islenos were farming an average of only 7 hectares (17.3 acres) at the time, so their acreage cut was quite minimal. The isleno who would lose the most land was partially compensated through a generous reimbursement of Bs 112,000 (U.S. $24,889) for fixed capital improvements. Five of the original subsistence farmers left at the time of reform, preferring to take up land elsewhere. They were each given a "severance pay" of Bs 2,000 (U.S. $444).

The first step in the settlement process was to deforest the land, divide it, and give clear title to the 30 original occupants who wanted to remain. This group received the best land in the sindicato-supervised drawings. By early 1960, 200 other local campesinos had requested land. Thirty of these had worked for IAN during preparation of the land and they also drew for parcels. Thirty-four others were chosen by interview. Fifty campesinos were resettled from elsewhere in the state of Aragua, to bring the asentamiento up to capacity—144 parcels. Although 25 of these parcels were abandoned in the next few years, in 1967 a land invasion reoccupied them. The 25 campesinos who left their parcels failed for several reasons. Most had come from more temperate regions and were unable to make the necessary shift in technology to tropical agriculture. Little guidance was offered them, and they were allocated the worst land as well. Credit was extended for only two years. Interviews with some of these farmers revealed that they were better off before being resettled on the asentamiento and that they were bitter about the failure of the sindicato to help them further.

Social Structure and the Sindicato. As a group, the farmers on Ruiz Pineda were not greatly different from peasants on other settlements in Venezuela.[2] Their level of education was about the same as the general norm: 41% were illiterate; 35% had three years or less of primary education—not sufficient to produce functional literacy; while 24% had from four to six years of primary schooling. The low educational level was to some degree a function of the fact that the heads of families in

Ruiz Pineda tended to be slightly older (50 years) than the national settlement average of 43.

Prior to the sindicato, there was little community organization. In the Barbacoas area, as in most of Venezuela outside the coffee and cacao areas, the hacienda system never developed. About half the settlers were subsistence farmers before. The rest worked occasionally on large farms. Though subservience developed in this rural milieu, it was not the paternalistic dependency found in so many other areas of Latin America where the hacienda system was strong. The church was not strong in Barbacoas and did not provide a nucleus for a community social structure either. Geographical mobility was extremely common among Venezuelan peasants and in Barbacoas village loyalties and traditions had not developed at the time the settlement was founded. Even the local government did not provide a nexus for social organization. The local town council was in the hands of large landlords and storekeepers from the town. It concerned the subsistence farmers only insofar as they paid nominal rent for plots of the town's land. Although they resided in the town of Barbacoas, there was no strongly articulated social structure in which the peasants participated prior to 1958. No groups, loyalties, or common experiences bound the local peasants together.

The Sindicato Agropecuario de Barbacoas was one of the first founded in Aragua State. The initiative came from the state headquarters of the Venezuelan Campesino Federation (Federacion Campesina de Venezuela—FCV) in Maracay, which sent organizers to Barbacoas. At that time Accion Democratica (AD) was in the process of rebuilding its peasant base of support (first developed during 1945–48) in preparation for the national elections, which named Romulo Betancourt as president. The vehicle for this was the FCV, which the party largely controlled. The organizational pattern in Barbacoas was similar to that in other areas of Venezuela. The organizers sought out local political leaders of AD and enlisted their cooperation in calling together the peasants to found a union. It then entrusted local party leaders with overseeing the nascent organization.

Some 375 area subsistence farmers were induced to join the Barbacoas sindicato by promises of improvement in their deplorable living conditions.[3] The larger farmers generally did not become very actively involved. Through the years the sindicato evolved from an organization that focused on the consignment of land to one that was the vehicle through which government programs worked. In particular, the sindicato functioned as a channel for administering government credit and such technical inputs as mechanized seeding, fertilizers, etc. The sindicato used these functions to reward activist members. There was clear relationship between sindicato membership and the receipt of government credit and technical assistance.

The secretary general was the principal leader through all of this.

He was a storekeeper, with time to spare for his sindicato and, at the time of this study, was the local party leader and the district agrarian secretary. These activities were inextricably linked in that his evident effectiveness in mobilizing government aids to sindicato members had been largely predicated on his political capacity and "connections." His leadership was paternalistic—he was regularly consulted by farmers for advice on minor day-to-day problems—to the degree that it prevented both the development of self-reliance on the part of the farmers and the training of any other potential leaders.

Production Experience through 1964. Since land was given out in June 1961, it was too late to plant maize.[4] But IAN prepared the soil for sesame, which was to be seeded in October or November, and gave each farmer a credit of Bs 150 (U.S. $33) for each hectare to be planted. Nearly all this credit was in fact used for subsistence expenses during the first year.

In 1962 cotton and maize were planted. For each hectare of cotton, a farmer was loaned Bs 500 (U.S. $111); for each hectare of maize or sesame he planted, he was granted a credit of Bs 300 (U.S. $67). Even though the year was quite productive, a total of Bs 16,000 (U.S. $3,556) of outstanding loans remained uncollected.

In 1963 IAN again assumed responsibility for soil preparation with machinery, but since it experimented with different varieties of rice during that year on Ruiz Pineda, it did not charge the asentados for this service. Based on the results of these experiments, it was decided in 1964 to seed rice of variety number 501 on 312 hectares (771 acres) of savanna land. Seed was purchased and dispatched to a private drier, a practice aimed at promoting good germination. When the seedbed was ready, the IAN extensionist who went to get the seed from the drier found that it had been sold. He immediately ordered seed of a different variety—no more of the 501 variety was available. But this seed arrived too late for planting and it was returned. Thus the "rice farmers" were forced to leave their parcels idle and live on the subsistence payments the government supplied.

This brief background sets the stage for the following detailed analysis of the 1965 and 1966 crop years, during which weather conditions, according to extension personnel, were "normal."

USE OF FACTORS OF PRODUCTION AND CREDIT IN FARM PRODUCTION.
Central to success in farm settlements as in all agriculture is effective use of factors of production and credit. On Ruiz Pineda, land and labor were the main agricultural resources, with some use of machines for plowing, weeding, spreading pesticides, and water pumping. High levels of output depend on the most productive combi-

nations of resources used to the limit of their availability. Did land limit the settlers from increasing income further on Ruiz Pineda or were there shortages of labor at peak labor demand periods? How well did the cropping patterns spread labor use relatively evenly over the year? Credit makes possible the acquisition of additional resources. To what extent was it used on the settlement? How was it arranged and was it paid back? Examination of these and other questions about the use of the factors of production and credit on the settlement will provide necessary information for a later analysis of factors associated with settler success.

Land and Labor

Land and Labor Use on Ruiz Pineda. There were about 165 total person-years of labor available for the 119 farms making up Ruiz Pineda during 1965 if we assume a 300-day work year and an 8-hour work day. This includes the potential work force of the male farmers and the labor that could be supplied by their sons 15 years of age or older who lived on the farm, were not in school, and depended on their parents for support. Hence, average labor availability was 1.4 person-year equivalents per farm.[5]

But during 1965 parceleros and their families worked more off their farms (32 person-years) than on them (25 person-years). Nearly two-thirds of the off-farm work was in agriculture. Between 30 and 40% of this was wage work on neighbors' land.

Considering labor use on and off the farmer's own land, then, only 51 person-year equivalents of the 165 total available were spent in remunerative employment. This means that only 35% of the labor available within the settlement in 1965 was used; 65% was idle. The average farm operator worked on his farm about 45 days. He worked elsewhere for 78 days and was idle an equivalent of 177 days. The explanation for this apparent idleness lies in the peculiarities of seasonal cultivation in this area and the cropping and management practices used.

In winter there is ample rain during the growing season so that irrigation in the Barbacoas area is not necessary. But during the dry period cropping is impossible without irrigation. While there is substantially more unused land in summer than in winter, there was idle land in both seasons.

Although 860 hectares (2,124 acres) had been divided into farms on Ruiz Pineda by 1965, 196 hectares (484 acres) were idle through desertion. Thus the 119 farmers in 1965 owned parcels whose area totaled 664 hectares (1,640 acres) (see Table 7.1). Of this, 614 hectares (1,516 acres) were usable for agriculture and about 275 hectares (679 acres) were irrigable with shallow wells (two or three meters deep). Only the irrigable land could be cropped in the summer dry season. But only 195 hectares (482 acres) were irrigated in 1965, and only 138 hectares (341

TABLE 7.1. Land use on the 119 occupied parcels, Leonardo Ruiz Pineda Agrarian Reform Settlement, Venezuela, 1965

	Ha	Acres
1. Total area	664	1,640
2. Usable area for agriculture	614	1,516
3. Area irrigable with shallow wells	275	679
4. Total irrigated	195	482
5. Irrigated land actually used year round	138	341
6. Total usable area (Items 2 and 3)	889	2,195
7. Area used in winter only	306	756
8. Area actually used[a]	582	1,438
9. Unused land resource (Items 6–8)	307	758

[a] Column 7 + (2 × Column 5).

acres) of this were actually used the year round. Of these 138 hectares (341 acres), about 84 (207.5 acres) were planted to permanent orchard crops; 54 (133.4 acres) were double cropped, with maize taking up the bulk of the land on most farms in winter and sesame and truck crops in summer (see Table 7.2). Nearly half the total area farmed in 1965— 306 hectares (756 acres)—was planted in winter only. Considering merely the land in farms in 1965—but including the double-cropping capability of the irrigated area—307 hectares (758 acres) were idle in that year. The inclusion of land potentially irrigated with existing deep wells and land idled by desertion in 1965 would raise this figure even higher.

Of the 614 hectares (1,516.6 acres) available for use in winter, 170 (419.9 acres) were unused in 1965; of the 275 (679.25 acres) irrigable hectares available in summer, approximately half were unused. Thus problems of idle land and, hence, idle labor, were more serious in the summer dry season than in winter.

Some farmers also utilized deserted but irrigable parcels on the settlement in the summer of 1965. This amounted to some 117 hectares (289 acres) of deserted land "borrowed" and planted in annual crops.

Summer farming is not more common on Ruiz Pineda because of the expense involved in irrigation—an outlay of Bs 4,000–5,000 ($889–$1,111) for well and pump. Sixty-three wells were dug on the asentamiento and farmers owned about 30 pumps that could be moved from well to well. In fact, however, most of these were out of order for one reason or another. In addition, truck crops had to be marketed through unstable and monopsonistic channels. Hence summer truck farming on Ruiz Pineda was largely limited to the "agricultural specialists," primarily the Spanish immigrants from the Canary Islands who had brought with them some experience and a great deal of ingenuity in this type of farming. Besides, and perhaps as important, they had access to private sources of operating capital and usually marketed their products in trucks they owned.

For the reasons given above, the dry season accounted for a great deal of the idleness reported in the last section and was the period of the year when most parcel holders and their families who did not have

TABLE 7.2. Use of cropped land, Leonardo Ruiz Pineda Agrarian Reform Settlement, Venezuela, 1965

		Total Acreage Used	Corn[a]	Sesame[b]	Beans	Rice	Millet	Other Grains	To-bacco	Vege-tables	Fruits	Bananas	Other Fruits	Natural Pasture
Rainy (*invierno*) season crops	Hectares[c]	359.75	155.82	109.75	36.43	26.50	21.75	9.50	...	...	...	...	...	...
	Percentage	100.00	43.30	30.50	10.10	7.40	6.00	2.60	...	...	...	...	...	...
Dry (*verano*) season crops	Hectares[c]	171.63	37.50	52.50	7.50	...	...	...	1.13	5.25	67.75	...	...	...
	Percentage	100.00	21.80	30.60	4.40	...	...	...	0.70	3.10	39.50	...	...	...
Permanent crops[d]	Hectares[c]	83.77	...	...	...	...	...	...	...	...	...	44.43	31.09	8.25
	Percentage	100.00	...	...	...	...	...	...	...	...	...	53.00	37.10	9.80

[a] For data on yields, see Table 7.3.
[b] Sesame is planted in the *Norte*—the last rain of winter—and grows and matures in summer. After germination, sesame needs no further watering. Thus the division of the sesame crop into *invierno* and *verano* is a bit arbitrary. Likewise, corn and beans may be grown in both *invierno* and *verano*, even though they are usually rainy season crops; the division was made according to when the interviewee claimed to have planted his crops.
[c] One hectare equals 2.47 acres.
[d] For purposes of land use evaluation, acreage in "permanent crops" should be multiplied by two since this land is used in summer and winter.

the necessary skills, operating capital, a pump, or a well had to attempt to hire out their own labor; they performed whatever menial work they could find in the community. If they had irrigated land, they often hired out both their land and their labor to the islenos.

Only 23 of the 119 settlers in 1965 farmed additional land in the summer. Fifteen of these used the land free of charge, courtesy of the sindicato, in what may have been an attempt to enlist greater support from the relatively more well-to-do. The other 8 participated in sharecropping-in-reverse arrangements. Land-borrowing islenos supplied the inputs, mechanical services, and technical expertise; the parcel owner supplied his land and labor and received 50% of the harvest. While this system held potential for spreading good marketing practices, it has not worked this way and will not do so in the future without better marketing arrangements. The parcel owner was at the mercy of the isleno's marketing skills and sense of fair play.

Although farms that raised summer truck crops used more labor per cultivated hectare than those planted to winter cereals, much otherwise heavily labor-intensive weeding was accomplished by machine and chemicals. This, coupled with the fact that the summer-farmed land was only about 20% of the winter-farmed land, made for serious unemployment in the summer on Ruiz Pineda.

Rainy season labor needs were also far from stable over the growing period and apparently were becoming more irregular as operations were increasingly mechanized. Only about 500 person-days were employed in seeding, and family labor was used at this time primarily for supervising machine work. Mechanization seems almost imperative as the work coincides with the first rains and must be fitted in between showers. Delays at this time of year are costly in terms of harvest. About 2,300 person-days were used for weeding and about 1,600 in the harvest. There was great idleness in the winter planting and postplanting period and in the period between weeding and harvest.

Rationality of the Labor Use Pattern. To discern whether there was overutilization or underutilization of labor in the various tasks performed over the year, an attempt was made to estimate the number of person-days required for the work, assuming (1) the same cropping patterns, (2) an average harvest, and (3) the current level of technology on the settlement. Since no ready coefficients existed that would meet the requirements of these assumptions, two agronomists who were familiar with Ruiz Pineda were asked to supply approximate calculations based on their experience with the settlement and the region.

Using this procedure, only weeding and harvesting labor use appeared out of line with estimated requirements (Fig. 7.1). In these operations, the estimates of labor needs were somewhat higher than actual use. Given the rough nature of the estimates, precise conclusions are impossible. However, one important fact is clear from this compari-

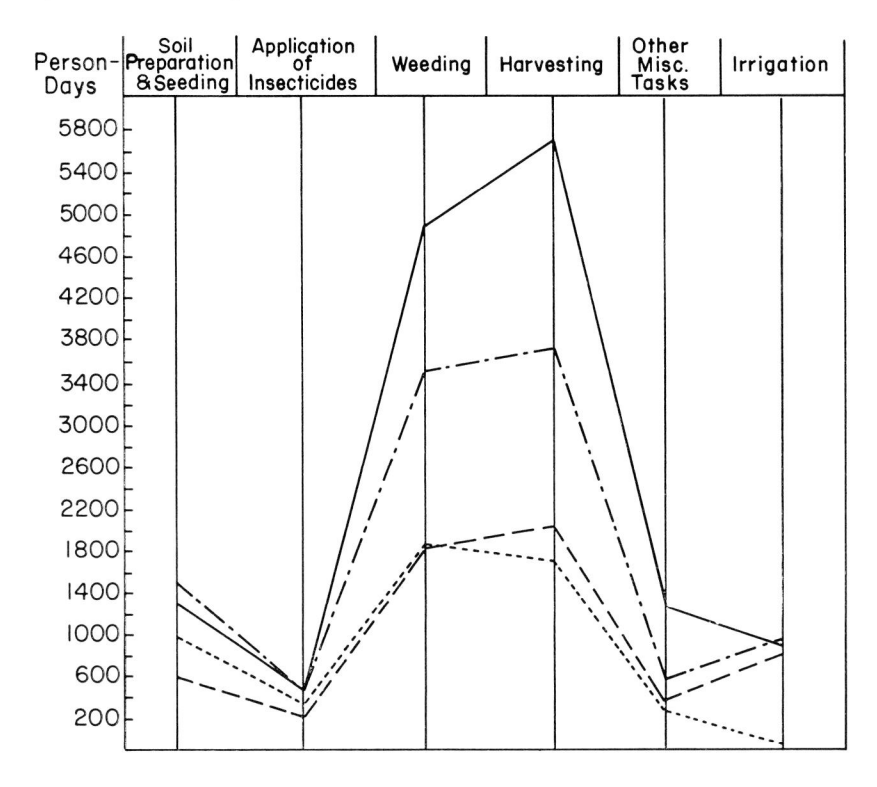

| Person-Days | Soil Preparation & Seeding | Application of Insecticides | Weeding | Harvesting | Other Misc. Tasks | Irrigation |

[Graph with y-axis values: 5800, 5400, 5000, 4600, 4200, 3800, 3400, 3000, 2600, 2200, 1800, 1400, 1000, 600, 200]

LEGEND
—— Agronomists' estimates of labor requirement
—·— Total labor use
——— Hired labor use
······· Family labor use

Fig. 7.1. Labor use compared to agronomists' estimates of necessities, Leonardo Ruiz Pineda Agrarian Reform Settlement, Venezuela, 1965.

son: labor use during the crop year is more or less according to need. It is probable, in other words, that all the labor used in 1965 was needed. Indeed, peak labor tasks could perhaps have been even more labor intensive than they were, with positive results.

As observed previously, in each working day the average farmer had 1.4 person-days of labor available to him. The labor requirements of permanent crops and livestock (spread relatively evenly around the year) reduce the available labor supply to about 1.3 person-days each day for seasonal tasks. During the winter weeding period, a total of approximately 1,100 person-days of family labor and 1,200 person-days of salaried labor were used. This means that between 19 and 20 person-days (2,300 ÷ 119) of weeding had to be accomplished on the average farm. About three-quarters of this (or about 15 days) had to be done at about the same time. (The weeding of beans, other grains, and winter corn falls in roughly the same time period.) It was particularly important to accomplish the weeding speedily, for sudden rains might leave the fields impassable for days due to poor drainage. The average family could get the peak weeding done in 11 days (15 ÷ 1.4). Yet, instead of doing it all with family labor, about half the work was done by hired labor, which ran up cash operating costs and reduced net family income.

A peak labor period similar to weeding—with large amounts of hired labor—existed at maize harvest time. Certain institutional arrangements on the settlement caused labor requirements to become greatest during this season. The settlement had a husker-sheller, but it operated only during a specific period. Maize was picked by hand while the machine made the rounds of the farms. Trucks were then dispatched by the settlement to carry away the sacks of shelled maize to storage at the Banco Agricola y Pecuario (BAP) as soon as possible after the maize of all parceleros had been shelled. Accounts were settled when all maize from Ruiz Pineda had arrived in the BAP granaries. The quicker all the maize was trucked, the sooner the settlers received their payments. Thus there was pressure on the late harvesters. Weather also played a role. The October dry spell tends to be followed by a few final November rains. The objective is to harvest before these showers come, for they might further delay the maize harvest and payments.

The age of the labor force may also dictate use of some hired labor. The Ruiz Pineda settlement seems to have benefited older farmers more than younger ones: 61% of the parceleros were older than 42 years, while 39% were older than 56. Older farmers may need to hire more labor than younger men.

One factor that might modify the general conclusion (based, as it were, on an "average" situation) is the obvious one that family size does vary. The smallest family in the sample had one person-year of labor available while the largest had four. Even so, there was a marked tendency for unmarried sons 15 years old or over to want to earn some spending money. Thus, while three farmers in the sample each had three sons that were counted as part of the available labor force, all three farmers contracted some labor for the weeding and/or harvesting period while their sons periodically hired out to a neighbor. Meanwhile, these sons continued to depend on their fathers for their subsistence, but they did not get paid for work performed on the family farm.

Improving Labor Use with Present Cropping Patterns. Even with the winter cropping pattern that prevailed, there were ways in which peak labor requirements might have been evened off. These involved using more (rather than less) labor but distributing it more evenly over the growing season. There was a strong possibility that more rather than less labor in peak seasons would have improved yields. Because it occupies such a high percentage of the winter cropping area, maize is again used as a case in point.

The typical farmer on Ruiz Pineda chop-weeded his maize once during the growing season. With one chop-weeding—a process that does not kill the plant—the height of the weeds usually equaled that of the maize at harvest. Beside the reduction of yield due to competition from weeds, labor costs rise as maize picking is slow work when there is a rank growth of weeds. Furthermore, under these conditions, tractor costs for seedbed preparation for the following planting season are unnecessarily high because of the rank vegetation through which the machine must make its way. One solution to this problem is to weed maize at least twice, as demonstrated successfully by the best farmers on the settlement. Two weedings tend to even out the labor peak. And although each weeding takes less time, more total labor is used. Two weedings improve the harvest markedly and lower field preparation costs for the next crop.

During harvest, more flexibility in the machine operation could have evened off the labor peak. Accounts for early harvesters could presumably have been settled ahead of the remainder, and the husker-sheller could have operated more days. Maize varieties with different maturity dates might have been planted, which might also have helped encourage more farmers to plant sesame.

There was, however, an increasing tendency for another problem—inflexibility in the factor market—to complicate the picture. Wages in this area, at Bs 10–12 (U.S. $2.20–2.67), did not fluctuate much with demand, but machinery was available to the settlement at a subsidized rate, with a small down payment and low interest on the unpaid debt. Data from 1967 indicate that those parcel owners who hired laborers to chop-weed a hectare (2.47 acres) of maize paid twice as much in wages (assuming Bs 10 a day) to get the job done as those who rented a tractor and cultivator to do the job. Besides, since it breaks the soil, tractor cultivation resulted in a cleaner field and a faster operation. The price of labor, which appeared artificially high in view of the prevailing unemployment, and the price of capital, which was artificially low, promoted substitution of capital for labor, and more days of idleness resulted.

There were other practices that were wasteful of labor on Ruiz Pineda and that, moreover, were uneconomic even in terms of private accounting. Rice weeding is one example. In 1966 more rice was planted than in 1965. Postemergence herbicide spraying by helicopter in 1965 eliminated most weeds and the clean stand during the growing season contributed to a good harvest. An agricultural technician with the rough equivalent of a high school education in vocational agriculture pointed out the importance of a clean rice stand early in the season. In 1966 the settlers were promised helicopter spraying, but it came too late to do much good and was very expensive, about Bs 192 ($43) per hectare. If the farmers instead had used the available backpack sprayers combined with a little of their own labor (whose opportunity cost approached zero at this time of the year, since there were few competing jobs to do after planting), they would have at least halved their perhectare costs for the operation and insured the timeliness of the operation.[6]

Improving Labor Use through New Cropping Patterns. There seemed to be a good deal of rationality in the labor pattern on Ruiz Pineda, given the existing cropping pattern, techniques of farming, and capital and labor costs. In economic terms, the marginal productivity of labor was not zero. However, some very inexpensive changes in the winter cropping pattern might have made farm operations on the settlement more labor intensive and raised production and incomes. More pumps in working order would have meant that more truck crops, which were grown by the better-off farmers, would have been practical if the marketing problems could have been solved. A greater variety of crops per parcel would have spread out the weeding and harvesting peaks somewhat more. It must be admitted, however, that little research had been done on crop adaptability in the zone. The agronomist from the Ministry of Agriculture (MAC), who worked regularly in the zone, felt that plantains could have been grown, but his plans for a demonstration plot had not been carried out. Some cotton was planted in the early years of the settlement, but diseases and insects so plagued the crop that technicians—and farmers—were reluctant to rely heavily on it. Sesame, which was planted with the last winter rains and does not need water through its growing period, might have been attempted. But since sesame planting tends to coincide with maize harvest, those who grow maize usually do not plan to plant sesame. Yet, with judicious maize harvesting practices, sesame might provide one means of spreading labor requirements into the dry period. Multiple cropping, however, places a premium on rapid seedbed preparation and, hence, mechanization.

If the title problems of the settlement to the other town lands had been solved, it would have been possible to use more land so that livestock could also have become practical. Another apparently promising alternative was in the process of experimentation on Ruiz Pineda—the planting of orchard crops. The most successful of the islenos had planted his entire farm to bananas. He obtained land for annual crops in summer on the sharecropping-in-reverse basis described earlier. The most successful of the former subsistence farmers on Ruiz Pineda had also switched to permanent crops.

An important social benefit from this type of orchard crop was that the peak labor season for the harvest fell in the postcultivation slack period of winter. More operations of this type would eventually have been able to absorb underemployed local labor. Other orchard crops could also have been important from a labor-use standpoint. Some fruit, such as certain varieties of bananas, can be harvested throughout the year, thus using a more or less steady supply of labor. It was the successful experience of innovating farmers on Ruiz Pineda that encouraged the government to promise some assistance to fruit tree growers.

However, in 1966, only 84 of the 119 farmers on Ruiz Pineda had titles. Those who did not have clear rights to their land had no intention of making an investment in orchard crops.

Farm Capital and Credit

Types and Amount of Farm Credit. The mean value of capital per farm in 1965 was Bs 13,109 (U.S. $2,913) per parcelero. This included orchards, barns, fences, farm implements, vehicles, livestock, input inventories, and irrigation systems but not land and infrastructural improvements made at the time of parcelization. Settlers did not pay for their land or infrastructural improvements and were not permitted to sell their parcels. Were a value assigned to "land plus improvements," it would increase the mean value per farm by about Bs 9,579 (U.S. $2,129).

Since this small average capitalization includes the plantations and vehicles owned by a small number of the parceleros, it is obvious that little capital is owned by the majority. The distribution of capital was highly skewed, in part reflecting the income distribution to be described later.

ORDINARY CREDIT AND THE EMPRESA CAMPESINA. With 6 hectares, land was not the major factor impeding agricultural development for the settlers on Ruiz Pineda; operating capital and management skills seemed to have become the principal bottlenecks. BAP tried to provide credit to small farmers, unsupervised until 1963, but credit was actually available only to a small group of hand-picked farmers. In 1965 no one on Ruiz Pineda was receiving such credit.

BAP's policy was to give short-term production credit only to those who had little or no prior debt. Using this criterion, very few settlers on Ruiz Pineda in 1965 would have been able to obtain credit, as was the case in most other settlements in the country. Indeed, only 12 Ruiz Pineda farmers were free from debt at the beginning of 1966—largely because they ran their farms with their savings and did not depend on borrowed funds. With these credit policies BAP aided a few successful farmers, but little latent management was developed among the majority of small farmers. And the income gap separating the successful and the unsuccessful grew wider each year.

Under these credit conditions, the vast majority would not have had enough capital even to plant their winter crops. BAP attempted to meet this problem by softening its policies somewhat in the mid-1960s. "Empresas campesinas" were founded among the best credit risks on some settlements—only the above-mentioned 12 on Ruiz Pineda—to "take the responsibility" for the credit program. This "innovation" brought more credit to the settlement in 1965 than in the past and, as mentioned previously, strengthened the hand of the sindicato president.

However, even this program was beset with difficulties. The plan called for credit to come in three installments to coincide with the periods of peak labor needs; in fact, it often came too late. The payments were too small to cover all costs so farmers had to borrow and/or cut corners. Family needs were so great that some or all of the cash went for immediate consumption. Low yields produced a repayment rate of only about 36%, and by the end of 1965 the settlement had an outstanding BAP debt of Bs 221,819 (U.S. $49,293) for production credit received.

THE CIARA DIRECTED CREDIT PROGRAM AND THE UNION DE PRESTATARIOS. In 1966 the "directed credit" program promoted and supervised by CIARA (Centro de Capacitacion e Investigacion Aplicada en Reforma Agraria—a semiautonomous public foundation) was introduced on Ruiz Pineda. The CIARA program operated with BAP funds loaned to groups of farmers on the basis of a detailed plan developed for each participating farm on the settlement. The agricultural extension agent (perito agricola) and an officer of the sindicato (usually the secretary general) discussed cropping alternatives with each farmer well in advance of the planting season. In accordance with CIARA's one-step-at-a-time policy, the cropping alternatives open to the farmers in the first year were quite circumscribed; thus parceleros who wanted to grow nontraditional crops were invariably turned down. CIARA's first priority was to close the wide gap between current and potential productivity in the traditional crops in which all campesinos had prior experience and which would not entail learning new technologies and patterns of work. As before, only rainy season crops were financed. For Ruiz Pineda this meant upland rice in the savanna and corn in the lowlands near the river. Those who had prior experience or special interest were permitted to grow sesame. An overall plan was drawn up for the settlement and forwarded for review at the regional level. Any changes were discussed with the farmers involved, and the whole plan— with its associated inputs—was discussed with and approved by the farmers in a meeting.

The campesinos were formally organized into a Union de Prestatarios (union of borrowers). Of the 144 parceleros on Ruiz Pineda, 111 joined the union and 107 actually got credit. (Because of the liberalization CIARA represented, this number included some who still had debts outstanding with other credit agencies.) The union did not involve mutual responsibility for debts but did provide mutual assistance, pooling of orders, etc. Credit was closely supervised and largely in kind, unless farmers had to pay labor or had agreed upon subsistence loans.

BAP issued to the Union de Prestatarios the total amount of credit called for; the agronomist ordered all inputs in truckloads and they were delivered promptly to each settlement, unlike the situation in 1964 when the seeds failed to arrive on time. At the same time, a local bank account in the name of the Union de Prestatarios was opened. The union drew checks on it—which had to be signed by two of its elected officials—to pay for machinery rental, for land preparation, for paying day labor, and for subsistence payments. To avoid delay in availability of cash, BAP and CIARA signed an agreement that BAP must supply funds to local banks within five days after a lump sum request was filed. It appears to have worked successfully in 1966.

The total credit made available by BAP was Bs 300,167 (U.S. $66,704), an average of Bs 3,086 (U.S. $686) per borrower, or Bs 745 (U.S. $166) for each harvested hectare ($67/acre). This was about three times the previous year's level. Interest at 3% per annum (the rate provided by the agrarian reform law) was discounted for the six-month growing period. The 107 borrowers paid back a total of Bs 232,194 (U.S. $51,635) or Bs 524 (U.S. $116) for each harvested hectare ($47/acre)—a repayment rate of 68%, leaving campesinos with a debt of Bs 221 (U.S. $49) per harvested hectare ($20/acre), up from 1965's Bs 167 (U.S. $37) ($15/acre). Because of the experimental nature of the CIARA program, the 1966 repayment performance of the asentamiento did not prevent BAP from authorizing total credits of Bs 353,900 (U.S. $78,644) in 1967, more than in 1966. Slightly fewer acres—again mainly maize and rice—were planted in 1967 than in 1966.

Credit and Productivity. The first year of a novel, highly planned and directed program such as the one CIARA sponsors is likely to have its difficulties. To permit a more penetrating analysis of this year of the credit program, focus is now placed on improvements in production over time and on various cost relationships.

MAIZE (CORN). An analysis of the 1966 accounts of 25 settlers who grew 114 hectares (282 acres) of maize (over half the total maize acreage) allowed determination of production and expenses per hectare for this group. They seemed to be representative of the others.[7] In 1966, for these 25 farmers, maize grossed Bs 513 per harvested hectare (U.S. $46 per acre), including both maize sold and that held for use at home. An average of Bs 411 per hectare (U.S. $37 per acre) was spent (including credit in kind) to produce maize, hence Bs 102 per hectare (U.S. $9 per acre) remained to pay for family labor, management, and the small amount of farm capital. In the previous year, 1965 cash production costs were estimated at Bs 255 per hectare (U.S. $23 per acre) and gross

TABLE 7.3. Yields of maize (corn) and rice per harvested hectare, by yield strata, Leonardo Ruiz Pineda Agrarian Reform Settlement, Venezuela, 1965 and 1966

Commodity	Production Strata	1965 Yields kg/ha	1965 Yields bu/acre	1966 Yields kg/ha	1966 Yields bu/acre
Maize (corn)	Lowest Third	200	3.2	496	7.9
	Middle Third	992	15.9	1,033	16.5
	Upper Third	1,255	20.1	1,728	27.6
Rice	Lowest Third	a	a	613	12.1
	Middle Third	...	...	1,418	28.1
	Upper Third	...	...	1,837	36.4

[a] Too little rice was planted in 1965 to allow a realistic yield calculation.

income was Bs 300 per hectare (U.S. $27 per acre), leaving a margin of only Bs 45 per hectare (U.S. $4 per acre).

The entire maize yield spectrum moved up in 1966 (Table 7.3). One cause of this was the rise in yield-increasing inputs. Since on this part of the settlement the soil is relatively homogeneous, asset wealth was not too skewed, and the amount of owned capital was similar, differences in yields can be attributed to the management practices of farmers themselves. These practices can be expected to improve.

RICE. In 1966 accounts of 20 settlers who grew 112.5 hectares (278 acres) of rice were examined—slightly under half the total rice acreage. Their harvests grossed Bs 570 per hectare (U.S. $51 per acre), but total direct operating costs were Bs 735 per hectare (U.S. $66 per acre), producing a cash deficit of Bs 165 for every hectare harvested (U.S. $15 per acre). Data allowing comparison of costs per hectare on Ruiz Pineda with those of other areas of Venezuela reveal that on Ruiz Pineda costs for field preparation, seeding, harvesting, and herbicides were relatively high, while those for fertilizer were relatively low; this probably indicates that CIARA and MAC made some errors in the amounts of inputs prescribed. Table 7.3 shows the range of yields.

On farms with low gross production, the ratio of credit delivered in cash to gross production was high. This would indicate that there is some advantage to delivering credit in kind, at least until farmers become more production oriented. Perhaps bad and obviously uncollectable debts should be written off. Farmers often reason that if they produce more they will simply have to forfeit more in repayment of these debts, and they will still have to await a cash advance to carry them through the next agricultural year.

Information on 1967, when cash credit was more severely circumscribed than in 1966 and 1965, showed some unexpected side effects. In addition to using the cash for consumption purposes, settlers paid hired laborers with this money. There was a tendency to hold consumption constant and move to more mechanized processes, not only because of the relatively low cost of the operations (mentioned in the previous section) but because credit could be obtained for these operations.

ANALYSIS OF FACTORS ASSOCIATED WITH SETTLER SUCCESS

Effect of Particular Variables on Income. In this section, some of the independent variables associated with economic success on Ruiz Pineda are identified. Some variables are rejected that did not seem to be related to the dependent variable—income—the indicator of economic performance chosen in this study. Because average data tend to hide part of the picture, in the following section two measures of central tendency are used.

Land Capability. There was some heterogeneity of soil types on Ruiz Pineda—bottomland is more fertile on Ruiz Pineda than the highland savanna. Yet, discussion in this study has assumed homogeneity. This assumption has basis in fact. Parcels of poorest land quality were abandoned in 1965. Also in the 1965 sample, net farm and disposable family incomes were, in fact, higher in the savanna than in the bottom land, though the differences were not significant.[8]

This does not imply that agronomists were incorrect in their land capability assessment but rather that most farmers in the valley and in the savanna operated their parcels so far under potential that land quality had not yet become an influencing factor.

Technical Assistance. Settlers in the sample were asked whether they had received technical assistance in 1965. Nine responded positively and 19 negatively. The mean net farm income of the two groups was virtually the same and the median was actually higher for those who did not receive any assistance. It thus appears that technical assistance—defined as visits by an official extension agent—was not related to level of farm income on Ruiz Pineda in 1965.

This result does not imply that technical assistance was unnecessary. It may, however, indicate (1) that short visits—the kind most generally practiced by the extension service in this area—and the type of technical assistance given were not sufficient for the job at hand; and (2) that the extension people had not fully gained the confidence of the settlers so that advice, even though it may have been useful, was not heeded.

"Additional" Land. Those settlers who farmed additional land in 1965 were not always the best entrepreneurs of Ruiz Pineda. Some who acquired additional lands in 1965 did not farm them well and fell into the bottom income quartile. While mean income for those who farmed additional lands was high in relation to the overall mean, their median

income was close to the overall median; thus there is no significant statistical difference in either net income or disposable farm income between those who had and those who did not have additional land.

This result does not negate the supposition that the trend toward mechanization on Ruiz Pineda may result in the future in larger farms through land borrowing, rental, or sharecropping-in-reverse arrangements. But it does indicate that it was possible to make an adequate income by farming the basic parcel only. One settler who owned no additional land, for example, earned a net farm income of Bs 13,737 (U.S. $3,053) by farming his 6 hectares (14.8 acres) intensively in summer and winter. Also most farmers in the top net income quartile did not farm additional lands.

Land Titles. The 17 settlers in the sample who held title to their farms had a mean net farm income of Bs 2,237 ($497), while the 6 who had not yet been awarded titles had a mean net farm income of only Bs 318 ($71) (those who farmed additional land are omitted from this comparison). However, median net farm income was rather similar and the difference in income was not statistically significant.

Education. Amount of education of the settlers appeared to have some bearing on performance, but the relationship was not statistically significant. While the 18 best-educated parcel holders in the sample had from three to six years of education and showed a much higher mean income than the more poorly educated group, they were quite randomly distributed along the range of net incomes, and the medians were quite similar. The same relationships occurred in the case of disposable family income.

Spanish Immigrants Versus Former Subsistence Farmers. As was pointed out earlier, the recent Spanish immigrant earned significantly higher incomes than the former subsistence farmers. Indeed, islenos' mean net farm income was nearly ten times that of the others and their disposable family income was about six times as great.

Intensity of Land Use. Intensity of land use significantly influenced income. Those settlers who did not crop any of their land but rather allowed livestock to graze on "natural pasture" earned an average of Bs 785 (U.S. $174) in net farm income—Bs 131 per hectare (U.S. $12 per acre). Off-farm sources provided more than two-thirds of their total incomes, a mean disposable family income of Bs 2,548 (U.S. $566). Devoting the parcel to cropping in only one season of the year (winter or summer but usually winter) actually resulted in a negative mean net farm income for the 13 cases in this category. Their mean disposable family income was only Bs 1,001 (U.S. $222). Thus this group relied on off-farm sources not only to cover the deficit resulting from their farm operation but to provide family subsistence.

The 12 most successful farmers on Ruiz Pineda in 1965 planted annual crops in both winter and summer or they grew a permanent orchard-type crop in combination with one-season or two-season field crops. These settlers were well above the mean net farm income for all farmers. In view of the high statistical significance of these relationships, the figures demonstrate clearly the crucial economic importance of full land resource use.

Purchased Inputs. Inputs of labor, improved seeds, pesticides (fertilizer was not used on Ruiz Pineda in 1965), and contracted machinery work seemed to have affected production and, hence, incomes quite markedly. The mean labor input for the top half in the labor use scale was four times as great as among the lower half, whose average net farm income was virtually zero. Moreover, farmers who spent more on hired labor per hectare of land were likely to have larger incomes.

Even though fertilizer was not used in significant amounts in 1965, the level of use per hectare of other technical inputs did seem to influence yields. This conclusion is apparently at variance with the observations in an earlier section where it was shown that expenditures for yield-increasing inputs on maize did not vary much through a wide range of yields. However, data now being discussed include all crops grown on Ruiz Pineda in 1965.

The amount of directly productive capital owned by a settler was not clearly associated with his income. However, the amount of machinery work for which he contracted seemed to reveal a different picture. When the settlers were ranked according to the expenditures per hectare for hiring machinery it was noted that the top half spent five times as much, and their farm income was nearly six times more than that of the bottom half.

Association of Factors. A number of factors that had some bearing on the economic performance of farmers on Ruiz Pineda in 1965 have been examined. Some, such as land capability, the kind of technical assistance offered in 1965, education, ownership of certain kinds of capital, utilization of additional lands, and possession of titles, were rejected as not being clearly related to income in the year under examination. But in the case of intensity of land use, the use of certain inputs, and national origin, fairly clear relationships to economic performance were established.

Were any of these factors associated? Factors seeming most important in the previous analysis were placed into categories to determine into which category each of the twenty-eight sample cases fit (Tables 7.4a, 7.4b). Inserting the mean incomes into each category cell gives an indication of which group of factors is associated with various degrees of economic performance.

The first table shows net farm income (income earned by all farm

TABLE 7.4a. Association of factors with parcel holders' net farm income, 28 farms, Leonardo Ruiz Pineda Agrarian Reform Settlement, Venezuela, 1965 (bolivars)

	Net Farm Income			
	Less off-farm work[a] N = 16		More off-farm work N = 12	
	Uses yield-increasing inputs[b]	Uses negligible yield-increasing inputs	Uses yield-increasing inputs	Uses negligible yield-increasing inputs
MORE FARM WORK[a] N = 15				
Intensive Cropping[c]				
Hires labor or uses machinery[d]	N = 1 3,324 ――― 3,324[e]			
Hires little labor or machinery	N = 2 5,201	N = 2 198 ――― 2,258		
Extensive Cropping				
Hires labor or uses machinery		N = 1 ―66 ――― ―66		
Hires little labor or machinery		N = 2 598 ――― 598	N = 1 902	N = 1 133 ――― 380
LESS FARM WORK N = 13				
Intensive Cropping				
Hires labor or uses machinery	N = 2 25,851	N = 1 3,776 ――― 18,492	N = 1 13,737	N = 1 351 ――― 8,382
Hires little labor or machinery				
Extensive Cropping				
Hires labor or uses machinery		N = 3 ―1,407 ――― ―1,407	N = 1 ―510	N = 1 ―1,780 ――― ―986
Hires little labor or machinery		N = 2 382 ――― 382		N = 6 255 ――― 255

[a] The average family works 64 days on the farm (Less Farm Work = Works fewer than 64 days on the farm; More Farm Work = Works 64 days or over on the farm. The average family works less off-farm work = under 50 days, more off-farm work = 80 days or over.

[b] Settlers are considered as falling into this category if they are in the top quartile of those who use yield-increasing inputs (fertilizer, improved seed, insecticides).

[c] If settlers have an average-sized farm (approximately 6 ha), and/or have additional lands and do not leave more than 0.75 ha idle besides having two-season cropping or one- or two-season cropping and permanent orchard crops, they are considered to have an intensive cropping pattern.

[d] Settlers are considered as falling into this category if they meet one of the following qualifications: (1) own a tractor; (2) are in the top quartile of those who contract for custom machine work; (3) are in the top quartile of those who own directly productive capital; (4) are in the top quartile of those who hire labor.

[e] The figures under the lines are the means for both halves of each cell.

TABLE 7.4b. Association of factors with parcel holders' disposable family income, 28 farms, Leonardo Ruiz Pineda Agrarian Reform Settlement, Venezuela, 1965 (bolivars)

	Disposable Family Income			
	Less off-farm work[a] N = 16		More off-farm work N = 12	
	Uses yield-increasing inputs[b]	Uses negligible yield-increasing inputs	Uses yield-increasing inputs	Uses negligible yield-increasing inputs
MORE FARM WORK[a] N = 15				
Intensive Cropping[c]				
Hires labor or uses machinery[d]		N = 1 3,324		
		3,324		
Hires little labor or machinery	N = 2 5,201	N = 2 378		
	2,364			
Extensive Cropping				
Hires labor or uses machinery		N = 1 234		
	234			
Hires little labor or machinery		N = 2 490	N = 1 4,622	N = 1 2,133
	490		2,933	
LESS FARM WORK N = 13				
Intensive Cropping				
Hires labor or uses machinery	N = 2 25,851	N = 1 3,776	N = 1 19,137	N = 1 5,651
	18,492		13,743	
Hires little labor or machinery				
Extensive Cropping				
Hires labor or uses machinery		N = 3 −1,407	N = 1 9,090	N = 1 1,220
	−1,407		6,139	
Hires little labor or machinery		N = 2 462		N = 6 1,976
	462		1,976	

[a] The average family works 64 days on the farm (Less Farm Work = Works fewer than 64 days on the farm; More Farm Work = Works 64 days or over on the farm. The average family works less off-farm work = under 50 days, more off-farm work = 80 days or over.

[b] Settlers are considered as falling into this category if they are in the top quartile of those who use yield-increasing inputs (fertilizer, improved seed, insecticides).

[c] If settlers have an average-sized farm (approximately 6 ha), and/or have additional lands and do not leave more than 0.75 ha idle besides having two-season cropping or one- or two-season cropping and permanent orchard crops, they are considered to have an intensive cropping pattern.

[d] Settlers are considered as falling into this category if they meet one of the following qualifications: (1) own a tractor; (2) are in the top quartile of those who contract for custom machine work; (3) are in the top quartile of those who own directly productive capital; (4) are in the top quartile of those who hire labor.

[e] The figures under the lines are the means for both halves of each cell.

resources used) and the second table shows disposable family income (net farm income plus income earned off the farm). The first major column of each table enumerates those families devoting less time than the average to off-farm work. The second major column lists those families devoting more time than the average to off-farm work. Each major column is divided into two subcolumns showing those settlers who use yield-increasing inputs (i.e., who are in the top quartile of yield-increasing input users) and those who use negligible quantities of yield-increasing inputs (i.e., who are in the bottom three quartiles of yield-increasing input users).

The rows represent the following three characteristics: (1) more or less than 64 days of work on the farm; (2) intensive or extensive cropping pattern; and (3) hiring labor or using machinery. Definitions of these terms are found in the footnotes for the table.

The following are some general, at times overlapping, conclusions that may be drawn from this factor grouping exercise (data in Table 7.4a are examined unless indicated otherwise):

1. The yield-increasing inputs that were used had an important bearing on performance. In the five categories that varied internally in Table 7.4a only by the use of yield-increasing inputs, users showed much larger net farm incomes than nonusers (Bs 5,201 [$1,156] versus 198 [$44] in line two, etc.).

2. If a farmer had an intensive cropping pattern, he may have substituted hired labor and machinery for his own labor. The most successful farmers also used yield-increasing inputs. The three cases that did less farm work, had an intensive cropping pattern, hired labor and machinery, and worked fewer person-days off the farm had an average net farm income of Bs 18,492 ($4,109). Two cases with similar characteristics, except that they worked more than the average number of days off the parcel, appear in the top quartile of net farm income (Bs 8,382 [$1,863]).

3. Ignoring the amount of off-farm work, the performance of the thirteen families who worked less than the settlement average of 64 person-days on their farms *and* had an extensive cropping pattern was little different from the five who worked *more* than 64 days and had an extensive cropping pattern. The chart indicates that misuse of the land resource spells failure regardless of the number of days the settler says he devotes to his operation. Devoting labor to extensive operations does not seem to increase incomes. In order not to be dependent on borrowing or subsidies, if a farmer elects to have an extensive farming operation, he must, at a minimum, work off the farm, as ten of those with extensive cropping patterns did in 1965. The eight farmers who had extensive farming patterns and did not work off the farm had negligible incomes.

4. Only two parcel holders did more farm work and at the same time more off-farm work. Because of their extensive cropping pattern

and lower-than-average yields, their farm work seems to have come to naught and left them with low net farm incomes (Bs 902 [$200] and Bs 133 [$30]) and, hence, with low farm labor productivity. Forced to work off the parcel to support their families, these parcel holders raised their disposable family incomes to Bs 4,622 ($1,027) and Bs 2,133 ($474), respectively (Table 7.4b).

Two families who did less farm work had an extensive cropping pattern and hired labor or machinery to replace their own labor. But they compensated for the negative net incomes on their own farms by working off the farm and earning disposable family incomes of Bs 9,090 ($2,020) and Bs 1,220 ($271), respectively (Table 7.4b). Another six fell into the extensive cropping category except for their decision not to contract for much machinery or labor or use yield-increasing inputs. Their net farm incomes averaged only Bs 255, ($57), but their disposable family incomes averaged Bs 1,976 ($439) (Table 7.4b).

5. Three of the least successful farmers on Ruiz Pineda did less farm work, had an extensive farming pattern, raised costs by hiring labor or utilizing machinery, and did not compensate for their lack of success on the farm by doing much off-farm work. These three farmers, whose average net farm income and disposable family income was a negative Bs 1,407 ($313), certainly represented "hard-core poverty" and perhaps chronic incapacity to earn a living. Two more with an extremely low mean net farm income (Bs 382 [$85]) also fall into this category. Their farm income was higher only because they did not raise their costs by contracting for inputs that replaced their own labor.

HIGHLY SKEWED INCOME

Income Before and After Reform. Most of this analysis of results of the reform refers to incomes of settlers in 1965 and 1966. Data already presented indicate that the income picture improved somewhat in 1966 and that further gains were probably made in 1967. Mean disposable family income in 1965 seemed to have exceeded 1960 (prereform) income by Bs 570 (U.S. $127) (Table 7.5), but large differences between mean and median incomes indicate a highly skewed pattern of distribution.

Two-thirds of the settlers asserted that they earned less disposable

TABLE 7.5. Mean and median disposable family income, 28 farms, Leonardo Ruiz Pineda Agrarian Reform Settlement, Venezuela, 1960 and 1965

	1960[a]		1965		Difference	
	Bolivars	Dollars	Bolivars	Dollars	Bolivars	Dollars
Mean	3,542	787	4,112	914	570	127
Median	3,000	667	1,568	348	−1,432	−319

Note: Net farm income plus income earned off the farm.
[a] Subjective estimates of the settlers.

TABLE 7.6. Net farm and disposable family incomes, 28 farms, Leonardo Ruiz Pineda Agrarian Reform Settlement, Venezuela, 1965

	Net Farm Income				Disposable Family Income			
	Mean		Median		Mean		Median	
	Bolivars	Dollars	Bolivars	Dollars	Bolivars	Dollars	Bolivars	Dollars
First quartile	11,178	2,484	5,188	1,153	13,476	2,995	7,752	1,723
Second quartile	1,028	228	902	200	2,990	664	3,324	739
Third quartile	38	8	30	7	1,060	236	1,220	271
Fourth quartile	−965	−214	−576	−128	−771	−171	−216	−48
Overall	2,194	488	382	85	4,112	914	1,568	348
Overall without the 8 isleno families	1,354	301	133	30	2,734	608	1,322	294

family income in 1965 than before the reform. However, the 1965 data are based on detailed income analysis, while the prereform figures represent subjective estimates of the settlers. It is quite possible—even probable—that prereform figures were overestimated. Recollection of many past situations is doubtless biased by a "halo effect" which is unwarranted by the facts.

Income Distribution. Considerable inequalities in 1965 between settlers were apparent in both net farm income and disposable family income. Skewness was large even within the first quartile for both net farm income and disposable family income.

The drop-off of net farm and disposable family income between the first and second quartiles, considering both means and medians, is very marked (Table 7.6). Mean net farm income for the second quartile was less than 10% of the top quartile, and median income was also markedly inferior. In the fourth quartile, which showed negative values for both mean and median net farm incomes and disposable family incomes, settlers paid for the privilege of working or their labor literally pushed them into debt, assuming this debt has to be paid back.

If the net mean farm income in the fourth quartile is considered as zero, about 90% of the total net farm income generated on Ruiz Pineda in 1965 accrued to the upper 25%, or about thirty farms. This situation is somewhat less extreme when disposable family income is considered; for the upper quartile produced about 70% of the total mean disposable family income.

If the eight Spanish immigrant families (islenos) are excluded, the mean net farm income falls from Bs 2,194 (U.S. $488) to Bs 1,354 (U.S. $300), while the median falls from Bs 382 (U.S. $85) to Bs 133 (U.S. $30). This indicates the extent of the economic success of the islenos, who represented only about 7% of the settlers and farmed only 13% of the total cultivated land but earned about 50% of all the net farm income on Ruiz Pineda in 1965. As the former subsistence farmers were more apt to turn to off-farm sources to supplement their incomes than the Spaniards, the islenos earned only 40% of all disposable family income.

When incomes were low, farmers tended to participate little in the market—they supplied few goods to the urban consumer and demanded few purchased goods. When gross incomes were high, the reverse was true. The top gross income quartile supplied about 86% of the total marketings from Ruiz Pineda in 1965.

Management and Labor Income. Sources of income and average returns for settlers' work during 1965 are displayed in Table 7.7. It is worth pointing out that the average labor income per day, Bs 3.9 (slightly

TABLE 7.7. Average returns to operator's labor and management, 28 Farms, Leonardo Ruiz Pineda Agrarian Reform Settlement, Venezuela, 1965

	Mean Net Income as Base		Median Net Income as Base	
	Bolivars	Dollars	Bolivars	Dollars
A. Net farm income	2,194	488	382	85
B. Five percent of average capital (excluding land) per asentado (depreciation)	66	15	66	15
C. Farm labor income[a] (A − B)	2,128	473	316	70
D. Value of dependents' work (number of days worked × Bs 10)	120	27	106	23
E. Labor income of operator (C − D)	2,008	446	210	47
F. Labor income of operator per day worked (210/45 days)[b]			4.6	1.02
G. Family earnings for off-farm work			1,186	264
H. Dependents' work			18	4
I. Operator's income for off-farm work (G − H)			1,168	260
J. Income of operator per day worked off-farm (1,168/78 days)			15.0	3.33
K. Total disposable labor income of operator (E + I)			1,434	319
L. Average labor income per day operator worked (123 days)			11.6	2.58
M. Average labor income per day (365 days)			3.9	0.87

[a] The term "labor income" is used broadly to also include returns to management. The interest rate of 5% is very arbitrary. Three percent is charged on the settlement for operating credit. Because the amount of owned capital is so small, the interest rate would not appreciably affect the conclusions.

[b] All data for "average number of days worked" used in this analysis are *means;* it was not possible to obtain the corresponding medians but it is believed that the two measures do not differ greatly in this case.

under $1.00), noted in line M is a median figure; the lower-income half of campesinos on Ruiz Pineda had considerably less to live on.

Where Do the Poorest Farmers Obtain Their Subsistence? The less successful a farmer on Ruiz Pineda was, the more he relied on government credit. The average farmer in the two lowest net income quartiles borrowed more than twice as much from BAP as did the average farmer in the top quartile. On the average, the unpaid balance due to BAP matched the net farm income deficit rather closely.

While the bottom quartile of net income earners defaulted on government borrowing to support their family, it is difficult to see where those with a negative disposable family income got enough to survive. The data available do not permit a precise determination of where this survival income originated during 1965, but the practices of borrowing from relatives and padrinos (wealthy patrons) and of buying at local stores on credit with high interest rates are strong in the community. Certainly those in the bottom quartile were entangled in a web of borrowing from which they would find it extremely difficult to extricate themselves.

CONCLUSIONS. The conclusions of this study are offered in three topic areas: general institutional and organizational arrangements, improving productivity and income, and relating to long-range policy.

In the organization of Ruiz Pineda settlement, the sindicato played a key social role. The case may indicate that at the outset of an agrarian reform settlement, when experimentation with new forms of social organization is occurring, a strong, almost autocratic, organization like the sindicato may be necessary to give the peasants cohesiveness in the struggle for a share of agrarian reform benefits. At the same time, such an organization may provide a solid base for later collective efforts more directly related to farming operations. But it is equally evident from the case that such an organization may become dysfunctional as the organizational requirements of the settlement become greater. A different type of leader is required for the administrative tasks of a cooperative than for a sindicato. The function of the latter is brokerage, and a leader must be articulate and have political connections. By contrast, the skills required for farming cooperatives are more technical and administrative in nature and call for developing more member self-reliance. When a single leader, whose bases of power are his political connections and charisma, attempts to undertake an administrative role as well, the result may well become—as in Ruiz Pineda—inefficiency, favoritism, and paternalism. Similarly, the political role discourages delegation of authority. On Ruiz Pineda there was no actual or potential successor to the 1965 leader.

There would appear to be two alternatives for the future: one, a differentiation of organization function, with political bargaining left to the sindicato and its political leaders, and human development and administrative matters left to another organization with a distinct type of leader. The other alternative would entail the sindicato's taking on the character of a cooperative with genuine member support and participation. One should not, however, understate the difficulties and the strain on the existing social structure that this latter might imply. Doubtless, this process would take a number of years, but a strong government program in favor of cooperative development—based, perhaps, on the CIARA-type directed credit program initiated in 1966—would be essential. For example, there was no reason why the government could not have begun insisting on more member participation; after all it had a certain leverage in the credit sources it possessed. One cannot hope for a full-blown, multifunctional cooperative immediately, but partial steps could be taken in that direction. Members already had experience with a kind of cooperative credit and had purchased some inputs collectively. This was a promising beginning. In time, the cooperative would have to take up marketing functions and, it would seem, should provide a channel for technical information to be passed from the extension agent to the farmers through a series of selected officers who could be trained to assume roles as para-extensionists. This would necessarily involve some erosion of the power of the secretary general of the sindicato.

The results of this study point up the importance of searching for ways to diversify and intensify farm operations on settlements to promote fuller employment and increased incomes. As a minimum on Ruiz Pineda, some low-cost changes in farm practices were certainly possible. For example, technical analysis indicated that two weedings of corn would have reduced competition from weeds and increased yields. This practice could also have reduced the peak labor need somewhat and spread the labor requirement more evenly over the growing season, thus promoting fuller employment. The net result would have raised incomes.

The complications inherent in this conclusion should be recognized, however. While changing corn cultivation practices would have made traditional winter cereal farming more labor intensive, mechanization was offering an individually profitable alternative to greater labor use. Indeed most successful colonists on Ruiz Pineda did use machinery together with their intensive cropping pattern. Farm implements could be purchased by the settlers at a subsidized rate, with low interest, and with small down payments. Meanwhile, wage rates were sticky. Thus underpriced machinery and labor, which was probably overpriced considering its abundance, fostered the substitution of machinery for labor. On Ruiz Pineda, settlers could cultivate their maize with a rented machine at half the cost per hectare of hired labor. Also, since the coming of the comprehensive credit program in 1966, services such as tractor work were able to be secured on credit while cash for subsistence and to pay workers was becoming more difficult to acquire.

Not all mechanization used on the settlement was cost reducing, however. Helicopter spraying of rice with herbicides doubled the per-hectare cost of this operation, considering that backpack sprayers and ample labor were available. It would thus have been advisable to "cost out" all technological innovations before adoption on Ruiz Pineda. Some machinery operations that may be considered primarily as labor-replacing also have important yield-increasing functions: maize must be planted quickly so that rains do not slow the process and cut into yields, and tractor cultivation breaks the soil and eliminates weed competition more effectively than the traditional machete and garabato system.

How credit costs can be effectively reduced without leaving the campesinos destitute was a central concern of planners working with the Venezuelan reform. Rather than choking off credits, better planning and administration might have allowed capital and land to yield a higher product and income (as was being demonstrated on the settlement). The data justify some pessimism, however, regarding the possibility of tangibly raising the net farm incomes of all reform beneficiaries. Indeed income became quite skewed in the reform process as some took advantage of new opportunities and some did not. This suggests more study of the reasons why some fall so markedly behind even after getting land subsidies and credit. It may be that direct income subsidies to the small, hard-core poverty group are the most practical—and the cheapest—way to tie this small group closer to the market economy. This implies, however, that most of the new landowners can and must become more self-reliant. A government policy allowing a large group to become perpetually dependent on services that the state currently supplies will be self-defeating in the long run.

The analysis suggests that improving the productivity per hectare of the traditional crops was not adequate for the future. A more intensive cropping pattern utilizing much of the currently idle land and labor resource in summer and winter was needed. This would have called for the planting of summer crops and the provision of irrigation and other purchased inputs (especially fertilizer) for more plots. It would also have required more knowledge of the summer fruit and vegetable market in Caracas, where these commodities were sold, or the undertaking of some major market reforms. The provision of credit for the summer growing season would have helped. In turn, a need for more summer cropping management skills was also indicated. There were also several alternatives to more annual summer crops. One was planting permanent fruit trees. Another was expanding livestock—and even crop production—on the large land area that was still in dispute. A large part of the disputed land was suitable only for livestock grazing. Through the sindicato, members ought to have been able to arrive at some arrangement for common grazing. Intermediate-term credit would become important at this stage. Before this, however, the legal problems holding up transfer of this land had to be resolved. Considering the large number of sons who would come of age in 10 years, it would have been a mistake to divide the remaining ejido land in a permanent fashion among the current settlers if and when it became available. Rather, it might better have been used in common or on a cash-rent basis until the sons came of age and could receive their own grants.

POLICY IMPLICATIONS. The case of Ruiz Pineda seems to contain some general lessons for the reform process. Land, by itself, will not provide sufficient incomes. It must be accompanied by an adequate, properly supervised credit program—one that gets inputs to the farmers, makes sure they are correctly used, and does not serve only the most able. As the cropping pattern is intensified, more labor should theoretically be used. But if there are factor price distortions this may not happen.

Government land reform agencies must be truly committed to their task, and settler organizations that are democratic in their nature and organization seem to be a *sine qua non* for successful reform.

Market structure problems can be just as difficult to solve and just as exploitive as land tenure structures; when land tenure problems are bettered, markets usually must also be reformed.

When the postreform structure is the individual plot, there is a tendency for incomes to become skewed—maybe highly so—as some take advantage of new opportunities and are able to circumvent other existing institutional problems and some are not.

NOTES

1. Some detailed case studies may be found in the references in Land Tenure Center, *Colonization and Settlement: A Bibliography*, Training and Methods Series, No. 8, Madison, Mar. 1969, and two supplements dated Jan. 1971 and Apr. 1972. A particularly useful Venezuelan case is John Mathiason and Eric B. Shearer, "Caicara de Maturin: A Case Study of an Agrarian Reform Settlement in Venezuela," CIDA, 1967 (Mimeographed). I have attempted to bring together some generalizations about colonization and settlement in Latin America in "Colonization: Alternative or Supplement to Agrarian Reform in Latin America," in *Land Reform in Latin America: Issues and Cases*, edited by Peter Dorner, Land Economics Monographs No. 3 (Madison), 1971, pp. 207–25.
2. Most of the data in this chapter were obtained from detailed interviews with 28 settler families in 1966. These constituted 24% of the 119 families on the settlement in that year. The sample was stratified according to family size, preinterview subjective information, and relative income. For consistency in comparisons an exchange rate of U.S. $1.00 = 4.5 bolivars is used.
3. By 1965 the number of active members had dropped to 196. While some of this may be due to disillusionment, it mainly reflects the breaking up of the original sindicato into several smaller units.
4. In this area, "winter," the rainy growing season, runs from Apr. or May to Sept. or Oct. "Summer," the dry season, encompasses the remainder of the year.
5. The "farm" includes the official parcel plus any additional lands the farmer and his family may rent or "use." This distinction is explained later in the discussion.
6. They ingenuously came to call backpack sprayers "manocopteros" (handcopters) because their first experience with spraying was more streamlined.
7. All settlers who appeared in the 1965 stratified sample (note 2) were selected first; to make up the remainder of this sample for the analysis of enterprise accounts, every settler was taken in the order in which he appeared in the settlement's record book until the total of 25 was reached.
8. The Mann-Whitney U test was used to test significance. The reader is referred to William C. Thiesenhusen with Ricardo Alezones, Ramon Pugh, and John Mathiason, "Leonardo Ruiz Pineda: A Case Study of a Venezuelan Agrarian Reform Settlement," Research Paper No. 7 (Mimeographed),

Dec. 1968, CIDA/CENDES, Pan American Union, Washington, D.C., p. 54, and subsequent tables.

REFERENCES
1. Alezones, Ricardo, et al. *Seis trabajos sobre reforma agraria.* CENDES/CIDA, Vol. 7. Caracas, 1969.
2. CIDA/CENDES. *Venezuela: Notas preliminares sobre algunos aspectos de la reforma agraria.* Version preliminar. Caracas, 1969.
3. Consejo de Bienestar Rural. *Present Status and Possibilities of Agricultural Development in Venezuela.* Caracas: Ford Foundation, 1967.
4. *Gaceta oficial de la Republica de Venezuela, Ley de reforma agraria.* No. 611 extra ordinario, Mar. 19, 1960.
5. Lizardo, Pedro Francisco. *Reforma agraria en Venezuela, una revolucion dentro de la ley.* Caracas: Instituto Agrario Nacional, 1964.
6. Land Tenure Center. *Rural Development in Venezuela: A Bibliography.* Training and Methods Series, No. 20. Madison, July 1972.
7. Powell, John Duncan. *Political Mobilization of the Venezuelan Peasant.* Cambridge: Harvard Univ. Press, 1971.
8. Thiesenhusen, William C., with Ricardo Alezones, Ramon Pugh, and John Mathiason. "Leonardo Ruiz Pineda: A Case Study of a Venezuelan Agrarian Reform Settlement." Research Paper 7, Dec. 1968 (Mimeographed). CIDA/CENDES, Pan American Union, Washington, D.C.

CHAPTER 8

Changes in Ejidal Farming in Northwest Mexico's Modernized Agriculture: The Quechehueca Collective, 1938-1968

DONALD K. FREEBAIRN

BACKGROUND. Growth in the Mexican economy has been spectacular from the 1930s to the present. The gross national product rose at about 6% per year, the capital stock increased at about the same rate, and the structure of the economy has been dynamic, with manufacturing and construction providing increasing shares of the national product. The traditional sectors, particularly agriculture and mining, have dropped to more minor positions in the sectoral balance. These dynamic aspects of the Mexican economy provide the setting for an exploration of ejidal farming in northwest Mexico—a case study of agricultural development among the many possible alternatives.

It is precisely the nature of the general economic and political environment that permits an interpretation of a single example and generalization about the processes and problems of agricultural development. It is my intention to explore and identify the developing problems related to public agricultural policy in a country that has enjoyed a great measure of success in its recent economic development. In fact, it is because the society is rapidly modernizing and is achievement oriented that looking at its experiences may be worthwhile.

DONALD K. FREEBAIRN is Associate Professor, Department of Agricultural Economics, Cornell University, and was formerly Director, Latin American Studies Center, Cornell University. He is currently Associate Editor of the American Journal of Agricultural Economics. He began his research in Mexico while Agricultural Economist with the Rockefeller Foundation 1956–1964.

Although central attention will be given to the agrarian reform sector, it is impossible to understand the growth, development, and current problems of that sector without extending the description to agriculture in general and even to the emerging problems of the national economy. In the thirty years from 1940 to 1970, the Mexican economy grew from 20 million inhabitants with an average per capita income of roughly U.S. $240 (1970 prices) to almost a 50 million population in 1970 with a per capita income of U.S. $640. Almost all students of this growth would agree on the importance of structural transformation, the most important elements of which include the building of basic social capital, development of the incipient industrial sector, agrarian reform, formation of a growing and competent group of technicians and entrepreneurs, a modern financial system, and a competent public administration [14, 17, 21].

Over the past years there have been a great many changes in public policies influencing the rate and style of development. Heavy public investment in infrastructure provided not only the beneficial installations but also a large number of forward and backward linkages favoring economic development. For example, substantial investments in the construction of roads and bridges provided a secure market for expanded cement and steel production and at the same time lowered the supply prices of agricultural and other inputs for industry because of reduced transportation costs.

One of the recognizable limitations following a long period of successful development is the apparent unwillingness of public bodies to shift the public policy instruments responsible for past success. Policies initiated in the thirties and forties served well in their time but do not relate well to changed conditions. For example, new investments in infrastructure, as important as they may be in the resolution of specific problems, no longer carry the same forward and backward linkages as was the case thirty and more years ago. And import substitution in consumer goods industries, which served as a powerful stimulus to industrial development in the past, cannot reasonably be expected to serve as a powerful motor of development in the present.

Conditions and policies in the agricultural sector are not greatly different. The sector is generally credited with having played an important role in the progress of the Mexican economy. It was through rigorous application of agrarian reform laws that a number of structural rigidities were broken, which limited the possibilities of general economic growth. Thus forces were released that encouraged expansion of agricultural production and increased factor mobility not only in the labor force but also in capital, with resultant increases in managerial capacities.

Mexico's agrarian reform was based on the Constitution of 1917. The specifics are outlined in the Agrarian Code with latest reformulation occurring in 1971. The principal direct instrument of the agrarian reform was the *ejido,* an agrarian community that received and held land under any one of three basic conditions. According to Whetten, "lands may have been received as an outright grant from the government or as a restitution of lands that were previously possessed by the community and adjudged by the government to have been illegally appropriated by other individuals or groups; or the community may have received confirmation by the government of titles to land long in its possession. . . ." The term *ejidatario* refers to an individual who has participated as a beneficiary in a grant of land in accordance with the agrarian laws. The totality of ejidatarios participating in a given grant, together with their families and the lands they receive, constitute an ejido. Thus the term *ejido* refers to a community, while *ejidatario* refers to a specific individual [23].

Ejidos are formed on the basis of a petition to the state agrarian affairs office; members are listed in successful applications on the basis of an *ad hoc* agrarian census of the population center formulating the petition. In established ejidos, members are able to nominate their successors, usually a son (ejidal rights are not divisible), and the ejido may apply for an amplified grant to absorb new members. Amplification is not frequent because of the shortage of lands subject to expropriation.

The breaking up of the great landed estates and the broadening of ownership in rights in land gave Mexico a new rural structure. From 1915 to 1969 approximately 75 million hectares were transferred in ejidal grants, with about 2,800,000 direct beneficiaries (Table 8.1). Of equal importance has been the impetus given to the residual private sector, particularly the substantial number of moderately sized to larger farms. The stronger rural structure resulting from the agrarian reform provided the political base from which a developmentally biased overall agricultural policy could be formulated, the principal elements of which have included extensive water resource development, farm credit, price guarantees, the sponsorship of agricultural research and input supply, and other production-supporting activities. The result has been sustained growth of agricultural products, at an average rate of 4.5% each year, permitting the sector to respond to the needs of a rapidly growing

TABLE 8.1. Ejidal land grants and number of beneficiaries in Mexican agrarian reform, 1915–69

Years	Land Transferred Hectares	Acres	Direct Beneficiaries (no. of people)
1915–20	382,000	943,000	77,000
1921–34	10,639,000	26,278,000	870,000
1935–40	20,137,000	49,738,000	776,000
1941–58	17,182,000	42,439,000	458,000
1959–69	27,229,000	67,256,000	607,000
Total	75,569,000	186,655,000	2,788,000

Source: Centro de Investigaciones Agrarias, *Estructura Agraria y Desarrollo Agricola en Mexico.* Mexico, 1970, pp. 85–87.

urban population and to supply raw materials for domestic industries and for export [12].

Notwithstanding the success from the point of view of providing for national needs, there has been an increasing concern that agricultural policies, not unlike those for other sectors of the economy, may not be appropriate for the changed conditions in the nation. The principal effects of the agrarian reform have run their course. With the demonstrated ability of the agricultural sector to meet product demands, attention has shifted to a whole new gamut of undertakings. Expansion of internal demand for agricultural products and increased employment opportunities both within and outside agriculture have become more critical questions than the earlier ones related to production.

In this study our attention centers on the Mexican ejido. We use a case study of one of the modern and successful production-oriented ejidos, Quechehueca Collective in Sonora, against which to review the accomplishments of a long history of agricultural modernization and to trace the consequences of this capital-intensive development to issues of current national importance. In this respect, we will trace the development of the ejido in the Yaqui Valley of Sonora, one of the most modernized production zones of the country, and look with greater detail at the organization and development of Quechehueca Collective. Against this backdrop we will raise questions about the effectiveness of a capital-intensive agricultural development strategy in fulfilling national objectives. In addition and because of the general interest of the question, we will reflect on the institution of the ejido as a part of national development strategy.

EJIDAL FARMING IN THE YAQUI VALLEY
Development of Irrigation and Agriculture in the Yaqui Valley. The Yaqui Valley of Sonora State is a region that illustrates many aspects of Mexico's modern agricultural development. It is located on the periphery of the high population, central plateau region and has relatively low population densities; its emergence as an important agricultural region dates back only about eighty years. Since then, substantial investment in resource development has been made, technologically modern production practices have been facilitated and encouraged by public and private institutions, and an expanding capital-intensive agriculture has been developed. (In 1970, 25% of national wheat production and 10% of the cotton production originated in the valley.) The valley is typical of the new agriculture formed in northwest Mexico that has contributed so substantially to the country's agricultural growth [17].

No single factor has been more important to this growth than the development of the region's water resources. Crop farming began shortly after 1890 when the first colonists planted on the flats along the river bed, taking advantage of seasonal flooding for growing short-season crops in the basically desert region. It was in this year that the first concession for colonizing a major fraction of the valley was granted. Unable to successfully engage in large-scale water and land development, the concessionaires sold their rights to a New York banking group, which formed the Sonora-Sinaloa Irrigation Company. This company constructed the first 40 kilometers (25 miles) of the "Canal Principal" for the Yaqui irrigation system. In 1904 the Sonora-Sinaloa Irrigation Company entered receivership and its rights were sold to the Richardson Construction Company, a California-based construction and land development company. They in turn formed the Compania Constructora Richardson, S.A., and negotiated a new contract with the Mexican Ministry of Agriculture in 1909 permitting the company to engage in colonization of Yaqui Valley lands and utilize 3,900 million cubic meters of water annually. The concession provided that the company could not sell more than 2,000 hectares (approximately 5,000 acres) of irrigated lands to one person (or land company). Under the terms of the concession, the Richardson company laid out the grid of land divisions, roads, canals, and town borders that mark the region to this day. The company constructed a diversion dam in the river bed and developed distribution canals.

By 1926 there were close to 40,000 hectares (99,000 acres) under irrigated cultivation. In this year the Mexican government, noting that the company had failed to respect the terms of the concession, particularly the maximum size of parcel being sold, and also preoccupied by the Richardson company's apparent practice of favoring non-Mexicans in their sales, ordered cancellation of the concession, purchased all shares of the company, and turned over the company with all its assets to the Nacional Financiera (their recently established government development bank) to be continued as a land development and colonization company. Under a reorganization of public credit agencies in 1936, the Nacional Financiera was no longer permitted to carry out development activities related to land colonization. The shares of the Richardson company were therefore transferred to the National Agricultural Credit Bank, which assumed control of the company. Some years later this control was given to the National Irrigation Commission and, in 1951, all related activities were placed under the newly established Ministry of Water Resources.

During the 1930s the Public Water Resources Agency assumed responsibility for expanding the irrigation facilities for the valley; over the years it has built two major storage dams with associated canals and drains—the Angustura finished in 1941 and the Alvaro Obregon in 1952. These two storage dams have permitted the expansion of the area under irrigated cultivation to about 220,000 hectares (544,000 acres); climatic conditions permit double cropping with some crops, and water permitting, more than half the land could produce two harvests in any given year. However, available water supplies do not normally permit two harvests.

Estimates of growth in the area under cultivation and shifts in cropping composition are available for 1925–70 (Table 8.2). These data highlight two points: first, farmers in the private and ejidal sectors expanded the acreage of crops harvested rapidly in accordance with the availability of water. Between 1952 and 1954 as water from the Alvaro Obregon dam became available for irrigation, farmers doubled the amount of land cropped. Hence, in only two cropping seasons farmers put under the plough, leveled, built the required tertiary canals, expanded the on-farm capital and labor resources, and financed a doubling of the area's agriculture—a notorious example of a response to economic opportunities in agriculture. Second, these same farmers adjusted the composition of cropping in accordance with their perceptions of production opportunities. Rice and wheat were the predominant crops in the 1920s and 1930s; in the early 1940s flax substituted heavily for wheat when international markets for linseed oil were strong and when at the same time the wheat varieties became increasingly susceptible to leaf and stem rusts; in the early 1950s cotton entered the region's product mix, once again in response to strong international market opportunities, and flax was dropped as a major crop. At this time wheat increased again, as effective agricultural research developed disease-resistant varieties and government-guaranteed prices made it a more profitable crop than rice. During the 1960s a broader range of crops entered the cropping structure of the valley, which, while remaining predominantly a wheat-cotton area, saw both maize (corn) and soybeans forcing inroads as market limitations thwarted continued high production of wheat and both production problems and weak international markets caused a drop-off in the acreage planted in cotton.

Formation of Ejidos in the Valley. The Yaqui Valley of Sonora was one of the regions affected by the expanded agrarian reform activities under the Lazaro Cardenas administration (1934–40). By the mid-1930s a modern, capital-intensive agriculture had been established in the valley. While it is true that there were a number of farms well above the legal limit of 150 irrigated hectares (370 acres), the region had not developed a latifundia structure—agriculture was clearly organized under a modern capitalist orientation, with farms being well capitalized and farm laborers being paid comparatively high wages. Northwestern agriculture was establishing itself as a distinct fraction of the national agricultural sector, and it was laying claim to a right to be different and to be exempt from application of the agrarian code. There were two arguments for exemption. The first was a rationale of productivity; it was held that breaking up established farms in important agricultural regions would cause a serious decline in production, threatening the supply of domestic foodstuffs, but even more seriously reducing exports of crops with consequent implications for foreign exchange earnings. Second, particularly in the Yaqui Valley region, it was argued that the terms of the con-

TABLE 8.2. Area planted to principal crops, Yaqui Valley, Sonora, Mexico, 1925–70

Crop Year	Total	Cotton	Rice	Wheat	Flax	Sesame	Chick pea	Maize (Corn)	Soybean	Cartamo	Others
1925–26	37,033	...	12,606	15,586	...	...	1,615	2,329	...	...	4,897
1926–27	41,590	...	17,343	14,950	...	...	1,107	1,437	...	...	6,753
1927–28	44,113	...	15,248	17,969	...	...	162	1,612	...	...	9,122
1928–29	47,557	...	12,851	15,553	...	...	865	2,495	...	...	15,793
1929–30	46,788	...	6,939	20,929	...	...	63	3,110	...	...	15,747
1930–31	47,579	...	11,422	20,271	278	...	263	7,024	...	...	8,321
1931–32	43,681	...	14,762	12,263	2,508	242	143	3,727	...	...	10,036
1932–33	41,159	...	9,500	19,794	164	5	21	5,633	...	...	6,042
1933–34	47,123	...	11,084	28,558	360	2	122	1,878	...	...	5,119
1934–35	47,053	...	15,071	25,486	20	...	5	1,784	...	...	4,397
1935–36	53,108	...	14,892	32,958	60	...	...	2,066	...	...	3,132
1936–37	54,729	...	13,887	32,973	...	881	...	2,438	...	...	4,550
1937–38	56,295	...	18,131	34,040	...	752	...	1,876	...	...	1,496
1938–39	53,879	...	12,999	35,381	...	782	...	3,233	...	...	1,484
1939–40	62,561	...	20,098	38,110	...	881	...	2,438	...	...	1,034
1940–41	60,874	...	24,325	31,299	...	1,156	188	1,873	...	...	2,033
1941–42	65,989	...	25,880	30,226	1,455	613	654	1,652	...	...	5,509
1942–43	71,807	...	30,331	12,620	21,512	1,917	...	1,301	...	...	4,126
1943–44	77,496	...	31,030	21,019	13,299	1,901	...	4,928	...	...	5,319
1944–45	71,827	...	33,631	14,348	12,243	1,749	...	6,026	...	...	3,830
1945–46	86,614	...	28,593	35,274	4,874	2,696	...	8,636	...	...	6,541
1946–47	102,754	...	37,721	33,450	11,367	11,367	...	4,126	...	...	4,723
1947–48	89,920	...	43,428	21,414	13,260	5,254	...	3,626	...	...	2,808
1948–49	115,845	...	42,387	25,223	23,148	17,299	...	4,943	...	...	2,845
1949–50	130,668	3,679	57,340	47,981	7,398	10,318	...	2,661	...	...	1,291

216

TABLE 8.2. *(continued)*

Crop Year	Total	Cotton	Rice	Wheat	Flax	Sesame	Chick pea	Maize (Corn)	Soybean	Cartamo	Others
1950-51	123,852	21,940	30,872	46,811	13,615	3,252	...	6,104	...	...	1,258
1951-52	106,061	24,654	13,414	50,783	2,604	6,647	...	6,235	...	...	1,724
1952-53	126,027	42,658	14,389	56,755	6,099	1,180	...	3,056	...	...	1,890
1953-54	154,427	45,376	3,020	94,283	...	2,405	...	4,804	...	...	4,539
1954-55	209,493	86,874	4,149	113,267	157	436	...	2,597	...	...	2,013
1955-56	213,749	31,935	8,197	154,039	128	7,290	...	9,605	...	...	2,555
1956-57	221,848	49,695	1,609	143,110	252	2,271	...	15,418	...	...	9,493
1957-58	212,594	74,014	1,877	105,126	821	335	...	18,382	...	...	12,039
1958-59	226,492	47,672	4,263	130,500	543	3,697	...	26,600	...	...	13,217
1959-60	221,311	78,975	9,207	90,799	6,298	9,323	...	15,270	2,992	408	8,039
1960-61	258,916	56,041	14,519	110,685	2,274	22,047	...	23,016	8,574	862	20,898
1961-62	255,626	64,336	...	114,546	368	18,931	...	20,276	28,558	1,191	7,420
1962-63	234,853	47,226	...	143,504	208	2,100	...	36,134	570	74	5,037
1963-64	256,079	61,017	...	134,016	290	162	...	53,961	1,166	194	5,273
1964-65	263,913	53,265	...	138,392	76	4,863	...	44,186	17,344	72	5,715
1965-66	226,112	64,815	...	85,716	1,541	2,592	...	10,976	28,478	12,897	19,097
1966-67	291,041	47,546	...	136,696	1,180	11,227	...	41,574	34,732	5,979	12,157
1967-68	303,461	73,528	...	110,000	1,133	9,037	...	20,920	72,964	5,638	10,241
1968-69	323,094	49,692	...	129,449	437	8,934	...	11,316	107,220	4,266	11,780
1969-70	299,100	34,561	...	135,870	2,412	11,729	...	15,000	75,228	10,739	13,561

Source: Data for the years 1925–67 were obtained from the Ministry of Water Resources, Cd.Obregon; those for the period 1967–70 from the Ministry of Agriculture, also in Cd.Obregon.

cession granted to the Richardson Construction Company as well as the terms of Richardson's contracts with the colonists permitted the larger size of farm. Hence, it would be unlawful to confiscate these properties.

Peasants had, however, formed applications to receive land grants in accordance with the agrarian law, and they insisted that the articles of the constitution must be followed. Through errors in formulating the applications and through administrative inaction, decisions were held off from the period of the early twenties to the mid-thirties. With the exception of the ejido "Cajeme," which received a grant of desert lands outside the perimeter of the Richardson colonization scheme in 1924, all applications were sidetracked until 1935. In this year, two ejidal grants were made to the ejidos Bacum and Cocorit, both of which were located at the periphery of the Richardson land grid and where the lands were irrigated by a secondary canal system. All other pending applications were denied.

This resolution was highly unsatisfactory to the peasants and increased the level of tension within the area. Agricultural workers insisted that their constitutional rights to land be respected; colonists insisted that the terms of their concessions be defended and that their modernized production systems be maintained for the benefit of the nation. The Farmers' Association requested that a commission be formed to investigate and report on the conditions of the original Richardson concession and the subsequent presidential decrees made in 1926 and 1928 firmly establishing the inviolability of the Richardson land schemes' interests. At the same time the association offered its cooperation in helping resolve the land problems. In concrete terms the Farmers' Association agreed that its members would withdraw from cultivation (in proportion to the extension of their own farms) sufficient land to make enough water available for a proposed set of ejidal districts. They also promised to provide the land and money necessary to permit the lands in the proposed districts to be cleared, complete with irrigation facilities, and ready for cultivation. In return, the association requested that the proposed districts not be interspersed with the established farms and that the remaining areas be respected as continuing private farming areas. This plan, however, was at variance with the agrarian code providing for a dispersal of the ejido grants throughout the cultivated area; communities were to be granted land as close as possible to the population center in accordance with the availability of lands subject to expropriation from privately held farms.

The study commission was set up, and among other things it attempted to evaluate the distribution of land holding among the colonists within the Richardson land grid (Table 8.3). It was further reported there were eighty-five land holders with more than 150 hectares (370 acres), with an average of about 320 hectares (790 acres) per farm.

TABLE 8.3. Distribution of land holding within the Richardson land grid, Yaqui Valley, Sonora, Mexico, 1935

Size of Properties		Total Land in Size Group	
Hectares	Acres	Hectares	Acres
Less than 100	Less than 247	13,915	34,370
101–150	248–370	2,752	6,794
151–200	371–494	3,890	9,608
201–400	495–988	9,079	22,425
More than 400	More than 989	14,102	34,832
		43,738	108,033

The commission also carried out an agrarian census to identify the potential number of agrarian reform beneficiaries. Using the established requirements, they identified a total of 3,266 potential beneficiaries. The agrarian problem remained unresolved until 1938 when the government, taking account of the earlier studies and the prevailing political environment, decreed that the agrarian laws would be enforced and that the area-wide resolution of the agrarian problem would follow the mandates of the code, that is, that communities would be granted lands from their immediate environs and that ejidos would be distributed across the entire valley. A total of 2,160 ejidatarios were named to enjoy land rights and the grants included 17,400 hectares (43,000 acres) of irrigated land plus 36,000 hectares (89,000 acres) of adjoining nonirrigated lands. For the most part a given ejido enjoyed contiguous lands, but this was not always possible. The grant of the nonirrigated lands had little immediate economic significance in 1938, but as the irrigation networks were expanded, these potentially fertile lands gave the region's ejidatarios one of the country's biggest land endowments and the region's ejidal agriculture a special character.

The Ejido Credit Bank was the agency responsible for organizing and facilitating the development of a viable ejidal farming sector. The bank organized the newly founded ejidos into Local Societies of Collective Ejidal Credit to facilitate obtaining farm machinery and working capital and to provide for the means of sustenance until the ejidatarios could harvest their first crop. These societies had a much broader mandate than that of merely handling farm credit for the new group of farmers. The societies were, in effect, production cooperatives that constituted the administrative structure of the ejidos as farming units. Basically, the following norms determined the system of organizing a farm [3].

1. Each cooperative society consisted of the members of the parent ejido. The society was formed without member capital, each initiating its activities with credit from the Ejido Credit Bank. All members of the society accepted joint and unlimited financial responsibilities for the society and societies were organized for an indefinite time.

2. Ultimate authority for decisions rested in the General Assembly, where actions were taken by majority vote and where each member had one vote.

3. The profits of the society were to be distributed among members in accordance with the number of days worked.

4. An Administrative Commission elected by the membership at large was responsible for the management of the society. This commission, in turn, elected from its membership a Chief Delegate who was the principal administrative officer of the society. As a protection against abuse, the General Assembly also elected a "vigilance committee," which was responsible for seeing that the members' interests were not violated by the Administrative Commission.

5. Daily work routine was supervised by a Work Foreman, who was also elected by the General Assembly.

6. Technical direction for agricultural, financial, and marketing activities received direct assistance from the field officer of the Ejido Credit Bank. All monetary transactions of the society were reviewed by the local field officer of the bank.

These organizational norms gave the collective ejidos a particular structure for carrying on daily operations. A salient feature is that members had two sources of farm income, they received a conventional wage payment and, at the end of each fiscal period, a proportion of the society's profits based on the number of days worked.

As mentioned, all ejidos in the Yaqui Valley were organized as collective societies at their formation in 1938. There were in total fourteen ejidos, with 2,160 members and almost 18,000 hectares (44,500 acres) of

TABLE 8.4. Ejidal land grants and development of land resources, Yaqui Valley, Sonora, Mexico, 1938–43.

Ejidatarios	Number	
Ejidos formed in 1938	14	
Ejidatarios at establishment	2,159	
Ejidatarios at 1941 census[a]	1,810	
Land in ejidos (1938)	*(ha)*	*(acres)*
Irrigated	17,417	43,020
Desert lands	36,099	89,164
Total	53,516	132,184
Land brought under irrigation, 1938–43	8,344	20,610
Irrigated land in 1943	25,761	63,630
Land per ejidatario		
Land grant per ejidatario in 1938	8.07	19.9
Original land grant per member based on 1941 census	9.62	23.8
Land brought under cultivation, 1938–43 per ejidatario in 1941 census	4.61	11.4
Irrigated land endowment per ejidatario in 1943 based on 1941 census listing	14.23	35.1

Source: Ejidal Credit Bank study [3].

[a] Some of the original members abandoned their ejidos in the early years. The Agrarian Department carried out a formal census in 1941, redefining those who maintained land rights.

irrigated lands (8.3 hectares [21 acres] per member) plus 36,000 hectares (89,000 acres) of unimproved desert lands. Implementation of the agrarian reform laws transferred almost one-third of the valley's agriculture into the ejidal sector and put it under a distinct form of social organization, the cooperative production unit. Changes of this type have important implications for a region's production, and the performance of agriculture under this kind of social and organizational change has always been of interest. We are fortunate that the Banco Ejidal study, cited earlier, includes data on the performance of the ejidal sector in the regional agriculture from 1938 to 1943 (Tables 8.4 to 8.6).

The data are suggestive of the nature of early ejidal agricultural development in the valley. The new societies had numerous problems in their first years. They had to develop a farm organization; involve members of widely varied backgrounds and capacities as productive members of the cooperative community; obtain control over needed capital and technical knowledge; decide on rates of expansion of their productive base at the expense of current income; and work out social relationships with other farming interests, with political pressure groups, and with governmental agencies. The data in the tables suggest that the new sector was successful in getting started. Among other things, the ejidos expanded their land base; they obtained crop yields higher than those registered by the established farmers in the region; and they witnessed

TABLE 8.5. Indicators of farming efficiency, collective ejidos in the Yaqui Valley, Sonora, Mexico, 1938–43

Comparative Crop Yields

Crop	All Valley (kg/ha)	All Valley (bu/acre)	Ejidal (kg/ha)	Ejidal (bu/acre)
Wheat	770	11.6	820	12.3
Rice (paddy)	1,640	32.5	1,690	33.4

Loan Repayments 1938–43

Concept	Mexican Pesos[a]
Total money loaned, 1938–43	22,580,000
Recuperated	15,978,000
Not yet due (Dec. 31, 1943)	4,711,000
In arrears	1,893,000

Recuperation of Loans by Year, 1938–43

Year	Recuperations as a percentage of loans coming due in the given year	Recuperation as a percentage of all loans due
1938	0	0
1939	78	66
1940	74	69
1941	66	68
1942	120	83
1943	104	89

Source: Ejidal Credit Bank study [3].
[a] Money in current monetary value.

TABLE 8.6. Farm earnings for ejidatarios, collective ejidos in the Yaqui Valley, Sonora, Mexico, 1942–43 (1942–43 money values)

Labor	Numbers	
Number of ejidos reporting	14	
Number of members who worked	1,712	
Average days worked per member working	184	
Total work-days worked	315,105	
Gross earnings	Pesos	Dollars
Gross earnings received (1942–43 value)	1,291,229	266,233
Total distributed profits (1942–43 value)	1,378,190	284,163
Sum of farm earnings received by members (1942–43 value)	2,669,419	550,396
Farm earnings		
Average ejidatario earnings per day worked (1942–43 value)	8.47	1.75
Average ejidatario farm earning for the year (1942–43 value)	1,559	321.00
Average daily earnings (365 days/year) (1942–43 value)	4.27	0.88
Minimum daily agricultural wage established by law for the zone (1942–43 value)	2.70	0.56

Source: Ejidal Credit Bank study [3].
Note: During 1942–43 the rate of exchange was U.S. $1.00 = Mexican pesos 4.85.

improved capacity in paying back bank loans. By the fourth and fifth years they had begun to make substantial repayments on earlier years' indebtedness; members' farm earnings were substantially higher than the area minimum wage; and a number of social benefits evolved that had not been available in the prereform period, including village schools, medical clinics, and a small hospital in Ciudad Obregon.

These accomplishments might lead one to believe that the successful start would have established a base from which the collective ejidos of the Yaqui Valley could have developed into a significant production and social force in Mexican agriculture. This was not the case. In fact, throughout the founding years there were strong underlying problems; many centered on the questions related to the form of social organization—cooperative or individual. Others included area-wide production problems, such as serious rust infestations on wheat causing low yield, and doubts concerning the integrity of the directive committees and government agency officials. The area also was not isolated from the national political arena, where the pattern of long-term national development was being influenced by the interplay of established interests and contrasting views of what Mexico might look like twenty-five years hence. For the most part, these were the vocalized points of reference for the actions that were to follow. I would suggest, however, that many of these issues were the surface points of discussion for a deep-seated lack of confidence on the part of the ejidatarios as to where they might fit into the picture of Mexico's modern agriculture.

Beginning in the mid-1940s and continuing through the 1960s the ejidal sector suffered under repeated periods of economic and social instability. During the 1940s the collective societies began to dissolve, most usually separating between those who wanted individual parcels and those who wanted to continue their cooperative farms. There have been cases also, where the decision to dissolve came because the members were unable to work together and wanted to set up separate administrations on a smaller scale, even though both sides were convinced of the convenience of cooperative farming. By 1970 no original ejido in the Yaqui Valley remained as a single collective farm. Of the original 2,160 ejidatarios granted land rights in 1938, only 40 have had a continuing history of working under strictly defined cooperative norms, and even this one constant group has been described as being more nearly capitalist *corporative* than *cooperative* in nature [8]. But more than just the integrity of the originally organized cooperative farm has been involved. Although the agrarian reform program was carried out under the banner of "land and liberty" where the call was for the benefits of the land to accrue to him who worked it, much of the ejido land in this valley has been rented recently to adjoining farmers, and an additional large segment has been farmed under contract, with the owners of the usufruct rights having only the most cursory involvement in the production processes. Even on the collective farm, which we will review in detail, over three-quarters of the work force in 1968 was made up of hired workers, almost none of the physical (as contrasted to administrative and supervisory) work was done by members, and only 20% of the members worked at all on the farm. Some years ago the bylaws were changed so that the profits of the farm were shared equally among members without reference to days worked; most members, in effect, live off their income from land rent.

Before leaving consideration of the region as a whole, it is important to point out that the agrarian reform beneficiaries in this region were favored by the continued development of the region's resources. Since the land grants were made, two storage dams have been completed, the first providing a major increase in stored water, permitting much more equal water distribution during the course of the year for the established agricultural region, and the second (the larger of the two) permitting a doubling of the area under cultivation. This provision of irrigation facilities for lands that were formerly desert greatly increased the land resources of the ejido sector. Some ejidos in 1968 had almost 50 hectares (123 acres) of irrigated land per member, and the great majority had between 20 and 30 hectares (50 and 74 acres). The failure of a strong ejidal sector to develop under these most favorable circumstances provides a serious challenge to this type of organizational strategy.

THE QUECHEHUECA COLLECTIVE—GROWTH AND DIVISIONS. Ejido Quechehueca was formed in 1937 under authorization from the governor of the state of Sonora and was a part of the agrarian reform activities carried out in the Yaqui Valley at the behest of General Lazaro Cardenas, president of Mexico from 1934 to 1940. The actual Presidential Resolution, confirming the actions of the state government was dated January 5, 1938. It provided that Ejido Quechehueca be made up of 183 beneficiaries and that the land endowment would be 1,472 hectares (3,640 acres) of irrigated lands and 4,000 hectares (9,800 acres) of unimproved desert that could be used for grazing the ejido members' animals, plus a school parcel. The irrigated lands had been expropriated from several farming corporations having land in excess of that permitted by the agrarian laws and that surrounded the small population center; the nonirrigated lands were expropriated directly from the land development corporation.

As was true for all the ejidos in the Yaqui Valley, Quechehueca was organized as a collective or cooperative production unit. This was as President Cardenas desired, and there is, through much of the literature on Mexican agrarian reform, the insistence that the collective production system was inherently superior for both the needs of the country and the peasant farmers [1, 3, 6, 20]. The evidence is clear that great numbers of ejidatarios were not so convinced. Within ten years of formulation, most of the ejidos had divided into two or more societies: one was usually a collective structure and the other had individual operation of parcels. Quechehueca maintained its unity from the time of formation in 1937 until 1948 when it divided into two societies, one naming itself the Aguila with individual operation and the other continuing under the name of Quechehueca with collective exploitation, but it was still technically a single ejido. In 1950 it formally divided into two ejidos: the Ejido Aguila with 75 members, 2267 hectares (5,600 acres) of land, and individual operation; and the Ejido Quechehueca with 107 members (plus the school plot), 3,205 hectares (7,920 acres) of land, and a collective farming organization. Once again in 1957 the Ejido Quechehueca divided into two groups (but not two ejidos): one, Quechehueca No. 1 with individual organization and 61 members, and the other, Quechehueca Collective with a collective structure and 41 members. It is this latter group that serves as the present case study.

We are fortunate that a number of detailed studies had been carried out at different times permitting us to look at the growth and development of agricultural organization, productivity, and farm income levels for the ejidal sector of the Yaqui Valley and for Quechehueca Collective in particular. I have cited earlier the Banco Ejidal study [3], but there are others. Works by Andrade and Freebairn, Fernandez y Fernandez, and Silva treat this region specifically [2, 8, 19]. In a broader sense, the work by Erasmus and the criticism of it by Huizer are also relevant [7, 13].

A number of the elements that contributed to the fundamental structure of northwest agriculture held for this case study of the Quechehueca Collective, and it is perhaps useful to point them out again.

TABLE 8.7. Characteristics of Quechehueca Collective, Yaqui Valley, Sonora, Mexico, 1942 and 1968 (1968 money values)

	1942		1968	
Number of Members	184		40	
Land Resources	Hectares	Acres	Hectares	Acres
Irrigated land at time of grant	1,472	3,636	320	790
Lands brought under cultivation	1,289	3,184	868	2,144
Nonirrigated lands	2,711	6,696	0	0
Total land	5,472	13,516	1,188	2,934
Capital Resources	Pesos	Dollars	Pesos	Dollars
Farm Machinery and equipment	...	...	2,960,000	236,800
Buildings and land improvements	...	...	135,000	10,800
Vehicles	...	...	350,000	28,000
Office equipment	...	...	64,000	5,120
Total farm capital	3,100,000	248,000	3,509,000	280,720
Labor Employed (in work-days)				
Administrative	...	...	3,851	
Regular and temporary workers	...	...	30,973	
Cotton picking	...	...	23,841	
Total		45,167	58,665	
Work-days employed per ha of irrigated land		16.8	49.4	
Land Use	Hectares	Acres	Hectares	Acres
Wheat	285	704	566	1,398
Rice	1,300	3,211	...	...
Cotton	400	988	584	1,442
Flax	700	1,729	...	...
Soybeans	...	...	428	1,057
Maize	...	...	340	840
Total	2,685	6,632	1,918	4,737
Farm Production		Metric Tons		Metric Tons
Wheat		237		1,860
Rice		2,255		...
Flax		579		...
Cotton (seed)		279		1,413
Soybeans		...		902
Maize		...		1,465
Member Earnings	Pesos	Dollars	Pesos	Dollars
Annual wage and profit income per member	2,192	175.36	56,241	4,500
Average daily income (365 days)	6.00	0.48	154.09	12.33
Regional daily minimum wage (365 days)	2.70	0.22	30.00	2.40

Source: Data for 1942 are derived from the Banco Ejidal study [3]; those for 1968 were obtained from the society's accounting records and personal interviews both in the ejido and in public offices.

Note: The 1968 exchange rate was 12.5 pesos = $1.00.

TABLE 8.8. Per member characteristics of Quechehueca Collective, 1942 and 1968, Yaqui Valley, Sonora, Mexico

	1942		1968	
	Hectares	Acres	Hectares	Acres
Land Resources				
Irrigated land at time of land grant	8.0	19.8	8.0	19.8
Lands brought under cultivation	7.0	17.3	21.7	53.6
Nonirrigated lands	14.7	36.3	0	0
Total land	29.7	73.4	29.7	73.4
	Pesos	Dollars	Pesos	Dollars
Value of Farm Equipment (1968 money values)	17,400	1,392	87,725	7,018
Labor Employed	Work-days 245		Work-days [a]	
	Hectares	Acres	Hectares	Acres
Land Planted	14.6	36.1	48.0	118.6

[a] Most employment was nonmember hired labor.

We are dealing with a region far separated from the principal population center of the country; the countryside is basically desert and its development into an agricultural emporium has been dependent on water resource development. Because of the long distance from national markets, the product mix has been staples, for both domestic use (grains and oilseeds) and export (cotton). From the beginning, agricultural enterprise in both the established private sector and the ejidal sector had been capital intensive and technologically modern. Forming the ejidal sector into cooperative farming units, and charging the Ejidal Bank to provide the necessary technical and financial support to facilitate this kind of agricultural organization, set the formal structure of a modernized and technical agriculture very early in the region's development.

The data in Tables 8.7 to 8.9 summarize the comparative farm organization for Quechehueca Collective for over 25 years of its history. The development of the ejidos' land resources was well under way by 1942, five years after establishment. The ejido, with Ejido Credit Bank technical and financial support, had established a series of pumping stations that almost doubled the land under irrigation. The farm also had a substantial complement of heavy equipment and machinery, a total of 478,000 pesos worth was reported for the end-of-year inventory in 1942 (roughly equivalent to U.S. $100,000 at 1942 prices). The cropping system was relatively straightforward in the early years, with rice, flax, and wheat predominating. Quechehueca was one of the few farming units in the valley planting cotton in 1942; as such, it was experimenting with a crop that was to become increasingly dominant in the regional cropping pattern. In that year, however, the experiment was

TABLE 8.9. Crop yields and loan repayments, Quechehueca Collective and Valley average, Yaqui Valley, Sonora, Mexico, 1942 and 1968

	Ejido		Valley Average	
	(kg/ha)	(lb/acre)	(kg/ha)	(lb/acre)
1942 Crop Yields				
Wheat	832	742 (12.4 bu)	774	690 (11.5 bu)
Rice	1,735	1,548 (34.4 bu)	1,582	1,411 (31.4 bu)
Flax	827	738	682	608
Cotton (seed)	699	624		
Loan Repayment Rate[a]	94%		89%	
1968 Crop Yields				
Wheat	3,286	2,931 (48.8 bu)	2,838	2,531 (42 bu)
Cotton (seed)	2,240	1,998	2,579	2,300
Soybeans	2,107	1,879 (31.3 bu)	2,365	2,110 (35.2 bu)
Maize (corn)	4,309	3,844 (68.6 bu)	3,800	3,390 (60 bu)
Loan Repayment Rate[a]	100%		92%	

[a] Ejido Credit Bank payments as a percentage of loans falling due for the periods 1937–43 and 1965–69.

an expensive luxury, for it contributed a substantial loss to the ejidos' financial results. And, as was true for the entire valley, wheat yields were extremely low. Traditional varieties were not resistant to the rust pathogens endemic to the region. Rice, however, yielded well and flax had a strong market in these early years.

The farm unit provided an estimated 254 days of employment for members. We do not know the extent to which nonmembers worked on the farm, and while it is possible there would be some peak-time outside workers required, the spread of seasonal work over farm crops with little or no double cropping suggests there would not have been a great deal. The low cotton crop yields obviated the need for many temporary workers, even for cotton picking.

Intertemporal comparisons of farm management effectiveness are difficult to make. I have chosen three indicators: two compare the Quechehueca Collective's accomplishments with the average circumstances in the valley and another compares member earnings from the ejido with the statutory minimum wage. In 1942 this ejido compared favorably on each of the measures. Crop yields on the collective farm were better than those obtained generally in the valley. Their loan repayment record was better than the average and their payments in 1941 and 1942 covered not only loans falling due in these years but made significant reductions on previous years' bad debts. And the income obtained by members was over twice that received by those few agricultural laborers who were able to find full-time work. Reasonable wages, full-time employment, an increasingly demonstrated debt-paying capacity, a technically satisfactory agriculture, and a rapidly expanding production base all promised a successful future to this farm. Yet, during the following ten to fifteen years the production unit underwent two major reformulations. The data for 1968 indicate the kind of farm organization under recent circumstances. The essential elements established twenty-five years earlier still hold. The farm operates on a capital-intensive basis, it has slightly higher than average area yields, it has a record of full repayment of bank credit providing a good credit rating, and member farm earnings are both absolutely and relatively high.

It may fairly be asked if those who chose to follow individual cultivation of their parcels did better. We do not have the information for ejidatarios who chose this path to compare to the results obtained on Quechehueca Collective. Data from two studies do give some indications, however, particularly with respect to income generated and member participation [2]. To make income comparisons it is necessary to inflate the income-generating capacity identified in the Silos-Freebairn study of individually cultivated ejido parcels, which was based on the valley average of 18 hectares (45 acres) per parcel, for members of Quechehueca Collective enjoy the product from a comparatively large 30 hectares (74 acres) of land per member. The income-generating capacity for an equivalent 29.7-hectare (73.4-acre) parcel under individual cultivation would have been approximately 51,500 pesos (U.S. $4,120). This is quite comparable to the 56,241 pesos (U.S. $4,500) per-member earnings obtained in Quechehueca Collective in 1968. (Ejidatario earnings were also quite similar between the individually farmed parcel and the collective farm in the Silos-Freebairn study [18].)

Ejidatarios also have the alternative of renting their parcels. Although the opportunities for legally exercising this alternative are restricted, rentals are commonly reported. Rent is most commonly specified in a peso payment per crop planted, although there are share rental arrangements. About one-fourth of all ejido lands in the valley were reported rented out in the Andrade and Freebairn survey [2, p. 34]. Income from cash renting would be somewhat less than that from directly operated farms. Using going cash rent rates and the same cropping pattern and resource endowment as that of Quechehueca Collective, farmers would receive approximately 33,500 pesos (U.S. $2,680) if they rented out all their land. The lower annual income from renting would be somewhat compensated by the elimination of farming risks and the complete absence of ejidatario capital, labor, or management participation. With respect to income earned by ejidatarios from their farming operations, we may conclude there are no notorious differences between those who operate their parcels individually and those who choose to operate within a cooperative farming structure. Cash rental of the parcel produced less income but reduced the ejidatario's obligations in the production processes.

A second major comparison may be made with respect to ejidatario participation in the farming activities. The issue is to measure the degree to which the system of farm organization may contribute to the socially healthy end of substantial member involvement in farm production processes. The data show that ejidatarios on individually parceled

TABLE 8.10. Availability of ejidatario family labor and its utilization on individually parcelized ejidos in the Yaqui Valley, Sonora, Mexico

Class of Worker	Work-months of Work Potential[a]	Work-months Spent on the Parcel	Work-months Worked off the Farm	Work-months Idle
Ejidatario (men)	27,400	14,300	5,600	7,500
Wife	400	100	...	300
Sons	13,300	7,000	1,700	4,600
Other family members	3,400	1,400	600	1,400
Ejidatario (women)	500	100	100	300
Totals	45,000	22,900	8,000	14,100

Source: Farm survey by Andrade and Freebairn, 1965 [2].

[a] The numbers are expanded from a probability survey carried out in the Yaqui Valley; details on the sampling procedure are given in the original report [2].

ejidos report approximately one-half the potentially available family labor employed on the farm enterprise (Table 8.10). A further breakdown of the time spent by ejidatario family labor on the parcel showed that only 4,800 work-months of the 22,900 dedicated to the farm were spent on what could be considered normally productive farm activities. Over 80% of the time dedicated to the farm was spent in supervising machine-hired services, obtaining credit, making marketing arrangements, and other like activities. On balance, in a carefully carried out survey of ejidatario's time utilization, Andrade and Freebairn demonstrated that only about 10% of the productive energies of the member families were used in direct farming operation on the parceled ejidos [2].

A study by Silva gives approximately comparable data for Quechehueca Collective [19]. Using the daily worksheet from the collective's accounting office, Silva determined that members worked on the farm less than one-half of the potentially available work-days. Of the days worked, only about one-half were spent on farming operations, with the rest spent on managerial and supervisory tasks. He also reported that the ejido required more work-days for the field labor in given crops than the average for the valley (for example, 9 work-days per hectare [3.6 work-days per acre] devoted to wheat vs. 7 work-days for the valley, and 92 work-days per hectare [37 work-days per acre] of cotton vs. 68 for the valley). This greater use of labor than the regional average suggests that some jobs may have been created for members, and this has been suggested as being the case in field inquiries. With respect to the heavy administrative component on the collective farm, it should be clarified that we are dealing with a large and complex farming unit. Over a hundred work-years of employment are provided on the farm and so large an enterprise may well justify the employment on managerial and supervisory tasks of about one-fourth of the members' labor supply. By comparison, the managerial tasks on the 20- to 30-hectare (50- to 74-acre) individually operated ejidal parcels, where most farming operations are carried out by custom hire, are almost nonexistent.

What does follow is that on both collective farms and individually operated parcels, ejidatarios themselves do little of the actual farm work. At the same time, whether by choice or by necessity, members and their families are unemployed about one-half of their potential work time. The evidence is clear that the farming system employed, that is, a highly modern, capital-intensive agriculture, has not provided the agrarian reform beneficiaries with steady and productive employment. Members' earnings are high by Mexican agricultural standards, but these are largely influenced by the extraordinarily large land base of this group of ejidatarios.

Ejidal farm organization in northwest Mexico has been strongly criticized because it does not comply with the original philosophical formulation of the reform. The concept was of a group of landless agricultural workers being banded together in a collaborative production enterprise. Some used the term "haciendas sin hacendados" (that is, the efficiency of large-scale enterprise without the stigma of the single owner). Today in the northwest only a small fraction of ejidatarios are organized in cooperative farming units; and whether in this form of farm organization or not, they do not, for the most part, actively work on the farm. Most of their earnings are rental income. Recognizing the inconsistency of this arrangement with the reform philosophy that the benefits of land should accrue to him who works it, we must accept that there may be enough extenuating circumstances to provide justification. Under any circumstances, what is important is whether the entire system of production can reasonably be able to offer promise of a socially desirable strategy of development. It is this criterion that should now guide evaluation.

OVERVIEW. Mexico's agrarian reform has developed a life of its own and all too frequently the issues surrounding the rights in land have found themselves separated from the rest of society's pressing social, economic, and political problems. The record indicates that in the beginning this was not so; the formulators of the Constitution of 1917 were preoccupied with the necessity to get the war-ravaged countryside back into effective production of the goods needed for both domestic use and export. The Zapatista forces were interested in the rights of the peasants, who had either lost out to the encroachments of the hacienda in the Porfirio Diaz regime or who had never had very substantial rights. The thrust, then, was the need to formulate a land policy that would provide a flow of goods and yet simultaneously satisfy the call of the less advantaged peasants for a participative share in the national society.

The formula adopted was a dual-structured agrarian system providing for a private proprietorship sector and an ejidal sector. The great haciendas were to be broken up because they held little promise of being able to respond to the national product needs, but a strong residual private sector was to be maintained. In answer to the peasant call for "land and liberty," the ejidal sector was established. This sector was to provide some stability to the society and a sense of participation and security to the peasants who received land rights. In the early years the ejido grants were not expected to provide full productive employment to the recipients. It was expected that ejidatarios would work on the privately held farms in the region and use their ejidal allotments to provide a subsistence for themselves and their families. It was not until the mid-1930s that policy shifted to call for the establishment of economically viable ejidal land grants. In this sense the 8-hectare (20-acre) grants made in the Yaqui Valley met the new norm. The fact that substantial additional desert lands were opened to irrigation was a fortuitous accident for this group of reform beneficiaries.

Mexico's experience in agrarian reform has generated a substantial amount of external interest. The operation of two landholding structures—one private, the other ejidal—has attracted a number of scholars to attempt comparative evaluations. Typical of these studies is that of Dovring, which uses census data to compare crop yields between the two sectors [4]. Considering the reliability of the basic data and the fact that production from ejido lands rented by the private sector are reported as ejido production (thus confounding the comparison being attempted), it is not surprising that no significant differences were identified. Using the considerably more sophisticated returns to all factors (rather than just crop yields), Mueller drew about the same conclusions—that there are no notorious differences in factor productivity between the two sectors [15].

Studies of this type have been criticized by Weckstein as failing to capture the essential elements of a comparison between the two subsectors of Mexican agriculture [22]. He points out that the two subsectors are formed by quite distinct institutional arrangements and that as a consequence producers in each of the two sectors face completely different factor markets and even in some instances final product markets. As a consequence, the two sectors are substantially insulated from one another. Weckstein's formulation of the problem is a substantial contribution to understanding ejidal vs. private farming in Mexico because his evaluation includes the full set of supporting mechanisms for each of the systems.

It is precisely in the framework of the full set of supporting mechanisms that one sees how the two sectors function in contemporary Mexico. While the definitive study has yet to be carried out, a number of students of Mexican agricultural development suggest that the public policies related to agriculture have been almost exclusively directed toward increasing production and that fostering a small modern technologically advanced and capital-intensive subsector consisting almost, although not completely, of the larger farmers in the private sector has been the instrument of these production-expanding policies [6, 11, 12,

14, 21]. The effort to foster rapid expansion of production in a limited number of regions and for a few farmers within these regions by selectively providing the supporting mechanisms of a modernized agriculture —irrigation, applied agronomic research, chemical and mechanical inputs, agricultural credit, guaranteed prices, and market services—has brought with it a pronounced concentration of the benefits from the progress in Mexico's agriculture.

Increasingly, there is a call for a broadening of participation, but it is difficult to shift away from the programs that have been successful in meeting the national product needs in years past. And, as has been the theme throughout this case discussion, land policy and agricultural policy must be understood with reference to the overall national society. The policies for this sector must make sense in terms of what is planned and desired for the society in general. The overriding issues of the day are increased employment opportunities for a rapidly expanding work force, a broadening of the participation in the benefits from economic growth and progress, and an increasing democratization in political, social, and economic affairs. What is done in agriculture must be coordinated with what is planned for the total economy. Except in the continuation of the status quo, there are few guidelines as to the directions that may be followed.

One can conceive, however, of two alternatives that might be considered to bracket the range of alternatives. On one hand, policies might be followed that would tend to incorporate as many farmers as possible into a commercial and modestly productive agriculture. Not all would have the resources to qualify, but even for these, positive welfare-oriented policies might be followed that would tend to hold them in the countryside until they could be absorbed productively in urban and industrial society. The linkages to national policy supporting this kind of alternative are extraordinarily strong, for the number of farmers who can participate in the productive sector will be strongly influenced by the demand restraints defined, in part, by income distribution in urban society. At the same time, the number who can be held in reserve, awaiting their incorporation into the industrial sector and receiving welfare transfers from that sector, will depend on the degree of social and political democratization making these transfers possible.

At the other extreme of the range of alternatives, the path is not simple either. A forced urbanization policy could conceivably be followed that would work toward the rapid incorporation of the great mass of underemployed rural (and also marginal urban) workers into the industrial sector. Agriculture would purposefully employ relatively small numbers but would be highly modern and productive in structure. The capital-intensive modernization policies in agriculture followed over the past 30 years in Mexico would be accelerated and, based on a demonstrated capacity to produce, the society could be reasonably assured that its agricultural sector could respond to the product needs. Doubts probably need not center in such an alternative about the capacity of the residual agricultural sector to produce, but rather about the capacity of the rest of society to form the capital and build the structures permitting the forced urbanization to take place.

The role of the ejido as a structural element of Mexican agrarian society comes out differently depending on the direction events may take. The ejido is a good unit if Mexico chooses to expand the participation of small farmers in total national agricultural production. It would seem to be well situated also as an instrument through which a thoughtful welfare program might be structured. The ejido counts within its members perhaps about 1,600,000 active small farmers. Notwithstanding that about half again as many have abandoned their ejido rights, the institution has been credited with keeping a large number of farm families in the rural areas and away from the slums of the big cities. But there is a minimum of well-being against which it cannot hold the farmers and most particularly their children. Only a purposeful public health, housing, and educational program can be expected to hold populations in the least well-situated rural areas until they can be released and prepared to enter into more productive activities elsewhere. At the other end of the spectrum, if policies concentrate on a selective and modernized agriculture, few except the most privileged ejidatarios (some from the Yaqui Valley) would find a continuing role in agriculture. Under these circumstances, the ejido as an institution would have only modest viability.

Over the years, Mexican agriculture and particularly its ejidal sector has attracted international attention. A major reason it deserves this attention is that the society has demonstrated an ingenious capacity to be socially innovative. It was able in years past to draw on pre-Colombian and medieval Spanish landholding institutions as well as contemporary Western European ones to formulate its own distinct landholding structure. Today the country has an ample breadth of experience to shift land and agricultural policies in accordance with national objectives. The agricultural sector's dual structure permits either an accentuation of progress emphasizing production growth from a limited number of modern capital-intensive units or permits a shift to a wider participation in the national agricultural production by a greater number of less well-situated and smaller farmers. The direction of the policies will be determined at a broader level of generalization than the agricultural sector itself; it is comforting to know that experience exists in the countryside that can be used in the implementation of whatever programs of change are chosen.

REFERENCES

1. Agronomos Socialistas (Liga de). *La Comarca Lagunera*. Mexico, 1940.
2. Andrade, F. J., and Freebairn, D. K. *Economia Agricola en el Valle del Yaqui: Los Ejidatarios Individuales*. Folleto Tecnico Nr. 49, Instituto Nacional de Investigaciones Agricolas, Mexico, 1965.

3. Banco National de Credito Ejidal, S. A. *El Sistema de Produccion Colectiva en los Ejidos del Valle del Yaqui, Sonora.* Mexico, 1945.
4. Dovring, Folke. "Land Reform and Productivity in Mexico." *Land Economics* 46 (3, Aug. 1970).
5. Duran, Marco Antonio. *El Agrarismo Mexicano.* Siglo Veintiuno Editores, Mexico, 1967.
6. Eckstein, Solomon. *El Ejido Colectivo en Mexico.* Fondo de Cultura Economica, Mexico, 1966.
7. Erasmus, Charles J. *Man Takes Control.* Minneapolis: Univ. of Minnesota Press, 1961.
8. Fernadez y Fernandez, Ramon. "La Collectiva ha Muerto; Viva la Colectiva!" *Revista Chapingo,* Epoca II, 1 (3, July–Sept. 1961).
9. ———. *Propiedad Privada versus Ejidos.* Escuela Nacional de Agricultura, Chapingo, Mexico, 1954.
10. *Financial Times.* "Indian Agriculture: Mechanisation Creates a Labour Shortage." London, Feb. 9, 1972.
11. Flores, Edmundo. *Vieja Revolucion, Nuevos Problemas.* Juaquin Mortiz, Mexico, 1970.
12. Freebairn, Donald K. "Dichotomy of Prosperity and Poverty in Mexican Agriculture." *Land Economics* 45 (1, Feb. 1969).
13. Huizer, Gerrit. "Resistencia al 'Cambio' como una Potencial para la Accion Radical Campesina." *America Indigena* 30 (2, Apr. 1970).
14. Ibarra, David. "Mercados, Desarrollo y Politica Economica," in *El Perfil de Mexico en 1980* 1:89–199, Siglo Veintiuno Editores, Mexico, 1970.
15. Mueller, M. W. "Changing Patterns of Agricultural Output and Productivity in the Private and Land Reform Sectors in Mexico, 1940–60." *Economic Development and Cultural Change* 18 (Jan. 1970):2.
16. "Perfil Demografico de Mexico (II), Dinamica de la Ocupacion." *Panorama Economico,* May–June 1971, Mexico.
17. Reynolds, Clark W. *The Mexican Economy.* New Haven: Yale Univ. Press, 1970.
18. Silos, J. S., and Freebairn, D. K. *El Valle del Yaqui, Sonora, Su Desarrollo Agricola, Utilizacion de Recursos y Potencial Economico.* Colegio de Postgraduados, Chapingo, Mexico, 1970.
19. Silva, Hector. "Las Colectivas en el Valle del Yaqui, Sonora." *Tesis Profesional,* Escuela Nacional de Agricultura. Chapingo, Mexico, 1964.
20. Simpson, Eyler. *The Ejido: Mexico's Way Out.* Chapel Hill: Univ. of North Carolina Press, 1937.
21. Solis, Leopoldo. *La Realidad Economica Mexicana.* Siglo Veintiuno Editores, Mexico, 1970.
22. Weckstein, R. S. "Evaluating Mexican Land Reform." *Economic Development and Cultural Change* 15 (Apr. 1970):3.
23. Whetton, Nathan L. *Rural Mexico.* Chicago: Univ. of Chicago Press, 1948.

PART 4
Accelerating Production on Small Farms

CHAPTER 9

Policies and Programs for Small-Farm Development

ROBERT D. STEVENS

THE CHARACTERISTICS OF SMALL FARMS AND AGRICULTURAL DEVELOPMENT THEORY. The purpose of this chapter is to set guidelines for policies and programs that will result in accelerated agricultural output and income growth on small farms. These conclusions about effective government actions for small-farmer development follow from the theory of the transformation of traditional agriculture set forth in Part I and from the empirical analyses in the six detailed studies of Parts II and III. To gain focus, the following few paragraphs highlight resource and institutional characteristics of small-farm agriculture in low-income nations that limit growth and set forth the implications of agricultural development theory for government policies and programs for small farms. The central task of government is to facilitate the shift of small farms from a natural resource-based traditional agriculture to a science-based dynamic agriculture.

Resource and Institutional Characteristics of Small Farms Limiting Growth. The general resource characteristics and the institutional conditions surrounding the more than 100 million smallholders in developing nations are known from many studies, although detailed information about a large number of particular farming regions in the developing world is still lacking. The quantity and kind of resources on small farms that affect agricultural development can be summarized under the categories of labor, natural resources, and capital.

Labor resources on small farms in low-income nations have two principal characteristics related to accelerated growth. First, the supply of labor per unit of land is large in many areas, especially where population densities are high. Labor availability will continue to increase due to persistent high rates of population growth and limited urban job opportunities [9, 10]. Thus the increasing supply of rural labor will tend to keep labor costs low relative to land and capital. Hence, in these areas labor-intensive agricultural technology for small farms will, in many cases, provide the highest returns to farmers. The second general characteristic of small farms related to labor is of labor shortage during peak periods of labor demand, usually at planting and harvesting, due to the seasonal nature of agriculture. As the shortage of labor at peak labor demand periods often limits the total amount of crop production, investment in hand, small motorized, and other farm equipment or rental of large machinery that will reduce peak labor demands can permit major increases in agricultural production on small farms.

As natural resource availability per farmer and per rural person continues to decline in many small-farm areas associated with greater rural population densities, little productive agricultural land will remain unused, particularly in Asia. Under these resource conditions, small-farm development requires increased productivity per unit of land. Greater land productivity is obtained through higher yields, increasing agricultural production intensity through more double and triple cropping, and greater livestock production. In nations with lower population densities, particularly in some areas of Brazil and Africa, lands may be available for farm expansion and settlement. In these areas tough questions face government officials in determining whether greater output and income growth could be obtained from the use of given government resources to increase yields and crop intensity on presently farmed lands or by use of these resources for expansion, through settlement and other programs, onto presently unfarmed land that may be of lower productivity. The amount of investment required per settler to make new lands productive is often very high.

Capital resources and credit become limiting as the agricultural transformation accelerates. As the flow onto farms of purchased inputs increases, such as fertilizer and investment items, including all manner of mechanical equipment, the need for credit explodes. Lack of savings and the very high rates of interest charged by traditional moneylenders, often ranging from 30 to 60% annually, greatly limit the amount of capital available for increased production. Workable procedures for the delivery and repayment of credit in small-farm areas, therefore, become essential to rapid growth.

Institutional and cultural conditions within which small-farm agriculture operates may limit growth. In small-farm areas with a high level of farm ownership where the income earned by cultivators is largely retained, traditional views and practices related to the annual pattern of use of resources often constrain changes required for incorporation of new agricultural technology, slowing the adoption of new high return investments.

In many farming areas of the feudal Asian or Latin American types [20], rural societies that developed through the centuries sustained themselves with high levels of tenancy and, particularly in Asia, high rents (40 to 60% of the crop). These high rents pump a large share of small farmers' production off their farms to other members of the community. Not only do high rents paid by tenants reduce their income but when the objective is rapid growth in agriculture, many of these rental arrangements greatly reduce the economic incentive of tenant farm operators to adopt and invest in new production-increasing technology. Some kinds of changes in institutional arrangements, particularly for the control of land or flow of inputs, are likely to be required in small-farming areas to aid in accelerating the growth of income on small farms.

Agricultural Development Theory and Programs for Small-Farm Development. The theory of agricultural development set forth in Chapter 1 showed that small-farm agriculture requires a fundamental transformation of farming processes. The necessary change is from a technologically static agriculture dependent on traditional practices to a dynamic, market-oriented agriculture dependent on continuously produced new agricultural technology delivered to farmers. The shift is from self-sufficiency and largely subsistence farming to predominately market-oriented farming.

A guide for effective government policies and program thrusts is provided by this theory of the agricultural transformation. The center piece in the transformation is the creation of a growing stream of new science-based agricultural technology for small farms. Through new economic opportunities opened up by the delivery of new technology to farmers, successive adjustments are undertaken in farming activities to obtain the increases in income made possible by the more productive techniques. Associated with these actions is the necessary increase in the sale of products off farms to pay for the new inputs. Increasing needs for improved marketing systems result.

Closely associated with technological change in agriculture are institutional and value changes. In a few traditional agricultures, the new techonologies appear to fit so easily within the existing institutional and cultural configurations and the resultant distribution of benefits so well accords with group values that little institutional or cultural change appears needed. More usually the lack of congruence between the new technological opportunities and the institutions and cultural traditions of small farmers sets up conflicts related to the use of the new technology and the distribution of its benefits.

In the Hayami-Ruttan induced innovation model, the new profit opportunities are viewed as inducing changes in institutions so that individuals and society can take fuller advantage of the new technology. This theory of the cause of institutional change appears to be more relevant to the long run of decades. Criticisms by Beckford [4] and others emphasize continuing institutional rigidity in many developing societies that creates artificial constraints on the flow of factor supplies and resource use. They view institutional change of equal importance to technical change in accelerating growth. A large potential role for government policymakers in aiding institutional change that will facilitate small-farm development is apparent.

The theory and empirical studies presented in this book emphasize three additional general points relevant to policy and program plans for small-farm development. First, although theoretically possible, empirical studies have shown that in the foreseeable future there are limited economies of scale in agricultural production in most areas of developing nations. Hence small farms can compete effectively with medium and large farms, or state farms. As much of the data demonstrates that small farms have greater land productivity than large farms, farm enlargement is not likely to be associated with increased land productivity. Second, theoretical and empirical evidence demonstrates that the shift to science-based agriculture usually increases the demand for labor. Estimates of the potential increases in farm employment range from 25 to 300% (Chapter 1). Thus small-farm development has the potential of making a major contribution to reducing rural unemployment and disguised underemployment. However, serious threats to rural employment and political equilibrium are posed at times in particular small-farming areas by certain types of new agricultural technology often embodied in large machines such as combines and cotton pickers. Hence, governments have responsibility to monitor these threats and take necessary action to reduce the costs to farmers, laborers, and society of too rapid changes to more productive agricultural technology. Third, the material in Chapter 1 and the empirical studies provide evidence of the complex interrelated nature of the agricultural transformation. Thus policies and programs that have successfully influenced agricultural operations in past time periods are likely to require modifications in later time periods. (Gotsch provided a stimulating exploration of the interactions through time of technology and institutions in agriculture with emphasis on income distribution [12]).

POLICIES AND PROGRAMS FOR SMALL-FARM DEVELOPMENT.
A central conclusion of this book is that accelerated small-farm development depends on the right sets of government policies and programs for the particular developmental conditions. Small farmers have been shown to be caught very often in an equilibrium trap of stagnant technology. Small farmers have also been shown to be responsive to government actions that increase the local availability of new profitable investment opportunities produced by agricultural scientists and embodied in new inputs.

The specification of policies and programs set out here for action by government officials fits into the framework of the second part of the

Hayami-Ruttan induced innovation model [14]. In this model government officials, policymakers, and agricultural scientists respond to resource scarcities as indicated by the prices of resources and products in agriculture. The guides for action in this section are intended to clarify the inducements to which public sector actors should respond.

Comparing additional costs with additional returns provides the economic framework for decisions about government policies and programs. Stated more directly, what are the costs associated with using public resources to implement a certain program (or policy) as compared with the returns (benefits) to society from such a program? The formal estimating tool, social benefit-cost analysis, can provide estimates of the rate of return from action programs or projects. The World Bank, bilateral aid agencies, and the stronger national planning agencies use benefit-cost analysis to evaluate proposed programs to the extent possible and useful. Poor and wrong government policies for agriculture waste immense amounts of public and private resources. Too many poorly thought through government policies and programs or ineffectively implemented programs can be in some cases even more stifling to agricultural growth than a lack of needed programs.

Government Commitment and Ability to Act for Small-Farm Development. The extent of government commitment and ability to act to accelerate small-farm development is a fundamental variable affecting growth in small-farm areas. In low-income nations where government is often dominated by large farmers or urban professional and business interests, objectives and, more importantly, government policies and programs may be formed and carried out with little consideration of their effect on the large number of often politically inactive small farmers. Appropriate specific questions are: Were national price policies reviewed from the point of view to encouraging small-farmer production? Is the allocation of funds for research in agriculture made in relation to the needs of the small-farm areas of the nation as well as the large? In setting import and export policies and tariffs, is the need to stimulate small-farmer development considered? The study of small farms in southern Brazil by Rask (Chapter 4) illustrated a situation in which government price policies and credit programs were aimed at supporting the expansion of cattle and wheat enterprises of the large-farm regions. Little government action aided the different enterprises in the small-farm area studied where maize, soybeans, and hogs were most important.

A dualistic government policy and program strategy can be a solution as it has been in Mexico (Chapter 8), with some actions focused to aid large farms and others to aid disadvantaged rural farm people. Such a dualistic approach has some merit in at least assuring a certain amount of focus on the development needs of small-farm areas containing the largest numbers of rural citizens.

As applied to small-farm agriculture, a commonly accepted framework for developing effective government policies and programs includes four steps: (1) the establishment of general government objectives for small-farm areas; (2) the specification of constraints to government action, such as budget limitations, foreign exchange availability, trained personnel, etc.; (3) the planning of particular government policies and programs to reach the specified objectives. This integration of consistent sets of policies and programs has the purpose of creating an improved incentive environment for farm development actions by farmers; and (4) the development of specific projects as components of programs with activities designed to relax constraints on the transformation of small-farm agriculture.

High priority areas for government policy and program action to accelerate the development of small farms follow from the realities of small-farm agriculture illustrated in the empirical studies and from the nature of the agricultural transformation process. These high-priority areas are discussed below under the following six headings:

1. Land Reform and Institutional Change
2. Price and Tax Policies to Encourage Small-Farmer Production
3. Continuous Creation and Testing of New Agricultural Technology
4. Increasing the Availability of New Agricultural Inputs
5. Improved Product Marketing to Benefit Farmers and Consumers
6. Effective Organization of Government and Rural People to Facilitate Agricultural Development

Land Reform and Institutional Change. Types of land reform and institutional change in agriculture encompass a vast range from relatively minor adjustments in rules governing tenure arrangements to a complete shift to central government ownership and large-scale industrial style management of land as in the case of the Soviet State Farms. The overriding purpose of many land reforms is to redistribute rights to the products of the land so as to increase distributive justice. The transfer of agricultural assets in a land reform from one group to another is almost always a consequence of significant social and political changes at the national level, well illustrated by the ejido agrarian reform in Mexico analyzed by Freebairn (Chapter 8).

Rent Reform Essential for Growth in Some Areas. In some small-farm areas rent reform is critical for accelerated growth. Two types of reform may be needed: rent reduction and a shift from certain types of share-rent arrangements to fixed rents or types of share rent that do not dampen economic incentives to increased production. In many small-farm areas of the developing world, the evolution of traditional society and changes in supply and demand for land have resulted in high rents, from 40 to 60% and more of the crop. Tenants who pay high rental rates have so little capital to work with and such low incomes and savings that they have extreme difficulty in purchasing new, more productive agricultural inputs. These high rent farmers have little incentive to risk more of their meager resources in the production of crops from which they get such a small return. In these farming areas, rent reduction will accelerate agricultural growth as well as contribute to improved distributive justice.

A shift from many of the usual forms of share rental arrangements can stimulate the use of new, more productive off-farm inputs. A share arrangement found in many small-farm areas requires that the cultivator provide all or most of the inputs except the land, with the gross product of the land being divided in some proportion, say 40, 50, or 60% to the landlord. Under these rental arrangements, through production function analysis it can be demonstrated that tenants will achieve maximum income by using fewer inputs than an owner-operator. These share-rent arrangements, therefore, provide economic incentives to tenant farmers to produce fewer agricultural products per unit of land than they could profitably produce under alternative rental arrangements. A change to a fixed rental fee is one solution; another is to have the landlord pay for the same share of the inputs that he receives of the gross product. By shifting to tenure arrangements that provide maximum incentive to increase output per acre, increases in agricultural production can be accelerated in small-farm areas.

Land reforms, in which tenant cultivators have been able to obtain ownership of the land they till, have almost universally resulted in increased productivity per acre. Well-documented land-to-the-tiller reforms in Japan, Taiwan, and South Korea provide extensive evidence of accelerated growth on small farms after land reform.

Uncertainty about the Productivity Effects of Many Land Reforms. Much uncertainty surrounds the effects on land and labor productivity of different types of land reform, most of which are not well documented. The analysis of ejido collective farming in Mexico in this volume provides evidence of the mixed results of this particular reform. This form of collective farming did succeed in achieving a land productivity equal to the average of the individually operated ejido farms in the valley, although somewhat more labor was used per unit of land. In spite of this, the collective failed to keep the interest of the majority of its members, who withdrew to operate their land individually. Uncertainty of outcome of land reforms is also illustrated by the Thiesenhusen analysis of an agrarian reform settlement project in which land was fairly evenly divided but, after considerable government investment per farmer and a few years, a highly skewed distribution of income occurred (Chapter 8). The large literature on land reform includes some recent general works

[2, 8, 20, 26, 35]. This literature demonstrates that the transfer of rights to small farmers is not sufficient for accelerated growth. Effective policies and programs of the nature outlined below in the areas of price and tax policy, technology generation, input supply, and product marketing are also essential for rapid growth. An example of this kind of government action in support of land reform is provided by the complementary efforts made by the Mexican government to supply credit and other inputs in support of both collective and individual ejidal farms. Thiesenhusen's study of a land reform settlement project in Venezuela (Chapter 7) underlines the critical need for effective government action to contribute to the availability of appropriate technology, dependable input supply, and stable product markets.

Whether land reform, which transfers significant amounts of assets and rights to land between groups, should occur to reduce income disparities between groups in developing nations is outside the scope of this book. However, no matter what the resulting tenure arrangements, whether owner operated, tenanted, collective, commune, or state farm, the essential requirements remain for the transformation of the agricultural sector from one based on traditional technology and subsistence production to a primarily market-oriented science-based agriculture. These requirements are appropriate agricultural price and tax policies, the creation and delivery of new high productivity agricultural technology to farmers, and improvements in the marketing system for farm inputs and farm products.

Price and Tax Policy. Government policies to influence the prices of agricultural inputs and products and government tax policies have a major influence on the rate of small-farm development. Most developing nations have centralized governments that have taken actions greatly affecting the prices farmers pay for farm inputs and the prices received by farmers for their products. Many of the actions taken were for purposes unrelated to the requirements of the transformation of small-farm agriculture. A common policy has been to attempt to assure low food prices to urban citizens. Such actions usually provide a disincentive for increased production by farmers and a stimulus to urban migration and increasing numbers of unemployed in ever-expanding slums. Another common government action has provided large subsidies for tractors and agricultural machinery, encouraging large farmers to convert to mechanized farming, in some cases reducing employment in labor-surplus rural areas. The subsidy for tractor mechanization on the Venezuelan land reform settlement reduced labor demand and the income that could have been earned by the settlers (Chapter 7). Government actions to subsidize interest rates for agricultural credit have in many cases resulted in a transfer of government resources to large farmers with very little credit available to small farmers, particularly in some Latin

American nations. In other actions, tariffs on imported fertilizer to protect a high-cost domestic fertilizer industry have increased crop production costs and reduced farm output.

Price Policy Objectives. The central price policy objective should be to accelerate the agricultural transformation. To do so prices should reflect real resource scarcities and should be as stable as possible. With these price conditions farmers can achieve the highest levels of production and agricultural investment without distorting investments into high-cost enterprises, due to temporary subsidies or high price supports. When policies affecting the prices of inputs or products are proposed, careful analysis is also needed to assure that the targeted groups will benefit and that subsidies do not become an unreasonable drain on the central treasury as can be the case with fertilizer subsidies, for example. In nations with largely market economies where most of the small farmers in the developing world live, a useful subsidiary policy objective is to facilitate the functioning of farm input and product markets to aid in increasing price stability.

Price Policy Actions to Accelerate Small-Farm Development. Four specific types of government action to influence prices can aid small-farmer development:

1. Removal of policies and regulations that have reduced market competition and market performance and that have encouraged the development of monopolistic positions. Such policies and regulations often are left over from earlier periods in which they may have been useful, or they are based on misguided views about the nature of marketing and how to influence the marketing system to improve its performance. In many situations the removal of constraining rules, regulations, and controls will increase competition in the marketing system. A result will be lowered input and higher product prices for farmers that more nearly reflect real costs of production and marketing. Increased competition in markets leaves fewer opportunities for monopoly positions to be established.

2. Actions to reduce price instability in farm inputs. Government actions to assure the supply of new inputs such as fertilizer, high-yielding seeds, and pesticides and their delivery to local markets in small-farm areas are primary strategies to achieve an accelerating flow of science-based inputs onto farms. In the early phases of new input introduction before small-farmer demand has been established, fixing input prices and the supply of inputs through government channels can, in some cases, aid more rapid incorporation of the new inputs on small farms. But fixed prices for inputs, however low and subsidized, mean little if the inputs are not locally available. The study of the Venezuelan settle-

ment (Chapter 7) highlights the importance of consistency in policies for input supplies such as helicopter spraying, mechanization services, and credit availability. The Eckert analysis goes a step further by stressing that government price and other policies will need to be adjusted continually as changes in supply and demand conditions occur, due partly to the success of previous policies (Chapter 6).

3. *Temporary subsidies on inputs to encourage initial adoption.* Subsidies are often useful to encourage experimentation and initial adoption of new science-based inputs. After farmers have become knowledgeable about the production relations of the new inputs, a return to pricing on the basis of real resource scarcity will result in optimum development of small farms and the most productive use of national resources. An example of this policy is provided by Eckert (Chapter 6). During the first few years of the adoption of the high-yielding wheat varieties, the government provided a considerable subsidy for nitrogen fertilizer. This subsidy was later terminated.

4. *Aiding farm product price stability.* Appropriate government actions to aid price stability for export crops such as rubber, oil palm, bananas, tea, and cotton depend very much on the international market and the particular conditions in that market and industry; thus general policy prescriptions cannot be made. For staple food crops, however, government actions to increase food crop price stability can be outlined. Government actions to moderate crop shortfalls and surpluses will contribute most to food product price stability. The objective is to encourage levels of production that will equal demand at usual price levels and to moderate price fluctuations when large and short crops occur. The main areas of government action are to attempt to assure appropriate import and export flows and to carry out any government purchasing or sale of food crops that may be possible with limited government resources. Official fixing of floor and ceiling prices may or may not contribute to price stability, depending on the circumstances. The importance of risk avoidance for farmers was explored in detail by Norman (Chapter 3). Rask (Chapter 4) illustrated a case in which the farm product prices were assured for the large farms but not for the small farms. More detailed discussion of price policy is provided by Krishna [19].

Tax Policy. Realistic levels of taxation of agriculture can aid small-farm development in a number of ways. Insignificant and uncollected land taxes permit certain groups of farmers to reap windfall gains as they benefit from scattered government activity in the development and delivery of high-yielding inputs and from various forms of land development projects without contributing anything to the government treasury. The small industrial sector in agrarian countries cannot provide sufficient government revenue through taxes for the development of agriculture. Hence import, export, and sales taxes are usually relied on for government revenue in low-income nations. Although relatively easy to collect, these taxes reduce the total amount of economic activity and tend to be regressive, hitting the poor hardest. Marketing board taxes are often employed for export crops. These taxes reduce the prices received by farmers, causing reduced production.

As a minimum guide, agriculture should pay sufficient taxes to support government activity in the agricultural sector. In more developed nations, land taxes have been the most usual and effective form of taxing agriculture. Such taxes discourage wasteful use and underuse of land such as cattle ranching in good crop production areas. Increased government revenues from agriculture should be used to accelerate the production and distribution of new high productivity inputs to small farmers and the more rapid expansion of irrigation and other agricultural resource development programs. It should be fairly easy to appreciably increase land taxes in areas recently benefiting from new high-yielding varieties or from irrigation water [5, 21].

Continuous Creation and Testing of New Agricultural Technology. Policies and programs for agricultural technology development are central catalytic elements in plans for accelerated small-farmer development. The cause of rapid growth in agriculture, according to theory and historical experience, is the development and subsequent use by farmers of new high-return technology in agriculture. Theory and empirical studies (Chapters 3 and 5, for example) show that reallocation of resources presently available will not cause much growth in agriculture. In developing nations the speed of small-farmer development will be largely dependent on the effectiveness of government action to import, create, and test new agricultural technology. Little action in this area will result in halting, uneven spurts of "accidental" growth in some small-farm areas. Effective, dynamic, agricultural technology development for small farms can lead to continuous, balanced growth in small-farm areas.

Numerous studies have shown very high returns to the investment in new agricultural technology development, indicating that there are few fields that are likely to provide such a high return for the use of government resources [11].

For small farmers, perhaps the most important government action is the specific decision in agricultural technology policy to focus a certain amount of government research and development resources on the problems of small farmers. This may require concrete action to redirect the work of research personnel and organizations. With small farmers as a focus, the objective for government action should be to carry out agricultural technology creation, importation, and local adaptive testing that will be more productive when combined with the resources to which small farmers have access.

Agricultural Technology Tailored to Small-Farm Conditions. To develop agricultural technology suited to small-farm conditions requires detailed knowledge of the quantities and qualities of the resources available to the small farmers in the different areas of a nation: the labor supply, particularly in the periods of peak demand and slack periods; the quality of the land resources (including rainfall patterns and irrigation water supplies), current capital, and technology in use, plus any major institutional constraints that could affect the use of new technology. Increased knowledge of land resources requires soil and water surveys and the development of climatological data. Estimates of other resources are obtainable through different types of farm management and socioeconomic surveys of different small-farm areas. The importance of detailed knowledge of resource conditions in developing appropriate technology for small farms is demonstrated by Eckert (Chapter 6). In this case, the introduction of four-wheeled tractors for plowing wheat fields replaced bullock plowing and resulted in pressure to displace tenants who had traditionally plowed the land. In spite of this pressure, tractor plowing in the region studied did not cause labor displacement because labor was needed for harvesting. However, should mechanical harvesting be adopted, the prospect was for appreciable labor displacement. Rask (Chapter 4) demonstrated that most of the mechanical technology available in southern Brazil had little relevance to the small farms studied. A major constraint faced by the settlers of the Venezuelan land reform project was lack of tested agricultural technology adapted to that location (Chapter 7). Norman found that the labor shortage of the peak labor demand periods limited the amount of land that could be farmed and hence put a ceiling on family income (Chapter 3).

Creation and Importation of Agricultural Technology. Most agricultural technology is generated internationally but must be tested and adapted to each farming locality. In the past, estimates suggest that 95% of all agricultural research has been carried out in the more developed nations on temperate climate agriculture. Currently, the international agricultural research institutes are providing major leadership in the development of new technology for agriculture in tropical areas where low-income nations are located. A developing nation needs a proper balance of policies and programs for agricultural technology development that will draw effectively from the international research community and encourage the growth of its own capacity. The three phases of international technology transfer suggested by Hayami and Ruttan clarify government technology policy [14]. They propose that *material transfer* is the first phase in international technology transfer. It is characterized by the importation of new materials such as seeds, plants, animals, machines, and techniques associated with these materials with spotty adoption and use. *Design transfer,* the second phase, occurs as a nation develops the capacity to use blueprints, formulas, and books, and to copy, reproduce, or manufacture the kinds of materials previously imported. Systematic tests of field performance of new elements of agricultural technology are carried out in this phase also. In *capacity transfer,* the third phase, the nation builds up its indigenous scientific knowledge and professional capacity so that it can produce new locally adapted technology suited to local technical, economic, and social conditions.

In large nations, policies and programs for agricultural development should move as rapidly as possible to the third, capacity transfer, phase, as this level of technological ability will permit the most productive use of the agricultural resources in the many small-farm areas of the nation. In small nations not having the resources to develop a full range of scientific capability to provide technical leadership in all agricultural enterprises, tapping the right combination of the three sources of agricultural technology should be sought. The relative importance of different crops and the extent to which it is possible to rely on the international scientific community for agricultural technology development for particular ecological zones or crops will influence these policies [3, 11, 15, 16, 23, 28].

Risk Reduction through Local Adaptive Testing and Research on the Impact of New Agricultural Technology. A basic characteristic of much agricultural technology is the variability in its productivity from area to area depending on soil, climate, pests, and other conditions. Hence, crops, pesticides, and agricultural machinery that produce high returns in one area may not improve productivity in another. Risk aversion is a rational and almost universal characteristic of small farmers, particularly with respect to the family's subsistence food crops. If risk aversion is coupled with the location-specific characteristics of much agricultural technology, the need for systematic programs of local adaptive testing of new agricultural technology is clear. Norman concludes (Chapter 3) that the criteria for new agricultural technology should include an equal or smaller standard deviation in yields under farm operating conditions as well as higher productivity. The erratic farming results in the Venezuelan settlement project (Chapter 7) highlighted the great need of those farmers for locally tested high-return enterprises. Due to the complex timing of different agricultural activities and the sequential patterns resulting from rotational practices and crop-livestock interrelations, systems analyses of small farms may be necessary to understand the impact on small farmers of proposed changes in agricultural technology. The usefulness of this research approach is illustrated by the systems analysis of constraints on cattle and buffalo production in northeastern Thailand (Chapter 5).

The practice of testing new technology on farmers' fields, with the farmer carrying out the operations, is being accepted by professionals as necessary before conclusions can be made that new technology will be productive on small farms. Hence, government policies and programs are required that develop a national professional capability to carry out tests of new technology on farmers' fields. A usual approach is for scientists on experiment stations to include experiments on farmers' fields in their research. The Puebla project, in a recent innovative approach, employed adaptive research on new agricultural technology in trials on farmers' fields as part of an extension and input delivery project [7, 36].

Extension Roles in Technology Flow. In more developed nations, a major role of agricultural extension workers has been to provide a flow of information about new technology to farmers. A second role makes extension a channel to inform the research establishment about technical and other problems facing farmers. The poor performance of many extension services in low-income nations, especially with respect to small farmers, attests to the importance of carefully planned extension policies and programs so government resources may be used productively to carry out these needed functions. Effective extension personnel are in such short supply in most developing nations that they must work with groups of farmers, not with individuals—a mode used much in more developed nations.

A specific objective of extension work is to aid cultivators in obtaining better subjective estimates of profit and risk variability on their farms from the use of new technology or changed practices. An essential requirement for this task is the availability to the extension agent of knowledge of new agricultural technology that has high potential productivity in the farm area served. Trials on farmers' fields are almost always required to obtain this knowledge. A specific example of this need was provided by Rask's study. Information about the results of on-farm trials of hog-feeding practices was not available (Chapter 4). A second requirement for effective extension work is sufficient knowledge and ability on the part of the extension agent to competently demonstrate and instruct farmers in the use of the new technology. Many extension agents in low-income nations know less about the crops and farming practices than the farmers they are supposed to educate in the new technology. Until the extension agent can confidently demonstrate all aspects of the new technology, his influence on increasing technology flow to farmers will remain weak. The usual lack of tested new high-productivity agricultural technology for all parts of a nation supports Norman's advice that limited extension service capability should be concentrated on areas and enterprises in which there is current potential for rapid change (Chapter 3).

Increasing the Availability of New Agricultural Inputs. Once higher-productivity agricultural technology has been demonstrated, the major constraint becomes local availability of the necessary inputs. Local availability can be defined as within a distance that can be reached by usual transportation in a round trip during one day.

Because of the complementary nature of many of the new inputs, greater total net income to farmers and greater national agricultural production can be obtained if the necessary inputs are all available locally and *in the right proportions*. For example, the high-yielding wheat, maize, and rice varieties, without more fertilizer, usually produce little additional output. Likewise, when the available chemical fertilizer is distributed where traditional varieties are grown, relatively low increases in production have resulted. However, government policies and programs that succeed in assuring the availabilities of fertilizer and high-yielding varieties in localities result in very high returns on small farms, often with a doubling of production. Rask, in Chapter 4, observed that the small farmers in southern Brazil appeared to be losing opportunities for increased income by failing to employ all the complementary inputs in the new technology package. Eckert pointed out an associated government program problem. As one input package becomes successful, soil and pest conditions may change, requiring changes in the optimum package. In the case of the wheat area studied, as larger crops of wheat were taken off, shortages of phosphorus in the soil began to appear, requiring flows of phosphate fertilizer not previously needed (Chapter 6).

Alternative Approaches to Input Supplies. In many small-farm areas, a marketing system for modern inputs is poorly formed or nonexistent. One solution has been for the government, through the extension service or specialized agricultural input distribution organizations, to set up a monopoly to provide the necessary inputs to farmers. Although this policy and use of government resources may be able to deliver inputs effectively to farmers for some time, especially when inputs are in very short supply, eventually this or any other form of monopoly, public or private, tends to provide poorer and poorer service. Hence, the approach recommended here is policies and programs that will facilitate the development of multiple competitive input marketing channels, one of which might be governmental. Different types of organizational strategies have been employed for the delivery of inputs to small farmers. (The most notable and reasonably well documented include the Intensive Agricultural District Program in India; the Comilla Project, Bangladesh; the Puebla Project, Mexico; and the Minimum Package Program, Ethiopia.)

Government actions should contribute to input price stability and availability at the times needed. In the north of Nigeria, Norman emphasized that the availability of new inputs at the right price and at the right time often depends on improved rural infrastructures, particularly roads and communication facilities (Chapter 3).

Credit to Facilitate New Input Use. In the agricultural transformation the shift from traditional agricultural inputs produced on the farm to the purchase of large amounts of new, more productive industrially produced inputs, such as chemical fertilizer, creates a very large increase in cash and credit requirements by small farmers. Rask stressed this point as small farmers in southern Brazil were found to have accepted only those components of the crop technology package having a low cash outlay. One-fifth of the small farmers also reported capital constraints to the increased use of fertilizer (Chapter 4).

Policy and program approaches to the solution of credit bottlenecks for small farmers include expanding credit through private and public banking channels and methods that couple credit with input supply and sometimes extension. Great difficulties are faced in the development of viable credit organizations for small farmers. In spite of these difficulties, successful credit organizations have been developed for small farmers in a number of low-income nations including, for example, Bangladesh [25]. Credit coupled with input supply takes many forms, ranging from private credit through fertilizer dealers and other input suppliers to government-supervised credit in its myriad forms [32]. One form of private financing is illustrated by the contracting arrangements made by tobacco companies in southern Brazil (Chapter 4). The review by Thiesenhusen of the sequence of changes in the methods of providing credit to settlers in Venezuela provides insight into the complex issues in carrying out successful credit operations with small farmers (Chapter 7). A large capital flow through a central government credit mechanism was a basic source of accelerated growth on ejido farms in Mexico (Chapter 8).

Effective policies and programs for the delivery and repayment of credit in small-farm areas are often dependent on the extent to which the credit organizations fit within the particular cultural and institutional matrix of the farming area. Developing credit organizations adapted to local rural customs may require pilot programs and applied research, such as that carried out by the Bangladesh Academy for Rural Development, to determine what organizational methods are feasible among different groups. Government action and resources to encourage the development of such rural development research and training institutions can be an important element in accelerating small-farmer progress [30].

Improved Product Marketing to Benefit Farmers and Consumers. In reasonably competitive staple food markets, which appear to prevail in most developing nations, reduction in the costs of marketing will increase prices to farmers, or reduce agricultural prices for consumers, or both. The development of a "national marketing strategy" [27] can contribute to dynamic improvements in rural small-farm areas. Involved in this strategy are improved roads and communications and higher productivity and performance by private and public marketing organizations [1, 13, 17, 33]. Through appropriate policies and programs, governments can provide leadership in forcing increased pluralism and competition among market firms and somewhat better terms of trade for farmers as Eckert observed occurring in Pakistan (Chapter 6). However, government should focus its actions in marketing in high pay-off areas since developing nations have limited numbers of effective administrators. In most cases market performance is unlikely to be improved through government operation of marketing enterprises.

Specific examples of the kinds of changes in marketing that may be necessary are illustrated in the studies. Eckert pointed to the considerable expansion in wheat transportation and storage capacity required with the rapid introduction of high-yielding wheat in Pakistan (Chapter 6). The rapid increase in production of wheat also placed the government wheat price support program under considerable strain, with the government increasing its procurement to 30% of the marketed crop. Investigation of wheat export possibilities determined that the potential was small under existing price relationships. In the Venezuelan land settlement study, Thiesenhusen found that settlers were hampered by uncertain product markets and concluded that market structure problems can be just as difficult to solve and just as exploitive as land tenure structures. When land tenure problems are bettered, markets usually need reform (Chapter 7). Rask's study in southern Brazil illustrated the large impact of a new all-weather road in one region that contributed to more rapid increases in income in that region (Chapter 4).

Effective Organization of Government and Rural People to Facilitate Agricultural Development. The governments in a large number of developing nations are highly centralized with younger, less experienced, lower paid civil servants posted out from the capital city. With relatively small numbers of well-trained personnel in rural areas, effective administration of policies and programs is difficult. To increase the implementation capacity of rural areas, new mechanisms may be required for effective rural development actions. Considerable literature has been addressed to these problems [6, 18, 22, 24, 29, 30, 31, 34]. The Chinese commune and Israeli kibbutz systems for organizing rural people are held up by some as models of how to assure effective action for accelerated development. With scarce and uncertain quality government administrative talent in many small-farm areas, stronger organizational arrangements appear needed, including cooperatives, farmers' associations, and other local development-promoting organizations to greatly increase local policy and program effectiveness. Dynamic change in agriculture will require continuous local organization, training, and education. To achieve the goal of accelerated income growth on small farms, effective rural leadership and government organization is essential, for the complex agricultural transformation is a fundamental change in rural life spanning a number of generations.

REFERENCES

1. Abbott, J. C. *Marketing: Its Role in Increasing Productivity.* Rome: U.N. Food and Agriculture Organization, 1962.
2. Adams, Dale W. "The Economics of Land Reform." *Food Research Institute Studies in Agricultural Economics, Trade and Development* 12 (2, 1973): 133–38.
3. Barker, Randolf. "The Evolutionary Nature of the New Rice Technology." *Food Research Institute Studies,* 1971, pp. 117–30.
4. Beckford, George L. "Strategies for Agricultural Development: Comment." *Food Research Institute Studies,* 1972, pp. 149–54.
5. Bird, Richard M. *Taxing Agricultural Land in Developing Countries.* Cambridge: Harvard Univ. Press, 1974.
6. Blase, Melvin G. (ed.). *Institutions in Agricultural Development.* Ames: Iowa State Univ. Press, 1971.
7. Diaz-Cisnero, Heliodoro. "An Institutional Analysis of a Rural Development Project: The Case of the Pueblo Project in Mexico." Ph.D. dissertation, Univ. of Wisconsin, 1974.
8. Dorner, Peter. *Land Reform and Economic Development.* Baltimore: Penguin Books, 1972.
9. Dovring, Folke. "The Share of Agriculture in a Growing Population." *Monthly Bulletin of Agricultural Economics and Statistics* 8 (Aug.–Sept. 1959): 1–11. FAO, Rome.
10. Eicher, Carl, and Witt, Lawrence. *Agriculture in Economic Development.* New York: McGraw-Hill, 1964, pp. 78–98.
11. Evenson, Robert. "Technology Generation in Agriculture," in Lloyd G. Reynolds (ed.), *Agriculture in Development Theory.* New Haven: Yale Univ. Press, 1975.
12. Gotsch, Carl H. "Technical Change and the Distribution of Income in Rural Areas." *American Journal of Agricultural Economics* 54 (May 1972): 326–41.
13. Harrison, Kelly; Henley, Donald; Riley, Harold; and Shaffer, James. *Improving Food Marketing Systems in Developing Countries—Experiences from Latin America.* East Lansing: Latin American Studies Center, Michigan State Univ., 1974.
14. Hayami, Yujiro, and Ruttan, Vernon W. *Agricultural Development: An International Perspective.* Baltimore: Johns Hopkins Univ. Press, 1971, pp. 53–66.
15. Hayami, Yujiro, and Yomada, S. "Agricultural Research Organization in Economic Development: A Review of the Japanese Experience," in Lloyd G. Reynolds (ed.), *Agriculture in Development Theory.* New Haven: Yale Univ. Press, 1975.
16. "Intensification of Animal Production." *The World Food Problem,* vol. 2. U.S. Government Printing Office, Washington, D.C., May 1967.
17. Jones, William O. *Marketing Staple Food Crops in Tropical Africa.* Ithaca: Cornell Univ. Press, 1972.
18. Khan, Akhter Hameed. "Reflections on the Comilla Projects." Overseas Liaison Committee. American Council on Education, OLC Paper No. 3, Mar. 1974.
19. Krishna, Raj. "Agricultural Price Policy and Economic Development," in Herman R. Southworth and Bruce F. Johnston (eds.), *Agricultural Development and Economic Growth.* Ithaca: Cornell Univ. Press, 1967.
20. *Land Reform.* Washington, D.C.: World Bank, 1974, p. 13.
21. Lewis, Stephen R., Jr., "Agricultural Taxation and Intersectoral Resource Transfer." *Food Research Institute Studies* 12 (2, 1973): 93–114.
22. Montgomery, John D., and Siffin, William J. (eds.). *Approaches to Devel-*

opment: Politics, Administration and Change. New York: McGraw-Hill, 1966.
23. Moseman, Albert H. *Building Agricultural Research Systems in the Developing Nations.* Agricultural Development Council, 1970.
24. Mosher, A. T. *Creating a Progressive Rural Structure to Serve a Modern Agriculture.* Agricultural Development Council, 1969.
25. Raper, Arthur F. *Rural Development in Action.* Ithaca: Cornell Univ. Press, 1970.
26. Raup, Philip M. "Land Reform and Agricultural Development," in Herman R. Southworth and Bruce F. Johnston (eds.), *Agricultural Development and Economic Growth.* Ithaca: Cornell Univ. Press, 1967.
27. Rostow, W. W. *View from the Seventh Floor.* New York: Harper & Row, 1964, p. 135.
28. *Second World Conference on Animal Production.* Maryland: Bruce Publishing Co., 1969.
29. Stavis, Benedict. *Rural Local Government and Agricultural Development in Taiwan.* Cornell Univ. Press, 1974.
30. Stevens, Robert D. "Three Rural Development Models for Small-Farm Agricultural Areas in Low-Income Nations." *Journal of Developing Areas* 8 (Apr. 1974): 409–20.
31. Swerdlow, Irving. *Development Administration: Concepts and Problems.* Syracuse Univ. Press, 1963.
32. "Systems for Delivering Agricultural Credit," in *Agricultural Credit,* Washington, D.C.: World Bank, May 1975, pp. 51–63.
33. United States Department of Agriculture. *The Marketing Challenge: Distributing Increased Production in Developing Nations.* Washington, D.C.: Foreign Agricultural Economics Report 96, 1974 (originally published in 1970).
34. Uphoff, Norman, and Esman, Milton. *Local Organization for Rural Development: Analysis of Asian Experience.* Cornell Univ. Press, 1974.
35. Warriner, Doreen. *Land Reform in Principle and Practice.* Oxford: Clarendon Press, 1969.
36. Winkleman, Don. "Plan Puebla after Six Years," in *Small-Farm Agriculture: Studies in Developing Nations,* Agr. Exp. Sta. Bull. No. 101, Purdue Univ., Sept. 1975.

Index

Affluence: and food scarcity, 26, 27–28; and grain consumption, 26–27; and livestock consumption, 27–28
Agrarian reforms: in Mexico, 211–12, 215–23, 230–31; uncertainty about productivity effects of, 243–44; in Venezuela, 177–209. See also Quechehueca Collective; Ruiz Pineda; Yaqui Valley
Agricultural input. See Inputs, agricultural
Agricultural loans. See Credit, farm
Agricultural output. See Economic Efficiency; Marginal value product; Productivity; Yields per acre
Agricultural technology: dynamics in, 13–14. See also Modern technology; Technological change; Traditional agriculture
Agricultural transformation: economics of, 11–20; interrelated nature of, 19–20; of traditional agriculture, 3–24
Allocation of resources: adjustments in, 8; in Non Som Boon, 122–23, 135–36; in Sahiwal District, 166–68; and small-farm development, 247. See also Capital resources; Labor resources and use; Land resources and use; Water resources
Alto Uruguai, 97
Alvara Obregon Dam, 214, 215
Amish farmers, 15
Angustura Dam, 214
Animal fats, 49
Animal power: as agricultural innovation, 29; in Non Som Boon, 124, 125, 134; in Rio Grande do Sul, 100
Animal protein. See Protein, animal
Aquaculture, 41
ASCAR, 101
Aswan Dam, 37
Australia, as grain exporter, 42

Baan Phai, Thailand, 121
Backpack sprayers, 190, 206
Bacon, soya-based, 49
Bananas, 190, 191

Banco Agricola y Pecuario (BAP), 188, 191
Bangladesh: Academy for Rural Development, 252; rice production of, 52
Barbacoas, Venezuela, 178, 183
Beef: constraints on production of, 45; consumption in U.S., 27, 40, 49
Betancourt, Romulo, 178–79, 181
Birthrate: in China, 35; in European countries, 47; and nutritional diets, 48; reducing, in poor countries, 47; in U.S., 47
Boerma, A. H., 50
Borlaug, Dr. Norman, 35
Bovine production practices, 127–31. See also Buffalo; Cattle
Brazil: annual population growth of, 26; grain production of, 52; increasing cultivated area of, 52; small farms in southern, 92–114; and technological change, 92; and world population growth, 26. See also Lajeado, Brazil; Rio Grande do Sul
Brown, Lester R., 25–53
Buffalo: birthrates, in Non Som Boon, 130; characteristics of Thai, 117; number of, in Non Som Boon, t. 128; ownership of, in Non Som Boon, 127–28; production, in Non Som Boon, 115–41; use of, in Thailand, 118, 119

Campesinos, 180
Canada, grain consumption of, 26
Canals, in Sahiwal District, 157–59
Capacity transfer, 248–49
Capital resources: in northern Nigeria, 73–74; at Quechehueca Collective, t. 225, 226; of small farmers in developing countries, 6, 22, 238; and technological change, 22
Cardenas, Lazaro, 215, 224
Carryover stocks of grain, 42
Cash crops: of Dan Mahawayi, 76, 77, 82; of Lajeado, Brazil, 104, 106–7, t. 108; of Non Som Boon, 125; of Quechehueca Collective, 226–27; of Rio

257

Cash crops *(continued)*
Grande do Sul, 99; of Sahiwal District, 156
Cash expenses: of bovine production in Non Som Boon, 137–38; of Dan Mahawayi farmers, 74–75; of Lajeado, Brazil, farmers, t. 108; of Non Som Boon farmers, 135, 137–38; of northern Nigeria farmers, t. 73; of Rio Grande do Sul farmers, t. 108
Cattle: birthrates in Non Som Boon, 130; characteristics of Thai, 119; number of, in Non Som Boon, t. 128; ownership of, in Non Som Boon, 128; production, in Non Som Boon, 115–41; production returns on, in Non Som Boon, 136–39; regions in Rio Grande do Sul, 96
Cereals: advantages of new, 33–35; sustaining rising per acre yields of, 44–45. *See also* Dwarf rice; Dwarf wheat
Chemical fertilizers: as agricultural innovation, 29; in Dan Mahawayi, 74; and eutrophication of lakes, 44; in Lajeado, Brazil, 110, 111; and low yield of traditional seed varieties, 251; in Sahiwal District, 159–60; as technological innovation, 29; threat of, to streams and lakes, 38; *See also* Nitrogen fertilizers
China. *See* People's Republic of China
CIARA credit program, 192
Cobb-Douglas production function: and mixed cropping in northern Nigeria, 85–86; and wheat yields of Pakistan, 164–68
Commission agents, in Pakistan, 171–72
Community development programs, 5
Concentric ring theory, 64
Cooperatives. *See* Quechchueca Collective; Yaqui Valley, Mexico
Corn: farmers in Mexico, 36; nitrogen requirements of, 45; raising U.S. yields of, 3, 46. *See also* Maize (corn)
Cotton: in Dan Mahawayi, 76, 77; at Quechehueca Collective, 226–27; in Ruiz Pineda, 182, 190; in Yaqui Valley, 213, 215
Credit, farm: available to large vs. small farmers, 244; effect of government, in Venezuela, 206–7; and high interest rates of moneylenders, 6, 238; in Lajeado, Brazil, 101; to Mexican peasants in Yaqui Valley, 219; organizations for small farmers, 252; problems of Dan Mahawayi farmers, 74; requirements for new input use, 251–52; to Ruiz Pineda farmers, 182, 191–93. *See also* Loan repayments
Cropland, idled. *See* Idled cropland
Crop mixing. *See* Mixed cropping
Cropping patterns: in Dan Mahawayi, 76–79; in Non Som Boon, 125–27; at Quechehueca Collective, 226–27; in Ruiz Pineda, 188–91, 200, 201, 207; in Sahiwal District, 156–57. *See also* Mixed cropping; Single cropping
Crops. *See* Cash crops; Food and fodder crops
Cultivated acreage: expanding area of, 30–31, 36, 37; of Hausa dryland farmers, t. 67; increasing Brazil's, 52; intensifying Japan's, 31; intensifying U.S., 31; limitations to expanding, 44; of Non Som Boon, t. 126; of Yaqui Valley, 216–17
Cultural change, 8

Dan Mahawayi, Nigeria: cash crops of, 76, 77, 82; cash expenses of farmers of, t. 73, 74–75; credit problems of farmers of, 74; cropping patterns and yields of, 76–79, 83; crops of, 67, 76–77, 82; family income in, 79; family size and organization in, 68; farmland types in, 67; farm sizes in, 80–81; food crops of, 76–77, 82; and gross returns per acre, 84; hired labor in, 70; labor input and per acre yields of, t. 84; land availability and use in, 68–76; land-labor relationships in, 75–76; land ownership rights in, 66, 67; livestock investment in, 74; location of, 81; mixed cropping practices of, 77–79, 82, 83; off-farm occupations in, 70; population of, 65; seasonal employment problems of, 70–74; seasonality of farming in, t. 71; traditional farming in, 65–79; types of farm work in, 68, 70; use of family labor in, t. 69; work by male adults of, 70. *See also* Hausa dryland farmers
Day length, sensitivity of dwarf wheat to, 33
DDT, 39
De Boer, John, 115–41
Deforestation, and soil loss, 37
Demand. *See* Supply and demand
Design transfer, 248
Detergents, phosphates in, 39
Developed countries: grain consumption in, 48; meat consumption in, 27–28; population growth in, 26
Developing countries: capital resources of small farmers in, 238; credit needs of small farmers in, 238; efforts to modernize agriculture in, 31, 33; expanding food production of, 52–53; family planning programs in, 35; farm size and productivity in, 17–18; food production and population growth of, 31; grain consumption in, 48; introduction of new cereal seeds in, 31, 33; labor resources of small

farms in, 237–38; large-scale farming in, 6; mixed impact of green revolution on, 3–4; per person cost of literacy in, 47–48; poor performance of extension services in, 250; population growth rates in, 3, 4, 26; reducing birthrates in, 47; small-farm development in, 240–53; spread of new rice and wheat seeds in, 33
Disequilibrium, 14
Doka, Nigeria, 64, 65, 81, 82
Double cropping: increased labor demands of, 19; in Yaqui Valley, 214
Dovring, Folke, 231
Draft animals, 29. *See also* Animal power
Dryland farming, in northern Nigeria, 63–91
Duroc Jersey hog, 104
Dwarf rice: adoption of, in developing countries, 33; advantages of, 33; and increased demand for labor, 36; introduction and spread of, 34. *See also* Rice
Dwarf wheat: acreage, in Pakistan (1966–68), t. 161; adoption of, in developing countries, 33; adoption of, in Sahiwal District, 160–70; advantages of, 33; characteristics of, 33; early maturity of, 33; expanding impact of in Pakistan, 170–75; impact of, on Pakistan villages, 173–75; and increased demand for labor, 36; introduction and spread of, 34; introduction and spread of, in Pakistan, 153–55; irrigation needs of, 36; and landlord-tenant relationships, in Pakistan, 172; nitrogen fertilizer use with, 33; in Pakistan, 149–76; reduced sensitivity of, to day length, 33; in Sahiwal District, 160–70; vs. total wheat acreage in Pakistan (1965–70), t. 155; yields in Pakistan, 154, 155. *See also* Wheat
Dynamic agriculture. *See* Modern technology
Dynamics: in agricultural technology, 13–14; in small-farm agriculture, 143–47; of traditional agriculture, 55–61

Earnings, farm. *See* Income, farm
Eckert, Jerry B., 149–76
Economic efficiency: of dynamic agriculture, 15; of Non Som Boon farmers, 131–36; at Quechehueca Collective, 227–30; of Ruiz Pineda farmers, 195–97; of traditional farmers, 8; of Yaqui Valley farmers, 221–22
Economics of transforming traditional agriculture, 7–20
Ecosystem, agricultural stresses on, 36–39
Ecuador, and offshore fishing limits, 40
Education. *See* Literacy
Egg production, increased U.S., 30

Egypt: irrigation problems in, 37, 38; schistosomiasis in, 38
Ejidal farming: and agrarian reform, 211–12; changes in, 210–34; overview of, 230–33; at the Quechehueca Collective, 223–30; in Yaqui Valley, 213–23
Ejidatario, 212
Ejido Aguila, 224
Ejido Credit Bank, 219, 226
Ejido Quechehueca, 224. *See also* Quechehueca Collective
Ejidos, 212; early problems of, 222–23; evaluation of, as social institution, 233; formation of, in Yaqui Valley, 215–23
Empresa campesina, 192
Encosta Inferior do Nordeste, 97
Energy crisis, 45
Equilibrium: in supply and demand, 8–9; technical and economic, of small farmers, 6–7; in traditional agriculture, 8–9
Erosion, soil, 37, 44
Eutrophication, 37, 38–39, 44
Exchange of crops, 29
Exports: agricultural, of Thailand, 116; constraints on Pakistan wheat, 172–73; U.S soybean, 35; U.S. wheat, 46
Extension services: and flow of technological information, 250; and improvement of farmers' production, 5; in Lajeado, Brazil, 101; necessary for new inputs, 20; need for effective, in northern Nigeria, 89; in Ruiz Pineda, 195

Family goals, 82. *See also* Profit maximization; Risk aversion
Family labor: of Hausa dryland farmers, t. 69; at Quechehueca Collective, 229–30; in Rio Grande do Sul, 99; at Ruiz Pineda, 183, 184–86, 187–88
Family planning programs, 35
Family size: in Dan Mahawayi, 68; of Hausa dryland farmers, t. 66; in Ruiz Pineda, 188
Famine: ensuring against, 50–51; U.S. role in combatting, 42, 48
FAO, 50
Farmers Association (Mexico), 218
Farm mechanization. *See* Mechanization
Farm ownership. *See* Land ownership
Farm sizes: in Dan Mahawayi, 66; in Lajeado, Brazil, 101, 109; and productivity, in developing countries, 17–18; in Rio Grande do Sul, 98, 112; in Sahiwal District, 156; as structural variable, 93
FCV, 181
Fertilizers. *See* Chemical fertilizers; Nitrogen fertilizers

Fish: constraints on catch of, 45; farming, 41; future price of, 51; importance of, as protein, 40–41; in Japanese diet, 40–41; in Soviet diet, 40, 41; U.S. consumption of, 40
Fish catch: decline in world, 39–40; and eutrophication caused by chemical fertilizers, 38; falloff in world, 45; of Iceland, 40; of Soviet Union, 40; and use of chemical fertilizers, 38
Fisheries: cooperative approach to, 5; prospects for, 39–41
Flax, 215, 227
Food and Agriculture Organization (FAO), 50
Food consumption, altering patterns of, 48–50
Food demand: population growth and rising, 28; reasons for increased, 20. *See also* Food scarcities
Food and fodder crops: of Dan Mahawayi, 67, 76–77, 82; at Non Som Boon, 125–26; at Quechehueca Collective, 226–27; in Rio Grande do Sul, 101, 102–4; in Ruiz Pineda, 194–95; in Sahiwal District, 156; in Yaqui Valley, 216–17, 219
Food reserve system, world, 50–51
Food scarcities: and altering consumption patterns, 48–50; caused by affluence, 26, 27–28; caused by population growth, 29, 35–36; emerging global, 46; in 1973, 25–26; reasons for, 25–26; and rising prices, 25
Ford Foundation, 33
France, 28
Freebairn, Donald K., 210
Fulani farmers, 64

Gandu, 68
Gaud, William, 34
Genetics, 13, 29
Global poverty, 47–48
Government: action to influence prices, 245–47; and costs of modern technology, 240; credit, in Ruiz Pineda, 74; credit activities, in Dan Mahawayi, 74; credit programs, as benefit to large farmers, 6; and delivery of new inputs to small farms, 251; and effective organization of rural people, 253; price policies and small-farm development, 244; research of small-farm problems, 247; and small-farm development, 240–53; subsidy of fertilizers in Pakistan, 170–71; tax policies, and small-farm development, 246–47; test of new technology, 249–50
Government policies and programs: and economic growth in Mexico, 211; and small-farm development, 240–53

Grain: annual American consumption of, 26, 49; consumption in poor countries, 26, 48; consumption in rich countries, 48; consumption and rising affluence, 26–27; exports of Latin and North America, 41–42; percentage of, in human diet, 26; requirements and rising income, 27; reserves, downward trend of, 42–44; stocks, in principal exporting countries, t. 43; world consumption of, 42; world reserves of, 42
Grazing land: full use of world's, 45; in Non Som Boon, 130–31, 140; in Rio Grande do Sul, 96
Great Britain, and Icelandic fishing, 40
Green revolution, 31–36; and advantages of new cereal varieties, 33; assessing the results of, 35–36; defined, 34; effects of, 34–35; impact of, on Non Som Boon, 140; impact of, on unemployment, 36; mixed impact of, on developing nations, 3–4
Gross returns, per person-hour, 84

Haciendas, 230
Hanwa, Nigeria, 64, 65, 81
Hausa dryland farmers, 63–91; crops of, t. 67; family characteristics of, t. 66; land resources of, t. 66; land use by, t. 67. *See also* Dan Mahawayi, Nigeria
Hayami, Yujiro, 12, 17, 248
High-yield rices. *See* Dwarf rice
High-yield wheats. *See* Dwarf wheat
Hired labor: in Dan Mahawayi, 70, 72; in Rio Grande do Sul, 99; in Ruiz Pineda, 188, 200, 201; in Sahiwal District, 157
Hogs, raising of: in Lajeado, Brazil, 104–5; in Rio Grande do Sul, 99
Hypotheses for change in small-farm agriculture, 5-7

IAN, 178, 179, 180, 182
Iceland, fishing off, 40
Idled cropland, U.S.: decrease in, 43; returning to production, 51; use of U.S., 43; withheld from production (1961–74), t. 52
Illiteracy, 48; in northern Nigeria, 64; in Ruiz Pineda, 180. *See also* Literacy
Income, farm: composition of, northern Nigeria, 79; of Dan Mahawayi farmers, 79, 81–82, 87–88; distribution, Ruiz Pineda, 203; effect of variables on, Ruiz Pineda, 195–97; highly skewed, in Ruiz Pineda, 201–5; of Lajeado, Brazil, farmers, 107, t. 108; at Quechehueca Collective, 227, 228; raising of, in northern Nigeria, 87–88; in Rio Grande do Sul, 100; in Ruiz

Pineda, 196, 201–5, 206, 207
India: community development programs in, 5; effect of monsoons on agriculture of, 35; green revolution in, 36; increasing cereal production of, 51–52; wheat production of, 34, 36
Inputs, agricultural: access of large farmers to, 36; access of small farmers to, 36; adjustments of farmers to, 20; and agricultural transformation, 14; external suppliers of, 13; government fixing of prices of, 245; government supply of new, to small farms, 251; and increased labor demands, 19; institutions and flow of, 17; local availability of new, 250; and need for extension services, 20; reducing costs of, to small farmers, 21; relationship of, to outputs, 17–18; technological, and increased labor demands, 19; temporary subsidies of, 246
Insecticides, 39, 111
Institutions: in agricultural change, 15–17; credit, 6; as growth-limiting factor, in developing countries, 238; influence of, on technological change, 93; and new agricultural inputs, 17; and new inputs in Lajeado, Brazil, 101, 110; and response to agricultural change, 17; in Rio Grande do Sul, 112–13; and technological changes on small farms, 239–40
Instituto Agrario Nacional (IAN), 178, 179, 180, 182
Interest rates: and farm mechanization, 36; of moneylenders, 6, 238
Internal combustion engine, 30
International Agricultural Research Centers, 13
International Rice Research Institute (IRRI), 13, 33
IR-8. *See* Dwarf rice
Irrigation: as agricultural innovation, 28–29; canals in Sahiwal District, 157–59; of dwarf wheats in Sahiwal District, 168–70; needs of new seeds, 36; problems, 37–38; at Quechehueca Collective, 226; at Ruiz Pineda, 184; in Sahiwal District, 157–60, 168–70; and schistosomiasis, 38; as technological innovation, 28–29; tubewell, in Sahiwal District, 159–60; in Yaqui Valley, 223
Islam religion, 151
Islendos, 178, 180
Iyali, 68

Japan: cost of increasing rice yield per acre in, 45; egg production of, 30; fish consumption in, 40–41; intensifying cultivation in, 31; population growth in, 28; rising affluence of, 28; yield-raising agriculture in, 37
Java, irrigation problems in, 37

Kenaf, 124; cropping practices of, 126–27; production in Non Som Boon, 120, 125; yields, in Non Som Boon, 132
Khon Kaen, Thailand, 121
Klinkenberg, K., 64

Labor displacement, 19
Labor productivity: of Amish farmers, 15; effects of land reforms on, 243–44; of Non Som Boon farmers, 134
Labor resources and use: in Dan Mahawayi, 70, 72; of Hausa dryland farmers, t. 69; in northern Nigeria, t. 69, 70, 72, 88; at Quechehueca Collective, t. 225, 229–30; in Rio Grande do Sul, 99; in Ruiz Pineda, 183, 184–86, t. 187, 188–91, 200, 201; in Sahiwal District, 157; on small farms in developing nations, 237–38.
Lajeado, Brazil: altitude variations in, 101; cash crops of, 106–7; crops of, 101, 102–4, 106–7; dairy cows in, 105–6; farm characteristics in, 103; farming returns in, 107–8; farm sizes in, 101, 109; food crops of, 102–6; hog raising in, 104–5; location of, 100–101; rainfall in, 101; settlers of, 101; small farms in, 101; soils of, 101; tobacco farming in, 106–7
Landed estates, Mexican, 212, 230
Land-labor relationships, in Dan Mahawayi, 75–76
Landlord-tenant relationships, in Pakistan, 173
Land ownership: broadening of, in Mexico, 212; in Dan Mahawayi, 66, 67; distribution of, in Yaqui Valley, 218–19; in Ruiz Pineda, 178–79, 190, 191, 196, 207
Land productivity: of large farms vs. small farms, 240; uncertain effects of land reforms on, 243–44. *See also* Double cropping; Mixed cropping; Yields per acre
Land reform: government agencies for, 208; and institutional change, 242–44; in Mexico, 211–12, 215–23, 230–31; in Venezuela, 178, 207–8
Land rentals, in developing countries, 239
Land resources and use: in Dan Mahawayi, t. 67; and decreasing area for crop production, 44; of Hausa dryland farmers, 66–67; in Lajeado, Brazil, t. 103; at Quechehueca Collective, t. 225, t. 226; in Ruiz Pineda, 183–84, 196–97; of small farms in developing nations, 238; in Yaqui Val-

Land resources and use *(continued)* ley, t. 220. *See also* Rainfall; Water resources
Lard, 49
Large farmers: and access to inputs, 36; in developing countries, 6; in Pakistan, 160–61; in Rio Grande do Sul, 100, 112–13
Latin America, as grain exporter, 41–42
Law of the Sea, 51
Leonardo Ruiz Pineda. *See* Ruiz Pineda
Limited scale economies, 17–18
Linear programming test, 86–88
Literacy: in China, 48; cost of universal, 48; level of, in Pakistan, 20; per person cost of, in developing countries, 47–48
Livestock Breeding Center, 123–24
Livestock products: consumption of, in high-income countries, 28; consumption of, and rising affluence, 27–28; importing countries of, 28; returns to Thai farmers, 136–39; of Soviet Union, 41; in Thailand, 117, 123–25, 136–39. *See also* Buffalo; Cattle; Hogs
Loan repayments, 6; at Quechehueca Collective, 227; in Yaqui Valley, 222
Local Societies of Collective Ejidal Credit, 219
Low-income countries. *See* Developing countries
Luxembourg, low birthrate in, 47
Lyallpur, Pakistan, 156

Maize (corn): in Brazil, 102–4, 107; in Lajeado, Brazil, 102–4, 107; in Mexico, 215; in Rio Grande do Sul, 99; in Ruiz Pineda, 182, 188, 189, 193–94; yields in traditional vs. modern agriculture, t. 10
Malaria, 38
Mangla irrigation reservoir, 37
Marginal factor cost (MFC): of nitrogen fertilizer in Sahiwal District, 167; of resources in crop production, Non Som Boon, 136; of water in Sahiwal dwarf wheat crop, 169, 170
Marginal value product (MVP): of land and labor in Dan Mahawayi crops, t. 76; of land and labor in northern Nigeria crops, t. 86; of nitrogen in Sahiwal District dwarf wheat, 166–68; of resources in Non Som Boon crops, 135–36; of water in Sahiwal District wheat, 169
Marketing: changes in, institutions, in Pakistan, 171–72; of farm products in Lajeado, Brazil, 101, 102; improved, 252–53
Material transfer, 248
Measure, units of, in Pakistan, 176 n 1

Meats. *See* Beef; Cattle; Hogs; Livestock products
Meat substitutes, 49
Mechanization: needs of small farms in developing countries, 238; in Non Som Boon, 124; in Pakistan, 174–75; at Quechehueca Collective, 226; in Rio Grande do Sul, 93, 96, 100, 112; in Ruiz Pineda, 186, 206; and use of new seeds, 36
Mellor, J. W., 7, 73
Mexican wheat. *See* Dwarf wheat
Mexico: agrarian reform in, 211–12, 215–23, 230–31; capital-intensive agriculture in, 232–33; corn farmers in, 36; and development of dwarf wheat, 33; economic growth of, 210, 211; population growth of, 26, 211. *See also* Ejidal farming; Quechehueca Collective; Yaqui Valley, Mexico
Mexipak. *See* Dwarf wheat
MFC. *See* Marginal factor cost
Milk production: in India, 29; in Lajeado, Brazil, 105–6; in Rio Grande do Sul, 99; in U.S., 29
Mixed cropping: in Dan Mahawayi, 77–79, 82, 83, 84; and income security in northern Nigeria, 85, 86; in Lajeado, Brazil, 102; production function test of rationality of, 85–86; and profit maximization in northern Nigeria, 86; in Rio Grande do Sul, 97, 112
Modern technology: adapting to small farms, 21; and capacity transfer, 248–49; creation of, for small-farm development, 247–50; efforts to introduce, in poor countries, 31, 33; farmers' perception of, in Lajeado, Brazil, 111–12; future use of, in Non Som Boon, 139–41; government actions to supply, 245–46; impact of, on Non Som Boon, 40; importation of, for small-farm development, 248–49; and increased labor demand, 18–19, 240; and increasing output in northern Nigeria, 89; increasing yields of, 15; in Lajeado, Brazil, t. 94, 109–12; and land design transfer, 248; and large farmers in southern Brazil, 96; and local availability of inputs, 250; and material transfer, 248; need for, in northern Nigeria, 89; in Non Som Boon, 139–41; at Quechehueca Collective, 226; in Rio Grande do Sul, t. 94, 96, 100, 109–12; and rural unemployment, 240; in Sahiwal District, 159–60; tailored to small farms, 247–50; testing impact of, on small farmers, 249–50; yields of, compared to traditional agriculture, t. 10. *See also* Technological change
Moneylenders, 6, 238

INDEX

Monsoons, 35
Moslem religion, 64
Mueller, M. W., 231
MVP. *See* Marginal value product

New seeds. *See* Seeds, new
Nigeria, northern: crops of, t. 67; farm capital of, t. 73; farm expenses of, t. 73; Hausa dryland farming in, 63–91; improving per acre yield in, 81; labor inputs and yield per acre of, t. 84; land use in, t. 67; low farm incomes of, 88; marginal value products of land and labor in, t. 86; use of family labor in, 69. *See also* Dan Mahawayi, Nigeria
Nile Valley, 37
Nitrogen fertilizers: with dwarf wheat, 33; and rising energy costs, 45; with soybeans, 46; with traditional wheat varieties, 33; use of, in Pakistan, 163–64, 168. *See also* Chemical fertilizers
Nonfamily labor. *See* Hired labor
Non Som Boon: allocation of resources in, 122–23; bovine production practices of, 127–31; cropping practices of, 125–27; crop profits in, 132–33; cultivated acreage in, t. 125; description of, 120; farm incomes of, 122; farm production system of, 122–23; farm products of, 122–23; impact of green revolution on, 140; location of, 120–21; major crops of, t. 126; map of, 121; resource use in, 131–36; technological changes in, 123–25
Norman, David W., 63–91
North America, as grain exporter, 41–42
Nutritional diet: in China, 48; cost of, 48; importance of vegetable oils in, 49; and lowering of birthrates, 48; and meat substitutes in American, 49; in Pakistan, 149; simplifying, in rich countries, 48–50

Oceans, as protein source, 39
Off-farm work: of Dan Mahawayi farmers, 70, 71, 79, 81–82; of Ruiz Pineda farmers, 183, 200, 201
Orchard crops, 190–91
Output, agricultural. *See* Economic efficiency; Productivity; Yields per acre
Overfishing, 39, 40, 51

Pakistan: adoption of dwarf wheats in, 160–70; changes in marketing institutions of, 171–72; community development programs in, 5; dwarf wheat vs total wheat acreage (1965–70) in, t. 155; foodgrain self-sufficiency program of, 153–54; geographical variations of, 151; impact of dwarf wheat on, 170–75; irrigation projects in, 37, 157–60; Islam religion in, 150; landless labor in, 174; languages of, 151; literacy in, 20; rainfall of, 151; rice production of, 149; rural economy of, 150; territories of, 151; transportation in, 150–51; wheat imports of, 153; wheat marketing problems of, 172–73; wheat production of, 34, 149, 152, 154–55. *See also* Punjab; Sahiwal District
Partition, 152
Pastureland. *See* Grazing land
Peasant farms. *See* Small farms
People's Republic of China: literacy in, 48; nutritional diet in, 48; reduced birthrates of, 35
Per capita income: in Mexico, 211; and rising grain consumption, 27. *See also* Income, farm
Persian wells, 169, 170
Person-hour input, t. 75, 84
Person-land ratio, in Thailand, 116
Pesticides, 29, 38, 44
Philippines: eutrophication of lakes and ponds in, 38; fish catch of, 37; high-yield rice and labor demands in, 19; population growth of, 26; rice production of, 19, 34; use of chemical fertilizers in, 37
Phosphates: in Pakistan soil, 171; U.S. banning of, in detergents, 39
Policies and programs for small-farm development, 237–55
Poor countries: abandonment of unproductive lands in, 37; cereal production of, 35; grain consumption in, 26; high population growth of, 26; population growth of, 26, 47; potential of, 51–53. *See also* Developing countries
Population density, in northern Nigeria, 80–81
Population growth: alleviating pressures of, 46–50; countries contributing to world, 26; future, of developing nations, 3; in Mexico, 211; in poor countries, 26, 47; and pressure on food scarcity, 25–33; in Punjab, 152; reducing, 46–47; in rich countries, 26; U.N. projection of, 44
Pork, 40
Potato yields, t. 10
Poultry: consumption in U.S., 27–28, 30, 40; production in Japan, 30; production in U.S., 30
Poverty, global, 47–48
Price: of fertiliziers in Pakistan, 170–71; food, and scarcity, 25; and output, 21; stability, for export crops, 246;

Price *(continued)*
  for staple food crops, 246
Price policies, government: needed for small-farm development, 245–46; objectives of, 245; and small-farm development, 244–45
Production economics theory, 8
Productivity: accelerating small-farm, 21–22; bases of estimates of, 9; and educational inputs, 20; effects of land reforms on, 243–44; and farm size, 17–18; increased, and world food supply, 30; increasing, of traditional farmers, 11; in Lajeado, Brazil, 102–8, 109–10; low, and slow growth, 9–11; need to increase, 20–21; in northern Nigeria, t. 86; in Pakistan, 166–68; in Rio Grande do Sul, 99, 100; in Ruiz Pineda, 207; traditional farmers' low, 9. *See also* Economic efficiency; Yields per acre
Profit maximization, 83, 85–87
Protein, animal: and constraints on beef production, 45; and constraints on fish catch, 45; and constraints on production of, 45–46; growing demand vs. lagging supply of, 46; increasing world demand for, 40; oceans as source of, 39; production constraints on, 45–46; and soya-based meat substitutes, 49. *See also* Fish
Puebla project, 250
Punjab: dwarf wheat adoption patterns in, 160–70; expanding use of dwarf wheat in, 170–75; farm resource adjustments in, 163–70; impact of dwarf wheat on, 170–75; increase in wheat acreage of, 152–53; population growth in, 152; tradition and change in Sahiwal District of, 155–60; wheat improvement program in, 150–55. *See also* Sahiwal District
Pure stands. *See* Single cropping

Quechehueca Collective, 223–30; capital-intensive agriculture of, 226; characteristics of, 225; cotton production of, 226; cropping system at, 226–27; crops of, 226; crop yields of, t. 227; divisions of, 224; growth of, 223–24; irrigation at, 226; modern technology at, 226; original provisions for, 224; per member characteristics of, t. 226; rice yields of, 227

Rainfall: in Barbacoas, Venezuela, 183; in Lajeado, Brazil, 101; in Pakistan, 151; in Rio Grande do Sul, 97; in Ruiz Pineda, 186; in Thailand, 120; of Zaria area, Nigeria, 64
Rask, Norman, 92–114
Rationing, food, 25

Rent reforms, 242–43
Rheinhart's Ballad, 29–30
Rice: in Bangladesh, 52; consumption in Thailand, 134; and cost of increasing yield in Japan, 45; in Mexico, 215; in Non Som Boon, 125, 132, 133–34; in Pakistan, 149; in Philippines, 34; at Quechehueca Collective, 227; in Ruiz Pineda, 182, 189–90, 194–95; in Thailand, 116; yields in traditional vs. modern agriculture, t. 10. *See also* Dwarf rice
Richardson Construction Company, 214, 218
Rich countries: low population growth of, 26; simplifying diets in, 48–50
Rio Grande do Sul: agriculture in, 93–98; characteristics of small farms in, 98–100; crop diversification in, 99; dairy herds in, 99; farming regions of, 95; farm size in, 98, 112; geographic regions of, 95, 96; home consumption in, 99–100; income levels in, 100; increased number of farms in, 98; institutions and technological change in, 112–13; labor supply and use in, 99; large farms in, 93, 100, 112; livestock diversification in, 99; location of, 96; maize yields of, 99; mixed farming in, 112; rainfall in, 97; settlement patterns of, 96; small farms in, 93–94, 97–98, 112; small- vs. large-farm production in, 112; soils of, 97; soybean yields of, 99; terrain of, 94; types of farming in, 97–98; use of new technology in, 112; wheat yields of, 99. *See also* Lajeado, Brazil
Risk aversion: of Dan Mahawayi farmers, 82, 83; of Pakistan farmers, 161–62, 168; of Rio Grande do Sul farmers, 113; of small farmers, 249; and subsistence farming, 3
Rockefeller Foundation, 33
Ruiz Pineda: and CIARA credit program, 192–93; crops of, 185; early development of, 179–80; family size in, 188; founding of, 178–79; improving labor use in, 188–91; labor use in, 183, 184–86, 190–91; land use in, 183–84; location of, 178; new cropping patterns needed in, 190–91; population of, 178; production experience of, 182; rationality of labor use in, 186–87; sindicato in, 181–82; size of, 178; social structure of, 180; summary of, 205–7
Ruttan, Vernon W., 12, 17, 248

Sahiwal District: adoption of dwarf wheat in, 160–70; canal irrigation in, 157–59; cash crops of, 156; farm size in, 156; food and fodder crops of,

INDEX

156; irrigation in, 156, 157–59; traditional cultivation practices in, 156–57; tradition and farming change in, 155–60
Schistosomiasis, 38
Schultz, T. W., 7–8, 11, 12
Security motivation, 82, 83, 85, 86, 88
Seeds, new: advantages of, 33–35; farmers who benefit most from, 36; and increased labor demands, 36; and increased yields, 13, 33–35; and irrigation needs, 36; in Lajeado, Brazil, 110, 111; in Punjab, 160–75. *See also* Dwarf rice; Dwarf wheat
Sesame, 182, 190
Sharecropping: lack of economic incentives in, 243; in Rio Grande do Sul, 98; tobacco, in Brazil, 106–7
Sheep, 96
Sindicato, 179, 180–82, 205
Single cropping: in Dan Mahawayi, 77; in more developed nations, 79; in northern Nigeria, 86
Small farmers: and access to inputs, 36; capital shortages of, 6; economic technical equilibrium of, 6–7; vs. large farmers, 6; and moneylenders, 6, 238; as poor decision makers, 5–6. *See also* Small farms
Small farms: accelerating production of, 21–22, 237–53; creation of modern technology for, 248–49; credit needs of, 238; defined, 4; development and creation of new technology, 247–50; development, policies, and programs for, 237–55; development and price policies, 245–46; development and reducing rural unemployment, 240; development and tax policies, 247–48; dynamics in agriculture of, 143–47; effective government programs for, 242; growth-limiting factors of, 237–39; impact of green revolution on, 4; importation of modern technology for, 248–49; and improved product marketing, 252–53; labor resources on, 237–38; in Lajeado, Brazil, 102–8; vs. large farms in land productivity, 240; major hypotheses for change in, 5–7; in northern Nigeria, 80–81; in Pakistan, 161–62; programs for development of, 239–40; reducing input costs to, 21; and rent reforms, 242–43; in Rio Grande do Sul, 93–94, 97–98, 112; in southern Brazil, 92–114; and technological change in Brazil, 92. *See also* Small farmers; Traditional agriculture
Smith, Adam, 13
"Snail fever," 38
Social structure: in Dan Mahawayi, 65, 68; in Lajeado, Brazil, 101; of Mexican ejidos, 233; and responses to agricultural change, 15; in Ruiz Pineda, 178–82
Soil loss, 37
Soil types: in Lajeado, Brazil, 101; in Ruiz Pineda, 195; in Thailand, 120
South Asia, green revolution in, 3
Soviet Union: annual population growth of, 26; collective and state farms of, 18; fish consumption in, 40, 41; and fishing off U.S. coast, 40; large farming units in, 6; livestock industry of, 41; virgin lands project of, 38; and world population growth, 26
Soya-based meat substitutes, 49
Soybeans: in Lajeado, Brazil, 104; in Mexico, 215; nitrogen fertilizer use with, 46; as protein source, 46; in Rio Grande do Sul, 96; U.S. exports of, 35, 46; U.S. per acre yields of, 46
Spraying, crop, 190, 206
Stevens, Robert D., 3–24, 55–61, 143–48, 237–55
Subsidy, government: of fertilizers in Pakistan, 170–71; in Ruiz Pineda, 182; temporary, on inputs, 246
Subsistence farming: in Dan Mahawayi, 73–74; in Non Som Boon, 122; and risk aversion, 3; in Ruiz Pineda, 178, 181, 204–5; static yields of, 3. *See also* Risk aversion
Sugarcane: in Dan Mahawayi, 77, 79, 81, 84; yields in traditional vs. modern agriculture, t. 10
Supply and demand: adjustments to changes in, 14–15; equilibrium in, 8–9
Swamp buffalo, 117–18

Tax policy, and small-farm development 246–47
Technological change: forms of, 93; global effects of, 36–39; and government actions to assure, 245–46; of greater benefit to large farmers, 36; and institutional and value changes, 239–40; major advances in, 28; and solution to food shortages, 35; use of, in increasing yields, 30–31. *See also* Modern technology
Tenancy laws, in Pakistan, 173
Tenant farming and rent reform, 242–43
Thailand: agricultural changes in, 119–20; buffalo in, 117–18; cattle in, 119; farm sizes in, 116; general information on, 116; income growth in, 116; interrelationships of crop-bovine production in, 139; natural vegetation of, 120; physiographic regions of, map, 118; population of, 116, 119; rainfall in, 120; as rice exporter, 116; size of, 116; soils of, 120; topography of, 120; transportation in, 120–22. *See also* Non Som Boon
Thiesenhusen, William C., 177–209

Third world. *See* Developing countries; Poor countries
Tobacco farming: in Lajeado, Brazil, 101, 106–7; in Rio Grande do Sul, 98, 100
Tractors, 100, 140
Traditional agriculture: and change in social and economic variables, 7–8; complexity of, 19–20; dynamics of, 55–61; economic efficiency of, 8–9; economic equilibrium of, 7–9; economics of transforming, 11–20; hypotheses for change of, 5–7; increasing productivity of, 11; low capital formation in, 73; low productivity of, 9; model of, 7–11; in northern Nigeria, 63–91; in Pakistan, 155–60; and rate of return on investment, 9, 11; in southern Brazil, 92–114; transformation of, 3–24
Transformation of traditional agriculture, 3–24
Transportation: in Pakistan, 174; in Thailand, 120, 121–22
Truck farming, 184, 186
Trucks, 124
Tubewells, 159–60, 169, 170

UAR. *See* Egypt
Unemployment: impact of green revolution on, 36; and small-farm development, 240
Union de Prestatarios, 192–93
United Arab Republic. *See* Egypt
United States: agriculture and world food needs, 41–44; aquaculture in, 41; birthrate of, 47; corn yields of, 29, 45; egg production of, 30; fish consumption of, 40; food consumption patterns of, 26, 27–28, 48–50; grain consumption in, 26; as grain exporter, 42; idled cropland in, 42, 43, 51, 52; livestock consumption of, 27–28, 49; poultry consumption of, 27–28; role of, in combatting famine, 48; role of, in expanding world's food supply, 52; soybean crop of, 35, 46; wheat exports of, 35; yield-raising agriculture in, 31
U.S. Agency for International Development, 52
USSR. *See* Soviet Union

Vegetable oils, 49
Vegetable proteins, 49
Venezuela, 177–209. *See also* Ruiz Pineda
Venezuela Campesino Federation, 181
Village relationships: in Dan Mahawayi, 65, 66; in Lajeado, 101; in Non Som Boon, 120–23; in Ruiz Pineda, 178–82
Von Liebig, Justus, 29

Wages, farm: in Non Som Boon, 134; in Ruiz Pineda, 189; in traditional vs. modern agriculture, t. 58. *See also* Income, farm
Watermelons, 125, 127, 132
Water resources: adaptation to scarcity of, in Sahiwal District, 158–59; availability of, 44; decreasing, 44; in Yaqui Valley, 213–14. *See also* Irrigation; Rainfall
Weckstein, R. S., 231
Welsh, Delane E., 115–41
West Germany, birthrate of, 47
West Pakistan. *See* Pakistan; Punjab; Sahiwal District
Wheat: in India, 34–35, 36; in Mexico, 213, 215; in Pakistan, 34, 149, 151, 152–53, 172–73; at Quechehueca Collective, 227; in Rio Grande do Sul, 96, 99, 100; in Sahiwal District, 156–57; traditional vs. dwarf wheat, t. 10, 161–62; U.S. exports of, 35. *See also* Dwarf wheat
Whetten, Nathan L., 212
World fisheries. *See* Fisheries
World food bank, 50
World food reserve system, 50–51
World food supply: constraints on expanding, 44–46; cost of increasing, to extant species, 38–39; growing pressures on, 25–53; and U.S. agriculture, 41–44; ways to expand, 30

Yaqui Valley, Mexico: agricultural development in, 213–14; colonization of, 214; cotton production of, 213; crops of, 186–87, 213, 215, 216–17; cultivated acreage in, 216–17; development of land resources of, t. 220–21; distribution of land holdings in, 218–19; early problems of ejidos in, 222–23; ejidal farming in, 213–23; irrigation development in, 213–14, 223; location of, 213; principal crops of, 186–87; wheat production of, 213
Yields per acre: corn, U.S., 29, 45, 46; improving, in northern Nigeria, 81; kenaf, Non Som Boon, 132; maize, Ruiz Pineda, t. 194; of mixed cropping, Dan Mahawayi, 84; in modern vs. traditional agriculture, t. 10; at Quechehueca Collective, t. 227; rice, Japan, 45; rice, Non Som Boon, 133; rice, Rio Grande do Sul, 99; rice, Ruiz Pineda, t. 194; slowdown in cereal, 44–45; soybeans, U.S., 46; watermelon, Non Som Boon, 132; wheat, Pakistan, t. 152, 155; wheat, Rio Grande do Sul, 99

Zaria area, Nigeria, 64
Zero population growth, 47